HORACE ON
POETRY

HORACE
ON
POETRY

PROLEGOMENA TO THE
LITERARY EPISTLES

BY

C. O. BRINK

*Kennedy Professor of Latin in the University of Cambridge and
Fellow of Gonville and Caius College*

CAMBRIDGE
AT THE UNIVERSITY PRESS
1963

PUBLISHED BY
THE SYNDICS OF THE CAMBRIDGE UNIVERSITY PRESS

Bentley House, 200 Euston Road, London, N.W. 1
American Branch: 32 East 57th Street, New York 22, N.Y.
West African Office: P.O. Box 33, Ibadan, Nigeria

©

CAMBRIDGE UNIVERSITY PRESS

1963

Printed in Great Britain at the University Press, Cambridge
(Brooke Crutchley, University Printer)

CONTENTS

v

Contents

PREFACE

For some years I have been preparing a commentary upon the literary epistles of Horace. This book was begun as a brief introduction to it. By the time I had written less than fifty pages I had come to understand that no perfunctory introduction could possibly do what it should do—set the stage for both Horace's literary criticism and the poetry of these poetic letters. We have lost the tradition of classical literary criticism; but Horace presupposes it. Writers of the eighteenth century could still happily take the tradition for granted. Writers of the nineteenth and twentieth centuries cannot and do not. Hence the dispute and the controversy that clog every line, almost every word, of these epistles. Rather than unload the controversies on an edition of the letters, I chose to scrap what I had written and start afresh. The result is a lengthy book, and a book presenting an argument. No one can help that, if he wants to peel the crust of scholarly controversy off some fresh and engaging works of poetic art.

The chief source of Horatian literary criticism is the *Epistula ad Pisones*, known as *Ars Poetica* to most ancient and modern readers alike. It is the *Ars* therefore that stands in the centre of this book. So far that poem has defeated all attempts at analysis. No one critic has convinced his *confrères* that he can trace the sequence of its thought, the arrangement of its content, and the principles of its structure. And yet the poem has less than 500 lines, and on the face of it few passages present serious difficulties of interpretation. Hence a feeble scepticism is rife: we are told that no coherent sequence of thought can be established; the only arrangement that can be traced legitimately is a lack of arrangement. But Horace was one of the most architectonic of poets. Whatever his deficiencies may have been, lack of structure and plan is not among them. Suppose the alleged disorder is merely on the surface. Suppose the alleged disorder is itself part of a poetic plan. Then there would be no need for the alternative—either look for the prosaic order of a treatise throughout, or if you do not find it throughout, then be prepared to find no order whatever. The coherence of prose is one thing; the coherence of poetry is another. Some elements reminiscent of the order of prose there may be; but equally these elements may not be incompatible with a larger poetic plan. If there are features that remind the reader of the structure of a literary treatise, then by all means let us notice them. But these features make the *Ars* as little into a systematic exposition as their absence would cause the *Ars* to be a shapeless medley of literary topics. Analysis will go seriously wrong when these false alternatives are proposed. (Part I)

A simple underlying plan can be established, I believe, by reading the poem and nothing but the poem. Once this is done, however, adventitious information may be sought. There is much in this poem that is obviously traditional. Neoptolemus of Parium was one of many critics who wrote about these traditional matters. An ancient commentator tells us that in writing the *Ars* Horace drew on Neoptolemus. Horace may be set beside the surviving pieces of Neoptolemus' work; both Horace and Neoptolemus may be set beside Aristotle's *Poetics* and *Rhetoric*, the archetypes of ancient literary criticism. How far can the *Ars* be used as a quarry from which information on Neoptolemus may be extracted? How does Neoptolemus Resuscitated compare with the *Poetics* and *Rhetoric*? In an investigation dealing with fragmentary material it is essential to distinguish between evidence and hypothesis. I offer a hypothesis; but I shall attempt to distinguish it from the evidence. Over a century of modern study the two have got badly entangled. (Part II)

What did Horace the literary critic do with the legacy to which he and his contemporaries were heirs? Is our evidence sufficient to separate Horace from the tradition on which he relied? Horace's views can be abstracted not only from the

Ars but from the literary satires and the letters to Augustus and Florus. Do the views so abstracted square with the literary criticism of the *Ars*? Is the *Ars* in fact just another 'literary epistle'? I shall try to answer these questions by considering first the literary satires and the letters to Augustus and Florus (Part III), and next by setting the *Ars* against that background. (Part IV, ch. 1)

The *Ars* like the rest of the literary essays offers poetic criticism in the shape of poetry. How did Horace make his literary criticism into malleable material for his poetry? In particular, is the *Ars Poetica* a versified treatise, *Ars*? Is it a poem? No one can believe that the few obvious and rigid lines of demarcation that are traced in the first section of this book would have satisfied so subtle and flexible a maker of patterns as Horace. What then are the less obvious and more poetic patterns in the *Ars*? (Part IV, ch. 2)

Such are the preliminaries of analysis and aesthetics, literary history and literary criticism, on which the writer of a commentary should seek to satisfy himself and his readers. He may then turn to what, for us, is perhaps the most puzzling and intriguing of Roman poems. A line-by-line commentary may help to gain or regain that intimate understanding, now lost, of a poet who could make the stuff of poetry out of his own reflections on poetry. For the *Ars* is not only literary criticism versified. It is more than that—a poem that in many essential features exhibits the qualities which it debates: a poetic mirror of the ancient view of poetry.

Like all students of Horace, I am in E. Fraenkel's debt. Although my views on the literary *Satires* and *Epistles* differ from his, I have benefited greatly from the profound scholarship and the feeling for Latin poetry that make the reading of his *Horace* an education.

Many friends in this university, in this country, and abroad, have helped me by discussing and challenging my conclusions. F. Solmsen in particular has read and commented on an earlier

Preface

draft; his familiarity with ancient rhetoric and literary theory has been invaluable to me. While drafting part of this book, during a year of scholarly leisure at the Institute of Advanced Study at Princeton, I much profited from discussing some of the Aristotelian problems with H. Cherniss. My colleagues G. S. Kirk and F. H. Sandbach have read my typescript and my proofs respectively; they have sharpened many an ineffective argument and have mitigated some pernicious over-statements.

The bibliography is based on materials collected and arranged by my wife. In compiling the indexes I was assisted by Miss M. Webb, College Secretary of Gonville and Caius College.

C.O.B.

CAMBRIDGE
December 1962

ABBREVIATIONS

AAM	Abhandlungen der Akademie ...in Mainz
AGG	Abhandlungen der Gelehrten Gesellschaft zu Göttingen
AJP	American Journal of Philology
APA	Abhandlungen der Preussischen Akademie
BVSA	Berichte über die Verhandlungen der Sächsischen Akademie
CP	Classical Philology
CQ	Classical Quarterly
CR	Classical Review
CW	Classical Weekly
EC	Les Études Classiques
GR	Greece and Rome
H	Hermes
HS	Harvard Studies in Classical Philology
J-B	Jahrbuch, Jahrbücher
JP	Journal of Philology
MH	Museum Helveticum
N.F.	Neue Folge
NGG	Nachrichten der Gelehrten Gesellschaft zu Göttingen
P	Philologus
PIR	Prosopographia Imperii Romani
PW	Philologische Wochenschrift
R-E	Paulys Real-Encyclopädie d. classischen Altertumswissenschaft: Neue Bearbeitung
REA	Revue des Études Anciennes
REL	Revue des Études Latines
RFIC	Rivista di filologia e di istruzione classica
RM	Rheinisches Museum
RP	Revue de Philologie
SBBA	Sitzungsberichte der Bayerischen Akademie der Wissenschaften
SBPA	Sitzungsberichte der Preussischen Akademie der Wissenschaften, Berlin
SI	Studi Italiani di filologia classica
TAPA	Transactions...of the American Philological Association
WS	Wiener Studien
YCS	Yale Classical Studies

PART I

ORDER AND DISORDER IN
THE 'ARS POETICA'

CHAPTER I

HAS THE 'ARS POETICA'
A STRUCTURE?

Reliqui libri τεχνολογίαν *habent, ut scis.* Thus Cicero, alluding to the second and third books *De Oratore*.[1] *Technologia*, technology in its ancient meaning, denotes the content of treatises or of lectures or of disputations between experts. The mature writings of Cicero are not textbooks or lectures; nor indeed are the disputants in these dialogues experts. Greek theory had to be handled afresh if it was to become viable for Romans and for *homines nobiles*. To handle it so is a fundamental concern of Cicero, and more than anywhere in the *De Oratore* and the *De Republica*. If a modern writer would give him his due as an author he needs to notice two things above all—the stuff of the textbook, and likewise the economy whereby the *technologia* becomes part and parcel of a Ciceronian *sermo*.

The *Ars Poetica* too employs a conversational procedure, though Horace here converses in the form of a letter. It too offers the teachings of Greek *technologia*. Its addiction to technicality is greater than that of any of the other literary satires or epistles. On the other hand the conversational and apparently inconsequential manner equals if it does not surpass that of the other works on poetry. Moreover, there is a third element in the *Ars* which recalls the rest of his talks and letters. Horace employs conversation as material for poetic patterns which are flexible and complex.

It is a mistake to underestimate this complexity. If the conversational graces alone are considered, both the poetic patterns and the underlying *technologia* will not receive their due share of attention; and likewise if the poetic pattern or the literary theory is unduly isolated.

[1] Cic. *Ad Att.* IV, 16, 3.

3

That a *technologia* underlies the *Ars* seems to me undeniable. But, in a sense, it has become part of a Horatian *sermo*, that is, of Horatian poetry. The question then is, in what sense. At present disagreement is rife on what the underlying theory is and how much of it Horace employs—if indeed he employs it at all. Clearly a fresh analysis of the *Ars Poetica* is required. It must ascertain one thing above all. Does the poem itself, without the assistance (or hindrance) of extraneous criteria, reveal any vestige of arrangement or plan?

The beginning of the work is full of pitfalls—so I propose to begin at the end, which is less controversial, and work my way back to the beginning. It is pleasant to start with a topic that is agreed. All critics who recognize some sort of a literary plan in the *Ars* admit that lines 306–8 indicate a new subject. 'Though writing no poetry myself, I will teach the poet's job and profession' (*munus et officium, nil scribens ipse, docebo*); 'where to acquire the substance of poetry' (*unde parentur opes*); 'what nurtures and forms a poet'(*quid alet formetque poetam*); 'appropriateness or its opposite in poetry' (*quid deceat quid non*); 'perfection and imperfection in a poet', that is, the end of the poetic process (*quo virtus, quo ferat error*). Here two conclusions may be drawn: (1) in this passage Horace is enunciating a subject or subjects, and (2) in this passage Horace is enunciating a subject, or subjects, on which the *Ars* has not pronounced earlier in this general way.

As for the former, the enunciation of a subject: from here onwards, all the way to the end, 309–476, these general principles are discussed: no one doubts that, unless he doubts the presence of any plan in the *Ars*. As for the latter, since the whole of a *Poetics* is indicated by these words, we must expect, and indeed find, similar topics touched on before 306; but they are not discussed with the same kind of generality— 'what should a poet do to fulfil his function?' Hence it follows that those who say that the poem has no plan whatever must draw in their horns somewhat: there is at 306 an indication that here Horace approaches his subject from a

4

different angle than he did before, or at any rate claims to do so; and that is valid up to the end of the poem.

Having made this point I must qualify it. Line 306, though grammatically independent, does not mark the beginning of a logical period. It concludes a comparison between the teacher of poetry and a whetstone. The whetstone cannot cut but it can sharpen; the teacher cannot write verse though he can sharpen poetic ability in others. This in turn is the upshot of another sentence starting at 295, *ingenium misera*, etc., which ironically declines the title of poet because Horace is unwilling to forgo purging in the Spring: he is unwilling to retain that surplus amount of bile from whence comes (poetic) genius. Declining the antics of unkempt geniuses, he pretends he cannot be a poet. 295 then, with its humorous antithesis between sane craftsmanship and romantic dabbling, is the true beginning of the new section—and even that only in a manner of speaking. For the preceding argument which clearly belongs to quite a different context (a comparison of Greek and Roman drama) is with obvious deliberation so shaped as to end with a similar antithesis between careful rule and careless licence.

The result of our discussion so far should satisfy most readers. There is a final portion in the poem. It comprises lines 295–476, 182 lines or rather more than one third of the poem. (A third would make 158 or 159.) The result has always satisfied those critics who take the *Ars* to be a textbook versified, for they all say that a new part begins at 295 and, according to their idea of the textbook, they call it the final chapter. At any rate they must be right in calling it a section because the beginning of a new portion is indicated at 306, and that is the final portion of the poem, dealing with the very general precepts that are to help the poet to fulfil his function. There is deliberate order here; indeed subjects with the flavour of the textbook are announced in the driest manner. And yet the opposition, too, may find some grounds for satisfaction. For the transition from one portion of the poem to the next is carefully masked. The new section does not begin at 306 but 11 lines before, at 295. Moreover, the preceding context that ends at 294 dovetails into the present section. That is achieved by the simple device of gliding from a chosen aspect of one subject to a like one of the next—call it conversational, paratactic, or whatever label is at hand. The textbook is played down by this conversational and partly humorous way of constructing the link—but it is a link for all that, joining two distinct portions of the poem. There are many ways of constructing links and this happens to be the one chosen by Horace in this Epistle, presumably because it is suited to a conversation or a letter or a poem.[1] From these considerations it follows that although both parties have usefully drawn attention to different features of the *Ars* (the one to its divisions, the other to its lack of divisions) these features are not mutually exclusive, and the final portion of the poem shows in fact both features combined. A more commonsensical, and less dogmatic, approach will surely make allowance for both.

The character of the final section has been made so clear by Horace that few readers overlook it. It is in entering on the earlier portions of the poem that we get into deep water. How far back can we trace the large context that ends at 294? Lines 275–94 compare Greek and Roman drama; the point of the comparison lies in the antithesis 'artistic discipline *versus* licence'. This antithesis, I have asserted, makes the link with the final portion of the poem, and it comes to the fore in the preceding section on metre, 258: the careless workmanship of Accius and Ennius. But the section on metre, lines 251–74, is itself part of a context on drama, chiefly tragic, 179–274. This context is recognized by all as a unity of sorts; all the way Horace talks about tragedy, comedy, satyric drama. The context harbours some difficulties—but these lie elsewhere than in the question of unity. So here we have *one* context: a run from 179 to 274, followed by the comparison of

---

[1] This 'gliding' procedure is, I take it, one of the points scholars have in mind in denying hard-and-fast divisions in the *Ars*.

Greek and Roman drama, to 294. It is introduced by precepts on how to hold an audience's attention, 153–78. This is one of several passages of the *Ars* in which character is discussed. If character is consonant with a person's age (and there are four such 'ages') attention will not wander—or so Horace asserts. The passage clearly forms part of the section on drama, hence the section may be extended back to 153 and we may assert that there is a run from 153 to 294.

So far so good. Line 153 however is less straightforward. What are the difficulties? There is a break here, but is it a major one? Admittedly, the point is marked by a new start, and an address: *tu quid ego et populus mecum desideret audi*. And yet a comparison with the final section of the *Ars* makes against the assumption of a major division here. At the beginning of the final section we found a topic that was entirely new, though linked in various ways with what precedes it. Here on the other hand the rules for tragic drama follow on after the content of epic or drama has been discussed (119–52), and both sections alike (119–52 as well as 153 ff.) exemplify the general reflections and precepts about subject-matter, whether freely invented or traditional. This suggests that drama and epic are not discussed in two self-contained portions of the *Ars*. What is decisive from 119 onwards is subject-matter, either *per se*, in the construction of a 'plot', epic or dramatic; or else, in the final product exhibiting the plot, that is, the epic poem or drama. If that is true, it follows that subject-matter is the hallmark of a whole section of the *Ars*—subject-matter, that is, considered either *per se*, or as organized in the epic poem or the drama (chiefly tragic), the two major genres.[1]

---

[1] J. Vahlen saw this point clearly, *Ges. Phil. Schr.* II, 160, where he writes about the passage 119–52. 'Und fragt man nach dem Inhalt desselben, so ist es nicht zutreffend zu sagen, es handle von Drama und Epos, obwohl es von Epos und Drama spricht, sondern wir werden uns, denke ich, korrekter ausdrücken, wenn wir sagen, Horaz habe den Stoff der Dichtung und die Behandlung des Stoffes (die *materies* und *tractatio*) zum Gegenstand seiner Darstellung genommen... exemplifiziert am Drama und an der epischen Dichtung.' Vahlen also noticed that the lines 119–294 form *one* coherent context, *op. cit.* pp. 768–9. So others have said more recently.

The section so defined runs from 119 to 294. It is the penultimate section of the *Ars*, comprising 176 lines, a little less than the final section of 181 lines, yet more than one third of the poem. Its close, at 294, we have considered. Its initial point, at 119, resembles the beginning of the last part of the poem (at 294) in two respects. It starts abruptly on an entirely new tack—*aut famam sequere aut sibi convenientia finge*; moreover, here as there, Horace has secured a kind of connexion by linking the subjects on either side of the divide. Before 119, where he talks about diction, he demands that style should conform to character, and the characters that he considers are types.[1] Now the divide—a new subject, and the would-be writer is addressed: 'make the matter of your poem conform to tradition or if you invent it do so with consistency'. After the divide, talk is about character again: this time Horace is not concerned with diction but with plot; and the characters are not types but persons, individuals, the agents of a story or myth: Achilles, Medea, Ino, Ixion, Orestes.

Once it is agreed that Horace did not discuss drama and epic in self-contained sections, but used them to exemplify general observations on the subject-matter of poetry, the major difficulty of this portion of the *Ars* is resolved. Flexibility is thus restored to Horace. We need no longer charge him with inconsistency if he joins general remarks on the subject-matter of poetry with specific remarks on certain kinds of poetry. Nor need we, after the event, restrict Horace to *one* kind of poetic genre when he was talking of several. *Aut famam sequere aut sibi convenientia finge*, | *scriptor* (119–20) is a general injunction which may, but need not, be subsumed under the head *imitatio*. His own words show that Horace for one did not subsume it. Moreover, this injunction applies to several branches of poetry. When Horace continues, at 120,

[1] 114, god or hero: *divus* (not *Davus*, as at 237, although some codices say so) *an heros*; 115, age: old man and youth; 116, station in life: lady and nurse; 117, occupations: trader and farmer; 118, national types.

honoratum si forte reponis Achillem, he certainly recalls the
Achilles of epic poetry, perhaps also of dramatic. But two
lines farther (*sit Medea ferox,* etc.) he pronounces on a number
of characters whose associations are dramatic rather than
epic. At 125 he is clearly speaking of drama (*scaenae committis*), and at 129 he brings the *Iliacum carmen* to the stage.
Yet a few lines farther again he exemplifies from Homer and
the cyclic epic (136–52). And at 153 he definitely turns to the
stage, and although chiefly talking of tragedy, he glances at
comedy as well, and satyric drama gets a sizeable passage to
itself.

How incisive is the break at line 153? This is not easy to tell.
The incision is made manifest by Horace's manner of talking
—*tu quid ego et populus mecum desideret audi.* I have argued what
makes against the assumption of a major break. On the other
hand the incision must have some force. The subsequent section on drama twice mentions style.[1] If content were still the
only concern of this section (as it was from 118 to 152), the
discussion of style would conflict with this topic—words
against matter. The contradiction would have been easy to
avoid. It is not so avoided; but it needs to be noted how the
topic of style is introduced.

The two passages in the section on drama that deal with
style are 217–19 and 234–50. The main subject in the former
case is however music, within the wider context of the chorus
of drama. 'Heady eloquence' (*facundia praeceps*), is said to be
one of the concomitants of degenerate music. The main subject in the latter case is satyric drama and its diction is considered along with other features of that kind of drama. In
both cases Horace discusses style, but as a corollary of a larger
subject. In this regard the cases differ from such discussions
of style *per se* as are found in an earlier portion of the poem.

---

[1] At first sight a passage in the discussion of content may also refer to style:
A.P. 136–7. But Horace is criticizing the exaggerated grandeur of a 'cyclic'
prooemium. The point here is the layout of the poem and how to work up to a
climax.

The intrusion is only an apparent intrusion; the stylistic passages are incidental in the context of the dramatic genres.

The precepts on drama (153 ff.) appear therefore to fulfil two functions. They are linked with the discussion on content (119 ff.); on the other hand they are set sufficiently apart to allow the poet to discuss various aspects of the dramatic genres. These aspects include the diction of these genres, whereas diction is excluded from the discussion of content (119–52). Both portions of the poem together (from 119 to 294) direct attention, first to content or plot, exemplified from narrative and dramatic poetry, and secondly (from 153 onward) to various features of the dramatic genres. Why in the second portion attention is restricted to the dramatic genres is not explained. Nor indeed is it explained why in the first portion Horace should be concentrating only on epic *and* drama. His readers however would have assumed that epic and drama were the two chief genres in which a plot is organized; for in their experience that was the case. Once this assumption is made the transition from two genres exemplifying content, or plot, to the especial problems concerning one of them is not unduly hard.

Penetrate beyond line 119, still moving towards the beginning of the poem, and the state of affairs will be found to change abruptly. There is a long stretch where we hear no more about content, but everything concerns style. That this applies to the 'link passage' on types of characters, just before 119, I have noted. But that passage is part of a larger context in which 'appropriate style' is discussed and the criterion of suitability changes. Style according to such features as age, sex, social station, was noted just now.[1] Before that it is style according to the emotions that are portrayed;[2] before that, according to the circumstances of the characters, in the different genres of writing: the examples come from tragedy and comedy.[3] Metre also affects suitability of style.[4] Metre in

---

[1] Above, p. 8, on *A.P.* 114–18. [2] *Ibid.* 99–113. [3] *Ibid.* 86–98.
[4] *Ibid.* 73–85, on the various metres 'suitable' for various genres.

turn is not considered *per se* but as a stylistic feature of words in verse. Hence two passages on words precede, one on 'composition' (when words are linked in a phrase), and another on the choice of words.[1] Finally, arrangement is closely allied to style, and at 42–4 three lines (half humorous: *aut ego fallor*) on *ordo* precede the section on style. Horace himself leaves no doubt that arrangement and style have to go together: 40–1, 'a writer who selects a topic which he can master will fail neither in his style nor in the lucidity of his arrangement' ('nec facundia deseret hunc nec lucidus ordo')—to be followed in inverse sequence first by *ordo* (42–4) and next *facundia* (from 45 onward). Hence another section may be asserted, this time on style (and arrangement), from the middle of 40 to 118: the briefest of the three (79 lines).

We are now left with this problem: what does Horace convey in the first forty lines? Lines 40–1 are a 'link passage'. 'A writer selecting a topic which he can master will fail neither in his style nor in the lucidity of his arrangement' ('cui lecta potenter erit res, | nec facundia deseret hunc nec lucidus ordo'). *Cui lecta potenter erit res* continues the injunction of lines 38–40: 'Writers, choose a subject which is equal to your powers and examine at length what burden your shoulders can or cannot bear' ('sumite materiam vestris qui scribitis aequam | viribus, et versate diu quid ferre recusent, quid valeant umeri'). And after line 40 *facundia* and *ordo* are immediately taken up.

It was unfortunate that the occurrence of the words *materiam* (38) and *res* (40), and indeed the whole tenor of the preceding passage, reminded E. Norden of the rhetorical topic *de inventione*—that is, the chapter in the Graeco-Roman courses on rhetoric that is concerned with the finding of subjects and arguments for a speech. This occurrence muddled analysis for half a century. In 1905 Norden affixed the label

---

[1] *Ibid.* 45–72. The first two lines should be in the order 46/45, as Bentley saw and some recent editors do not, although Vahlen explained the matter so fully that one is surprised to find a point left to explain. Cf. *Ges. Phil. Schr.* I, 452–5.

de argumentorum tractatione et inventione to lines 1–41,[1] and in spite of some protests most critics followed suit.

Norden's suggestion is untenable. The denial that Horace dealt with the heading of subject-matter in the penultimate section (119 ff., where he clearly did so) is complementary to the assertion that he dealt with it in the initial section (where he clearly did not).[2]

A close reading of the first 37 lines of the poem reveals moreover that there is here no technical talk about subject-matter as opposed to style. The celebrated passage about the purple patch (14) shows that: it concerns matter, arrangement, *and* style. *Res, facundia,* and *ordo* are brought together at 40–1:

> cui lecta potenter erit *res*,
> nec *facundia* deseret hunc nec lucidus *ordo*.[3]

Matter, arrangement, and style, are the subjects of this introductory section, but only inasmuch as they are affected by the principles of unity and wholeness. It is the fundamental role of these two principles that Horace wants to inculcate: lines 8–9 *uni...formae,* 19 *nunc non erat his locus,* 23 *simplex dumtaxat et unum,* 29 *rem...unam,* and 34 *ponere totum.* Unity and wholeness, or the appropriateness of each part of a poem to each other part, are among the principles underlying the technical disquisition that is to follow; so most appositely, Horace places them at the beginning. Whether this introductory section is taken as one, from line 1 to line 37, or as subdivided (1–23, 24–37), the function of the passage remains the same. At the end of this short introductory section of the *Ars* Horace deftly shifts his emphasis: artistic unity recedes; now the

---

[1] E. Norden, in the paper cited below, p. 20.

[2] Thus Vahlen remarked in his critique of Norden's paper, *Ges. Phil. Schr.* II, 762, 'Wie *sachlich* die Wahl des Stoffes zu treffen sei, erörtert er hier nicht, sondern sucht vorab darzulegen, welche Vorteile aus einer subjektiv glücklich vollzogenen Wahl sich ergeben'. This assessment however requires some modification, see below, p. 25, n. 4.

[3] At *Ep.* I, 19, 27 and 29 the three rhetorical data are contrasted: *modi* and *carminis ars* as against *res* and *ordo.* But in the initial portion of the *Ars* they qualify only as vehicles of poetic unity.

critic is troubled by the craftsman's failure to create an artistic whole:

> infelix operis summa quia ponere totum
> nesciet. (34–5)

Hence the new injunction, to choose a topic within one's powers; and this precept gives rise to the subsequent technical talk on order, style, and content.

This then is my suggestion. Whatever was done by the poet to smooth out the rigidity of this division, the *Ars Poetica* has an underlying threefold scheme[1] preceded by a brief introduction. The introduction comprises the first forty lines; it demands unity of poetic conception—a demand closely relevant to the rest of the poem. It is followed by the first part, on order and style, 40–118;[2] the second part, on how to organize a sizeable subject and on what Horace regards as the major genres of poetry so organized, 119–294; and finally the third part, on general questions of poetic criticism, 295–476. In each case the new section is linked with the preceding by a passage that may belong to either.

I arrived at these results by the process of analysing the poem and nothing but the poem. These results suggest three observations. (1) Analysis has tended to go awry because extraneous criteria have been applied to a poem which, on the face of it, does not conform to them. (2) In suggesting that the *Ars* is either an inconsistent medley of literary topics *or* a systematic exposition, students of Horace have chosen false alternatives. Both contentions are justified up to a point but neither is fully justified. The qualities that the disputants picked out as conclusive—'gliding transitions', on the one hand, and a 'layout' on the other—are both present in the work. Disguised transitions do not necessarily produce a 'medley' nor does a modicum of order in the arrangement of topics necessarily produce a systematic exposition. In each case the demonstration amounts to a *non sequitur*. (3) Analysis

---

[1] Or fourfold, if line 153 marks a stronger break than I think it likely to mark.
[2] Or two parts, if 42–4 are believed to form a 'section'.

has failed to distinguish between two kinds of arrangement: the pedestrian, which rigidly conforms to a few large subject-headings, and the poetic, which spurns such subject-headings. The former is likely to have been traditional in literary and rhetorical theory; the latter is not likely to have been traditional. Horace has tended to push the former into the background while bringing the latter to the fore. Since both principles are present in the *Ars*, it is possible to checkmate every argument based solely on one principle, by urging the opposite argument based solely on the other. Much analysis has consequently come to nought. In order to avoid this logical deadlock, it will be expedient to explore separately the traditional order which Horace applied as far as it suited his poetic purpose, and the poetic order for which the literary tradition is but malleable material. I propose to discuss the literary tradition in the second section of this book, and Horace's own procedures in the third and fourth sections. But first of all, in the next chapter, attention needs to be drawn to the premisses of what is known as the 'analytic' study of the *Ars*.

CHAPTER 2

THE ANALYTIC PROCEDURE AND SOME ANALYSES

Analysis came into its own when Horace's literary criticism had suffered an eclipse—in the nineteenth century. This statement is less paradoxical than it might appear to be. Certainly, for centuries close study had been devoted to the *Ars* even more than to the other critical poems of Horace. But close reading and analysis are not the same thing. It was the substance of the teaching and the elegancies of its poetic presentation that attracted poets, literary critics, and scholars. Now both the teaching and the presentation had become irrelevant or suspect. The link with the Horatian tradition had snapped. Scholars could feel free to ask large questions concerning that tradition. The *Ars* as a whole could become an object of dispassionate study. Detachment and precision however are hard to attain. Analysers too had their presuppositions. And confusion rather than coherence of statement has been the outcome of a century's analyses. A vast bibliography now blocks the road to the *Ars Poetica*. It will be necessary to clear a path through this jungle of contradictory opinions before we can usefully approach a work of literary criticism which is first and foremost a work of poetry.

Not that the basic assumptions were new. A reading of the commentaries of the sixteenth and seventeenth centuries, even of the eighteenth, readily shows that the Aristotelian background and the rhetorical affiliation of the *Ars* were then commonplaces.[1] But the Italian commentators and their successors looked to the *Ars* for poetic laws and precepts. Even where the poem was recalcitrant they naïvely converted

---

[1] The early commentaries have now been conveniently summarized. Cf. below, p. 79, n. 1.

it into a system of rules, without much regard as to how and where such rules appeared in it. Moreover, so long as Horace and Aristotle talked about similar matters in a similar vein, this accord could be noted. When they did not, Aristotle and to a lesser degree Cicero were made to supply Horace's supposed deficiencies, and *vice versa*. The *Ars* was wanted for a purpose and there was little interest in how it achieved that purpose. In the nineteenth century needs and interests changed. Critics no longer required systems of rules, from Horace or Cicero, from Aristotle or anyone. What they wished to determine was something new. Horace—a deliberate composer if ever there was one—had put his coherent literary criticism in the seemingly incoherent manner of the *Ars Poetica*. How was this manner to be explained? Over a century, from about 1860 to about 1960, scholars have made attempts to explain the structure of the poem *either* as a treatise versified *or* as a medley of divers literary topics.[1] But the *Ars* is not a treatise, although it contains elements of a treatise, nor is it a literary medley, although Horace employs the inconsequential manner when it suits his poetic purpose. So common sense suggests.

About the middle of the last century three different lines of approach to the *Ars* had been adopted by different scholars. The first was textual—the attempt by transposition and emendation to rid the poem of apparent contradictions and discrepancies. The procedure could not then be called new; few things in Horatian studies could.[2] But it did not become

---

[1] R. K. Hack, 'The doctrine of literary forms', *HS*, xxvii (1916), 14, caricatured the procedure in this manner.

   (*a*) The *Ars Poetica* is an εἰσαγωγή.

      All εἰσαγωγαί are written in strict accordance with a fixed rhetorical scheme.

      Therefore the *Ars Poetica* is written in accordance with a fixed rhetorical scheme.

   (*b*) The *Ars Poetica* is an *epistula*.

      All *epistulae* are written in a loose conversational style.

      Therefore the *Ars Poetica* is written in a loose conversational style.

[2] Much earlier, Daniel Heinsius was said to have 'attempted to evade the charge (of unfolding the order of this epistle) by having recourse to the unprece-

a fashion until 1850 or so. Its most thorough-going practitioner was the Dutch critic, P. Hofman Peerlkamp.[1] For a time many others followed suit. Soon however another fashion set in, different in everything except dogmatism. Nowadays professional transposers are rare though not extinct.[2] To my knowledge there is only one place in the poem where transposition of lines has a chance of convincing more critics than the one who made it—and that is an exchange of two adjoining lines, first proposed by Bentley. I refrain from argument therefore. What needs to be done is to understand the difficulties; it is not to remove them by main force.

Such violent methods did not commend themselves to a second group of scholars, also writing about the middle of the last century. Not only did they disapprove of these solutions, but they denied that there was a problem to solve. This view again has a long and varied history. The elder Scaliger only put by way of epigram what had been commonly held by scholars of the Italian and French renaissance: 'nam et Horatius Artem quum inscripsit, adeo sine ulla docet arte, ut Satyrae propius totum opus illud esse videatur.'[3] That the *Ars* was *sine arte tradita*[4] seemed evident to these critics. But thence they would proceed to what (they thought) should be their true concern—to draw the outlines of a Horatian system

dented and uncritical expedient of a licentious transposition'. Thus Richard Hurd in his commentary (3rd ed., 1757, vol. I, p. vi). Dacier condemned Heinsius for a different reason: 'L'ordre qu'Heinsius y a voulu mettre, ne sert qu'à relever & à faire mieux connoître la beauté du desordre dans lequel Horace l'a laissé' (*Œuvres d'Horace*, VIII, 1735, p. 71).

[1] In his edition (Leyden, 1845).

[2] Cf. L. Hermann's edition and translation, Coll. Latomus, VII (Brussels, 1951).

[3] Julius Caesar Scaliger, *Poetice* (1561), at the end of his introductory *Epistula ad Sylvium Filium*. Thus, for example, Robortelli in introducing the paraphrase of the *Ars* appended to his edition of Aristotle's *Poetics* (1548): 'Nuncuerò quis credat hominem doctissimum de arte tam confuse fuisse locutum.' The intelligent men said so; the others assumed it but glossed it over.

[4] Thus the same Scaliger in Book VI, ch. 7, of his *Poetice*. 'De arte [i.e. Horatii] quaeres quid sentiam. Quid? equidem quod de arte sine arte tradita. Nam quod principium? nempe Satyrae.' There follows a conspectus of 36 unconnected items and the remark, 'Haec est Horatii ars: quam si praeceptores nostri nobis olim ad hunc modum partiti essent, eius sane facies nota fuisset', etc.

of literary criticism. Similar views persisted well into the eighteenth century. According to Pope,

> Horace still charms with graceful negligence,
> And without method, talks us into sense.

And Dacier like many others admired *la beauté du desordre* of the *Ars*, never doubting that Horace yet wanted to make sense. In the nineteenth century scholars certainly agreed that Horace had not set out his views coherently. But now they would not accept the corollary; that there was a 'system' at the bottom of this 'Satyra'. If *Ars sine arte* expressed the Renaissance assessment of a didactic *sermo*, scholars of the nineteenth century soon satisfied themselves that Horace had offered no coherent argument but that he knew how to be inconsequential in a charming way.[1] Some of our contemporaries agree, although they use more contemporary language to express their agreement.[2] The proposition takes account of some features of the *Ars*. Yet it neglects the coherent and systematic features which the poem also contains.

Finally analysis proper, the search for a principle, or principles, of arrangement, on the assumption that the sequence of verses is in the main Horatian and that the poem has got an underlying plan which can be traced.[3] The most thoroughgoing of analysers, E. Norden, dated this procedure from a brief and unassuming paper of J. Vahlen's, of 1867.[4] Other scholars were more spectacular—and made more mistakes.

---

[1] 'Form der Formlosigkeit' is how K. Lehrs described the style of the *Ars* although in his edition of 1869 he did his best, by transposition, to put right any assumed deficiencies. In 1880 O. Weissenfels argued elaborately that Horace's inconsequential chatting was the chief attraction of the poem, see 'Aesthetisch-kritische Analyse der Ep. ad Pisones von Horaz', *Neues Lausitzisches Magazin*, v (1880), 118–200. More recent publications of this kind are too well known to call for mention here.

[2] See below, p. 34.

[3] The simple expedient commended by Henry Nettleship proved too simple and mechanical. He tried to persuade an Oxford audience in 1882 that the *Ars* consists of a string of originally Greek texts to which Horace in each case adds his own comment. Cf. H. Nettleship's *Lectures and Essays* (1885), pp. 174, 183.

[4] J. Vahlen, 'Bemerkungen zu Horatius' De arte poetica', *Ges. Phil. Schr.* I, 443–61 (from *Zeit. Öster. Gym.* xviii (1867), 1–16).

The Analytic Procedure and some Analyses

To these scholars I shall turn first, noting at the same time their assumptions.

Aristotelian affiliations and a rhetorical background determined the structure of the *Ars*. That seemed indubitable to many students about the turn of the present century. These assumptions prompted some of their analyses. The first section of the *Ars*, according to N. Wecklein writing in 1894,[1] largely reproduced the six constituent parts of tragedy, from Aristotle's *Poetics*.[2] The topics were familiar to earlier commentators. For more than four centuries scholars had been used to arranging them alongside their Horatian counterparts. But now Aristotle was called in to elucidate the composition and coherence of large portions of the *Ars*—or of the whole poem. Some details apart, Wecklein's argument does something to explain the sequence of topics in the first half of the *Ars*.[3] It does not explain the *Ars* as a whole. His main sections on Greek theory and on Roman practice (1–219 and 251–476), linked by a discussion of satyric drama—these topics scarcely add up to Horace's *Ars Poetica*.[4]

Only a few years later, in 1897, the arrangement of topics was set in a clearer perspective. T. Birt made a strong case for two related theses: the *Ars* has a recognizable arrangement of topics, and, the arrangement of the whole poem is bipartite.[5]

---

[1] N. Wecklein, 'Die Kompositionsweise des Horaz und die Epistula ad Pisones', *SBBA* (1894), pp. 397–418.

[2] The topics of style and thought would be at the bottom of *A.P.* 46–118; plot, at 119–52; character, at 153–78, the visual element, at 179–201, and music, at 202–19.

[3] Lines 99–118 are not however related to Aristotle's διάνοια; the Aristotelian ὄψις does not fully explain the items at 179–201; most important of all, as a subsequent chapter will show, the relevance of Aristotle's *Rhetoric* is ignored.

[4] The bearing of drama on Horace's arrangement of his topics had been mooted by a number of writers in the eighteenth century, such as Richard Hurd in this country and the poet Wieland in Germany. Satyric drama in particular was considered from that angle by T. Fritzsche, shortly before Wecklein: cf. *P*, XLIV (1885), 88–105.

[5] Theodor Birt, 'Über den Aufbau der Ars poetica des Horaz', in A. Dieterich, *Pulcinella* (1897), pp. 288–301. Birt was certain that he could deal with the *A.P.* in its transmitted order. But since lines 136–52 did not fit his preconceived scheme he decided to place them, *more Peerlkampiano*, after line 44.

A boundary line is drawn at line 295. What comes before it (he asserts but does not argue) is an *ars poetica* proper; what comes thereafter deals with generalities, under the heading of 'poet'. The Aristotelian character of the first part is taken for granted. Moreover, Birt forestalled Norden not, be it noted, only in asserting the bipartite division into *ars* and *artifex*, but also, like many critics before him, introduced the rhetorical schema of *inventio* (1–41), *dispositio* (42–4), and *elocutio* (45–118). Thus a large part of the *Ars* was linked with a rhetorical order of things. The treatise begins at the beginning: *inventio*, or 'content', a rhetorical topic, is thought to lead off at line 1. These assertions were to bedevil discussion for a long time to come.

Scholars were still busy elaborating the suppositions of Wecklein and Birt[1] when a fresh impetus came from a paper of Eduard Norden's.[2] Thus in 1905, for better or worse, a new era in the study of the *Ars Poetica* began.[3] This statement may seem to be surprising in view of what has been said earlier. If Norden had indeed been forestalled in the essentials of his analysis, why was his influence paramount for as much as half a century? The answer may well be this. At the beginning of the century the rhetorical tradition which critics and scholars of earlier days could take for granted had been abandoned. Norden sought to demonstrate by way of analysis that the *Ars* cannot be understood without the assumptions of a rhetorical tradition. It is advisable therefore

---

[1] Wecklein repeatedly returned to the problem, especially in *P*, LXVI (1907), defending his position, which Norden (incorrectly) had described as 'altogether fanciful', *ganz abenteuerlich*. Birt reasserted his own opinions, cf. *RM*, LXX (1915), 540. K. Welshofer (*Die A.P. des Horaz*, 1898), and A. Patin (*Der Aufbau der A.P.*, 1910), tried to proceed on the old assumptions, the former before, the latter after, Norden. A. Kiessling noted the bipartite division in his commentary of 1898, but refrained from pursuing its implications.

[2] E. Norden, 'Die Composition und Litteraturgattung der Horazischen Epistula ad Pisones', *H*, XL (1905), 481–528.

[3] This is so much the case that scholars do not now hesitate to date 'the analytic approach' from the publication of this paper. So for example E. Burck, in his new edition of Kiessling and Heinze's commentary (1959), p. 402, 'Am Anfang steht der epochemachende Aufsatz Ed. Nordens', etc.

to distinguish between the details and the general nature of his theory. The former may have been forestalled by his predecessors and moreover is at times incorrect. The latter may be too narrowly conceived; but the assertion of a rhetorical background may contain an important truth.

Apollonius ὁ εἰδογράφος wrote in the early Alexandrian age. Norden was a modern εἰδογράφος.[1] He sensed 'literary forms' (εἴδη), in any writings which he considered—the *genus* epic, hymnic, didactic, ethnographic, and so forth. He attempted to determine the character of a piece of ancient verse or prose by explaining its traditional features. This procedure may do good or evil. It may promote the error that the dissection of a work of literature will result in a tidy separation of traditional and individual portions. But good writing is an entity and all of a piece. As the poems of Horace show, its traditional features need not be less personal than its individual. On the other hand the procedure may have its uses when a tradition has been lost or is misunderstood. Such is the case of the rhetorical tradition which lies at the root of all ancient literary criticism.

Two questions then arise. Were there such traditions as Norden asserted? If there were, what is the relevance of any traditional features to a given piece of writing? These questions are not easily answered. Norden certainly did not answer them. It may be doubted if either he or his critics were fully aware of their nature.

On the first count, Norden noted that Horace had adopted a bipartite division according to *ars* and *artifex*. By this he meant that the specific details of the poet's craft were discussed under the former heading, the more general problems of poetic criticism under the latter. Noting the same division in certain works that purported to instruct in the arts or

---

[1] Norden's *eidologische Literaturbetrachtung* in the context of Latin letters has been justified by W. Jaeger, on the grounds that 'Latin literature had inherited its stock of literary forms ready-made from the Greeks', cf. 'Die klassische Philologie an der Universität Berlin, 1870–1945', in *Studium Berolinense* (1960), p. 476. Norden's assumptions were strongly attacked by R. K. Hack, *op. cit.* pp. 2–5.

sciences, he proceeded to classify them by this division. He described them as introductory or (to employ John Skelton's neologism) *isagogical*; likewise he described the *Ars* as a *commentarius isagogicus de arte poetica per epistulam ad Pisones*.[1] Yet the writings that have a measure of resemblance to the *Ars* can be called introductory only by a stretch of meaning; hence they do not offer a valid criterion. Εἰσαγωγαί, 'Introductions', seem to have been published first by the Stoics, a pedagogic sect.[2] Adherents of other schools and writers on various topics followed suit. Nothing survives that might serve to distinguish between these introductory writings and full-blown *artes*, in Greek τέχναι, treatises or textbooks. On the first count therefore Norden failed to prove his case. There was a confusion at the root of his inquiry. What he proved differed from what he meant to prove. He did prove that the pair *ars–artifex*, not unnaturally, had some place[3] in writings upon τέχναι or *artes*. But when that pair puts in an appearance, it does not necessarily make its *locale* into a *commentarius isagogicus*.[4]

Moreover, Norden's documentary evidence was late. The complete loss of all early Hellenistic εἰσαγωγαί or for that matter τέχναι rendered it impossible for him to offer other evidence. But it also renders it impossible now to tell *how* the pair *ars–artifex* was applied in the books in which it was used.

---

[1] *Op. cit.* p. 528.

[2] Thus Chrysippus' Περὶ τῆς εἰς τὰς ἀμφιβολίας εἰσαγωγῆς and other logical writings *ap.* Diog. L. VII, 193 ff. (*SVF*, II, pp. 6–7); moral inquiry is indicated by ἐν τῇ εἰσαγωῇ τῇ εἰς τὴν περὶ ἀγαθῶν καὶ κακῶν πραγματείαν, with a telling anecdote, *ap.* Athen. IV, 159 (*SVF*, III, p. 196, 17). Cf. Norden, *op. cit.* p. 521, *Agnostos Theos*, p. 108, n. 1, H. Dahlmann, *AAM* (1953), p. 111, n. 2. For Posidonius' εἰσαγωγή on style, see below, p. 65.

[3] It had some place. Precisely what place, is a different question, raised soon after Norden, and here discussed in my last chapter.

[4] This is not to deny that several features of the *Ars* would very well suit 'isagogics' in a less specific sense. The *Ars* is dedicated to Piso and his two sons and the poet addresses the elder son with particular emphasis. A youthful addressee would naturally suit the tenor of didactic writings. But there are more ways than one of being magisterial. Cicero addressed the *De Officiis* to young Marcus. But that does not make it a *commentarius isagogicus* in Norden's sense of the term. In fact it is much closer to a didactic treatise.

Talk about the criteria that might guarantee at once the deductive infallibility and moral sufficiency of what was named τέχνη—that is a characteristic of Attic, in particular Platonic, philosophy. But before Attic philosophy had come into being, information and instruction were purveyed by such 'technicians' as doctors, rhetoricians, and mathematicians. And it continued to be purveyed after Socrates, Plato, and Aristotle had established their new methods of inquiry. Some Hellenistic scholars, for example, might ignore *a priori* arguments, and restrict themselves to the facts required by the learner or the expert. Others might pay lip-service to the philosophical attainments that were rapidly becoming common property. Before displaying their scholarly wares they might lead off with some innocuous generalizations as to the nature of the technique, the truth the technicians could attain, and the good purpose they had in view. Others, more philosophically-minded still, might take the *officia artificis* seriously enough to discuss them more fully. This was likely to happen in such centres of learning as Alexandria or Pergamum, where Attic philosophy made some impression on the new scholarship. A measure of philosophical discussion might become an integral part of scholarly work, affecting the manner in which topics were offered and arranged. Thus in some cases the pair *ars–artifex* would determine the plan of the writings, in others it would not. Norden simplified the problem unduly, for he wrote his paper before attention had been drawn to the Aristotelian element in Alexandrian scholarship and criticism, although he, perhaps more than most, was prepared to appreciate the rich and diverse nature of Hellenistic writing. It is now the best part of scholarly caution to allow for these several contingencies. The evidence will have to be scanned afresh from more than one angle.

Norden then asserted that the whole structure of the *Ars* was erected on a traditional base and divided according to the pair *ars–artifex*. I have hinted in the first chapter that this is true up to a point. Further discussion will define this observation more closely. Moreover, Norden reaffirmed the findings of some of his predecessors: what he considered the first 'section' (again to be taken as a whole) reflects another traditional and rhetorical distinction—the sequence of content—arrangement—style, *inventio—ordo—elocutio*. Here too difficulties arise because he approached the poem from the side of the tradition, and the rhetorical, not the literary, tradition at that. He did not pause to ask precisely what tradition Horace had turned to and what he had made of it.

Protests were not long in coming. Scholars like Wecklein and Birt had made up their minds on the *Ars* and did not feel inclined to change them.[1] More important than that, now the very scholar demurred whom Norden had claimed as the only pioneer in analysis—his predecessor in the Chair of Lachmann and Haupt at Berlin. Johannes Vahlen, intent on proving Horace's perfection, had many years before subjected a sizeable portion of the *Ars* to a minute examination.[2] He had satisfied himself that this part of the *Ars* at any rate was not *sine arte tradita*. Most of it, he argued, has a single subject—poetic style.[3] Horace's discourse, he summed up,[4] proceeds by a natural and simple progression of thought from the choice of words and their combination to their metrical shape, which must be appropriate to each chosen genre. Appropriateness also must regulate the colouring, *color*, of the style itself. For tragic elevation is on the whole alien to the plainness of comedy, although the situation of the plot may on occasion raise the tone of comedy and lower the tone of tragedy. Finally, style needs to be appropriate to the momentary emotions of the characters of drama as well as to their ethos. Vahlen's demonstration is simple and it carries conviction.

---

[1] Cf. above, pp. 19–20.

[2] J. Vahlen, *Ges. Phil. Schr.* I, 443–61 (cited above, p. 18, n. 4) on *A.P.* 46–118.

[3] J. Vahlen, *op. cit.* I, 460. This includes metre, for at times ancient critics defined poetic style as words in metre. Cf. Ar. *Poet.* 6, 1449*b* 35, where he defines (poetic) style as τὴν τῶν μέτρων σύνθεσιν, 'combination of metres'.

[4] *Op. cit.* I, 460 f.

A like analysis had never before been achieved in this field. Nearly forty years later it impressed Norden, and also R. Heinze, the editor of Kiessling's standard commentary. But when it appeared, in 1867, its impact was negligible.

One cause of this neglect may well have been that Vahlen failed to interest himself, or his readers, in the implications of the Horatian argument. He had traced what amounted to a theory of poetic style. He had even referred to the passage of Aristotle's *Rhetoric* which provides the wider, literary, context of this theory, or of a large part of it.[1] But Vahlen would have no truck with rhetoric. He asserted that the argument of the *Ars* was poetry, not a rhetorical treatise.[2] Yet the sequence of thought which he traced was prosaic rather than poetic, and one would like to know where the alleged poetry came in.

Small wonder therefore if after a lapse of many years the Professor Emeritus felt embarrassed by the daring construction which his successor, Norden, had placed on this sound piece of *Textphilologie*. His second thoughts rapidly followed Norden's paper.[3] Now the narrow base from which he had operated stood open to view. Vahlen could have corrected the details of Norden's rather summary procedure while yet admitting that his successor had observed the literary significance of his own stylistic observations. He did indeed put right some of the details of Norden's analysis.[4] But details,

---

[1] Ar. *Rhet.* III, 7, cited by Vahlen, *op. cit.* I, 460, had not been unknown to the earlier commentators. Cf. below, p. 97, n. 2.

[2] Vahlen, *op. cit.* I, 460.

[3] Vahlen, 'Über Horatius' Brief an die Pisonen', *Monatsber. Berlin Ak.* (1906), pp. 589–614 (*Ges. Phil. Schr.* II, 746–74).

[4] Most convincingly in the delimitation of the various 'sections'. Norden laid himself open to attack when he maintained that the passage *A.P.* 1–41 dealt with the set item of technical rhetoric, called *inventio* or content. Vahlen countered (*op. cit.* II, 762) that it does nothing of the kind. When Horace enjoins on the poet to stick to his last, he is not legislating on *inventio*. Such legislation does however come at 119–52, 'aut *famam* sequere aut sibi convenientia *finge*' (cf. above, p. 12). It is even more surprising that Vahlen's observation, though repeated by Heinze and independently by P. Cauer, was consistently neglected until almost thirty years later it was made on different grounds by P. Boyancé; see below, pp. 32 f. But even here where Vahlen was evidently right he was not fully aware of Horace's argument. The difference between the two passages is not that the one is 'sub-

however important, are one thing; the fundamental problem, which Norden raised, is another. Here Vahlen's criticism was fumbling. It is impossible, he argued, in writing about poetry, to separate *ars* from *artifex*: hence Norden's bipartite division is not acceptable.[1] The point has been repeated only too often.[2] It would apply with equal force to all the undoubted cases of *ars–artifex* which Norden cited from writings on a large variety of arts. But it is irrelevant for all that. What matters is not whether the traditional distinction is clumsy, even illogical, but whether Horace employed it, and if he did how he employed it. Hence the awkwardness with which Vahlen first rejects Norden's contention; next, accepts it with so small a modification as not to matter; and finally leaves it all undecided so long as no doubt is cast on the poetic stature of the *Ars*.[3]

More intelligent criticism came from a lesser scholar. Paul Cauer readily accepted Norden's division into *ars–artifex*, but he doubted its application to the details of the poem.[4] He raised a question which even now has not been answered. If the unity of the work really depends on this simple rhetorical schema, why is the schema not brought out more clearly?

Cauer started his professional career as a schoolmaster. It may be that having to teach schoolboys he had good reason to notice what the experts were apt to overlook: the rhetorical schema (if it is applied at all) does not explain the *Ars* as we have it. It only explains that element of it which is in fact rhetoric applied to poetry. Wherever (says he) Horace saw fit

jective' and the other 'objective'. Rather it is contingent on the different premisses of Horace's literary doctrines: one deals with the unity of poetic conception, the other with the subject-matter of a poem.

[1] Vahlen, *op. cit.* II, 767 ff., 773.

[2] Particularly by readers who feel offended in their poetic taste by this curious distinction. So for example R. K. Hack, *op. cit.*

[3] Vahlen, *op. cit.* II, 773. 'Doch wie dem sei (denn ich wage nicht, zu entscheiden), den Brief an die Pisonen betrachte ich als eine Dichtung, die alle Anforderungen an ein Kunstwerk erfüllt.'

[4] P. Cauer, 'Zur Abgrenzung und Verbindung der Theile in Horazens Ars Poetica', *RM*, N.F. LXI (1906), 232–43.

to remind his readers of that element—a mode of teaching in which they as much as he had been brought up—he would do so, unobtrusively;[1] elsewhere he would not do so. Cauer considered two, and only two, of the devices which Horace employs in separating or connecting the parts of his poem.

One is the 'gliding transition' on which a great deal has been written since, not always with the acknowledgement due to Cauer's paper. Does, for example, the 'section on the poet' begin where Horace marks it clearly, at 306, *munus et officium nil scribens ipse docebo*? Scarcely, since this line is itself part of a longer sentence, just as that sentence is part of a longer train of thought, taking the reader right back to the preceding context, on the sufficiency of the poetic workshop in Greece and Rome—be it lines 295 or 289.[2] In this and many like passages the transition is so managed as to make it impossible to indicate the end of one and the beginning of another context: a clear sign that Horace at any rate did not encourage a cut-and-dried arrangement by textbook headings.

A second device is equally Horatian but even less amenable to hasty or prosaic simplification. Often (says Cauer) the poet offers, on the face of it, no connexion whatever between two topics.[3] He knew where he was going and it is up to the reader to take what hints he can in order to gather the drift of the poem. The appearance of a brusque abruptness is perhaps even more frequent than its opposite, the appearance of a gliding transition. When external links are absent, this may but need not always mean that two items are therefore unconnected. On the contrary the transition of thought may and often does proceed under the surface.[4] Cauer exemplifies particularly from the last part of the *Ars*, where thought seems to jump uncontrolled from one thing to another. His point is

---

[1] Cauer, *op. cit.* p. 242. 'Wenn sie [i.e. the readers] nur leise erinnert wurden, so wussten sie Bescheid; und sie wollten nicht laut erinnert sein.'

[2] Cf. above, p. 5.

[3] Cauer, *op. cit.* p. 238.

[4] Cauer, *op. cit.* p. 243, says perceptively, 'die verbindenden und gliedernden Gedanken sind ins Unbewusste geschoben'.

worth noting, for if there are jumps he showed that a number of them at any rate are not uncontrolled.

Thus within a year from the date of Norden's publication both Vahlen and Cauer had felt stimulated to raise some fundamental questions as regards this most difficult of all Horatian poems.[1] The former rejected Norden's pronouncements, the latter accepted them, with some qualifications. The stimulus however was insufficient to bring them face to face with the essential problem. Vahlen failed to account for a most puzzling fact. When all the needful corrections are made Norden's rhetorical schema for the *Ars* shares essential features with his own, which he said was not rhetorical. Cauer made a distinction between the exigencies of a treatise and of a poem. Yet he noted no more than two poetic features, however reasonable this restricted enquiry may have been in a brief paper. Neither of them asked the question whether Norden's bipartite scheme could possibly be the only ordering principle. In the event, Cauer was largely disregarded by the analysers, while Vahlen's authority paradoxically served to confirm Norden's authority. For although they held seemingly contrary views, they concurred in the same *non sequitur*. Either (they argued) the *Ars* was a kind of literary treatise—in which case a technical schema could be assumed—or it was not—then the schema was out of place. The choice does not apply. The *Ars* could be a kind of treatise without the schema and conversely it could hint at the schema without being a treatise. The problem was too narrowly conceived.

[1] The changes relevant to our problem which R. Heinze introduced into his new edition of A. Kiessling's commentary were made in 1908 and he made no changes thereafter. They are largely based on Vahlen, although Heinze was even more reluctant than the master to come to grips with the true difficulties of Norden's analysis. But unlike Vahlen he largely accepted the sense of Norden's bipartite division; a similar view is erroneously ascribed to Vahlen by E. Burck in his bibliographical appendix of 1959 (p. 403). The *ars–artifex* scheme was however wholeheartedly welcomed by K. Barwick, in 'Die Gliederung der rhetorischen τέχνη und die horazische Epistula ad Pisones', *H*, LVII (1922), 52, and by G. C. Fiske and Mary A. Grant, in 'Cicero's *Orator* and Horace's *Ars Poetica*', *HS*, xxxv (1924), and their later publication on 'Cicero's *De Oratore* and Horace's *Ars Poetica*', *Univ. of Wisconsin St.* xxvii (1929).

The Analytic Procedure and some Analyses

The argument might yet have been followed to its logical, Horatian, conclusion. But an unexpected discovery turned attention back to the technicalities of Greek literary criticism and away from Horace's poetry. By 1908 the pronouncements of Norden, Vahlen, and Cauer, had opened up a new line of scholarly inquiry. In the same year a young German student of papyri, Christian Jensen, started work upon the literary remains of Philodemus. Literary criticism was not Jensen's *forte*. He worked it up *ad hoc*, competently but at a middling level of critical understanding. He set out to read the papyri; and he approached their content by fitting Norden's new theories to his own new readings. He scored a remarkable success in deciphering not only the name of Horace's reputed authority in the *Ars*—one Neoptolemus of Parium—but in finding literary theories held by Neoptolemus and shared by Horace.[1] These the reader will find discussed fully in a subsequent chapter. What is relevant here is the bearing of the new readings on the analysis of the *Ars*.

Jensen's arithmetic does not seem to have been equal to his palaeography. For he found no difficulty in the equation, $3 = 2$. Philodemus said that Neoptolemus' division of the art of poetry was tripartite; it consisted of *poema*, *poesis*, and *poeta*. The meaning of this curious division will be considered in my next chapter. Only one aspect needs to be considered here. Jensen took Neoptolemus to denote the style and the content of verse by the terms *poema* and *poesis* respectively. *Poema* and *poesis* together could then denote all the technical details of the poet's craft while *poeta* could denote the more general questions of poetics. Now that *poema* and *poesis* may stand together *vis-à-vis* *poeta*, who will deny? That occasionally Neoptolemus may so have grouped them, there is some slight indication.[2] But that Neoptolemus' triad should be thus

[1] His findings were first published in a paper after the First World War, 'Neoptolemus und Horaz', *APA* (1918), later in his edition of the 5th Book of Philodemus, *De Poematis*, under the title *Philodemos über die Gedichte, Fünftes Buch* (1923).

[2] Philod. *De Poem.* v, col. xi, 5, p. 29, ed. Jensen (1923), ἀτόπως δὲ καὶ τὸν τὴν τέχνην καὶ δύναμιν ἔχοντα τὴν ποιητικὴν εἶδος παρίστησι τῆς τέχνης μετὰ τοῦ

29

reduced is not at all indicated. Jensen took it for granted.[1] Rather the juxtaposition of three, not two, elements is reported and attacked by Philodemus.[2] This difficulty alone should have caused Jensen to loosen up Norden's schema of *ars–artifex*. He might then have shed some light on Horace's less hidebound procedure. But Jensen had made up his mind. He claimed that Neoptolemus corroborated Norden's account of the *Ars* and in consequence he largely reproduced Norden's analysis.[3]

The procedures of Norden and Jensen gained much approval in the twenties.[4] Two large works of the thirties standardized their conclusions along with their false premisses.[5] A. Rostagni and O. Immisch opened up the wider, philosophical, vistas of ancient literary criticism, where there had been a certain narrow departmentalism before them. But their analyses of the *Ars* are rigid and unconvincing.

Rostagni set out to divide the poem into sections: a desirable task if it is undertaken with some tact and skill. But he drove a coach-and-four right through the poem. *Disiecti*

ποήματος καὶ τῆς ποιήσεως. If τὴν τέχνην here comprises *poema* as well as *poesis* a twofold order would be obtained. Cf. below, p. 58.

[1] Jensen, *op. cit.* pp. 100–5.   [2] Cf. below, p. 58.

[3] His only serious correction of Norden's work was prompted by Vahlen and Cauer: he rightly placed a new context at *A.P.* 119, not like Norden at 131, cf. Jensen, *op. cit.* p. 122, n. 2. The subtler points of Vahlen and Cauer left him unimpressed. He was unshaken in his belief that he was dealing with an isagogic treatise.

[4] The theories of Norden and Jensen formed the basis for an elaborate comparison between the *Ars* and Cicero's *Orator* and *De Oratore*; cf. Mary A. Grant and G. C. Fiske, in the publications cited above, p. 28, n. 1. There are many undoubted likenesses between the writings of Horace and Cicero; some of them of great interest and significance. But so far as the structure of the *Ars* is concerned the likenesses are insignificant. The two scholars were careful not to define too closely Horace's assumed degree of reliance on Cicero. Nevertheless they clearly ascribe much importance to the 'parallels' which they discuss. Their argument is vitiated not only by their uncritical adherence to the teaching of their predecessors. They also tend to ignore the marked differences between rhetorical theory on the one hand and rhetoric applied to poetic criticism on the other. Since rhetoric is concerned in both cases the basic similarity may deceive the unwary. But the differences had been established in literary criticism for centuries before Cicero and Horace.

[5] A. Rostagni, *L'Arte Poetica di Orazio* (1930); O. Immisch, *Horazens Epistel über die Dichtkunst, P*, Supp. vol. xxiv (1932).

membra poetae were seen scattered right and left. His paragraphing is a model of how a Horatian *sermo* should not be paragraphed.[1] Immisch, publishing a commentary without the text, did not fully paragraph the poem. But his definitions of the key terms *poema* and *poesis* are fanciful—one is surprised that he did not attempt to define *poeta* in the same fashion. He like Barwick and Rostagni added a section on *imitatio*.[2] His analysis differs from those of his predecessors chiefly in these details. But on the whole he too adhered to Norden's teachings.[3] A confrontation with Norden of Jensen, Rostagni, and Immisch will confirm the identity of views despite some considerable disagreement on details.

Norden, 1905	Jensen, 1918	Rostagni, 1930	Immisch, 1932
Ars (Poetica) 1–294	*Ars (Poetica)* 1–294	*Ars (Poetica)* 1–294	*Ars (Poetica)* 1–294
partes poeticae	ποίησις, *on content, order*	ποίησις, *on content, order*	ποίησις, *on poetry*
1–130			
1–41 content	1–44	1–45	1–46 content
42–4 order			and order
	ποίημα, *on style*	ποίημα, *on style*	
45–130 style	45–118	46–127	47–118 style
genera poeticae	*genera poeticae*		119–52 imitation
131–294	119–294	128–52 imitation	
			ποίημα, *on the genres*
epic	epic		
drama	drama	153–294 drama	153–294 selected genre, drama
Artifex, poeta 295–476	*Artifex,* ποιητής 295–476	*Artifex,* ποιητής 295–476	*Artifex,* ποιητής 295–476

[1] I cite one glaring inconsistency. Norden had walked across a clearly marked boundary line, at *A.P.* 118, believing that style was discussed from 45 to 130. Jensen heeded Vahlen's and Cauer's warnings; he concluded the topic of style at 118. Rostagni did not; he reproduced something like Norden's division, and believed that discussion of style ran on as far as 127. Then a cut, in the middle of a context, and a new section (on imitation) is supposed to begin at 128. This mistake at any rate is avoided by Immisch.

[2] Barwick in the paper cited above, p. 28, n. 1.

[3] In his table of contents, p. viii, Immisch puts forward the tripartite order of

This identity of views despite considerable disagreement on details has proved a *hereditas damnosa* to Horatian studies. The leading scholars whose views are summarized in my diagram agreed on one fundamental proposition. They found the true unity of the poem in Norden's bipartite *schema isagogicum*, and modified it so as to accommodate Neoptolemus' tripartite schema. But they could not agree on how to apply either or both. One suspects that they had not decided whether they were analysing the *Ars* as Horace has left it, or a literary theory to which Horace may have attached great or small importance. It seems that this literary theory existed in antiquity. But if it did, then both questions need to be answered. To treat them as one and the same question (whatever the answer) is to invite disappointment and cause confusion. Analysis has made little headway since Rostagni and Immisch precisely because of this awkward difficulty. Work in the 1930's still tended to concentrate on the Hellenistic, and only by implication on the Horatian, side of the problem.

How mechanically literary theories had in fact been applied to the *Ars* was demonstrated in 1936 by P. Boyancé.[1] Jensen and Rostagni were fully satisfied that Norden's schema was applicable both to Neoptolemus' triad and to Horace's *Ars*. They assumed that the poet had begun the poetic treatise at the beginning; and since Norden had equated the initial forty or so lines with the rhetorical topic of *inventio*, or the finding of subject-matter, they in turn equated this portion of the *Ars* with Neoptolemus' *poesis*, dealing with subject-matter, and the subsequent portion with *poema*, dealing with style. Immisch was even more strong-minded. He decided that the label *poesis* should be affixed to Horace's discussion of subject-matter *and* style *and* imitation (*A.P.* 1–46, 47–118, 119–52,

---

poesis–poema–poeta; at p. 9 he reduces it to what he calls 'Norden's *schema isagogicum*', equating *ars* with *poesis* plus *poema*, and *artifex* with *poeta*. Jensen, *SBPA*, (1936), p. 292, agreed with the former proposition, at p. 293 with the latter.

[1] P. Boyancé, 'À propos de l'Art poétique d'Horace', *RP*, x (1936), 20–36.

respectively), reserving *poema* for an (assumed) middle portion on poetic genres (153–294). Boyancé convincingly demonstrated that *poesis* is not likely to have been the first item of Neoptolemus' triad. Rather there is a presumption in favour of the order, (1) *poema*, on style, (2) *poesis*, on content, (3) *poeta*, on general questions of poetic criticism. He was convincing too in his treatment of the initial forty lines of the *Ars*. If Neoptolemus' terms have any relevance to Horace at all, then *poema* must be the label for the stylistic problems of lines 45–118 (plus 'arrangement', *ordo*, at 41) whereas *poesis* must apply to the problems of the plot at 119.[1] Thus the initial portion of the poem remains outside the technicalities indicated by Neoptolemus' *poema* and *poesis*, as indeed its topics would lead one to expect.[2] On this foundation Boyancé might have dealt successfully with most of the relevant problems. Regrettably however he did not extend his researches to the whole of the poem. Thus once more an opportunity was lost. Nor was he equally happy in discussing the Hellenistic theories associated with *poema* and *poesis*. These are defects; but they should not be allowed to detract from the elegant and just critique of assumptions that had been rashly made and too readily received.[3] What in fact the main 'sections' would be if note were taken of Boyancé's observations W. Schmid indicated in a brief paper;[4] *A.P.* 45–118 would correspond to Neoptolemus' *poema*, 119–294 would correspond to his *poesis*, and 295 ff. to his *poeta*.

[1] It does not however follow that the passage beginning at *A.P.* 119 only deals with drama, as Boyancé concluded.

[2] Cf. below, pp. 137–9. So in fact both Vahlen and Cauer had surmised before Neoptolemus had been called up from the shades.

[3] This is not to say that the unfounded assumptions of Jensen, Rostagni and Immisch were never to be heard of again. Domenico Bo, *Q. Orazio Flacco, Satire, Epistole, Arte Poetica* (1956), assigns *A.P.* 1–41 to *poesis*, 42–294 to *poema*; he writes as though no one since Rostagni had laboured in this field. G. Stégen, *Les épîtres littéraires d'Horace* (1958), canonizes Immisch in the same manner, assigning 1–152 to *poesis*, and 153–294 to *poema*.

[4] Wolfgang Schmid, 'Nugae Herculanenses', *RM*, XCII (1944), 53–4.

This simple application to the *Ars* of the terms of Greek literary criticism could now no longer carry conviction. Too many flaws had been discovered in the argument propounded by Norden and his successors. The stage was set for reaction; and reaction took various forms.

First of all a complete denial of anything reminiscent of the order of a textbook could be made. The relation between Horace's poetic order of things and the arrangement of a Greek textbook had never been satisfactorily explained. A relationship was assumed but not defined. It was open to scholars to deny the existence of a problem. Horace had never troubled himself about the technical procedure of Greek literary criticism; modern scholars need only follow his example. Outstanding, perhaps unique, among those who argued in this vein was F. Klingner.[1] The objection to modern research was that it ossified the flexible organism of a poem. Very well, it was argued, let us soften the hardened structure. Instead of its bone and cartilage Klingner proffered an *Ars Poetica* that was all skin and surface; the skeleton that should bear the burden was pushed into a cupboard. There it has remained ever since. This chapter deals with the structure of the poem; there would seem to be no call for a mention of his essay,[2] were it not for one unexpected agreement with his predecessors. The poem, says he, is after all divided according to *ars* and *artifex*—a curious opinion to hold, since the *artifex* context is no more, and indeed no less, marked off from the rest than some other parts of the poem.

A second way of dealing with the impasse seemed more attractive at first sight. The analysers had been accused of substituting a prosaic and rigid schema for Horace's poetic and flexible order. Could not this be remedied by establishing the poetic and flexible order of the poem—its poetic unity? But when such attempts were made the difficulties of the *Ars* were

---

[1] F. Klingner, 'Horazens Brief an die Pisonen', *BVSA*, 88, no. 3 (1936), 1–68.
[2] It will have to be mentioned again in a more relevant context, see below, p. 244.

seen to be bypassed rather than solved. For it is not a foregone conclusion that Horace, as was now asserted, had employed a single device in order to shape the multiplicity of his topics. Nor indeed is it easily seen how the poetic unity of the *Ars* can be even considered if some of the observable elements of the ancient literary tradition are jettisoned.[1]

Finally for the most radical solution of the problem—and the most unconvincing. This requires a detailed examination. For it not only involves an attempt to eliminate Norden's exaggerated rhetorical schema and Neoptolemus' triad, but affects the whole traditional foundation of a work that patently rests on a literary tradition. H. Dahlmann made this attempt.[2] He advanced three arguments which he considered foolproof. Are they? And if they are, how relevant are they to the problem?

His first argument impugns Norden's *schema isagogicum*.[3] The *ars–artifex* schema, says he, is not 'isagogic' because it does not suit the earliest titles of εἰσαγωγαί that are known.[4] Had he been content to make this point he would have done useful service. I should go even further than that. Since, as

---

[1] W. Steidle's little book, *Studien zur Ars Poetica des Horaz* (thesis, Würzburg, 1939), is the most competent attempt of this kind. Steidle worked sensibly on the interpretation of the text; his line of attack was that marked out by Vahlen and Heinze. He also made some progress in demarcating the contexts of the first part of the poem. The sequence of topics is further clarified—unity, order, *decorum* in style, followed by subject-matter, at 119. Yet he takes the short view of the poem as a whole. No attention is paid to the problems of Neoptolemus' triad. The poetic unity of the *Ars* is said to lie in the postulate of 'appropriateness', *decorum* or τὸ πρέπον. That this may be so had been argued with varying degrees of cogency by W. Kroll, R. Philippson, M. Pohlenz, R. K. Hack, Mary A. Grant and G. C. Fiske. A detailed but somewhat involved comparison between Cicero's and Horace's views on *decorum* had been offered by L. Labowsky, *Die Ethik des Panaitios* (1934). Now Steidle sought to represent this concept as the decisive feature of the poem. Other features found little consideration. It is not surprising that an intelligent reviewer remarked, amusingly if not very helpfully, that it is always expedient to fall back on τὸ πρέπον when everything else fails: see J. Tate, *CR*, LIII (1939), 192.

[2] H. Dahlmann, 'Varros Schrift "De poematis" und die hellenistisch-römische Poetik', *AAM* (1953), no. 3.

[3] Dahlmann, *op. cit.* p. 111, n. 2.

[4] Dahlmann, *loc. cit.*; some of the titles are cited above, p. 22, n. 2.

3-2

I have argued above,[1] nothing is known of any of these early 'Introductions', there is no call to associate any known schema whatever with these writings. The pair *ars–artifex* then is not likely to be 'isagogic', whatever else it may be. But this result has little relevance to the Horatian problem since the *Ars* may be arranged according to *ars–artifex*, whether the distinction is isagogic or not.

Dahlmann however is not content with this restricted type of conclusion. He argues further that the *Ars* (like Quintilian's *Institutio*) is too personal a work to have been conceived on traditional lines.[2] He hardly considers the more likely contingency that Horace may have made reference to *ars–artifex* or a like distinction *because* it was a traditional feature of a literary treatise, *ars* or *techne*. But judgement here surely depends on whether we have reason to believe that Horace thought it worth his while to allude to traditional features, whether 'isagogic' or not.

Dahlmann apparently believed that his third argument was sufficiently strong to take care of the previous point as well. He contends that even if Horace's poem resembled a traditional *ars* more than he thinks it does, this resemblance would not prove a traditional layout, whether twofold or threefold.[3] For just as others before him he was impressed by the extant specimens of textbooks or treatises, late though they are. Such specimens as the scholia to Dionysius Thrax do indeed make reference to *ars–artifex*, and the like. The references however amount to no more than generalities about a skill or about the subject of a branch of learning, and about the training and aims of those who profess it. These generalities are of an abstract nature; they rarely touch the subject-matter of the treatise. The points are made in the introductions of these

[1] Above, p. 22.
[2] Dahlmann, *loc. cit.*
[3] Dahlmann, *loc. cit.*, citing J. Börner, *De Quintiliani inst. or. dispositione* (thesis, Leipzig, 1911), and others. Heinze gave some publicity to Börner's observation in the introduction to his commentary on the *Ars*, where a similar argument is presented.

works; they are made in a perfunctory manner and do not normally interfere with the plan of the treatise itself. Most of these writings are no more than summaries. The rich flow of earlier scholarship is reduced to a thin trickle, and what thought there was in the earlier models is reduced to a few handy definitions. Yet Dahlmann is ready to accept the scribblings of these hacks as a criterion, as the 'norm of an ancient treatise'. His conclusions are what conclusions from false premises are bound to be. Horace and Quintilian were not hacks; so he concludes that any approximations to any type of treatise they may offer must be 'untypical'. Hence if Horace's *Ars* or Quintilian's *Institutio* shows traces of a threefold structure or of the schema *ars–artifex*, these traces are 'untypical'. One more step is now needed to make confusion complete. Since the late specimens of the genre are not arranged in bipartite or tripartite fashion, Neoptolemus' triad cannot have had anything to do with the layout of his treatise. Neoptolemus too must have been content with a perfunctory reference to *poema–poesis–poeta* in his introduction. Neoptolemus' triad is 'typical' and not therefore used as a principle of arrangement; Horace's triad which is so used has already been declared 'untypical'; *ergo* Horace must be dissociated from Neoptolemus.

I find myself unable to accept this manner of reasoning. The skeins of the argument have become badly entangled. Unravelling them one finds the following separate skeins.

(*a*) *The plan of Hellenistic treatises.* This item largely calls for an argument on general grounds. I have presented such an argument earlier in this chapter.[1] My conclusion allows for the possibility, even the probability, that pairs such as *ars–artifex* or triads such as *poema–poesis–poeta* were employed to give some coherence to the layout of a treatise. The tradition must not be judged by late and desiccated specimens. The case for any specific treatise has to be made on its own merits.

[1] Above, p. 23.

(*b*) *The specific evidence for Neoptolemus' triad.* The evidence
should not be judged by the stylistic properties of late scholiasts and grammarians. The details of the case will be presented in the chapter devoted to Neoptolemus of Parium.
I there argue that the most satisfactory explanation of the
ancient evidence makes against Dahlmann's conclusion:
Neoptolemus' treatise seems to have differed from the late
specimens adduced by Dahlmann in that it appears to have
been arranged according to the triad, *poema–poesis–poeta*.[1]

(*c*) *Structural elements in Horace's 'Ars'.* These are different
matters again. It is misleading to speak of *the* structure of the
Ars as though Horace had written a textbook and not a
poem with a multiplicity of formal elements. My first chapter
was concerned with those elements to which the technical
character of an ancient, literary, treatise may be ascribed.
I concluded that a tripartite structure of this 'technical' kind
underlies the *Ars*. I did not attempt to assess the importance
that Horace may have ascribed to these elements. Dahlmann
has proved that late scholiasts and grammarians do not use
the traditional principles in the same way as Horace does.
This neither proves nor disproves Horace's use of traditional
principles in his own way. It only proves that these men did
no longer apply the same larger principles to their work as
some of their more intelligent predecessors had done.

Neglect these distinctions and confusion will ensue. Confusion has ensued. I believe that the dissociation of Horace's
triad from that of Neoptolemus begs the question.

Dahlmann acknowledges a twofold or threefold order of
subjects in Horace (and Quintilian); yet he writes it off as 'by
no means typical' because it does not occur in any earlier writer.
But whether the schema occurred in any earlier writer is
precisely what we wish to find out: it cannot be both known

---

[1] Since the bipartite and tripartite schemes are often confused in modern discussion the following proviso may be added. The pair *ars–artifex* is not necessarily
identical with *poema–poesis* as against *poeta*. Moreover, although Neoptolemus'
terms have a rhetorical tinge they were drawn from poetry: *poema–poesis–poeta*.

and unknown.[1] Vahlen contradicted the results of his own analysis when he at once affirmed and denied the new teaching.[2] Dahlmann contradicts his own argument when he at once accepts and rejects the use of Neoptolemus' scholastic triad. Having denied that the triad, *poema–poesis–poeta*, could have been used by Neoptolemus as it appears to be used by Horace—that is, as a schema underlying his treatise—he yet reached the following conclusion. 'Apart from the lack of an especial section on *poeta*,[3] the arrangement of Neoptolemus' *Ars Poetica* will have corresponded wholly to that of his successor Horace.'[4] Does it follow, then, that Neoptolemus did and did not arrange his work under general headings? Since both inferences cannot obtain simultaneously, one of them needs to be jettisoned—the sequel will show which. In spite of this fundamental contradiction, Dahlmann's treatise has been commended. It is said that it 'stands not only chronologically at the end of a long line of such studies, but in a

---

[1] Cf. *op. cit.* p. 111, n. 2, 'Quintilians institutio und Horazens Brief verkörpern eine durchaus eigentümliche und keineswegs typische Form der technischen Lehrschrift, die in der Poetik nicht vor Horaz, in der Rhetorik nicht vor Quintilian und sonst überhaupt anscheinend nie nachweisbar ist...'. Is the upshot of this pronouncement that Horace and Quintilian invented this layout? Dahlmann does not say so, but E. Burck appears to hold this view. What in Dahlmann is no more than an implication, and in Heinze no more than a possible implication, Burck brings into the open; cf. his bibliographical appendix (*op. cit.* p. 418). 'Wenn die Ars aber nun dennoch, wie auch Heinze und Dahlmann nicht leugnen, die von Norden festgestellte Zweiteilung in *ars–artifex* aufweist, so liegt die Vermutung nahe, dass Horaz selbst diese Einteilung geschaffen hat.'

[2] Above, p. 26.

[3] It is hard to see why one is asked to ignore the third prong of Neoptolemus' triad but not equally the other two. Dahlmann's arguments are adduced, *op. cit.* pp. 99–111. They are further discussed below, pp. 72–3.

[4] Dahlmann (*op. cit.* p. 139, n. 1) has his own way of accounting for this correspondence without troubling Neoptolemus. The technical portion of the *Ars* (up to 294) is to be explained by direct reference to the three modes of imitation, in Aristotle's *Poetics*, ch. 1—the objects of imitation (ἅ), its medium, verse recited, sung, etc. (ἐν οἷς), and its manner, dramatic, narrative, etc. (ὡς). But at *Ars*, 40–294, Horace is applying plain rhetorical terms to poetry—cf. 40–1, *ordo*, *facundia*, *res*. How that squares with Neoptolemus and Aristotle will be debated in the next section. But it clearly does not square with the *Poetics*; for in that work Aristotle looked at poetry as modes of imitation, not chiefly as an expression and ordering of subject-matter.

39

certain respect, reasonably if provisionally, brings to a close this most controversial *Kompositionsfrage*.[1] It seems to me, on the contrary, that no tenable conclusion has as yet been reached.

The long and weary train of treatises and papers on the structure of the *Ars* has left confusion and illogicality in its wake. A fresh beginning will have to be made. And first of all some common sense will have to be shown in the questions we ask. It would be well if scholars could decide what they wish to do. Do they wish to treat the *Ars* as a quarry in order to unearth the kind of tradition in which Horace chose to work? Or do they wish to analyse Horace in order to determine what he made of that tradition? There is a case for undertaking both operations. But there is no case for the muddled thinking which mistakes a great poet for the tradition in which he worked, and the tradition for a great poet.

The survey of the second chapter and the analysis of the first have led to precisely the same questions. The *Ars Poetica* employs certain principles of arrangement which are related to conventional ancient literary criticism. The state of our evidence makes it hard but not impossible to determine what these conventions were. In the subsequent chapters I shall try to determine such conventions as are relevant to the *Ars Poetica*. For that purpose I will turn to Aristotle and Neoptolemus of Parium. Having determined these conventions I propose to ask what importance Horace ascribed to them in his literary criticism and in his own, poetical, scheme of things.

[1] So E. Burck (*op. cit.*, 1959, p. 417). K. Büchner endorses Dahlmann's pronouncements, cf. 'Humanitas Horatiana, *A.P.* 1–37', *Studia Classica*, Cape Town, I (1958), 70. N. A. Greenberg ('The use of Poiema and Poiesis', *HS*, LXV (1961), 263 ff.), extends an even more enthusiastic welcome to them.

PART II

THE TRADITION OF
LITERARY CRITICISM AND THE
'ARS POETICA'

NEOPTOLEMUS OF PARIUM

In my first chapter I analysed the *Ars Poetica* without paying attention to any matters extraneous to the poem. The result was not perhaps startling. It was certainly incomplete. But, for better or worse, it was derived from the poem and only from the poem. I used no technical language from literary criticism or rhetoric and I did not breathe a word about Horace's predecessors and the bearing their work might have had on his own pronouncements. Yet the *Ars* does deal with literary criticism, and the structure of earlier criticism may have left its mark on the structure of that work. This contingency explains why, in discussing recent analytic study, I had occasion to make reference to Neoptolemus of Parium.

The scholiast Porphyrion introduces his notes on the *Ars* with the following celebrated remark: 'in this book Horace has brought together the teachings of Neoptolemus of Parium on the art of poetry—not indeed all but the most outstanding' (*in quem librum congessit praecepta Neoptolemi* τοῦ Παριανοῦ *de arte poetica, non quidem omnia sed eminentissima*). Such information as this cannot help readers if they feel anyway lost in the maze of the *Ars*. But if they have a rough and ready map of the maze there may be some point in scanning extraneous information.

In the nineteenth century scholarly opinion was sharply divided over the validity of Porphyrion's information.[1] New

---

[1] W. Y. Sellar for example thus summarized one part of prevailing opinion. The 'purely didactic part' (about three-fifths of the poem) 'seems to be a *résumé* of Greek criticism on the drama, ultimately, perhaps, based on the doctrines of Aristotle; but, according to Porphyrion, really made up of selections from an Alexandrian critic, Neoptolemus of Parium' (*Horace and the Elegiac Poets*, 1899, p. 112). Contrariwise A. Michaelis expressed the opinion held by many doubters. 'Pauca igitur sunt quae aliqua cum probabilitate Horatius ex Neoptolemo *congerere* potuisse videatur, ut quod Porphyrio refert fumum potius quam lucem

evidence has accrued since; but it has not served to restore scholarly concord. The reverse is the case. Discussion between any two Horatian scholars makes it only too clear that we are far from agreement. But in spite of much effort the new evidence has not been fully digested. The present section therefore seeks to answer only one question. How far does the evidence, new and old, support Porphyrion's statement?

The Neoptolemus known before 1918 was a poet and grammarian. Our sources do not call him an Alexandrian;[1] but the character of his output points to Alexandria and so does his combining the writing and the criticism of verse. His literary remains had been duly assembled.[2] He had written a mythological poem about Dionysus;[3] also what appears to be a didactic poem, probably geographical, called 'Tricontinental'.[4] As a *littérateur* and 'grammarian' he had published books about epigrams[5] and about witty sayings;[6] and above all, the works for which he was best known, the *Homeric Glosses*,[7] and the *Phrygian Glosses*, in which he used the Phrygian language to explain the meaning of Greek words.[8] To a man

adferat nostrae quaestioni' (*Diss. de auctoribus quos Horatius in libro de arte poetica secutus esse videatur*, Kiliae, 1857, p. 16). Cf. the same writer's 'Die horazischen Pisonen', in *Commentationes phil. in hon. Theodori Mommseni* (1877), p. 421.

[1] E. Norden (*Antike Kunstprosa*, I, 1898, p. 189), and O. Stählin and W. Schmid (*Griech. Lit.* II, 1, 6th ed., 1920, p. 170), concluded that he must have belonged to the local, Pergamenian, school because he was born at Parium in the Troad.

[2] A. Meineke (*Analecta Alexandrina*, 1843, pp. 357–60) offered a critical if incomplete survey. J. U. Powell's later collection, made after the new material had accrued, cannot by any means be called an improvement (*Collectanea Alexandrina*, 1925, pp. 27–8). H. J. Mette's article in *R-E*, xvi, 2, 'Neoptolemos (II)', cols. 2465–70, presents the material competently; but his treatment of an important part of the evidence is hazardous, cf. below, p. 55, n. 1. He (like O. Immisch, in his commentary on Horace's *Ars*, and K. Latte, *H*, LX, 1925, pp. 1–13) draws attention to Neoptolemus' probable or possible links with Alexandria.

[3] Νεοπτόλεμος ὁ Παριανὸς ἐν τῇ Διονυσιάδι: extant one reference. Below, p. 47.

[4] For the title, Τριχθονία, see E. Maass, *Aratea*, 204; extant one fragment: cf. Powell's references, *op. cit.*, Neoptol. fr. 2, Euphorion, fr. 122; Wilamowitz, *Hellenist. Dicht.* II, 300, n. 2. Below, p. 47.

[5] Περὶ ἐπιγραμμάτων; extant one fragment. Below, p. 47.

[6] Περὶ ἀστεϊσμῶν; extant again one fragment. Below, p. 47.

[7] Περὶ γλωσσῶν 'Ομήρου, in at least three books. Below, pp. 47–8.

[8] Νεοπτόλεμος ἐν ταῖς Φρυγίαις φωναῖς. Below, p. 47; cf. J. Friedrich, *R-E*, xx, 1, 'Phrygia (Sprache)', col. 871.

writing in the time of Augustus he was worthy of note for his glossaries.[1] An ancient reference to his *Glosses* may also indicate his date, though not in a very helpful fashion. He appears to have been cited by Aristophanes of Byzantium[2] and that puts him in the third century, or at any rate before *c.* 180 B.C., the probable time of Aristophanes' death. The third century is also suggested by the character of his literary and scholarly production. By that I mean not only the grammatical and antiquarian studies that resemble those of the other Alexandrians, but the (apparently) learned character of his verse, and particularly the combination of that kind of verse with that kind of scholarship, which recalls the like (if larger and more important) output of such men as Callimachus and Eratosthenes.

But there appears to be one difference which is relevant to our discussion. For centuries scholars had known the one sentence of Porphyrion's commentary that linked Neoptolemus' name with the *Ars*, the sentence already cited on *praecepta Neoptolemi* τοῦ Παριανοῦ *de arte poetica*. Now this should have caused some surprise, as indeed it still might. For although the combination of versifying and antiquarian or grammatical studies is in the authentic Alexandrian tradition, the specific interest in literary criticism that is ascribed to Neoptolemus is perhaps a different matter. Certainly, Callimachus had pronounced on literary criticism; but apart

---

[1] So Strabo says, XIII, 1, 19, ἐκ Παρίου μὲν οὖν ὁ γλωσσογράφος κληθεὶς ἦν Νεοπτόλεμος μνήμης ἄξιος. I count eight references to him in the Homeric *scholia*, in other *scholia* where a reference to Homer is likely (Hesiod and Theocritus), and finally in Greek lexicographers. Mette gives a list of references in the *scholia* (*op. cit.* cols. 2465–6).

[2] Eustathius, on the word μολοβρός, Homer, *Od.* XVII, 219, ὄν, φησί (i.e. Aristophanes), Νεοπτόλεμος ἀναπτύσσων.... εἶπε κτλ. A. Nauck considered the citation improbable on chronological grounds and, unconvincingly, replaced φησί by φασί, *Aristophanis Byzantini fragmenta* (1848), p. 119, n. 70. F. Susemihl (*Gesch. d. gr. Lit. in der Alexandrinerzeit*, I, 373), suggested that Neoptolemus' interest in Phrygian glosses might have been stimulated by Callimachus' 'Εθνικαὶ 'Ονομασίαι. Mette (*loc. cit.*) suggested that Neoptolemus' polemic against ψυχαγωγία as the sole aim of poetry might have been induced by Eratosthenes who held that view. Neither suggestion can be proved and neither need imply an earlier date than the second half of the third century B.C.

from one book, whose nature, apparently, was polemical, Callimachus' criticism was that of a poet speaking in verse and using terms appropriate to verse.[1] But there is no indication that Neoptolemus' book was in verse.[2] It is true also that later Alexandrian critics considered poetic criticism a part of what they named γραμματική—according to Dionysius Thrax its sixth, final, and best 'part'.[3] Yet the remains of the early Alexandrians do not suggest that their critical interests prompted *praecepta de arte poetica*. Neoptolemus' book, if one is entitled to judge from the relevant portions of Horace's *Ars*, did not resemble Callimachus' critical pronouncements but had Aristotelian leanings. This feature might have recalled a figure betwixt and between the Aristotelian and Alexandrian schools, Praxiphanes of Rhodes, but Praxiphanes did not apparently write verse.[4] The evidence concerning Neoptolemus, then, admittedly slender before 1918, might have been just sufficient to raise some new questions about a formative period of Greek literary criticism of which little was known. On this showing the existence of a literary critic Neoptolemus could not be proved, on the other hand it could not be disproved.

The following are the fragments that were known at that time:[5]

[1] *CQ*, xl (1946), 16.

[2] This assumption used to be made: see for example F. Susemihl, *op. cit.* I, 406, n. 179[b]; but there is no evidence encouraging it.

[3] Dionysius Thrax, I, γραμματική ἐστιν ἐμπειρία τῶν παρὰ ποιηταῖς τε καὶ συγγραφεῦσιν ὡς ἐπὶ τὸ πολὺ λεγομένων. μέρη δὲ αὐτῆς ἕξ... ἕκτον κρίσις ποιημάτων, ὃ δὴ κάλλιστον πάντων τῶν ἐν τῇ τέχνῃ.

[4] For Praxiphanes, see *CQ*, xl (1946), 11–26.

[5] *Locus fragmentorum collectores effugit* is C. Wendel's note in the index of his edition of the *Scholia in Apollonium Rhodium*, with regard to the mention of one Neoptolemus, *schol.* II, 299. The discussion concerned a mythological detail in which Neoptolemus and Apollonius concurred; cf. Kinkel, *Epicorum Gr. frag.* I, *Carmen Naupactium*, fr. 3; Pherecydes, *FGH*, 3, 29 Jac.; E. Diehl, *R-E*, xvi, 2, Ναυπάκτια ἔπη, col. 1977, 9. A Neoptolemus without a distinctive label is more likely than not the well-known Parian; the concurrence with Apollonius may point to a poem. The reference was rejected by Meineke (*Anal. Alex.* p. 358). Choeroboscus' citation of one Neoptolemus (Cramer, *Anec. Ox.* II, 239) is yet more uncertain.

Neoptolemus of Parium

1. NEOPTOLEMUS, THE POET

Dionysias

Athenaeus, III, 23: Νεοπτόλεμος δ' ὁ Παριανὸς ἐν τῇ Διονυσιάδι καὶ αὐτὸς ἱστορεῖ ὡς ὑπὸ Διονύσου εὑρεθέντων τῶν μήλων καθάπερ καὶ τῶν ἄλλων ἀκροδρύων.

Trichthonia

Achilles, *Isagoga*, 22 (E. Maass, *Comment. in Aratum*, p. 51): ὅθεν καὶ Νεοπτόλεμος ὁ Παριανὸς ἐν τῇ Τριχθονίᾳ φησὶν 'τῷ πᾶσα περίρρυτος ἐνδέδεται χθών'.

Schol. A, Hom. *Il.* xviii, 490: φησὶ γὰρ ⟨?Νεοπτόλεμος ὁ Παριανὸς⟩ʿ 'Ὠκεανὸς ᾧ πᾶσα περίρρυτος ἐνδέδεται χθών'.

2. THE SCHOLAR AND GRAMMARIAN

De epigrammatis

Athenaeus, x, 81: Νεοπτόλεμος δ' ὁ Παριανὸς ἐν τῷ Περὶ ἐπιγραμμάτων ἐν Χαλκηδόνι φησὶν ἐπὶ τοῦ Θρασυμάχου τοῦ σοφιστοῦ μνήματος ἐπιγεγράφθαι τόδε τὸ ἐπίγραμμα·

τοὔνομα θῆτα ῥῶ ἄλφα σὰν ὓ μῦ ἄλφα χεῖ οὖ σάν·
πατρὶς Χαλκηδών· ἡ δὲ τέχνη σοφίη.

De facetiis

Stobaeus, *Florileg.* IV, 52, 24 (vol. v, p. 1080, ed. Hense): Νεοπτόλεμος ἐν τῷ Περὶ ἀστεϊσμῶν·

ὦ θάνατ' εἴθ' εἴης αὐτάγρετος, ὄφρ' ἂν ἑλοίμην
πρώτιστος· καί κ' ἐχθρὸς ἐὼν πολὺ φίλτατος εἴης.

De vocibus Phrygiorum

Achilles, *Isagoga*, 5 Maass, *op. cit.* p. 36 (on οὐρανός from ὄρος): ἐπεὶ ἀνώτατός ἐστι· τῷ δὲ ὄρῳ τὸ ἄνω δηλοῦν Φρυγῶν ἴδιον, ὡς Νεοπτόλεμος ἐν ταῖς Φρυγίαις φωναῖς.

Glossarium

Strabo, XIII, 1, 19: ἐκ Παρίου μὲν οὖν ὁ γλωσσογράφος κληθεὶς ἦν Νεοπτόλεμος μνήμης ἄξιος.

47

Neoptolemus' glossary contained at least three books. Apart from the eight citations in which the author's name occurs (with or without the title of the work), there must be many more where his name is not now extant. But anonymous material can be traced only when it resembles citations known to be derived from Neoptolemus.[1]

3. THE LITERARY CRITIC

?De Arte Poetica

Porphyrion on Horace, *A.P.* 1: 'in quem librum congessit praecepta Neoptolemi τοῦ Παριανοῦ de arte poetica, non quidem omnia sed eminentissima.'

The single item of the third section was taken out of its isolation when in 1918 Christian Jensen published the celebrated paper on Neoptolemus and Horace to which I referred in my last chapter.[2] He announced that in a papyrus of the fifth book of Philodemus' work 'On Poems' he had discovered not only the name of Neoptolemus but a number of fragments with a bearing on the *Ars Poetica*. It so happened that two papyrus copies of Philodemus' book had been preserved and in both cases the author's name and the title were extant. This was rare luck, only once repeated in the case of the Περὶ ποιημάτων, for the texts belong to the famous collection of Herculaneum[3] and it is well known that when these papyri were discovered in the eighteenth century most of them were cut up and usually the author's name and the title were lost. As in the other cases, we mainly rely on the copies made at the time by draftsmen who apparently knew no Greek—one copy preserved and published at Naples, the other preserved and first published at Oxford. Jensen collated the originals at Naples in 1908, but not in full, and was not able to complete

---

[1] For the citations, see Mette in *R-E, loc. cit.*   [2] Above, p. 29.

[3] It has been conjectured, with some probability, that the 'villa of the papyri' where the collection was found may have belonged to Philodemus' patron Piso. For a discussion and bibliography, see R. G. M. Nisbet's edition of Cicero's *In Pisonem* (1961), appendix IV, with brief bibliography.

the collation. The rolls may reveal yet more to the eyes of an experienced student of papyri, specially in the initial columns where Jensen's procedure has been very selective. The two papyri are known by the numbers 1425 and 1538.[1] The former has the title, Φιλοδήμου περὶ ποιημάτων ε̄, the latter, Φιλοδήμου περὶ ποιημάτων τοῦ ε̄ τῶν εἰς δύο τὸ β̄—that is, because of its length two rolls were used for the same book; the second roll is (partly) preserved and thus supplements the other papyrus towards the end of the book. Jensen's edition of 1923[2] juxtaposes, in two columns, N and O, the Naples and Oxford transcripts, and on the opposite side offers the editor's own readings of the papyri and his supplements along with a German rendering. In addition Jensen reprinted almost verbally his paper on Neoptolemus and Horace, and added others.

The most important of all the new readings is doubtless the name of Neoptolemus, in the tenth column of papyrus no. 1425. The lines in which it occurs (32–3) contain these letters: .]ΛΛΑΜΗΝϹ[......]⁻ΟΛΕΛ ΟϹ. At the beginning [ἀ]λλὰ μὴν is easily read. The next letter may be a sigma (Ϲ) or an incomplete omicron; which of the two is suggested by the next line beginning ΟΥΚΟ followed by the top part of Ρ, a gap of six or seven letters and an Є. Jensen's supplement, οὐκ ὀρ[θῶς ἔδοξ]ε, is very acceptable, particularly in view of what looks like an infinitive two lines down, [....]ʒε[ι]ν; the supplement [χωρί]ʒε[ι]ν is suggested by the content of the sentence. If this is so a grammatical subject is required for οὐκ ὀρθῶς ἔδοξε...χωρίʒειν. ΟΛΕΛ ΟϹ is preserved, the horizontal stroke before these letters is the top part of a Τ, and there are not many names ending in -τόλεμος, and accommodating the requisite number of letters. Of the eighteen named ending in -(π)τόλεμος that are listed in B. Hansen's *Rückläufiges Wörterbuch der griechischen Eigennamen*, only one—

---

[1] Descriptions are found in Walter Scott's *Fragmenta Herculanensia* (Oxford, 1885), pp. 75–6, and W. Crönert, *Memoria Graeca Herculanensis* (1903), p. 6.

[2] C. Jensen, *Philodemos über die Gedichte, Fünftes Buch* (1923).

Neoptolemus—is the name of a literary critic. I have little doubt that Jensen's supplement, ὅ [γε Νεοπ]τόλεμος, is right; Jensen's reading of the preserved letters is said to have been confirmed by A. Olivieri and V. De Falco who inspected the papyrus after Jensen.[1]

The proper name in this place is suggested not only by the sentence that has been discussed but by its wider context. Less than one-half of the (partly) extant 38 columns of papyrus no. 1425 consists of what may be called a single section (columns ix–xxvi). The earlier columns may contain some references to Neoptolemus and, I believe, a case for this may be made, at any rate as regards the column immediately preceding this section;[2] but I do not now propose to argue the matter since the name of Neoptolemus is preserved only in this section.[3] The section is introduced thus: 'Of those whose opinions are reported by Philolomelus some say…', τῶν το[ί]νυν παρὰ τῶι Φιλομήλ[ωι] γεγραμμένων οἱ μὲν…λέγουσι. The final sentence of the section, col. xxvi, runs as follows: 'hence after refuting the doctrines mentioned by Zeno we shall conclude this book which is too long already', ὥσ[τε] τὰς παρὰ Ζήνωνι δόξας ἐπικόψαντες ἤδη [με]μηκυσμένον τὸ σύγγραμμα καταπαύσομεν. Παρὰ Ζήνωνι corresponds to

[1] Thus P. Fossataro, *RFIC*, XLIX (1921), 252, n. 2. Olivieri also confirmed the τ of (Νεοπ)τόλεμος. The copyists of the Naples and Oxford transcripts did very badly here; the former saw only one stroke of the Λ, and the Є, whereas the latter identified ΟΔЄ instead of ΟΛЄ.

[2] At the beginning of col. xi Philodemus criticizes Neoptolemus for separating style and content. He reports that Neoptolemus said that style was οὐδὲν η[.........] ἢ πλείω, 'as we have noted earlier', καθάπερ ἐπενοήσαμεν (line 4). Jensen supplied the letters ἤ[ττω μερίδα]—'that style is not a smaller part (of poetics or verse) or even a greater'—remembering that at col. ix, 2–3 the same sense occurred in a like context. In the earlier place the words are almost fully preserved: αὐτὸ [τ]ὸ ποιεῖν οὐδὲν ἂν ἐλάττω λαβεῖ[ν] μερίδα ἀλ[λ]ὰ καὶ πλείω τὸ εἰς τοῦτο. This is likely to supply not only the letters missing in col. xi but explain the point of καθάπερ ἐπενοήσαμεν. If this is so, at any rate cols. viii–ix contained a discussion of Neoptolemus.

[3] A new collation of the earlier columns would be desirable before discussion is resumed. Jensen discredited his treatment of that section by ascribing its content first to Neoptolemus and later, even less convincingly, to Heraclides of Pontus— cf. C. Jensen, *RM*, LXXXIII (1934), 196, and 'Herakleides von Pontos bei Philodemos und Horaz', *SBPA* (1936), pp. 292–320.

παρὰ τῷ Φιλομήλῳ—apparently two authors of books (text-books, one presumes) from which Philodemus has selected the defendants for his (Epicurean) indictment. The doctrines of the defendants are reported (and refuted) not out of their own mouths but out of someone else's.[1] Knowing the strongly partisan character of Epicurean polemics, which is fully borne out by Philodemus' book, one concludes that the inter-mediaries were Epicureans as well. Philomelus is not other-wise known, but Zeno would then be the Epicurean philosopher who taught Philodemus and whose influence on Philodemus' writings is otherwise attested.[2] Not only the reports, therefore, but the Epicurean counter-arguments would seem to have been prefabricated.

The Philomelus section, unlike that taken from Zeno, is arranged according to the authors indicted: 'some say' (col. ix); 'Praxiphanes says' (col. ix); 'Demetrius of Byzantium writes' (cols. ix–x); Neoptolemus (cols. x–xiii); an author with Stoic leanings, probably Ariston (cols. xiii–xxi); Crates (cols. xxi–xxvi). Each of these sections is set off by a paragraph mark; as Jensen observed, there is such a mark before the Neoptolemus section, and after that a proper name ought to follow; so the wider context confirms what the remains of the sentence suggest.

It is doubtful whether the writers are set out in chrono-logical order or according to the schools to which they belong. They do seem to fall naturally into the latter. First Aristote-lians: 'some' writers, Praxiphanes, and Demetrius of Byzan-tium. Neoptolemus, who follows, cannot with certainty be assigned to the Lyceum but, as will be seen, he shares the Aristotelian tradition. And, thirdly, two Stoics. I am not equally certain that there is also a chronological sequence, as has been assumed.[3] Praxiphanes' *floruit* was *c.* 300 B.C.;

[1] Whether these opinions were reported more fully in a preceding portion of Philodemus' work in an open question. Cf. Jensen, 'Philodemos', p. 94; N. Greenberg, *HS*, LXV (1961), 287, n. 25.

[2] Scott, *op. cit.* p. 76; Jensen, *op. cit.* p. 95.

[3] Jensen, *op. cit.* p. 97, n. 2; R. Philippson, *R-E*, 'Philomelos'.

Crates, that is Crates of Mallos, comes bottom of the list, and last in order of time. If Ariston's name is rightly restored, and if he is the heterodox Stoic, he would be dated by his master Zeno, the founder of the Stoic school, (say) 280–260. Hence if the order is chronological, Neoptolemus, who precedes him in the list, could be dated to the first half of the third century. This is attractive for other reasons that will soon appear, but the combination of two different principles in the same list makes one wonder: the evidence is uncomfortably ambiguous.

If we can be satisfied, however, that we are in fact here dealing with a person called Neoptolemus (the label ὁ Παριανός is not affixed),[1] what are his teachings, and is he the author from whom Horace took *praecepta de arte poetica*, not indeed *omnia* but *eminentissima*? The latter question clearly cannot be answered as yet, and as for the former it will put the matter in its proper perspective if we remember the setting in which Neoptolemus' teachings are preserved, and the nature of the author who preserved them.

If Philodemus reported elsewhere more fully on Neoptolemus and others, these reports are not preserved. What we read in this section is a criticism of Neoptolemus and it is Neoptolemus twice removed. It is bits and pieces from Neoptolemus as selected and (presumably) criticized by Philomelus, as reported for the purposes of a critique by Philodemus. Neoptolemus' own book may or may not have been used by him. Of Philomelus nothing is known, although we may reasonably assume that he belonged to the Epicurean school. But the Epicurean bias of Philodemus is known. This bias has prompted his critique and it may have prompted the selection of his evidence. Nevertheless, the husk of Philodemus' critique can be peeled off. What then emerges is rarely a literal citation, though in most cases it is Neoptolemus' doctrine and terminology.

How much of Neoptolemus' doctrine and terminology

---

[1] It may have been affixed prior to this passage.

survives in Philodemus' critical setting? And, furthermore, how much can be known of Philodemus' own convictions which presumably formed the basis of his criticism? In the extant portions of the two papyri Philodemus never cites more of Neoptolemus' or any other adversary's doctrines than a phrase or two, or else a sentence or two, at a time. As for the statements which he so cites, he does not pause to consider what prompted them or what was their context. He searches for contradictions in the adversary's argument and he registers his disapproval. It used to be thought that he did no more, and consequently the value of his captious criticism was played down[1] until Augusto Rostagni made a case for a different view. He argued that Philodemus' own aesthetic doctrine had to be taken seriously. The Epicureans, he contended, differed sharply from the assessment of poetry that largely prevailed in the Graeco-Roman world. Rostagni therefore proceeded to reconstruct the dissenting views held by Philodemus.[2] It stands to reason that the Epicureans dissented in some questions of principle. But, as elsewhere in his work on ancient literary criticism, Rostagni asserted more than the evidence will yield. For few unambiguous statements of Philodemus' own doctrine are as yet known. His aesthetic views have to be inferred from the polemic which he directs against his adversaries. Hence the paradoxical position that more may be known about Neoptolemus' poetics, of which only a few lines are preserved, than about that of Philodemus, whose work is much better represented.

Terra firma appears only when Philodemus' polemical exercises are seen to have a foundation in the doctrines of

[1] For example, see Jensen, *op. cit.* p. 121, 'Nichts ist so erbärmlich und töricht wie die Wortklauberei dieses Graeculus, der die Anschauungen anderer aus zweiter Quelle übernimmt und sie verhöhnt und lächerlich zu machen sucht, weil sie nicht in sein enges Schulsystem hineinpassen'.

[2] A. Rostagni, specially in the following papers, 'Sulle tracce di un'estetica dell'intuizione presso gli antichi' (1920), 'Risonanze dell'estetica di Filodemo in Cicerone' (1922), 'Filodemo contro l'estetica classica' (1923–4), all of them reprinted in *Scritti Minori*, I, 356–446, also cf. *Arte poetica di Orazio*, Introd., ch. VII, 'Le critiche di Filodemo al sistema di Neottolemo'.

Epicurean philosophy. Unquestionable evidence is regrettably scanty in such basic matters as the relation between philosophy and poetry, or the 'function' of poetry.[1] It is more scanty still as regards the technical problems of literary criticism. Surmise plays a large part and opinions differ widely on the doctrinal interpretation that may be placed on polemical arguments.

The problems surrounding poetic form and subject-matter are cases in point. Philodemus rejects Neoptolemus' traditional separation of style and content.[2] Rostagni has made much of that, even to the extent of finding therein something like Francesco de Sanctis' and Croce's views on poetic imagination.[3] But precisely how much should be made of Philodemus' protests could only be determined if their general relevance to his Epicurean aesthetics were known. His protests however have a particular relevance as well. Skilfully, and (as will be seen) without attention to Neoptolemus' argument as a whole, Philodemus uses this matter as a debating point against his opponent.

In dealing with any critic whose opinions are preserved and assessed by Philodemus we have to reckon both with his debating points and his Epicurean yardstick. With regard to the latter we are handicapped by insufficient knowledge of his aesthetics; but we must at any rate allow for the possibility that his critique is inspired by the doctrines of his school. In applying his strictures he rarely takes account of the setting and the context in which he finds opinions that he considers

---

[1] Cf. the evidence on the former subject adduced by P. H. de Lacy, 'The Epicurean analysis of language', *AJP*, LX (1939), 85 ff.; P. H. de Lacy and E. A. de Lacy, *Philodemus: On Methods of Inference*, etc. (1941), pp. 140 ff., 149 ff.

[2] See below, pp. 61–2.

[3] Rostagni, above, p. 53, n. 2. Recently, C. Benvenga, *Rendiconti della Accad.... Napoli*, n.s. XXVI (1951), 251, and N. A. Greenberg, *HS*, LXV (1961), 283, have concluded on different grounds that Philodemus places greater stress on content than on style. So that, according to Philodemus, no reciprocal relationship between content and style would obtain. I doubt this conclusion although on the other hand I do not accept Rostagni's overstatements. Rather see P. H. de Lacy and E. A. de Lacy, *Philodemus: On Methods* (cited above, n. 1).

obnoxious. He either seeks out contradictions in the opponent's argument or he applies the yardstick of his own theory or indeed he does both. With this proviso I now propose to complete the third section of Neoptolemus' fragments. I refrain from putting the fragmentary remains into *oratio continua;*[1] this is not preserved in Philodemus and in some places may distort the evidence.

Column x: 1. [ἔδοξ]ε τὴν σύνθεσιν [τῆς λέξε]ω[ς τ]ῶν

Column xi: διανοημ[άτων χωρί]ζε[ι]ν, οὐδὲν ἤ[ττω μερίδα] λέγων αὐτὴ[ν] ἤ πλεί[ω].

2. [τὸν] τὴν τέχνην [καὶ τὴν δύν]αμιν ἔχοντα τ[ὴν ποι]-ητικὴν εἶδος [π]αρίσ[τησι] τῆ[ς] τέ[χ]νη[ς μ]ετὰ τοῦ ποιήματο[ς] καὶ τῆς ποιήσεως.

3. [τ]ὴν ἐργασίαν ποιητικὴν καλεῖ.

4. τῆ[ς] ποιήσεω[ς] εἶναι τ[ὴ]ν ὑπόθεσιν [μό]νον.

*Column xii:*5. ποή[ματος μό]νον τὴν [σύνθεσιν τῆς] λέξεως μ[ετέχειν ἀλλὰ μὴ] τὰς διανο[ίας καὶ........] καὶ πράξεις καὶ π[ροσω]ποποιί[ας].

6. καὶ [τοῦ ποιητοῦ ταῦ]τα καὶ [δὴ] κ[α]ὶ τὴν ὑπ[όθ]εσιν καὶ [τὴν σ]ύνθ[ε]σιν [εἶν]αι παντ[ὶ δῆλ]ον.

7. [μ]ὴ κοινωνε[ῖν] τῶι πο[ιητῆ]ι τ[ῶ]ν ἁμα[ρτ]ιῶν τὰ[ς ὑ]ποθέ[σεις] καὶ τὰ ποήμ[ατα].

8. [πρ]ωτεύ[ει]ν τ[ῶν] εἰδ[ῶν] τὰ ποιήματα.

?8(*b*). ἧι (i.e. τῆι ποήσει) καὶ τοῦτο

Column xiii: [προσ]ῆψεν.

?8 (*c*). εἰ δὲ πρὸς τ[ά.....]ήματα τὸ πεποι[ῆσθαι] συνέκρινε, τα[ὐτὸ καὶ πρό]τερον ἔλεγεν.

9. ἁρμονίαν ἢ συν[έχεια]ν καὶ τοῖς μ[εγάλοις πο]ήμασιν περιθή[σειν]

10. καὶ πρὸς ἀρε[τὴν δεῖν τ]ῶι τελείωι ποι[ητῆι μετὰ τ]ῆς ψυχαγω[γί]α[ς τοῦ τοὺς] ἀκούοντ[ας] ὠ[φελεῖ]ν καὶ χρησι[μο]λ[ογεῖ]ν

11. καὶ τὸν Ὅμη[ρον] [τ]έρπειν [τε καὶ ὠφελεῖν] τὸ [πλεῖ]ον.

12. μέ[γιστος] ἦν ποιητής (ὁ Ὅμηρος).

The introductory clause, [ἀ]λλὰ μὴν ὅ [γε Νεοπ]τόλεμος οὐκ ὀρ[θῶς ἔδοξ]ε, has been discussed earlier. What follows

---

[1] Mette's conjectural reconstruction (*op. cit.*, col. 2468) shows up the hazards of linking unconnected sentences or clauses reported by Philodemus.

falls into two parts, nos. 1–8 and nos. 9–12. Nos. 9–12, the items mentioned last by Philodemus, are the most informative: '(He said) that he[1] will bestow harmony or coherence also on large poems'; (secondly) 'that the perfect poet in order to fulfil his capacity must not only thrill his hearers but improve them and teach them a lesson'; (thirdly) 'that Homer is mostly pleasing as well as improving'; and (finally) that he (Homer) 'was the greatest poet'.

Jensen's supplements in this passage are, I think, certain, with two exceptions in the first line that require discussion. Instead of Jensen's συν[τέλεια]ν[2] I have tentatively inserted συν[έχεια]ν, a technical term of the rhetoricians for continuity, coherence, or 'close-fitting' of words or clauses.[3] This, in spite of the word τέλειος in the next line, seems to me slightly preferable, because of the similarity to ἁρμονία. The second supplement, Jensen's, is μ[εγάλοις] qualifying [πο]ήμασιν. The conjunction καί ('also', or 'even', in a certain kind of poem) makes μεγάλοις an attractive proposition although only the initial μ is preserved.[4] For 'small' poems stylistic finish, ἁρμονία, is a self-evident demand in the Hellenistic age: we are then left with poems of either medium or full length. Now μ[έσοις] is not only too short for the available space, but is surely excluded in a context in which its meaning is not defined, whereas the phrase 'long poem' is sufficiently clear to forgo such a definition. Moreover it fits the rest of the sentence, with its mention of Homer. If this is correct, the

---

[1] The grammatical subject is probably 'the poet', or 'the perfect poet'.

[2] The final letter, ν, was read in the papyrus by Jensen; O has Cl.

[3] So, for example, Dionysius of Halicarnassus, speaking of the 'smooth style' of Sappho, *De Comp.* XXIII, ταύτης λέξεως ἡ εὐέπεια καὶ ἡ χάρις ἐν τῇ συνεχείᾳ καὶ λειότητι γέγονε τῶν ἁρμονιῶν. I have not noticed the word in Philodemus, but συντέλεια is quoted by LS, 9th ed., from his *Volumina Rhetorica*, II, 86 (Sudhaus), where however the sense differs.

'Αρμονία in the sense of σύνθεσις, 'combination of words', was a subdivision (beside choice of vocabulary and figures of speech) of one of the 'virtues of style' (that of ornament) according to Theophrastus. But the supplement σύν[θεσι]ν which has also been mooted appears to be too short.

[4] Jensen's reading, M, corrected the A of the Oxford transcript and the ⌐ of the Naples transcript, which may be either an A or the beginning of a capital M.

key-term of Hellenistic literary controversy was discussed by Neoptolemus. Theoretically Callimachus and others endorsed the primacy of the long epic of Homer, but in practice eschewed it because it did not seem amenable to artistic harmony as they understood it. I accept, then, the supplement μεγάλοις, and append what I consider a probable explanation. I take Neoptolemus' sentence to be polemical in intent: not only did he consider the long poem worth attempting but he considered harmony and continuity (or else harmony and completeness) obligatory for it—ἁρμονίαν καὶ συνέχειαν (or συντέλειαν) καὶ τοῖς μεγάλοις ποιήμασιν περιθήσειν. This is Aristotle's position with regard to the large poetic forms reasserted against prevailing tendencies. Whether the supplement should be συν[έχεια]ν or συν[τέλεια]ν is uncertain. In either case the context needs to be taken into account. The sentence (9) is concerned with long poems; it adjoins a statement on the effect of Homer's poems (10–11) and the standing of Homer (12). In items 9–12 we may therefore be dealing with one context. The terms 'harmony and continuity' or 'harmony and completeness' perhaps extend from stylistic properties to the composition and unity of the poem as a whole.

The rest of the sentence (10 and 11) also has its tale to tell. Aristotle had sought to vindicate poetry against Plato's moral strictures—hence his analysis of the pleasure derived from poetic drama is concerned with its aesthetic as well as its emotional effects. Neoptolemus' combination of aesthetic and moral effects can scarcely be compared to Aristotle's. He is much more down-to-earth, even trivial. His attitude is *miscuit utile dulci* and, like Aristotle in other passages of the *Poetics*, he uses Homer to bear out his theory.

Items 1–8 form one context. No. 1 makes the fundamental distinction between thought (or matter, διανόημα) and style (σύνθεσις τῆς λέξεως) on which we have remarked before. This recalls the Aristotelian pair, διάνοια and λέξις; but the distinction is common to literary and rhetorical theory: it is in fact a rhetorical distinction. Items 1 and 9–12 together set

57

the tone. We are dealing with a theory, somewhat common-place in character, but perhaps saved from being a truism by its implied condemnation of contemporary, Hellenistic, taste. It restates classicist doctrine and recalls Aristotelian features in that doctrine.

Items 2–8 rest on the common distinction stated in item 1, that between style and content. The style in poetry is linked with the term ποίημα, the content with the term ποίησις; and the two are the sum total of the poet's craft, τέχνη. Poetry as craftsmanship or technique has a Graeco-Roman tinge. This view makes it less nonsensical than it would be otherwise if we now hear that the poet is considered something distinct from the art of which he is the practitioner and which would not exist without him. *Ars longa, vita brevis.* It is just like Quintilian's putting the orator (*orator bonus*) alongside the art of oratory that he practises.

Now for the few sentences, 2–8, expressing these general points. Item no. 2 reports Neoptolemus' division of poetry.

(2) [τὸν] τὴν τέχνην [καὶ τὴν δύν]αμιν ἔχοντα τ[ὴν ποι]ητικὴν εἶδος [π]αρίσ[τησι] τῆ[ς] τέ[χ]νη[ς μ]ετὰ τοῦ ποήματο[ς] καὶ τῆς ποήσεως.

He juxtaposes (or represents) the person who possesses the art of writing poetry and has the power to do so, as a species of the art, along with ποίημα *and* ποίησις.

The word 'juxtaposes' (or represents) must be put down to Philodemus, summing up Neoptolemus' teaching. But the fact of the juxtaposition which gives rise to a triad, and the terms employed for the triad, ποίημα, ποίησις, and ποιητής, belong to Neoptolemus. So does the word εἶδος, which appears to be his term for each of the three 'parts' or 'elements' of the art of poetry. That εἶδος was in fact Neoptolemus' term is shown by no. 8.

Items 3, 6 and 7 comment on the relation of the three 'aspects'.

(3) [τ]ὴν ἐργασίαν ποιητικὴν καλεῖ.

He names the workmanship ποιητική.

(6) [τοῦ ποιητοῦ]...τὴν ὑπ[όθ]εσιν καὶ τ[ὴν σ]ύνθ[ε]σιν [εῖν]αι.
παντ[ὶ δῆλ]ον. *Everyone recognizes that subject-matter and style
belong to the poet.*

(7) [μ]ὴ κοινωνε[ῖν] τῶι πο[ιητῆ]ι τ[ῶ]ν ἁμα[ρτ]ιῶν τὰ[ς ὑ]ποθέ-
[σεις] καὶ τὰ ποήμ[ατα].
*No instances of subject-matter and style have a share in the faults of
the poet.*

Philodemus takes his adversary to task for using the term
ποιητική for the 'workmanship' of the poet, whereas it was in
fact the whole art of poetry that should be called by that
name: εἰ δ[ὲ τ]ὴν ἐργασίαν ποιητικὴν καλεῖ, τ[ῆ]ς τέχνης
οὕτω προσ[αγο]ρευομένης, ἀ[γ]νοε[ῖ]. This is less cryptic than
it sounds if it is remembered that Neoptolemus, a man of
pigeon-holes, had subdivided his τέχνη ποιητική by juxtaposing the poet and the art that he practises. He then
required a term distinguishing the technique, ἐργασία,
practised by the poet from the other 'aspect' of poetry (the
poet himself) and called that technique ποιητική. A like
tendency will be observed under items 6 and 7 where he
assigned style and matter to the poet, but expressly distinguished the faults of 'the poet' from those inherent in the
elaboration of matter and style.

Under 6 subject and style are abstract terms, expressed by
ὑπόθεσις and σύνθεσις. Under 7 individual instances are considered and therefore ὑπόθεσις is thrown into the plural
whilst σύνθεσις is replaced by ποιήματα, 'verse'; the word so
used is the plural of ποίημα, in the rather technical connotation that is now to follow in the decisive items 4, 5, and 8.

(4) τῆ[ς] ποήσεω[ς] εἶναι τ[ὴ]ν ὑπόθεσιν μό[νον].
Subject-matter alone belongs to ποίησις.

(5) ποή[ματος μό]νον τὴν [σύνθεσιν τῆς] λέξεως μ[ετέχειν ἀλλὰ μὴ]
τὰς διανο[ίας καὶ........] καὶ πράξεις καὶ π[ροσω]ποποιί[ας].
Only verbal composition belongs to ποίημα, *but not thoughts* [and
] *and actions and characterizations.*

(8) πρ]ωτεύ[ει]ν τ[ῶν] εἰδ[ῶν] τὰ ποιήματα.
ποιήματα *are the first of the* εἴδη.

There is but one textual difficulty in the three items; that is the lacuna in 5. Jensen supplied the word τάξεις, thus: τὰς διανο[ίας καὶ τάξεις] καὶ πράξεις κτλ. Arrangement, τάξις, is not an impossible item to appear here, beside style, thought, action and character. Nevertheless, the supplement is uncertain for two reasons: arrangement is one of the traditional 'parts' of rhetoric that might have been applied to poetry here, but it is not the only point that could have been so applied; moreover, the lacuna, at any rate in the Naples and Oxford transcripts, looks larger than the six letters of τάξεις. So for the time being the lacuna had better remain open.[1]

Finally the two extracts, tentatively listed as 8 (*b*) and 8 (*c*).

(8 *b*) ἧι (i.e. τῆι ποήσει) καὶ τοῦτο [προσ]ῆψεν.

(8 *c*) εἰ δὲ πρὸς τ[ά.....]ήματα τὸ πεποι[ῆσθαι] συνέκρινε, τα[ὐτὸ καὶ πρό]τερον ἔλεγεν.

Even close scrutiny fails to clarify the meaning sufficiently. I refrain therefore from basing any conclusions on dubious evidence and I refer the reader to the discussion at the end of this chapter.[2]

Proceeding from his sharp, and to us unreal, distinction between style and matter, Neoptolemus now assigns each to a different pigeon-hole: style in poetry to what he names ποίημα, and subject-matter in poetry to what he names ποίησις. And further, he puts them in an order, placing ποιήματα first: πρωτεύειν τῶν εἰδῶν τὰ ποιήματα. Two matters here require notice. Neoptolemus directs attention to the abstract entities of content and style. It is true, neither the one nor the other can exist *in abstracto*. Both must be realized in verse. Nevertheless the argument of these two extracts, as far as it goes, deals with content and style; it does not deal with types of poems. Moreover, Neoptolemus seems to be careful not to equate style with *poema* and content with *poesis*.[3]

---

[1] See below, p. 102.   [2] See below, pp. 75–6.

[3] N. A. Greenberg, *HS*, lxv (1961), 280, has rightly drawn attention to the absence of an equation between *poema* and style, and between *poesis* and content. But I disagree with the conclusions he draws from that observation.

Rather he says that style 'belongs to' *poema* and content 'belongs to' *poesis*. Why Neoptolemus argued as he did, will be considered later. What matters is the curious distinction between ποίημα and ποίησις. I believe it to be more than a curiosity; and to make a case for this view I shall have to go farther afield.[1]

Philodemus altogether rejects Neoptolemus' triad and the functions assigned by him to ποίημα and ποίησις. He argues that ποίημα, like everything else expressed in poetry, belongs to ποίησις. This, he thinks, is shown by his definition, according to which ποίημα is part of a long poem, such as the first thirty lines of the *Iliad*, whereas ποίησις is a whole poem such as the *Iliad*. In fact, ποίημα, he says, is a wider term than ποίησις: you could apply either word to the *Iliad* but you would not call the first thirty lines a ποίησις. His own words are these.

θαυμα[στὸ]ν δ' αὐτοῦ καὶ τ[ὸ] τῆ[ς] ποήσεω[ς] εἶναι τ[ὴ]ν ὑπόθεσιν
[μό]νον καὶ τοῦ ποήματο[ς καὶ] πάντων ὅλως τῆς ποήσ[ε]ως ὄντων·[2]
ἡ μὲν [γὰ]ρ πόησις καὶ π[όημά γ' ἐστίν], οἷον ἡ 'Ιλι[άς], οἱ δ[ὲ

---

[1] The pair, *poema* and *poesis*, was discussed by F. Marx, n. on Lucilius, 338. It has been considered frequently since Jensen and Rostagni drew attention to its standing in ancient literary criticism. Apart from the recent editions of Horace's *Ars*, see P. Boyancé, *op. cit.* (1936); P. Giuffrida, *L'Epicureismo nella lett. lat.*, etc. I (1940), 76; C. Benvenga, *Rend. della Accad....Napoli*, n.s. XXVI (1951), 243 ff.; A. Ardizzoni, Ποίημα, etc. (1953); H. Dahlmann, *Varros Schrift 'de poematis'*, etc., *op. cit.* (1953), pp. 118 ff.; N. A. Greenberg, *op. cit.* (1961); M. Gigante, Σημαντικὸν ποίημα, *Parola del Passato*, XVI (1961), 40–53.

[2] The phrase containing the genitive absolute has been a bone of contention ever since Rostagni in 1924 (repr. *Scr. Min.* I, 440 n. 1) replaced Jensen's rendering by his own. Philodemus, he argued, was contrasting two mutually exclusive propositions of Neoptolemus, thus pointing to a contradiction in his argument. So that the genitive absolute would contain another 'fragment' of Neoptolemus— 'whereas (or, since) according to Neoptolemus...'. This has been accepted by Boyancé (p. 22), Dahlmann (p. 122), and Greenberg (p. 280) in the papers cited in the previous note. Giuffrida (p. 78, n. 1), Benvenga (p. 243, n. 1), and Ardizzoni (p. 19, n. 13) demurred—rightly, I think. For the alleged opinion of Neoptolemus is in fact indistinguishable from that of Philodemus. In order to impute it to Neoptolemus, Philodemus would have had to say so, having just reported that his opponent held the opposite view. But Philodemus does not say so. He uses the same form of personal dissent which occurs elsewhere in his writings, cf. cols. iv, 9, vi, 28, xiv, 20; not that he would refrain from reporting others using it, cf. col. xv, 1 and 5. The meaning should then be similar to that posited by Jensen— 'since (or, whereas) in fact...'. Rostagni's suggestion was based on the obscure passage, xii, 33–xiii, 4: *obscurum per obscurius*.

πρῶτοι] στίχοι τρι[άκ]οντα τα[ύ]της πόημα μ[έ]ν, οὐ μέντοι ποί[η]σις.[1]

Conversely, on criticizing Neoptolemus' use of *poema* a few lines below, he denies that poetic expression is separable from the 'action' or subject-matter expressed.

εἰ δ' ἐν [τῆι] λέξει πεποιῆσθαί τ[ι πρέ]πει, κἀνταῦ[θα νὴ Δί' οὐ]κ ἔστι τι πεποι[ῆσθαι το]ύτων χωρίς, ἀλλ' [ἴδι]ο[ν το]ῦ συνκεῖσθαι [τὴν] λέξιν τὸ συνκεῖσθαι [τὴν πρᾶξ]ιν εἶναι φαίνεταί μ[οι].[2]

Now on first acquaintance these distinctions seem utterly futile. Yet there is a trace of them in unaffected Greek usage. Some years ago we were reminded, *à propos* of Cicero's puzzling remark about *Lucreti poemata*,[3] that ποίημα, its plural ποιήματα, and the Latin counterparts *poema* and *poemata*, do not always square with the common renderings, 'poem' and 'poems'. The meanings differ according to the contexts; the instances range from an indistinct use of 'verse', or 'verses' (hence, part of a poem) to a distinct use of 'poem', long or short. The meaning underlying the various usages is 'words versified'. Ποίησις (it may be added) also may occasionally refer to a poem of any length. But the two words overlap only to that extent; otherwise they differ. For ποίησις either describes the poetic process of composing; or it expresses an abstraction: poetry; or finally it denotes poetic compositions *in toto*—the *œuvre* of a poet—or the whole of a single composition.[4] I have found no case in which ποίησις is applied to a line, or a few lines, of verse which are not a complete poem.[5]

---

[1] Philod. *op. cit.* col. xi, 26–xii, 1.   [2] *Ibid.* xii, 6–13.

[3] F. H. Sandbach, *CR*, LIV (1940), 75, writing on Cicero, *Ad Q.F.* II, 10 (9), 3, 'Lucreti poemata ut scribis ita sunt, multis luminibus ingeni, multae tamen artis'.

[4] See below, pp. 76–8, 'Ποίησις and the Lexicographers'.

[5] Ποίημα and ποιήματα are among the words denoting 'line', or 'lines', 'of verse'. Aeschines (*In Ctes.* 136) refers to ποιήμαθ' Ἡσιόδου and means the six lines of *Works and Days*, 240–3, 246–7; *In Tim.*, 129, τούτων τῶν ποιημάτων are the words introducing a comment on two lines of Hesiod, 763–4. Aristotle finds Solon's political views expressed ἐν τοῖσδε τοῖς ποιήμασιν ('Αθ. Πολ. 5, 3) and then proceeds to cite two couplets from a longer elegy. Hence Plato, *Parm.* 128a, ἐν τοῖς ποιήμασιν ἐν φῇς εἶναι τὸ πᾶν, although it may refer to the whole poem is best rendered by 'in your verses', and *Lucreti poemata* in the letter of Cicero mentioned above is, as Sandbach says, ambiguous.

Ordinary usage may thus explain why critics of the Hellenistic and Roman periods started to theorize about the inherent difference of the two words, and came to link them with their various literary theories. It is not only that ancient grammarians have a strange liking for them, but authors of repute, Greek as well as Roman, use them with much assurance.

The first after Neoptolemus to be known to employ the two words as literary terms is the poet Lucilius, who propagates so many Hellenistic ideas. In Book IX of his *Satires*[1] he defends himself against an ill-conceived attack. His opponent must have taken him to task for criticizing Homer; Lucilius replies that he had blamed Homer merely for specific stylistic flaws that may now and again appear in the body of a large literary composition, without affecting the whole of it.[2] The terms that he uses to clarify his own position are *poema* and *poesis*; his opponent,[3] he alleges, is unaware of the difference between the one (*hoc*) and the other (*illud*).

> non haec quid valeat, quidve hoc inter sit[4] et illud,
> cognoscis. (338–9)

Poema is a small part (of a large poem, that is) or else verse in a small compass, such as a poetic epistle.

> pars est parva....[5] (340)
> —epistula item quaevis non magna poema est. (341)

(Between the two passages, no doubt, Lucilius furnished other examples of *poema* that are now lost.) Over against *poema* stands *poesis*, a large literary unity, *opus totum* (342). The rest of this line, and the next, are doubtful in wording but the

[1] Lucilius, *Sat.* IX, 338–47 (Marx); Leo, *Röm. Lit.* 417, n. 4, Nonius, ed. Lindsay, III, 691 (428, 5 M.). Cf. 401–10 in E. H. Warmington's Loeb edition, *Remains of Old Latin*, III, 126.

[2] Commentators have long since pointed out that at *Sat.* I, 10, 50, Horace applies to Lucilius what Lucilius here seems to be saying about Homer. For a like, but not identical, argument, see Hor. *A.P.* 347–60.

[3] I do not here raise the question, recently much debated, whether the opponent is Accius or another critic.

[4] *intersiet illud* codd., *inter sit et* L. Deubner, *H*, XLV (1910), 311.

[5] The word after *pars est parva* appears variously as *poema* or *poesis* in the MSS.

sense is clear enough: the *Iliad* is described as whole and one, in the sense now established for ποίησις, and Ennius' *Annals* are compared with it in regard to that quality. After that the text is straightforward, except for the final word. *Poesis* then is an *opus totum*,

> et maius multo est quam quod dixi ante poema.
> qua propter dico: nemo qui culpat Homerum,
> perpetuo culpat neque quod dixi ante poesin:
> versum unum culpat, verbum, enthymema, *poema*.[1] (344–7)

From all this it appears that a century, or a century and a half, after Neoptolemus, Lucilius used the distinction between ποίημα and ποίησις in order to make a point that was important for the Hellenistic and Roman reader alike—I mean the difference between a piece of verse and a large poetic composition. Lucilius' paradigms for the latter are the *Iliad* of Homer, and the *chef d'œuvre* of the Roman Homer, Ennius' *Annals*. It is also noted that his usage of *poema* and *poesis* bears some resemblance to that of Philodemus. Like Philodemus he exemplifies from the *Iliad*. Like him, at any rate at first sight, he talks merely in quantitative terms. His *poema* may be either a *pars parva* (of a large work) or a short piece of verse, such as a poetic epistle. But careful reading dispels this impression. His criterion for *poesis*, too, has a qualitative side to it: it must be a unity, an *opus totum*; and this is borne out by what he says about Homer. So whilst the quantitative aspect, of which Philodemus makes so much, predominates in the few lines of Lucilius that are preserved, the qualitative is not by any means absent.

---

[1] The word concluding the extract, *poema*, is Leo's emendation for the MSS. readings *tema, tima, temalocum*, and *timalocumque*. Its virtue is that it repeats one of the two key words at the end of the context and sets it over against the other, *poesis*, at the end of the preceding line (cf. Ardizzoni, *op. cit.* p. 32, n. 3). *Tema* or *tima* will have to be explained in any case as a repetition of the latter part of (*enthy*)*mema*. *Locum* would then be understood as a gloss explaining *tema*. This seems to me preferable to such corrections as *locum⟨unum⟩* (F. Marx) or *locum⟨ue⟩* (Lachmann). Perhaps, in view of the jingle *versum...verbum*, the rhyme *enthymema, poema* commends rather than contradicts Leo's emendation.

The double-sided aspect of the matter becomes even clearer when we move another fifty years or so to the first century B.C., and hear Posidonius make the following distinctions, in an Introduction to Style, περὶ λέξεως εἰσαγωγή.[1] 'A ποίημα is a metrical or rhythmical way of elaborate speech, which exceeds the character of prose (rhythmical ⟨... and metrical⟩ as in "Great Earth and Air of Jove"). A ποίησις is a ποίημα that conveys a meaning and contains an imitation of things divine and human.'

ποίημα δέ ἐστιν (ὡς ὁ Ποσειδώνιός φησιν ἐν τῇ περὶ λέξεως εἰσαγωγῇ) λέξις ἔμμετρος ἢ ἔνρυθμος μετὰ σκευῆς τὸ λογοειδὲς ἐκβεβηκυῖα ([τὸ] ἔνρυθμον δὲ εἶναι τὸ 'Γαῖα μεγίστη καὶ Διὸς αἰθήρ'),[2] ποίησις δέ ἐστι σημαντικὸν ποίημα, μίμησιν περιέχον θείων καὶ ἀνθρωπείων.[3]

This account is more cut-and-dried than that of Lucilius; it comes, after all, from a textbook, not from a poem. Like Philodemus, he considers ποίησις a kind of ποίημα: it is more than just metrical and elaborate speech because it must 'mean something'; it has a matter to convey. *Il n'y a pas* ποίησις *sans* ποίημα—so Boyancé described this doctrine.[4] Ποίησις entails ποίημα; ποίημα however does not entail ποίησις. Here the likeness between the two accounts ceases.

[1] Diog. Laert. vii, 60.   [2] Euripides, *Chrysippus*, TGF², 839, 1 (Nauck).

[3] The wording of the extract is not certain in every detail. The term for stylistic elaboration is κατασκευή not σκευή, cf. the Stoic definition (Diog. Laert. vii, 59), κατασκευή δέ ἐστι λέξις ἐκπεφευγυῖα τὸν ἰδιωτισμόν. Hence G. Kaibel, *Proleg.* περὶ κωμ., AGG (1898), p. 21, and R. Reitzenstein, *M. Terentius Varro und Johannes Mauropus*, etc. (1901), p. 92, are likely to be right in printing κατασκευῆς; the μετασκευή of Dion. Hal. *De Comp.* 6 is quite a different matter. Rhythm and metre receive only one illustration between them. This may suggest a lacuna after ἔνρυθμον δὲ κτλ., making room for a second example. But Varro in a like definition (below, p. 66) does not even mention metre; he only notes *enrhythmos*. In any case the parenthesis containing the illustration is in *oratio obliqua* which may indicate a summary rather than literal citation. So perhaps no more is required than Kaibel's deletion of τό before ἔνρυθμον, thus shifting δέ to the second place of the parenthesis. F. Marx in his note on Lucilius, fr. 338, suggests τὸ λογοειδὲς ἐ. ⟨διὰ⟩ τὸ ἔνρυθμον· ⟨ποίημα⟩ δὲ εἶναι κτλ. This is mistaken ingenuity since the MS. text offers the traditional, bipartite, definition of poetic language, rhythm *and* stylistic elaboration.

[4] P. Boyancé, *op. cit.* (above, p. 32, n. 1), 28. This description applies more clearly to Posidonius (and Philodemus) than to Neoptolemus, Lucilius, and Varro, to whom Boyancé applies it as well.

For Philodemus is content largely to stress the difference in size between the two poetic forms. Posidonius does not mention size; he stresses the difference in kind. A ποίησις must convey a full, or complete, meaning. It must be σημαντικόν—which the metrical phrase from a chorus of Euripides is not. No illustration of ποίησις is supplied in this short extract and we are left to surmise whether his definition would be satisfied by the whole of a large composition or by a shorter piece—so long as its sense is complete. Now ποίησις is a poem 'containing a representation of things divine and human'.[1] This further qualifies σημαντικὸν ποίημα. It may hint at the former alternative in that the poem must be large enough to accommodate such a representation.

The last of the trio of writers we are considering is Posidonius' younger contemporary, Varro. He propounds the following doctrine in the Menippean satire, *Parmeno*.

poema est lexis enrythmos, id est verba plura modice in quandam coniecta formam; itaque etiam distichon epigrammation vocant poema.

poesis est perpetuum argumentum e rhythmis, ut Ilias Homeri et Annales[2] Enni.

poetice est ars earum rerum.

These formulas recall certain features of Posidonius' and Lucilius' definitions. Varro defines *poema* by rhythm (though he omits the specific term, metre) and by stylistic pattern.[3] This recalls Posidonius, but his illustrations for *poema* as well as *poesis* exhibit a mixture of elements both quantitative and

---

[1] I had noted the Stoic character of Posidonius' terminology. This is now discussed by M. Gigante, *op. cit.* (above, p. 61, n. 1), 40 f. Σημαντικόν is a term of Stoic, and previously Aristotelian, logic. 'Things divine and human' is a Stoic description of the world or universe. Gigante draws attention to an extract from Cleanthes, *SVF*, 1, 486 (Philod. *De Mus.* col. 28, 1) which shows some significant resemblances. But its differences should not be overlooked. And I should be chary of linking the Posidonius extract with the passages of 'Longinus', *De Sublimitate* that are cited in Gigante's paper.   [2] *Annalis*, Nonius, p. 428 (M.).

[3] *Modice* renders ῥυθμικῶς—*secundum modum et numeros*, as the *TLL, s.v.*, 1236, 54, puts it. *In quandam coniecta formam*, 'thrown into some shape', is closer to such terms as *figura* or *schema* than to Posidonius' elaboration of style. Cf. *facta quodam modo* and like expressions in Cicero (specially *De Or.* III, 184, citing Theophrastus); the Greek terms are λέξις πεποιημένη or ποιὰ λέξις.

qualitative which is reminiscent of Lucilius. *Poema* is illustrated by the elegiac couplet whereas Lucilius referred to the
(brief) poetic epistle. And like Lucilius he allows for size as
well as unity in illustrating *poesis* by the same paradigms of
epic unity on a large scale, Homer's *Iliad* and Ennius' *Annals*.
Again like Lucilius, he brings out the coherence and unity of
poesis: it is an *argumentum* and it is *perpetuum*. The adjective
recalls the tag employed for a long and uninterrupted narrative poem, *carmen perpetuum*.[1] Finally, he joins *poema* and
poesis in his definition of *poetice*: which recalls Neoptolemus'
way of defining ποιητική.

Here there are five statements concerning *poema* and *poesis*:
those of Neoptolemus, Lucilius, Posidonius, Varro, and
Philodemus. None is quite like any other, but all seek to
elucidate the nature of *poesis*, a poetic work which organizes a
'subject', and they do so in contradistinction to *poema*, a piece
of verse. The middle three, Lucilius, Posidonius, and Varro,
resemble each other more than any one of them resembles the
first or last of the quintet. For these three clearly define the
qualities of what they regard as two types of poetry, although
Lucilius and Varro pronounce on their size as well. There was
a tendency in the Greek language to avoid the word ποίησις
for verse on a small scale; and this tendency is utilized for a
literary theory that takes account not only of the scale of
poetic works but of their nature.[2] It will be seen that Lucilius,

---

[1] Horace, *Od.* I, 7, 6; Ovid, *Met.* I, 4, recalling Callimachus' ἄεισμα διηνεκές:
Pfeiffer on Callim. *Aetia*, I, fr. I, 3, and *H*, LXX (1935), 310.

[2] Later lexicographers and grammarians, undisturbed by these subtle distinctions, adhered to the simple difference between short and long poems. Some
however display more insight than others. Of the relevant passages assembled in
F. Marx's note on Lucilius, fr. 338, Diomedes' remark deserves notice: *poesis
contextus et corpus totius operis effecti ut Ilias Odyssia Aeneis* (*Gram. Lat.* I, 473, 19, ed.
Keil). To Marx's passages should be added particularly a London Scholion on
Dionysius Thrax (p. 449, ed. Hilgard), which expresses Diomedes' point more
clearly: ' ποίησις properly speaking is a self-contained subject expressed in verse,
with a beginning, middle, and end', ποίησις δὲ κυρίως ἡ διὰ μέτρων ἐντελὴς
ὑπόθεσις ἔχουσα ἀρχὰς καὶ μέσα καὶ πέρατα. Rostagni, *SI*, n.s. II (1922), 116
(repeated *Scr. Min.* I, 202) drew attention to this passage. For these compilations,
see also H. Dahlmann, *op. cit.* (above, p. 35, n. 2), pp. 118 ff.

Posidonius, and Varro, clearly have their various purposes in making reference to this theory, although, at any rate in the extracts that are preserved, only Lucilius tells his readers about his purpose.

The first and last of our five however seem to differ. In Neoptolemus' opinion ποίημα *concerns* only the style of verse, whereas ποίησις *concerns* its subject-matter.[1] In Philodemus' opinion ποίησις *is* a sizeable poem such as the *Iliad* whereas ποίημα *is* part of a long poem such as the first thirty lines of the *Iliad*. Yet this difference can be overstated.

As for Philodemus, his definition is not unambiguously quantitative; it would be surprising if it were. His two illustrations surely differ not only in size but also in completeness: the first thirty lines of the *Iliad* are not only short but a snippet. A qualitative element thus enters his argument. But it is part of his polemical case to lay strong emphasis on the quantitative side.

Neoptolemus alone among these five writers pays attention to the abstract features of style and matter. He does not identify *poema* with a small poem or with part of a larger, nor does he identify *poesis* with a large and unified epic poem such as the *Iliad*. All he is doing, at any rate in the two relevant excerpts, 6 and 7, is to discuss poetic features—wording and content. I refrain from concluding however that he did not elsewhere refer to the various types of poetry. In his definitions of *poema* and *poesis* (which are not preserved) he may have done so. I think this is probable. And in the important item 9 he does do so when he demands 'harmony also in long poems'. The question then arises—in which way did Neoptolemus if he so argued link these types of poetry with his propositions as regards style and content?

Four critics writing in the second and first centuries B.C.

---

[1] M. Puelma Piwonka, *Lucilius und Kallimachos* (1949), p. 138 n., remarks that Lucilius first attached an 'evaluation and a qualitative meaning' to ποίημα, which in Hellenistic literary criticism was restricted to neutral, quantitative, *Verwendung*. This is not borne out by the facts: whether Neoptolemus' teachings contained an evaluation is not known; but their character was certainly not quantitative.

propound various theories on the basis of two types of poetry. One of their types, named *poesis*, is large enough to call for the activities of ordering and organizing; the other, named *poema*, does not make such a call. Sometimes the qualitative element predominates, as in Posidonius; sometimes size predominates, as in Philodemus; and sometimes, as in Lucilius and Varro, both elements are equally to the fore. Neoptolemus antedates the four critics by a century or more and his teaching differs considerably. His definitions of *poema* and *poesis* cannot be compared with theirs, for they are unknown, although I shall argue that plausible guesses may be made. He propounds an artificial triad—*poema, poesis, poeta*—which is claimed to be the sum total of *ars poetica*, but which is not repeated by the other four critics. Again unlike them, he does not appear to make *poesis* entail *poema* but rather stresses the separateness of the poetic activities connected with them. Finally, he does not appear to link the size or completeness of poems with his propositions on *poema* and *poesis*.

Often when evidence is closely scrutinized new questions arise instead of solutions. I have presented the incomplete evidence as it stands and I have been at pains not to state more than it warrants. What is now required is an attempt to explain the evidence, in particular the features to which I have drawn attention. The evidence is there whatever we make of it. An explanation is hypothetical and may be rejected when it fails to explain the evidence. I conclude this chapter with three attempts at explanation.

The first concerns Neoptolemus' curious and artificial triad. What was it meant to achieve? There is special pleading here —a rather forced application of tendencies inherent in the Greek language. What was the purpose of the pleading? The normal, rhetorical, distinction between style and subject-matter strikes us as quite distinctive enough. But it did not so strike Neoptolemus. He separated the two even further, assigning style (in verse) to one poetic process, and subject-matter to another. If a person elaborately separates two things he presumably wishes to draw attention to their separateness. In the case of a critic separating style and content, this is likely to mean that he wishes to keep distinct the ability to create style, and the ability to organize a large subject, in verse. Here one of the gaps in Neoptolemus' account can be supplied by way of conjecture. As Boyancé has suggested, the notions of *poema* and *poesis*, which are known from the later writers on this subject, need to be linked with Neoptolemus' contrast between style and subject-matter.[1] Presumably he identified the ability to create style with the ability to write verse, or short poems (*poema*, in the later writers), and with it he contrasted the ability to write a unified poem on a large scale (*poesis*, in the later writers). It makes sense that he then proceeded to put together again what he had first put asunder—item 6, 'subject-matter as well as style belong to the poet'. Thus the triad, *poema–poesis–poeta*, would acquire some sense. But it would do so only if the organizing of a (large) subject is indispensable for the name and nature of poetry. As I have stressed before, there is no point in attaching much importance to the organizing of subject-matter in a small poem—simply because there is not much to organize. Item 9—harmony and consistency even in *long* poems—agrees with this assertion. My first suggestion then is this. The problems surrounding a large poetic unity are likely to have prompted the rigid distinctions made by Neoptolemus—problems that have some reality, however unreal and artificial the terminology which the critic chose to employ. If that be so, Philodemus was adroit in spotting the logical inconsistency of Neoptolemus' poetic doctrine but his criticism does not touch its substance.

[1] I regard this suggestion as (*a*) conjectural though probable, and (*b*) not inherent in the genitive absolute at Philodemus, col. xi, 29–31, which I believe expresses Philodemus', not Neoptolemus', thought; cf. above, p. 61, n. 2. It is not certain that Neoptolemus anywhere made *poema* a part of *poesis*, although the doubtful extracts, 8 (*b*) and (*c*), may imply that he related *poema* to *poesis*, cf. below, p. 75. It is certain that both, *poema* and *poesis*, are in 'the charge of the poet who has the art and the ability' (item 2). With these qualifications I would accept Boyancé's suggestions, *op. cit.* (above, p. 32, n. 1), p. 29.

Secondly, what is the historical setting of all this talk about 'the long poem'? The setting is not that of the *Poetics*, for Aristotle did not set the major poetic forms over against the minor. Epigram, elegy, and the rest, were still overshadowed by the large compositions of drama and epic. He takes it for granted that size, μέγεθος, is essential to drama, and that large composition, μακρὰ σύστασις, is essential to epic.[1] The outlook may have changed in the Lyceum of his successors.[2] It has certainly changed for Neoptolemus. For Neoptolemus could no longer take for granted the Aristotelian primacy of the large forms of drama and epic. What little we know about him suggests one thing—he was an Alexandrian in combining the output of learned verse and grammatical, or literary, lore.[3] He is dated to the third century, the century of Callimachus.[4] Literary talk of this kind centres around the same Callimachus. 'Short poem' and 'long poem' were, after all, the battle-cries of the two opposing factions in the tussles of the coteries. Callimachus' own position as the leader of a school advocating the highly-wrought short poem is too well known to require documentation. What needs to be noted, however, is that Callimachus' reactions to poetry on a large scale, and in particular to Homer, were, as they say, ambivalent. On the one hand, he expresses unbounded admiration for the divine poet, the consummate poet, θεῖος ἀοιδός, ἀοιδῶν ἔσχατος. As a scholar, no doubt, he bestowed the same care on Homeric verse as on other great poetry. But as a creative poet, and indeed as a critic setting the stage for his kind of poetry, he deems all heroic verse dead. No use here to make a distinction between Homer and his degenerate successors. No use to apply Aristotle's precepts, and improve on the lack of organic unity which marked the 'cyclic epic': the very concept of unity on which Aristotle's precepts are based is

[1] Μέγεθος of drama, Ar. *Poet.* chs. 4 and 6 ff.; μακρὰ σύστασις of epic, 24, 1460 *a* 3.
[2] For the question of the origin of Neoptolemus' triad, see below, p. 142.
[3] Above, p. 44.
[4] Above, p. 45.

suspect and untenable for a modern poet.[1] Contrast Neoptolemus. His whole argument may well be designed to clear a
place for the poet who is not content with the poetic technique
displayed in a ποίημα, a piece of verse such as a Callimachean
ὀλιγόστιχον, but can go on to use ποίημα as a base for
organizing ποίησις, Aristotle's large poetic unity. My second
suggestion then is this. The controversy between the Callimacheans and their adversaries which concerned the 'long
poem' also motivated Neoptolemus' literary theories. It
looks as though Neoptolemus took sides in this controversy.
He sympathized with the demands for highly wrought compositions. But he found them insufficient and restated the
claims of the Aristotelian classicists against the claims of the
Callimachean classicists.

A third suggestion is required. What is the role assigned to
the triad, *poema–poesis–poeta*, in Neoptolemus' poetics? Our
evidence, such as it is, encourages the belief that the triad
served Neoptolemus as chapter headings; his book was laid
out in accordance with the order, *poema–poesis–poeta*. This
simple and convincing supposition seems now to be discredited
because earlier scholars have tried to prove too much.[2]

The pair, *poema* and *poesis*, resembles the rhetorical distinction between style and subject-matter—a principle common
in the arrangement of rhetorical works, in Aristotle, Cicero,
and elsewhere. The writer of a poetics had to discuss style and
subject-matter—if he happened to adopt that rhetorical distinction. Suppose he does pronounce on style and subject-
matter. How can he help using these terms as chapter
headings once he has used them to define his poetic field?
According to Philodemus, Neoptolemus so defined his poetic
field (no. 1, above); he is likely therefore to have discussed his
subject under these headings, naming the one *poema*, and the
other *poesis*. Moreover the items assigned by Neoptolemus to

[1] Cf. *CQ*, XL (1946), 16 ff. For these and other reasons I find it hard to accept
the criticisms of that paper in M. Puelma Piwonka's book, *op. cit.* p. 330, n. 2.
I am not so unaware as he seems to imply that there is a difference between a
critic and a poet.　　　　　　　　　　　　[2] Cf. above, part I, ch. 2.

poesis—content, thought, plot, characters (no. 5)—cover virtually the whole (technical) field known from Aristotle's *Poetics*.[1] The only sizeable item that remains is style; and that, for reasons of his own, Neoptolemus reserved for what he called *poema*. The subjects of his discussion are then so closely defined by his verbal distinctions that I for one do not see how the substance of the book could have been arranged otherwise than is laid down by these distinctions. Philodemus violently castigates Neoptolemus for making the unnatural distinction between style and content (no. 1), and in the same breath censures him for juxtaposing the poet as a third aspect, εἶδος, along with style and content (no. 2). The same point would consequently seem to apply to the third prong of the triad as it does to the two others—with the proviso that, having dealt with the technical side of his subject, he now discusses some general aspects, such as poetic talent (no. 2) and the aims of a poet (nos. 10–12).[2] Finally, when he says, under (8), that 'verse has precedence among the constituent parts of poetry', πρωτεύειν τῶν εἰδῶν τὰ ποιήματα, that may be nothing but an Aristotelian way of describing the fundamental role assigned to poetic style—τὸ πρῶτον, or πρότερον, φύσει, as it were. But it seems more likely that first things also came first in treatment:[3] *poema*, the technique of writing in verse (without which there is no poem), followed by *poesis*, the subject-matter as organized in long poems, and finally *poeta*, the poet's talent, training, and aspirations.

These surmises are prompted by the evidence, but they go beyond it in an attempt at explanation. If they have some

[1] See below, ch. 2.

[2] H. Dahlmann holds however that there was nothing left to say on the subject of 'the poet', *op. cit.* p. 139, n. 1 (cf. above, p. 39). Why, it is hard to see. The *Ars* surely shows what matters could be debated under that heading. Whether they were so debated depends on the evidence. I find no conclusive argument in Dahlmann's general considerations, pp. 99 ff., why the evidence should be jettisoned in any specific case.

[3] P. Boyancé, *op. cit.* p. 32, reminded readers pertinently of what Aristotle said at the beginning of the *Poetics*, ἀρξάμενοι κατὰ φύσιν πρῶτον ἀπὸ τῶν πρώτων. G. F. Else's note on *Poet.* 1, 1447 *a* 12, adduces similar passages from other Aristotelian writings, *Aristotle's Poetics: The Argument*, p. 10.

validity, a touch of colour appears at a corner of the Hellenistic literary map which so far has been left blank. There were Callimachus and others with their small and elaborate poems. However great their admiration for Homer, the large scale of epic narrative was not for them—and they said so. There were Apollonius and others with large epic or dramatic compositions. They may have been sophisticated, *docti*, but they employed the forms which Callimachus and his colleagues had declared untenable for a modern poet.[1] There were again Callimachus and others combining scholarship and poetry—the Alexandrian pursuits. There was Praxiphanes of Rhodes who resembles the Alexandrian grammarians and men of letters: but he wrote no verse and in his teaching he remained on the Aristotelian side: a philosopher of the Aristotelian persuasion, whose name appears among the adversaries of Callimachus.[2] To all these Neoptolemus of Parium may now perhaps be added—an Alexandrian in his learned verse and in his scholarship; an Alexandrian, too, in the stylistic refinement which he demands of poems small and large; but an Aristotelian upholder of the long poem, and a believer in the unity of a large literary conception. If a final guess be made, he must have been essentially a middle-of-the-road man who whilst accepting contemporary taste in stylistic matters (and perhaps showing it in his own verse) was yet convinced that the day of the large-scale poem had not passed. He raised a problem—and it was worth raising; the great Romans raised it again, and to better purpose. But his nomenclature strikes one as artificial and jejune; so it may have been what he said rather than how he said it that attracted Horace to his textbook.

[1] This point is disregarded by F. Wehrli in his paper on 'Apollonios von Rhodos und Kallimachos', *H*, LXXVI (1941), 20. He argues that the lack of a monumental, Homeric, unity would have commended Apollonius' *Argonautica* to Callimachus. But, as Aristotle explains and Callimachus implies, there were two types of epic narrative: the large unity of the Homeric epic and the unilinear narrative of the epic chronicle which Aristotle calls 'cyclic'. Callimachus would have considered that Apollonius had jumped from the Homeric frying pan into the fire of the cyclic epic: ἐχθαίρω τὸ ποίημα τὸ κυκλικόν.   [2] *CQ*, XL (1946), 16 ff.

APPENDIXES

I. PHILODEMUS OR NEOPTOLEMUS?

(*See above, p. 60*)

Two dubious extracts, 8 (*b*) and 8 (*c*), were left over for examination.

(8 *b*) ἧι (i.e. τῆι ποήσει) καὶ τοῦτο [προσ]ῆψεν.

(8 *c*) εἰ δὲ πρὸς τ[α.....]ήματα τὸ πεποι[ῆσθαι] συνέκρινε, τα[ὐτὸ καὶ πρό]τερον ἔλεγεν.

Philodemus has told his readers that Neoptolemus separated the two activities involved in ποίημα and ποίησις. But how did Neoptolemus get himself out of the *impasse* in which his theorizing had put him? How did he relate ποίημα to ποίησις? That the two are closely related he must have known as well as anyone. The sentences printed above may deal with this very point; but unhappily the evidence is still obscure.

Commenting on the primacy assigned to ποιήματα by Neoptolemus in extract 8, Philodemus now questions whether that primacy relates to the order of composing or to the order of value—whether τὸ ποίημα is [τ]ῆι τ[άξει] πρῶτ[ο]ν or τὸ βέλ[τι]στον. To the former alternative he objects because of its strange terminology; to the latter because 'the greatest value' may rather be found in ποίησις than in ποίημα: εἰ δ[ὲ] τὸ βέλ[τι]στον, πῶς μᾶλλον τῆς ποήσεως, (8*b*) ἧι καὶ τοῦτο [προσ]ῆψεν.[1] Now τοῦτο may refer to ποίημα in the preceding sentence of Philodemus; in which case the meaning is that proposed by Jensen: 'to which (ποίησις) he had indeed joined it (ποίημα)'. But Philodemus does not say how Neoptolemus joined together what he had so strenuously separated. Or τοῦτο may refer to τὸ βέλτιστον: 'to which (ποίησις) he had indeed applied it (the description, "the best")'. But in the section on Neoptolemus there has been no previous mention of a scale of poetic values. Either interpretation will suit the hypothetical case which I have made in this chapter. In neither case however is there any certainty whether we are dealing with Neoptolemus' words or only with Philodemus' report on what he conceived to be Neoptolemus' teachings.

The second extract presents equal difficulties. Jensen assumed that Philodemus was here talking of the relation between style and content as he was in the preceding sentence. Hence his supplements,

[1] *Ibid.* col. xii, 3–xiii, 1.

75

εἰ δὲ πρὸς τ[ὰ διανο]ήματα τὸ πεποι[ῆσθαι] συνέκρινε, τα[ὐτὸ καὶ πρό]τερον ἔλεγεν, 'but if he compared the composition of verse with the thoughts (expressed), he has said the same before'. On the other hand, it may be argued that Philodemus is still attacking the primacy of ποιήματα in extract 8, and the supplement therefore might have to be replaced accordingly—πρὸς τά [γε ποι]ήματα is all that occurs to me. The reference would then be to Neoptolemus' opinion (discussed in col. xii) that πεποιῆσθαί τι depends on the style or ποίημα, not on subject-matter or thought or ποίησις. In either case συνέκρινε may call for a rendering that is closer to that of προσῆψεν in the previous extract. Neither suggestion is sufficiently established to serve as a basis for further conclusions.

The purport of extracts 8 (*b*) and 8 (*c*) therefore must remain in doubt. The extracts do not provide unequivocal information on how Neoptolemus related ποίημα and ποίησις.

II. Ποίησις AND THE LEXICOGRAPHERS
(*See above, p. 62*)

The editors of the ninth edition of Liddell and Scott's lexicon thus arrange the article on ποίησις: (1) fabrication, creation, production; (2) of poetry, (*b*) poetic composition, poem. This is not so much false as incomplete. As often in that dictionary the meanings are not clearly delimited and they are insufficiently illustrated by examples. It is in fact still necessary to consult Stephanus' *Thesaurus* and the indexes to the relevant writers; *OED*, s.v. *Poesy*, also proves useful.

(1) Plato (*Conv.* 205*b*) paraphrased the word by 'production', ἐργασία, 'the cause of all transition from non-existence to existence'. He may have been right in asserting that in common use the word was restricted to 'musical and metrical production'. Nevertheless, usage from the fifth century (when this and many abstract words ending in -σις were first recorded or coined) was in fact wider, cf. Herodotus, III, 22, 3 and Thucydides, III, 2, 2 as cited by LS⁹, and later examples. The same applies to ποίημα.

Not infrequently the meaning oscillates between (the act of) composing, and poetry in a general or abstract sense. Aristoph. *Ran.* 907, τὴν ποίησιν οἷός εἰμι, 'what sort of poet I am', may be explained as 'what I am as regards composing' or 'as regards poetry'.

(2) Ποίησις is widely used in the abstract or general sense of 'poetry'. Homer or an earlier poet is said by Herodotus, II, 23, to

have introduced a certain name into 'poetry', ἐς ποίησιν ἐσενείκασθαι. Thus ποίησις is contrasted with prose by Isocrates, *Panath.* 35, οἱ περὶ τὴν ποίησιν καὶ τοὺς λόγους ὄντες, and Plato, *Rep.* II, 366*e*; with philosophy by Aeschines, *In Ctes.* 108; with history by Aristotle, *Poet.* 9, 1451 *b* 6. Qualified by an adjective, noun, or pronoun, it specifies the various poetic genres; Pherecrates, 145, 10 (Kock), τῆς ποιήσεως | τῶν διθυράμβων and Plato, *Gorg.* 502*a*, thus specify dithyrambic poetry; Plato, *Theaet.* 152*e*, and Aristotle, *Poet.* 4, 1449 *a* 3, denote tragedy and comedy by ποίησις (ἑκατέρα); Plato, *Rep.* III, 394*c*, so denotes epic. It is semi-animate when the early poets are said to have 'created it out of extemporizing', Aristotle, *Poet.* 4, 1448 *b* 23. 'Poetry' may have appeared on the stage in the Ποίησις of Aristophanes (the same title is credited to a playwright of the 'middle comedy', Antiphanes); and poetry is 'ejected' from the ideal state, Plato, *Rep.* x, 607*b*.

Ποίησις may not only be poetic composition (and thus 'poetry' in a general connotation) but the body of the composition itself, as Isocrates, *Euag.* 9, διαποικίλαι τὴν ποίησιν, Aristotle, *Poet.* 23, 1459 *a* 37, (ἐπεισοδίοις) διαλαμβάνει τὴν ποίησιν (ὁ Ὅμηρος), or *ibid.* I, 1447 *a* 10. Cf. Plato, *Leg.* VIII, 829*e*, τῆς ἐν ποιήσεσι παρρησίας.

Hence ποίησις is frequently used with a collective notion and refers to 'the poetry', that is the whole *œuvre*, of a poet. Thucydides, I, 10, 3, speaks of the 'work' or 'poetry' of Homer in that sense: τῇ Ὁμήρου αὖ ποιήσει... πιστεύειν. Aristophanes makes Aeschylus claim, *Ran.* 868, that his ποίησις has not 'died with him', whereas Euripides' has, so that he can draw on it in the Lower World; at 1366 however the work, ποίησις, of each tragedian can be weighed on the scales. Thus Isocrates, *Panath.* 33, as regards the work of Homer, Hesiod, and other poets; cf. Plato, *Ion*, 531*d* (on Homer), *Tim.* 20*e* (on Solon) πολλαχοῦ... ἐν ποιήσει, Aristotle, *Poet.* 22, 1458*a*20 (on Cleophon and Sthenelus).

(*b*) Finally and infrequently ποίησις may be a single composition, and hence, like ποίημα, a particular 'poem'. Aristotle, *Pol.* v, 7, 1306*b*39, δῆλον... ἐκ τῆς Τυρταίου ποιήσεως τῆς καλουμένης Εὐνομίας. *Ibid.* IV, 11, 1296*a*20, is a doubtful case (cf. Ardizzoni, *op. cit.* p. 111), Σόλων τε γὰρ ἦν τούτων (i.e. τῶν μέσων)· δῆλον δ' ἐκ τῆς ποιήσεως. The same applies to ᾽Αθ. Πολ. 12, 1. Greek writings of the Roman period provide more examples.

So much for ποίησις in the fifth and fourth centuries B.C., from Herodotus to Aristotle. Throughout these two centuries the word is used without any especial finesse: ποίησις is not part of a technical vocabulary. Technicality so far as ποίησις and ποίημα are concerned is post-Aristotelian, although it cannot have been long after Aristotle in coming. Nevertheless, for all their artificiality the later distinctions have some basis in actual usage. (The early evidence as regards these two words has been unduly simplified in P. Chantraine's otherwise instructive account, *La formation des noms en grec ancien*, 1933, p. 287; but see the same writer's *Études sur le vocabulaire grec*, 1956, p. 20. Ardizzoni, *op. cit.* pp. 105–12, looks too hard for the later technical refinements in pre-Hellenistic prose; Greenberg, *op. cit.* pp. 267–8, avoids that mistake.) Ποίησις is used in a variety of meanings in the fifth and fourth centuries; but except for the action of composing, or the abstraction, 'poetry', all cases that have come to my knowledge relate to something *in toto*, be it composition or compositions. Some cases of ποίημα do and others do not. I suspect it is this nuance that made it possible for Hellenistic critics to foist unreal distinctions on real.

CHAPTER 2

THE 'RHETORIC' AND 'POETICS'
OF ARISTOTLE

Any reader who knows his *Poetics* and *Rhetoric* is likely to feel
that in the *Ars Poetica* he is traversing Aristotelian ground. In
the sixteenth and seventeenth centuries, when the ancient
tradition still persisted, literary critics used to draw freely
either on Horace *or* on Aristotle *or* on both; so that a modern
writer could speak of a fusion of Horatian and Aristotelian
literary criticism.[1] Yet, in defining Horace's debt to earlier
authorities, Porphyrion points to Neoptolemus of Parium,
not to Aristotle himself. Here there may be a chance of
tracing Horace's debt to both Aristotle and Neoptolemus.
The operation presupposes that the debt amounts to more
than an occasional borrowing from Aristotle. Likewise the
operation presupposes that the Aristotelian material must be
in harmony with what is already known about Neoptolemus'
literary criticism. Even so the result is bound to be hypothetical. I aim at a hypothesis which fits all the evidence
known from Aristotle, Neoptolemus, and Horace. The degrees
of probability that are attainable vary in the different portions
of the *Ars*. Clearly if all three authorities agree the margin of
error is bound to be smaller than if only Aristotle and Horace
are available for conclusions about Neoptolemus, or if there
is no Aristotelian evidence at all. Such virtue as my argument
may possess will be seriously impaired if the strictness that can
be attained in this kind of inquiry is overestimated; but the
same is true if it is underestimated.

[1] M. T. Herrick, *The Fusion of Horatian and Aristotelian Literary Criticism, 1531–
1555* (Univ. of Illinois Press, 1946). More recently *A History of Literary Criticism
in the Italian Renaissance* has been published by B. Weinberg (2 vols., Univ. of
Chicago Press, 1961), which offers a serviceable account of Renaissance commentaries, and comments, upon the *Ars Poetica* and the *Poetics*.

Modern critics usually hold that in poetry the meaning cannot be adequately stated apart from the poetic words conveying it. Ancient critics usually hold that it can be so stated. They talk of subject-matter and style; that is, their categories are rhetorical. The dissatisfaction with the rhetorical outlook has stimulated inquiry into the characteristic features of ancient literary criticism. No one could have been more dissatisfied with what he considered rhetoric where rhetoric should have no abiding place than Augusto Rostagni. When he edited the *Poetics* and the *Ars Poetica* some thirty years ago he strongly dissented from the objectionable separation of subject-matter and style.[1] At the same time he asserted that this distinction underlies Horace's *Ars*, so that we would in fact be dealing with a combination of rhetorical and poetic categories. This combination of categories he traced back to Aristotle's *Rhetoric* and *Poetics*. He was not indeed the first scholar to apply this, rhetorical, distinction to Horace. A perusal of editions and writings on the *Ars* from the sixteenth to the nineteenth centuries will show that; and after all E. Norden's analysis which set the fashion for a whole generation of students of the poem was based on the same rhetorical distinction.

But no one before Rostagni had linked these and the like theories with the philosophical context of Aristotle's *Poetics*— a context which explains both their genesis and their importance. Now it is one thing to sense the general relevance of these ideas, and quite another to determine their relevance to any specific work of literary criticism. For the former, scholars are indebted to Rostagni; for the latter, much of the essential spade-work still needs to be done. Many judges are agreed that Rostagni has been too hasty in assigning crucial ideas to Theophrastus; but since I believe that the outcome of

[1] In ch. IV of his 'Aristotele e l'Aristotelismo nella storia dell'estetica antica', *SFIC*, n.s. II (1922), now *Scr. Min.* I (1955), 161–88: 'Il sistema di Aristotele nell'unione della retorica con la poetica'; also his *Aristotele: Poetica* (1st ed., 1927), and *Arte Poetica di Orazio* (1st ed., 1930).

a truer assessment would be mainly negative it need not concern us here. We need however to learn to read the *Poetics* and the *Rhetoric* with the eyes of a Hellenistic reader. This should help in charting the more difficult territory in the *Ars*, if indeed there is anything in the assertion of an ultimate, Aristotelian, provenance of Horace's rhetorical theory of poetry. In particular we need to know how the fundamental division into content and style affects the *Rhetoric* and the *Poetics*—as we have already seen it to affect Horace's poem. Thus it would become possible to state more clearly what critics mean when they talk of a mixture of Aristotelian rhetoric and poetics in the *Ars Poetica*.

The *Rhetoric* has many complications that arise from the lack of a final literary plan. These it shares with the rest of Aristotle's treatises. But unlike many it has a simple underlying scheme. This scheme was imperfectly applied by Aristotle, but it proved nevertheless suitable for the purposes of those of his successors who were more interested in a straightforward presentation of certain basic precepts than in raising and solving intellectual problems. 'It is not enough to know what to say, but necessary also to know how to say it': thus Aristotle near the beginning of the third book of the *Rhetoric*.[1] This is the familiar distinction between matter and style on which I have commented before. Hence the division of the *Rhetoric* into content and diction: Books I and II on content, Book III on diction. As a concession to established rhetorical teaching, but equally as a critique of the professional rhetoricians, Aristotle also considers how to arrange what has been thought and expressed, and with arrangement he deals, briefly and polemically, in the last seven chapters of Book III.[2] These chapters ill fit the clear-cut antithesis of content and style—and little wonder. For traditional

---

[1] Ar. *Rhet.* III, 1, 1403 *b* 15, περὶ δὲ τῆς λέξεως ἐχόμενόν ἐστιν εἰπεῖν· οὐ γὰρ ἀπόχρη τὸ ἔχειν ἃ δεῖ λέγειν, ἀλλ' ἀνάγκη καὶ ταῦτα ὡς δεῖ εἰπεῖν.

[2] *Rhet.* III, 13–19, cf. the sentence concluding ch. 12, περὶ μὲν οὖν τῆς λέξεως εἴρηται καὶ κοινῇ περὶ ἁπάντων καὶ ἰδίᾳ περὶ ἕκαστον γένος· λοιπὸν δὲ περὶ τάξεως εἰπεῖν.

rhetorical teaching was not established on that basis. Independent information suggests that traditional teaching was based on the chief sections of a Greek speech, from the proem to the epilogue.¹ The teaching of rhetoric changed when Aristotle made it part of a larger setting which juxtaposed content, diction, and arrangement; but in the *Rhetoric*, and indeed after Aristotle, it retained some of its original characteristics.² Subsequent practice was complicated by the effect of two different traditions: the old *partes orationis* and the later, generalized, rules about *dispositio*.³ Complications as regards the placing of the items naturally followed. But Aristotle's threefold division underlies the later five-part order of rhetoric: content, diction, and arrangement, with the addition of memorizing and delivery. Cicero's definition in the *Orator* shows how the five Hellenistic 'parts' may be fitted into the triad: 'tria videnda sunt oratori—*quod* dicet et *quo* quidque *loco* et *quo modo*'.⁴

Now, once again, Aristotle is noticing prevailing conditions in the field of rhetoric. Political and forensic rhetoric exist for a purpose—to bring about the decision desired by the speaker. That is why attention to the argument is not enough. In order to sway the judge, the speaker must also appear to have

¹ The polemic of both Plato and Aristotle against the older rhetoricians is directed specially against teaching on the basis of μόρια τοῦ λόγου, cf. Plato, *Phaedrus*, 266 *d*–267 *a*; Ar. *Rhet.* I, 1, 1354 *a*–*b*; III, 13–14. The remains of the older rhetorical *artes* (among them those of Thrasymachus and Theodorus of Byzantium whose names are mentioned by Plato in this context) are assembled in L. Spengel's Τεχνῶν Συναγωγή (1828), and L. Radermacher's *Artium Scriptores*, *SBÖA* (1951). But the former is out of date and the latter is insufficiently annotated. For Theodectes' Isocratean rhetoric as Aristotle's source and the target of his criticism in the final section of the *Rhetoric*, see K. Barwick, *H*, LVII (1922), 13, 24 and F. Solmsen, *H*, LXVII (1932), 147. For the reflection of a whole course of rhetoric in the final section of Aristotle's work, see F. Marx, *BVSA* (1900), p. 245.

² Solmsen, *op. cit.* pp. 144–51. Solmsen too has traced the outlines of both traditions in post-Aristotelian rhetorical teaching, *AJP*, LXII (1941), 35–50, 169–90.

³ Barwick, *op. cit.* pp. 1–13. A further complication, insufficiently noted by Barwick, was Hermagoras' theory of rhetorical 'modes', or *status*; cf. Quintilian's *I.O.*, Book VII.

⁴ Cic. *Or.* 43. Opposition to the rhetorical triad is registered at para. 4 of Quintilian's instructive survey, *I.O.* III, 3.

the right personal qualities.[1] Hence the means of persuasion, πίστεις, are three in number. One lies in the character, real or apparent, of the speaker, another in the influence he exercises over his audience, a third in the proofs, real or apparent, advanced by the speaker.[2] This new triad adapts earlier and contemporary teaching on how character and emotion could be exploited rhetorically; it also offers an answer to Plato's criticism of that procedure of the rhetoricians.[3] The professionals do not seem to have been impressed; they tended to adhere to the simpler, pre-Aristotelian, routine of founding their teaching chiefly on those parts of rhetorical speech, *partes orationis*, to which it was thought to apply. But Aristotle's three modes of persuasion reappear in the triad of *probare*, *conciliare*, and *movere*, in Cicero's rhetorical writings.[4] Aristotle deals with them in the order of (1) *probare*, (2) *movere*, and (3) *conciliare*; moreover, he subdivides the proof into two kinds of propositions: specific, when they are tied to a particular subject-matter, and general, when they are not so tied.[5]

Such is the structure of Aristotle's *Rhetoric*. A threefold division into content, style, and arrangement; content defined as sources of persuasion and subdivided into specific propositions and general arguments; and the specific propositions

---

[1] Ar. *Rhet.* II, 1, 1377*b*21, ἐπεὶ δὲ ἕνεκα κρίσεώς ἐστιν ἡ ῥητορική (καὶ γὰρ τὰς συμβουλὰς κρίνουσι καὶ ἡ δίκη κρίσις ἐστίν) ἀνάγκη μὴ μόνον πρὸς τὸν λόγον ὁρᾶν ὅπως ἀποδεικτικὸς ἔσται καὶ πιστός, ἀλλὰ καὶ αὐτὸν ποιόν τινα καὶ τὸν κριτὴν παρασκευάζειν. From this and other similar passages Theophrastus appears to have derived the opinion that rhetoric and poetry differed from philosophy in the end at which speech, λόγος, was aimed; rhetoric and poetry aimed at (affecting) an audience, πρὸς τοὺς ἀκροατάς; philosophy at (explaining) a subject, πρὸς τὰ πράγματα: Theophr., ed. Wimmer, frs. 64 and 65.

[2] Ar. *Rhet.* I, 2, 1356*a*1, τῶν δὲ διὰ τοῦ λόγου ποριζομένων πίστεων τρία εἴδη ἐστίν· αἱ μὲν γάρ εἰσιν ἐν τῷ ἤθει τοῦ λέγοντος, αἱ δὲ ἐν τῷ τὸν ἀκροατὴν διαθεῖναί πως, αἱ δὲ ἐν αὐτῷ τῷ λόγῳ διὰ τοῦ δεικνύναι ἢ φαίνεσθαι δεικνύναι.

[3] The chief features of the evidence have been presented by F. Solmsen, *CP*, XXXIII (1938), 390–404. For Plato's criticism see *Phaedrus*, 266*c*, etc.

[4] Solmsen, *op. cit.* p. 396. There are numerous references to this triad; I note, particularly, Cicero, *De Orat.* II, 115; *Or.* 69.

[5] The distinction between general arguments and specific propositions, κοινοὶ τόποι and ἴδιαι προτάσεις, is set out at *Rhet.* I, 2, 1358*a*2.

subdivided into proof proper, emotion, and character.[1] This is simple and systematic—an order of things that would appeal to writers of textbooks. It is true, there are many discrepancies that greatly complicate this straightforward scheme.[2] These are matters that concern the student of the origins of Aristotle's *Rhetoric*. They would be irrelevant to an author who worked in the same tradition as Aristotle and, presumably, was concerned with the use to which he could put the book. It is not hard to see that at any rate the underlying scheme of the *Rhetoric*, in its present form, serves the purposes of a systematic textbook and its chief divisions could be made to fit the related topic of poetry. Both Neoptolemus and Horace applied to poetry such a rhetorical scheme as Aristotle's. Was it Aristotle's *Rhetoric* that served as a model for this arrangement? The headings are definite enough, and they differ sufficiently from what is known of the rhetorical practice of the time, to make this a reasonable *question*. But the *answer* must depend on a closer comparison with the *Rhetoric*. This will be attempted in the next chapter.

On a first reading, the *Poetics* seems to be laid out with even greater clarity than the *Rhetoric*. For what could be clearer and more straightforward than an analysis of all kinds of poetic imitation, or *mimesis*, issuing in an arrangement by genres: tragedy and epic, the 'serious' genres, in the extant first book; comedy, and perhaps iambic, in the lost second

[1] To put it schematically, content is discussed in Books I–II, style in Book III, chs. 1–12, arrangement, ch. 13 to end of Book III. The sources of persuasion are subdivided into specific propositions, I, 3–II, 18, and general arguments, II, 20 to end of Book II. The specific propositions come under three sub-headings—proof, I, 3 to end of Book I, emotion, II, 1–11, and character, II, 12–17.

[2] The fundamental distinction between matter, style, and arrangement, should have been made at the outset if Aristotle had felt it to be as fundamental as it appears to be. Yet it is not made until the end of Book II and the beginning of Book III. Nor are the other two principles of division which are mentioned in the last note combined without awkwardness. Cf. F. Solmsen, *Die Entwicklung der aristot. Logik und Rhetorik* (*N. Phil. Unt.* vol. IV), 1929, pp. 223 ff., who seeks to determine the various drafts of the *Rhetoric*—not always convincingly since even a fundamental discrepancy in thought does not necessarily correspond to a different draft.

book?[1] Yet, on closer acquaintance, one notices several features which would render the *Poetics* an unsuitable model for a textbook on poetry.

The introductory section on *mimesis* is not so clearly linked with the main section on tragedy as the writer of a textbook might have wished. Aristotle claims that the definition of tragedy which opens the main section is based on the preceding analysis.[2] The claim is not entirely justified. One essential element of the definition has no counterpart whatever in the initial section—I mean, catharsis.[3] Critics deal with the problem as best they can. But this is not the only stumbling-block. That tragedy must be 'complete, having magnitude', τελείας μέγεθος ἐχούσης, amounts to a new proposition. The phrasing of the sentence shows that Aristotle was aware of this. The initial section did not mention 'completeness'. But two remarks about 'magnitude' were made *en passant*, in the historical chapter 4, and size is discussed in the historical chapter 5.[4] The notion of completeness does not necessarily follow from the notion of size and the reader is not instructed until, in chapters 7–9, he comes to Aristotle's

---

[1] *Poetics*, ch. 4, contrasts the serious genres of tragedy and epic with others that lack 'seriousness': comedy and iambic. In Aristotle's account the historical line, 'epic to tragedy', is parallelled by another, 'iambic to comedy'. This lends some colour to the tenuous but not improbable indication of the Codex Riccardianus that not only comedy but the iambic genre as well was discussed in the second book of the *Poetics*: C. Landi, *RFIC*, n.s. III (1925), 551. There is little that can be known about the lost second book. But dogmatic denials are no better than dogmatic assertions. A. P. McMahon, *HS*, XXVIII (1917), 1; XL (1929), 97, and D. de Montmollin, *La poétique d'Aristote* (1951), p. 188, go beyond the evidence in denying the existence of a second book. Cf. *Gnomon*, XXIV (1952), 380, and G. F. Else, *Aristotle's Poetics: the Argument* (1957), p. 653.

[2] Ar. *Poet.* 6, 1449*b*22, περὶ δὲ τραγῳδίας λέγωμεν ἀπολαβόντες αὐτῆς ἐκ τῶν εἰρημένων τὸν γινόμενον ὅρον τῆς οὐσίας. The precise meaning of the sentence is not agreed. But no one doubts that Aristotle intended it to refer to the introduction, *Poet*. chs. 1–5.

[3] *Ibid.* 6, 1449*b*27 (μίμησις) δι' ἐλέου καὶ φόβου περαίνουσα τὴν τῶν τοιούτων παθημάτων κάθαρσιν. G. F. Else, *loc. cit.*, considers the whole clause a later addition, made however by Aristotle himself. This creates other difficulties, some of which may be seen in Else's discussion.

[4] *Ibid.* 4, 1449*a*13, κατὰ μικρὸν ηὐξήθη, *a*19, μέγεθος, and ἐκ μικρῶν μύθων; ch. 5, 1449 *b*12, ἔτι δὲ τῷ μήκει κτλ.; the text at *b*10, μεγάλου, is unsound.

philosophy of artistic unity. And there are various smaller discrepancies which also discourage the belief that the first two sections are, in fact, of a piece—although clearly Aristotle treated them as though they were.

Neoptolemus had put forward principles applicable to all verse, ποίημα and ποίησις; it appears that he had arranged his textbook in accordance with these principles. The argument of the *Poetics* rests on a set of general axioms. But Aristotle, for reasons of his own, propounded the axioms, not in the general context of his introduction but in the specific context of the one genre of tragedy. The axioms of completeness, organic unity, and universality—τέλειον, ἕν, ὅλον, καθόλου κατὰ τὸ εἰκὸς ἢ τὸ ἀναγκαῖον—are intended to be valid for poetry, not only for any especial kind of it.[1] Thus Aristotle's axioms in the *Poetics* would attract a critic like Neoptolemus, but Aristotle's very personal procedure in setting them forth would be less likely to do so.

Poetic style raises an even greater problem. Style as a general concept is neglected in the scheme of the *Poetics*. It is recognized (almost regretfully, one feels) as an element poetry cannot do without. It ranks fairly low in the hierarchy of the 'parts of tragedy'—third, after plot and character. It is set over against 'thought', as it is in the *Rhetoric*, and Aristotle draws on the rhetorical treatise when he comes to deal with thought embodied in speech.[2] Poetic speech itself is discussed in a manner reminiscent of the *Rhetoric*, and conversely Aristotle in the stylistic section of the *Rhetoric* refers to the relevant part of the *Poetics*.[3] But unlike the *Rhetoric*, the *Poetics* minimizes style. There was little use in this feature of

---

[1] At ch. 8 the principle of unity is exemplified from Homer and the epic. And ch. 9 debates *poetic* universality, 1451 a36, οὐ τὰ γενόμενα λέγειν τοῦτο ποιητοῦ ἔργον ἐστίν, ἀλλ' οἷα ἂν γένοιτο καὶ τὰ δυνατὰ κατὰ τὸ εἰκὸς ἢ τὸ ἀναγκαῖον.

[2] *Ibid.* 19, 1456a33, περὶ μὲν οὖν τῶν ἄλλων εἰδῶν ἤδη εἴρηται, λοιπὸν δὲ περὶ λέξεως καὶ διανοίας εἰπεῖν. τὰ μὲν οὖν περὶ τὴν διάνοιαν ἐν τοῖς περὶ ῥητορικῆς κείσθω· τοῦτο γὰρ ἴδιον μᾶλλον ἐκείνης τῆς μεθόδου. ἔστι δὲ κατὰ τὴν διάνοιαν ταῦτα ὅσα ὑπὸ τοῦ λόγου δεῖ παρασκευασθῆναι. For διάνοια in the *Poetics*, see Miss Dale's paper, cited below, p. 87, n. 1.

[3] *Ibid.* chs. 19–22, and four references to the *Poetics* in *Rhet.* III, 1 and 2.

Aristotle's work for a poet, who held that his craft, in the first place, consisted of words used in a certain fashion.

A book on the *Ars Poetica* is not the place for an elaborate argument on the *Poetics*. Elaboration would be needed if I tried to account for the curious features that make the *Poetics* such a difficult, and such a fascinating, book. Two points however require mention because they have a bearing on Neoptolemus and the *Ars Poetica*. One of them is the interest, partly metaphysical and partly empirical, which moved Aristotle to establish the exemplary character of one particular literary form—poetic drama, specially tragedy. This interest must have been at the root of Aristotle's concentration on drama and those elements of drama that will support a reasoned defence of the value of *mimesis*.[1] This interest, too, may have suggested the context of tragedy for the discussion of qualities that are poetic rather than narrowly 'tragic'. Tragedy simply displays them *a fortiori* in an exemplary manner.

The second point is of equal importance. The *Poetics* was not Aristotle's only attempt to pronounce on poetry. There were the three books *De Poetis*.[2] The two works must have differed in scope: our *Poetics* belongs to the *commentarius* type restricted to the school, whilst the *De Poetis* appears to have been a work of literary pretensions, in the form of a dialogue aimed at readers outside the school.[3] However early the

[1] I concur with Miss A. M. Dale's observations, in 'Ethos and Dianoia', *AUMLA, Journ. Australasian Universities*, XI (1959), 4: 'The new version of the metaphysical "mimesis" theory, which Aristotle uses in order to reinstate poetry high in the scale of human activities after Plato's attacks, leads to an almost exclusive attention to the least subjective aspects of poetry. The most obviously mimetic form, the drama, gets fullest discussion and highest marks, epic comes second, with dithyramb as a bad third and lyric either nowhere or subsumed vaguely under music. Now this *a priori* deduction from metaphysical principles is supported by the empirical facts of the contemporary scene, since the growing-point of new poetic life was to be found in the theatre, and Homer still remained an inexhaustible fount of inspiration, while personal lyric had not yet found its new Hellenistic forms', etc.

[2] περὶ ποιητῶν γ, in the lists of Aristotelian titles.

[3] The title occurs in the initial part of the lists which seems to contain writings of that kind.

original draft of the *Poetics* may have been, the *De Poetis* is likely to have preceded it—not only because the literary works are dated early. For the *Poetics* gives the impression of being silent or allusive on certain fundamental matters. On the other hand the fragments of the *De Poetis* suggest that in that work Aristotle had dealt with precisely those points— the justification of *mimesis* and the personal aspects of poets and poetry[1]—on which the other is silent or allusive. If the *De Poetis* preceded the *Poetics*, this may explain at once the allusive character of the introduction to the *Poetics*, and the discussion under a specific genre of what are in fact general poetic features. For the *Poetics* is primarily concerned with literary genres and takes for granted that the mimetic art of poetry is sufficiently justified. Rostagni has justly remarked that this twofold aspect—a more general and a more technical—survived Aristotle in ancient literary criticism.[2] Neoptolemus seems to have combined the two aspects in his critical work,[3] and Horace certainly combined in the *Ars* the more general aspect with a more specific.

It is now possible to sum up my imaginary case. If a literary critic such as Neoptolemus knew Aristotle's *Poetics*, his feelings in regard to that book must have been mixed. There must have been much that was likely to attract him; above all, Aristotle's wholehearted conviction that it was only the large genres that really mattered. Yet there must have been many reasons why he could not adopt a procedure which was closely bound up with the philosopher's aims and aspirations. The *Poetics* was not comprehensive enough as a model for general poetic criticism, for it probably supplemented on the technical side, as it were, the less restricted and more personal writing in the *De Poetis*. On the other hand it was

---

[1] It will be apparent that I accept A. Rostagni's general position as regards the scope of the *De Poetis*, but take exception to his 'reconstruction'. Cf. below, p. 126.

[2] A. Rostagni, *Scr. Min.* I, 262, 314, on the περὶ ποιητικῆς καὶ τῶν ποιητῶν of Heraclides Ponticus, which title may point to a combination of the two features. But nothing is known about Heraclides' book.

[3] Cf. above, p. 73 and the discussion below, pp. 126 ff.

probably not literary enough—philosophical speculation rather than literary criticism. Moreover the generality of the axioms on which it is based did not stand out sufficiently. The *Poetics* is based on a set of axioms of considerable depth and subtlety, but the argument is not arranged in accordance with these axioms. It is arranged according to poetic genres. In the extant part of the *Poetics* the exemplary genre of tragedy is employed as a yard-stick wherewith to measure the rest of poetry. Much is said in the section concerned with tragedy which in fact pertains *a fortiori* to the whole of poetry—or is meant to do so.

CHAPTER 3

NEOPTOLEMUS AND THE 'RHETORIC' AND 'POETICS'

Such are the outlines of the *Rhetoric* and the *Poetics* which a student of the *Ars* needs to bear in mind. A literary critic of the third century would have to grapple with some of the difficulties inherent in the two treatises if he felt sufficiently attached to Aristotelian, or Peripatetic, teaching. He could still make use of the *Poetics*. But if he were hankering after a more general and more practical procedure, he would have to turn the *Poetics* inside out and remember the more systematic if somewhat flat arrangement of the *Rhetoric*. Such a procedure would take the mainspring out of the *Poetics*; but the Aristotelian aspect of the matter is beyond the scope of this book.

I now propose to contrast the *Poetics* and the *Rhetoric* with the *Ars*. The fragments of Neoptolemus are sufficient evidence for some of the essential changes which Hellenistic critics found necessary before they could employ the Aristotelian treatises for their own purposes. The evidence does not warrant a 'reconstruction' of Neoptolemus' poetics. But at any rate some features of his book can be known and much can be learned about his poetic theory. Nor are all inferences equally certain or probable. At times three pieces of evidence conveniently come to hand: a passage from the *Poetics* or *Rhetoric*, a fragment of Neoptolemus showing Aristotelianism revised, and a passage of Horace showing his adaptation of Neoptolemus. Then, as I suggested earlier, we may hope to recover Neoptolemus' views. When there are only Horace and Aristotle to draw on, or, worse, if Horace is our only source, the degrees of probability will be appreciably smaller; much will depend on the Peripatetic or Alexandrian character of such passages of Horace.

The first chapter of this book submits proof for the proposition that the technical portion of Horace's poem is laid out according to arrangement, style, and content, *ordo–facundia–res*.[1] Arrangement and style are juxtaposed: *nec facundia deseret hunc nec lucidus ordo*.[2] Nevertheless, 'arrangement' is treated so perfunctorily in three lines that the triad seems whittled down to the bipartite scheme of style (with a brief aside on *ordo*—apparently a traditional topic that is not to be pursued any further) followed by content. The first chapter of the present section shows, in contrast to current opinion, that Neoptolemus arranged the material of his technical section similarly, subsuming stylistic problems under ποίημα and problems of subject-matter under ποίησις. There is no information on how he dealt with the traditional heading of τάξις or arrangement. Since Horace and Neoptolemus concur in employing what is really the bipartite scheme of style and content, Neoptolemus may well have preceded Horace in removing *ordo* from the main line of the argument. In the preceding chapter of this section I have been suggesting that Aristotle's *Rhetoric*, unlike the *Poetics*, employs a similar division although naturally the terminology is more adapted to rhetoric. Aristotle has a threefold division in which two of the components outstrip the third—style and content as against arrangement.[3] His nomenclature for the content of rhetoric is πίστεις, 'modes of persuasion', and for style and order, λέξις and τάξις. He places subject-matter first, and style and arrangement second and third. These headings (it has been argued above) differ sufficiently from the rhetorical practice of the time to suggest that it was probably Aristotle who first introduced them. In any case, the transference to

---

[1] Hor. *A.P.* 42–4, order, and 45–118, style; 119–294, subject-matter. For the relation of the examples 153 ff. to what they exemplify, see above, p. 10. It should be noted that arrangement and style respectively are named at the beginning of the relevant parts while content, *res*, is named at 40 but not at 119.

[2] *Ibid.* 41.

[3] Content is discussed in *Rhetoric*, Books I and II, style in twelve chapters of Book III, arrangement in the remaining seven chapters of the same book.

poetry from rhetoric called for a terminology that was adapted to verse: ποίημα, ποίησις.

The rest of Neoptolemus' technical jargon shows a like bias; it is Aristotelian with a difference. Diction, or style, is named σύνθεσις τῆς λέξεως, or simply σύνθεσις, composition.[1] Aristotle called it λέξις.[2] Both Aristotle and Neoptolemus set διάνοια, thought, over against λέξις; Neoptolemus also uses διανόημα. In the place of 'story' or 'plot', the μῦθος of the *Poetics*, Neoptolemus employs a more general term known from the *Rhetoric*: ὑπόθεσις, subiectum, 'subject'.[3] The term may have been applied to drama as early as the first generation after Aristotle.[4] 'Character' appears beside style, thought, and action, just as it does in the sixth chapter of the *Poetics*, though it is not called by its Aristotelian name, ἦθος, but by another, προσωποποιία. Finally, his name for the three mainstays of his system. Ποίημα, ποίησις, and ποιητής he calls εἴδη, or 'constituent elements'—just as Aristotle applied this term to the six elements or parts constituting tragedy.[5] Two of Neoptolemus' εἴδη are identical with Aris-

---

[1] Aristotle used σύστασις to denote the matter of a 'composition': *Poet.* 24, 1460*a*3, μακρὰ σύστασις, a sizeable composition.

[2] But in the *Poetics* Aristotle placed σύνθεσις alongside μέτρων and ὀνομάτων, also in other contexts alongside πραγμάτων or the like.

[3] Ar. *Rhet.* III, 2, 1404*b*15, lays down that because of the nature of its 'subject' the wording of prose should be plainer than the wording of verse: ἡ γὰρ ὑπόθεσις ἐλάττων. The notion in τὰ ὑποκείμενα πράγματα, at I, 1, 1355*a*36, may be compared. Ὑπόθεσις then is the matter or substance of discourse. Διάθεσις on the other hand (as F. Solmsen reminds me) is either 'arrangement', or the material as finally arranged and laid out—the economy of the content on which Aristotle legislates in the *Poetics*. Διάθεσις is the key-word of the telling anecdote about Menander, reported by Plutarch, *Glor. Ath.* 347*e*; cf. Phrynichus *ap.* Bekker, *Anec.* 36; Wilamowitz, Menander, *Das Schiedsgericht* (1925), p. 119. Jensen had a good case therefore when he supplied διάθεσις in Philodemus' critique of Neoptolemus, *De Poem.* v, col. xi, 13, μᾶ[λλο]ν γὰρ ἐχρῆν τὰς δια[θέσει]ς ποιήσεις [ἐπικαλεῖ]ν.

[4] *Hypothesis*, according to Sext. Emp. *Adv. Math.* III, 3, denoted the dramatic *peripeteia* and thus the plot of a tragedy or comedy: (καθὸ... λέγομεν) καὶ Δικαιάρχου τινὰς ὑποθέσεις τῶν Εὐριπίδου καὶ Σοφοκλέους μύθων. (Cf. F. Wehrli, *Dikaiarchos*, 1944, fr. 78 and p. 68.) From this it appears probable that Dicaearchus thus used the term in the first generation after Aristotle. Aristophanes of Byzantium and his successors certainly used it as a title for their ὑποθέσεις, cf. *R-E*, 'Hypotheseis', 414–24.

[5] *Poet.* 6, 1450*a*13, cf. 12, 1452*b*14, 25.

totle's (style and matter). Philodemus has pointed out how oddly the third εἶδος, 'the poet', consorts with the other two.

To judge from the *Rhetoric* Aristotle had many revealing things to say on the subject of language. In the *Poetics* he is brief, and obviously ascribed only a limited importance to the practical business of composing and writing. His successor Theophrastus gave much attention to the subject of style, apparently both rhetorical and poetic.[1] Neoptolemus, who was a poet, took the craftsman's interest in it. Earlier on I supported the suggestion that a curious bit of information is likely to tell us more about Neoptolemus' interest. Item 8 of my list (Neoptolemus, col. xii) lays down that 'verse' (τὰ ποιήματα) takes first place among the poetic elements (εἰδῶν).[2] It has been suggested that the sentence not only ascribes primacy to diction but is meant to indicate also the place assigned to the discussion of diction in his work on poetic criticism.[3] The Aristotelian order is thus altered, for in the *Rhetoric* subject-matter takes precedence over style—subject-matter, in Books I and II, precedes style (and order, τάξις), in Book III. This can now be further supported by the *Ars Poetica*. For the arrangement of the *Ars* (once the controversy over the initial and middle sections is settled) is precisely what we would expect if this suggestion were accepted: the discussion of style (and arrangement, *ordo*) precedes the discussion of subject-matter. So here again we should find that Neoptolemus, in using Aristotle, used him with a difference.

Up to this point of my argument Neoptolemus' Aristotelianism has been an inference which different judges might consider either weak or strong. Now however the combination of general Aristotelian features with the specific use of the *Rhetoric* presents evidence which I think is exceedingly hard to set aside. For the primary distinction between matter and

---

[1] Cf. J. Stroux, *De Theophrasti virtutibus dicendi* (1912), O. Regenbogen, *R-E*, Supp. VII, 'Theophrastos', 1522, 1527 ff.

[2] Above, p. 60.

[3] P. Boyancé, *RP*, Sér. 3, x (1936), 32, and above, p. 73.

diction was not the only thing on which Neoptolemus agreed with the *Rhetoric*, and which could be adapted to the criticism of poetry. Commentators of Horace have for a long time insisted on the likeness between the third book of the *Rhetoric* and the stylistic section of the *Ars*. This likeness needs to be considered next. Perhaps it may yet be given its due weight, even though we have now reached a section of the poem in which only two of the three witnesses are available—Horace and Aristotle.

In the first place, the sequence in the *Ars* closely resembles that of the third book of the *Rhetoric*. Horace, at *A.P.* 45–72, deals with the choice and the combination of words, ἐκλογή καὶ σύνθεσις τῶν ὀνομάτων. So does Aristotle, at *Rhet.* III, 2–6. Next, at *A.P.* 73–85, follows poetic metre, just as in the chapter next but one, at *Rhet.* III, 8, there follows a disquisition on rhythm in prose. This topic Horace, and perhaps Neoptolemus before him, placed immediately after the section on words—reasonably so, for style in verse according to the *Poetics* is combination of metres, τῶν μέτρων σύνθεσις,[1] and this fittingly follows the discussion of words. The final portion deals with 'appropriate style': how can diction be made to fit a given situation, and the emotions and characters of the persons who are involved in it? *A.P.* 86–118 deals, in this order, with situations, next with emotions, and last with characters. So does the chapter of *Rhet.* III which has just been omitted, that is, 7. For here too situations, emotions, and characters are rehearsed in the same order.

The *Ars* does not however represent anything like the full argument of the third book of the *Rhetoric*. In the first place, the initial chapter is jettisoned, as being concerned with the style of prose; so are chapters 10–12, for the same reason. We are then left with the three groups of subjects which tally in Horace (and *ex hypothesi* Neoptolemus) and Aristotle. But Horace is here strictly selective and consequently (on the assumption that he draws on Neoptolemus) it is easier to

[1] *Poet.* 6, 1449*b*34, λέγω δὲ λέξιν μὲν αὐτὴν τὴν τῶν μέτρων σύνθεσιν.

know what Neoptolemus adopted from Aristotle than what he did not. In the first group Horace concentrates on vocabulary and composition; he omits the Aristotelian discussion of metaphor in its entirety. Also such fundamental terms as clarity and ornament, σαφήνεια and κόσμος, are eliminated in this section and brought in on other occasions.[1]

Now for the content. In the first group of stylistic subjects *Ars* and *Rhetoric* partly diverge, Horace commenting on the style of verse, Aristotle on the style of prose. But the divergence between poetical and rhetorical theory does not go very far. Aristotle's point of view is rhetorical. He likes to explain the characteristics of prose style in contradistinction to poetry. He refers in Book III of the *Rhetoric* to the like chapters of the *Poetics*, just as he refers in the *Poetics* to the *Rhetoric*. Hence chapters 21 and 22 of the *Poetics* offer some relevant material. Talking of verse, Aristotle approves of 'all deviation from ordinary speech' within reasonable limits; this is matched by a large measure of disapproval in regard to the same licence in prose.[2] Newly coined words, πεποιημένα (a topic of especial interest to Horace), are among these deviations from ordinary usage.[3] Vocabulary and the use of

---

[1] For example, ornament, clarity, and ambiguity are noted at *A.P.* 447–9, 'ambitiosa recidet | ornamenta, parum claris lucem dare coget, | arguet ambigue dictum'. At *A.P.* 25 the correct use of language is by implication defined, in Peripatetic fashion, as the right mean between two faulty extremes; mistakes arise from inability to recognize the right mean, *specie recti. A.P.* 25 censures an offence against the Aristotelian *virtus orationis* of clarity. Brevity is intended, obscurity results; Aristotle was aware of the demands for conciseness (*Rhet.* III, 6, 1407*b*28), but if a speaker talks too much, he offends the grand law of all speech, not an especial *virtus orationis* as the Stoics, and some pre-Aristotelian critics, thought (*Rhet.* III, 12, 1414*a*25). *A.P.* 26–8 presupposes the three *characteres orationis. A.P.* 97, *sesquipedalia verba*, touches on the stylistic subject of long compound nouns; for the rhetorical use of διπλᾶ ὀνόματα, see *Rhet.* III, 2, 1404*b*29, etc.; for the poetic use of τριπλοῦν καὶ τετραπλοῦν καὶ πολλαπλοῦν ὄνομα, see *Poet.* 21, 1457*a*34, and Rostagni's note on *A.P.* 97. Also cf. *A.P.* 234.

[2] 'All deviation from ordinary speech' renders *Poet.* 22, 1458*a*23, πᾶν τὸ παρὰ τὸ κύριον. This is recommended, in moderation, for use in verse. *Rhet.* III, 2–6, largely dissuades such usage for prose, with the exception of metaphors.

[3] Newly coined words, πεποιημένα, are placed among the deviations from ordinary usage, τὸ κύριον, at *Poet.* 21, 1457*b*2.

words were much debated in the Lyceum. It is known that Theophrastus discussed the subject in his book on style, and discussed it like Aristotle with regard to both verse and prose. The Aristotelian traces in Horace's remarks are best explained by the tenor of Neoptolemus' discussion, although Aristotle's brevity in the *Poetics* and his preoccupation with prose in the *Rhetoric* do not provide sufficient material for comparison. About one thing however there can be no doubt. Horace, and *ex hypothesi* Neoptolemus, resolutely take up the Aristotelian principle of appropriateness, or πρέπον.[1] It was already conspicuous, beside 'unity', in Horace's introduction. Now it reappears in the first group of stylistic subjects,[2] it is uppermost in the second, on metre, and in the third group it retains the commanding position which it had in Aristotle's discussion of appropriate style.

Metre is the second subject in the section on style. Again Aristotle is exceedingly brief in the *Poetics*, and in the *Rhetoric* he has his ear cocked mainly for prose rhythm. So there is little to set over against the discussion in the *Ars*. However, we hear just enough from the master to be aware of the guidance which he gave to his disciples. Horace notes two points: the appropriateness of certain metres for certain matters and the identity of the 'inventors' who first used each

---

[1] Other schools than the Lyceum adopted and developed theories of πρέπον. The *Rhetoric* and the *Poetics* however show what the Aristotelian theory looked like. The resemblance between the *Ars* and the *Rhetoric* proves that here Horace is employing the Aristotelian, or at any rate Peripatetic, variety. The concurrence of Horace and Aristotle also adds a further item to the list of Neoptolemus' probable Aristotelianisms. W. Kroll, *Sokrates*, VI (1918), 93, and W. Steidle, *Studien zur Ars Poetica des Horaz* (1939), p. 47, have rightly stressed the Peripatetic context of the πρέπον in Horace's section on style; many others have not.

[2] Aristotle legislated that appropriateness should govern poetic deviations from common usage. By this he meant moderation: *Poet.* 22, 1458*b*11 τὸ μὲν οὖν φαίνεσθαί πως χρώμενον τούτῳ τῷ τρόπῳ γελοῖον· τὸ δὲ μέτρ⟨ι⟩ον κοινὸν ἁπάντων ἐστὶ τῶν μερῶν· καὶ γὰρ μεταφοραῖς καὶ γλώτταις καὶ τοῖς ἄλλοις εἴδεσι χρώμενος ἀπρεπῶς καὶ ἐπίτηδες ἐπὶ τὰ γελοῖα τὸ αὐτὸ ἂν ἀπεργάσαιτο. τὸ δὲ ἁρμοττόντως ὅσον διαφέρει κτλ. There is a similar implication in *Rhet.* III, 2–6. Horace likewise, *A.P.* 51, *dabiturque licentia sumpta pudenter*, and 53, *parce detorta*. But he further qualifies this moderation by defining the motive for new coinages as 'expressing recondite things'.

metre appropriately. Both are Aristotelian,[1] and in each case Aristotle left enough details undecided to stimulate research by Peripatetic and Alexandrian scholars. Such research, Peripatetic and Alexandrian, accounts for the scholarly material in Horace's section on metre. This is a post-Aristotelian feature which cannot well be doubted. But if there is this difference from Aristotle, there is also the close proximity to Aristotelian origins. And this again tallies with the revised Aristotelianism of Neoptolemus to which I have repeatedly drawn attention.

The third group of subjects establishes yet more conclusively the Aristotelian background of this section. 'Diction will be appropriate if it is expressive of emotion and character and is proportionate to the subject.' Thus Aristotle, introducing appropriate style in the *Rhetoric*.[2] But his examples give the impression that he is writing a (rhetorical) treatise on poetry, and not a manual for speakers in the law court or assembly. 'When I say proportionate I mean that great matters are not put in trivial language nor trivial matters in grand language,

---

[1] The 'natural aptitude' of certain metres for certain literary subjects is asserted at *Poet.* 4, 1449 a 22–8, in particular a 24, αὐτὴ ἡ φύσις τὸ οἰκεῖον μέτρον εὗρεν, and 24, 1459 b 31–1460 a 5, in particular 1460 a 3, ὥσπερ εἴπομεν αὐτὴ ἡ φύσις διδάσκει τὸ ἁρμόττον αὐτῇ αἱρεῖσθαι. Also the remarks on the ethos of metres, *Rhet.* III, 8, 1408 b 32–1409 a 1. For the motif of invention in this context see *Poet.* ch. 4; this need not be identified with the very general topic περὶ εὑρημάτων to which many Peripatetic scholars contributed. The Alexandrians inherited an interest in inventors of metres and literary genres from the Lyceum, and added much material to the Peripatetic stock. Didymus, ὁ χαλκέντερος, excelled also in this regard; Proclus' report, in Photius' *Bibliotheca*, p. 319, may be derived from him, cf. G. Kaibel, *AGG* (1898), p. 32. Research was controversial: different 'inventors' are named in the *Poetics*, the *Ars*, and later compilations. Horace's celebrated line, *grammatici certant et adhuc sub iudice lis est* (*A.P.* 78) may point to a contemporary source—perhaps Didymus himself, or perhaps Varro. This does not by any means exclude a chapter of this sort at this place in Neoptolemus' book. Rather we get glimpses of the learned tradition at three different stages—Aristotle, Neoptolemus, and a contemporary of Horace.

[2] *Rhet.* III, 7, 1408 a 10 τὸ δὲ πρέπον ἕξει ἡ λέξις ἐὰν ᾖ παθητική τε καὶ ἠθικὴ καὶ τοῖς ὑποκειμένοις πράγμασιν ἀνάλογον. This chapter is noted in the standard commentaries on the *Ars*; Vahlen noted the 'parallel' in *Ges. Phil. Schr.* I, 460; but its relevance was better understood four centuries ago. Thus for example Jason De Nores correctly explains this portion of the *Ars* by comparing the context of the Aristotelian chapter: *In Ep.... De Arte Poetica*, etc. (1553), fol. 43 v.

and that a trivial noun is not decked out with an ornamental epithet.[1] Otherwise it tends to sound as though it came in a comedy, as in the poetry of Cleophon'—εἰ δὲ μή, κωμῳδία φαίνεται, οἷον ποιεῖ Κλεοφῶν, and a citation follows. Considering that these words come from the *Rhetoric*, they are surprisingly close to the context of poetry,[2] and surprisingly close, too, to Horace's words:

> versibus exponi tragicis res comica non volt;
> indignatur item privatis ac prope socco
> dignis carminibus narrari cena Thyestae. (89–91)

The *Ars* merely proceeds further on the road indicated by Aristotle, specifying the two styles as tragic and comic (or, as a Greek critic, probably Theophrastus, said, concerned with 'private affairs'),[3] and allowing for mutual encroachment between the two. The tragic examples are taken from plays on Thyestes, Telephus, and Peleus.[4]

The second postulate demands language appropriate to the emotions portrayed. An emotional speaker, says Aristotle, has his audience always with him—συνομοιοπαθεῖ ὁ ἀκούων ἀεὶ τῷ παθητικῶς λέγοντι, κἂν μηθὲν λέγῃ. Horace enlarges on this topic, 99–107, and so presumably did Neoptolemus:

> si vis me flere, dolendumst
> primum ipsi tibi; tum tua me infortunia laedent,
> Telephe vel Peleu; male si mandata loqueris,
> aut dormitabo aut ridebo. (102–5)

Telephus and Peleus however take the place of the pleaders in a court of law. The description of the emotions again is

---

[1] *Loc. cit.* τὸ δὲ ἀνάλογόν ἐστιν ἐὰν μήτε περὶ εὐόγκων αὐτοκαβδάλως λέγηται μήτε περὶ εὐτελῶν σεμνῶς, μηδ' ἐπὶ τῷ εὐτελεῖ ὀνόματι ἐπῇ κόσμος.

[2] The tragic writer Cleophon is also mentioned in the parallel chapter of the *Poetics* (22, 1458*a*20), λέξεως δὲ ἀρετὴ σαφῆ καὶ μὴ ταπεινὴν εἶναι. σαφεστάτη μὲν οὖν ἐστὶν ἡ ἐκ τῶν κυρίων ὀνομάτων, ἀλλὰ ταπεινή. παράδειγμα δὲ ἡ Κλεοφῶντος ποίησις καὶ ἡ Σθενέλου. The tendency of another remark on Cleophon is similar, *Poet.* 2, 1448*a*12: Ὅμηρος μὲν βελτίους, Κλεοφῶν δὲ ὁμοίους (εἴκαζεν).

[3] As Kiessling noted, the word *privatis* is likely to allude to the celebrated definition of comedy as ἰδιωτικῶν (= *privatorum*) πραγμάτων ἀκίνδυνος περιοχή, Diomedes, *Ars Gram.* III, ed. Keil, *Gram. Lat.* I, p. 488, 4.

[4] It may be remembered, for what it is worth, that the first two are titles of tragedies ascribed to Cleophon: *Suda*, s.v.

similar in both cases; but the psychology of the *Ars*, 108–11, is more sophisticated than what the *Rhetoric* offers; but that does not necessarily make it Stoic.[1]

The third postulate resembles the *Rhetoric* most closely. Language is characteristic, ἠθική, when it echoes faithfully each class and type of person. In this way, says Aristotle, it is made to carry conviction. He then rehearses the classes and types that he has in mind: the different ages: boy, man, old man; the sexes; and provenance, Laconian or Thessalian. Or else, types according to social station: rustic or cultured. Horace, and apparently Neoptolemus, slightly extend the same division, which partly fits tragedy and partly comedy, 114–18: god or hero, old man or temperamental youth, lady or nurse, travelling merchant or farmer, barbarian from Colchis or from Assyria, Greek from Thebes or from Argos. Such distinctions as these tend to proliferate and further refinements may be seen in the compilations of late antiquity.

At *A.P.* 118 the context of diction comes to a close. Various pieces of evidence, severally neither conclusive nor even suggestive, are now seen to support each other. The fragments of Neoptolemus suggest that he made diction, λέξις, one of the mainstays of the technical portion of his book. They also suggest that style preceded subject-matter in his discussion. Secondly, the *Ars Poetica*, considered on its own, bears out both the twofold division and the precedence of the section on style, with its corollary on 'order'.[2] Thirdly, it is hard to avoid the suspicion, once Aristotle's *Rhetoric* and *Poetics* are brought into the picture, that Neoptolemus' large headings are the headings of the *Rhetoric* transferred to verse. The application was made possible by the rhetorical character of Aristotle's doctrine of poetic style.

[1] W. Steidle, *op. cit.* p. 65, n. 68, argues against Stoic provenance and reasonably points to the Peripatetic context. Also cf. M. Pohlenz, *NGG*, N.F. III. 6 (1939), p. 197, *Die Stoa*, I, p. 39, II, p. 21.

[2] Τάξις was altogether a rhetorical term. It is not found in the *Poetics* where the structure of the plot provides all that is required on that score. Cf. above, pp. 91–3, and p. 91, n. 3, on διάθεσις.

If that were accepted, it would follow that in his section on style Neoptolemus was (directly or indirectly) indebted to the *Rhetoric* both for the general arrangement and for most of the material; only a small amount of the content may be derived from the *Poetics*. In spite of his indebtedness to Aristotle, however, he approaches his subject rather as a man of letters than as a philosopher. Being a poet he takes a greater interest in the practical business of writing. Being the author of a textbook he is concerned with the systematic order of topics. One senses a desire to dot the *i*'s and cross the *t*'s in those passages of Aristotle, both critical and historical, which are amenable to that treatment.

So far as the substance of Horace's critical doctrine is concerned, I find very little in the section on style which does not seem to be derived from Neoptolemus. Neoptolemus' teaching on diction, the agreement of Horace and Aristotle, and the manner of their disagreement—all this suggests to me only *one* conclusion: Horace (exceptions apart) has drawn on Neoptolemus' critical doctrine and, in turn, Neoptolemus' treatise was based (directly or indirectly) on Aristotle's rhetorical doctrine, recast so as to apply to the style of poetry.[1]

After style, the other member of the rhetorical pair—content or subject-matter. Such careful observers as J. Vahlen and R. Heinze had long since identified the elusive object where Horace had placed it—at line 119 of the poem. But so long as scholars believed that it was rather the beginning of the *Ars* that dealt with this topic, little headway could be made. That is not so any longer and discussion need not be deflected from the proper starting-point in Horace. On the Aristotelian side however it must be remembered that the notion of poetic subject-matter although rhetorical in origin cannot well be based on a Greek forensic speech. There is

---

[1] I have not here even mentioned the contingency that Horace himself adapted the *Rhetoric* and the *Poetics*. The *Ars* is clearly twice removed from Aristotle, and cannot therefore be used to prove that the *Poetics* (or for that matter the *Rhetoric*) was known to Horace. Cf. below, pp. 140–1.

nothing poetic in the 'modes of persuasion', or πίστεις, that supply the content of rhetoric in Aristotle's work. And true enough, with one significant exception,[1] the *Poetics* but not the *Rhetoric* makes further comparison with the *Ars* possible. To the *Poetics* I therefore turn, as *ex hypothesi* Neoptolemus or his predecessors turned at this point. The introduction on *mimesis* is not here involved; nor is the stylistic section, which has been used already to supplement the material of the *Rhetoric*. These irrelevancies apart, the whole of the *Poetics* could provide Neoptolemus with Aristotelian doctrine—if it could be recast sufficiently to serve the purpose of his own literary criticism. For Aristotle one exemplary genre, tragedy, provided a desirable approach and consequently some of his general propositions appear in the discussion of a specific genre. This approach was no longer desirable for Hellenistic critics. Some of these propositions seem to have been transposed from the specific context of tragedy to the general context of poetic subject-matter, where a literary critic would expect to find them. Whether they were in fact completely generalized is a different question.

The evidence for these surmises is found in the papyrus of Philodemus. For the general subject-headings of style and content, which were prompted by the *Rhetoric*, imply a shift of emphasis: what was in the *Poetics* a specific feature of tragedy now becomes a general feature of poetry, ποίημα or ποίησις. And that is borne out by the *Ars*. For although Horace occasionally glances at drama when he discusses diction, it is agreed that the whole section of the *Ars* deals rather with poetic diction than with the diction of *one* literary genre.

The metamorphosis of the pair, tragic content and style, into the pair, poetic style and content, is not the only shift of emphasis that is to be noted. Again the papyrus may lead the way. Aristotle, at ch. 6, begins the main section of the *Poetics* by enunciating a definition of tragedy, deducing six elements, or εἴδη, which are asserted to be essential to tragedy. They are

---

[1] I mean the four ages of man, at *A.P.* 156.

arranged in this order of importance: Plot, Character, Thought, Diction, Music, Staging. Now it should be noted that, in delimiting the field of poetic diction, Neoptolemus not only cut it off from subject-matter[1] but explicitly cut it off from thought, action, character—and one other item.[2] What that other item is, the papyrus does not, unfortunately, reveal; but seeing that the rest add up to four of the six elements constituting tragedy in the *Poetics*, and 'spectacle', ὄψις, is but a stranger in this company, music could be a possible claimant. But whatever the identity of the claimant was, here is surely another transference from the tragic to the general field of poetry. At the same time it is seen that whereas a definition of tragedy is not now extant either in Neoptolemus or in Horace, Neoptolemus allowed most of the tragic elements of chapter 6 to survive in a more general form.

It is the concern of chapters 7 and 8 of the *Poetics* to establish the concepts of unity and wholeness as fundamental for a plot which is well-shaped, which has the aesthetic quality of beauty. The parts of a unified whole should be so closely related to one another that none can be displaced or removed without affecting the others and thereby destroying the whole.[3] Aristotle reverts to this essential condition at various places of the *Poetics*. The papyrus of Philodemus suggests that harmony and continuity, or completeness, were postulated by Neoptolemus also for long poems. This may relate to the unity of the parts of such poems.[4] A study of the arrangement of the *Ars* earlier in this book has led to the conclusion that Horace placed this postulate in the introductory section of the poem.[5] Two arguments lend some probability to the assumption that

[1] Neoptol., no. 5 (col. xii) ποιήματος μόνον τὴν σύνθεσιν τῆς λέξεως μετέχειν as opposed to no. 4 (col. xi) τῆς ποιήσεως εἶναι τὴν ὑπόθεσιν μόνον.

[2] Neoptol., no. 5 (col. xii) continues after the words cited in n. 1, ἀλλὰ μὴ] τὰς διανο[ίας καὶ........] καὶ πράξεις καὶ προσωποποιίας. Jensen suggested τάξεις for the lacuna. For τάξις see above, p. 99, n. 2.

[3] Ar. *Poet.* 8, 1451a31, οὕτω καὶ τὸν μῦθον, ἐπεὶ πράξεως μίμησίς ἐστι, μιᾶς τε εἶναι ταύτης καὶ ὅλης, καὶ τὰ μέρη συνιστάναι τῶν πραγμάτων οὕτως ὥστε μετατιθεμένου τινὸς μέρους ἢ ἀφαιρουμένου διαφέρεσθαι καὶ κινεῖσθαι τὸ ὅλον κτλ.

[4] Above, p. 57, on Neoptol., no. 9.   [5] Above, p. 12.

Neoptolemus preceded Horace in assigning this prominent position to the Aristotelian principle. 'In sum [says Horace], no matter what the work may be, let it be of a piece and one' (*denique sit quidvis, simplex dumtaxat et unum*).[1] This sounds like the grand law of all poetry. Horace's words generalize Aristotle's argument. Unity in the *Poetics* is fundamental to the construction of a tragic plot, although Aristotle's intention is clearly to emphasize its general application. Unity in the *Ars* has been assigned the axiomatic role for poetry which Aristotle probably intended it to have, and it has been shifted to the most prominent position of the poem. This recalls the generalizing procedure which Neoptolemus applied to other Aristotelian principles. Moreover, although Neoptolemus tended to employ large concepts like style and subject-matter as his main headings, none of the main sections of his treatise has 'unity' as its main burden—and yet the principle is appealed to throughout. These two considerations make it probable that Horace followed Neoptolemus also in this regard, but there is no external evidence proving it.

Whether or no this placing may be ascribed to Neoptolemus, there can scarcely be a doubt that he believed in the wide application of Aristotle's principle of unity. The central section of the *Ars* suggests that he may also have retained certain features of the ninth chapter of the *Poetics*, Aristotle's assertion of poetic universality. *Difficile est proprie communia dicere*; so Horace at line 128. The translation of this puzzling sentence is still doubtful, but its true *context* cannot be considered puzzling any more, since Rostagni has linked it firmly with the poetic universal, καθόλου, of the ninth chapter of Aristotle's *Poetics*. A commentary will have to go into the details. Here it must be sufficient to say that Horace's concern is simply to warn the novice against inventing his own fiction because 'it is hard to lend individual features (*proprie dicere*) to what is common to many individual cases (*communia*)'. *Communia* and *proprie* presumably render the Greek words

[1] *A.P.* 23, with Bentley's *quidvis* in lieu of the vulgate *quodvis* or *quod vis*.

κοινά and ἰδίως. But the sense of Horace's words is close to Aristotle's argument. *Communia* are the features that possess generality, that are typical or universal, καθόλου; they are not individualized, καθ' ἕκαστον, like the happenings and personages of legend or history. *Communia* and *proprie* reflect the sense but not the wording of Aristotle's τὰ καθόλου and καθ' ἕκαστον.

The advice of Horace, and presumably of Neoptolemus, is to stick to what is already individualized, to avoid new stories. The skill of the poet must then prove itself in the treatment of prefabricated material. In the section 119–52, his advice is addressed to all poets who are tellers of long stories; at times dramatic composition is to the fore, at times epic.[1] Aristotle's advice, *à propos* of tragic plots, is different and more adventurous. 'In Agathon's *Antheus* both the names and the events are made up and the play pleases nevertheless. One must not therefore try to cling to the traditional stories which are the stuff of which the tragedies are commonly made. Indeed it would be laughable so to try, for even the familiar stories are familiar only to a few and yet please all.' Thus chapter 9 of the *Poetics*.[2] The topic recurs at chapter 14. Here Aristotle is determining the right manner of tragic incident. He desires to stress the tragic quality of acts of violence in a few, mythical, families; hence his peremptory advice against any change in the traditional plots that concern those families. This seems to be an emphasis on traditional plots, and it has put commentators in a quandary; for now Aristotle seems to reverse his earlier emphasis on fictitious plots. But better counsel has prevailed and it has been recognized recently that in this chapter, too, poetic imagination is not discouraged, although in accordance with the context it is not encouraged in the strong terms of the earlier chapter.[3]

---

[1] Dramatic, 125 *scaenae committis*, 129 *deducis in actus*; epic, 136 *scriptor cyclicus*, 140–52 Homer; neutral, 120 *scriptor*, and the general axioms, 119 and 128.

[2] Ar. *Poet.* 9, 1451 *b* 21–6.

[3] I am referring to *Poet.* 14, 1453 *b* 25, αὐτὸν δὲ εὑρίσκειν δεῖ καὶ τοῖς παραδεδομένοις χρῆσθαι καλῶς, and G. F. Else's discussion of the passage (*op. cit.* p. 416).

Unlike the *Poetics* then the *Ars* gives preference to familiar subjects. But the manner and setting in which the preference is expressed is thoroughly Aristotelian. It recalls the context of the *Poetics*. Once again this is Aristotelianism with a difference—in line with Neoptolemus' revisions of Aristotle's doctrine.

It may now be asked precisely how much of the doctrine of poetic universality is preserved in this section of the *Ars* (and *ex hypothesi* in Neoptolemus), and how much of Aristotle's doctrine underwent a revision. A glance at the section beginning at *Ars* 119 shows that the Aristotelian theory did not prove viable without a severe reduction. What savoured unduly of speculation and theorizing has been discarded. So it appears. But it is not for us to lay down *a priori* what ideas in the writings of the master may have seemed obnoxious to Alexandrian adherents of his. We can only turn to the *Ars* (which, I have been arguing, contains both Alexandrian and Aristotelian features), and verify the colouring of its Aristotelianism. There is no evidence that in this, technical, portion of the poem the more *recherché* features of Aristotle's thought are preserved. The content of poetry as a whole is no longer identified with universals, καθόλου, and poetic universality is not set over against non-poetic particularity, καθ' ἕκαστον. There is here no counterpart to the first sentence of Aristotle's chapter which lays down that it is the poet's job to say what might happen, and what is possible according to

Else proposes to co-ordinate the two phrases and to refer καλῶς equally to each of the two infinitives: εὑρίσκειν (καλῶς) and χρῆσθαι καλῶς. This seems to me worth considering, but it is perhaps unnecessary since Aristotle, who is here concerned primarily with certain features of the traditional stories, may surely stress the correct use of myths without wishing to discourage poetic imagination. Hence he could equally well say: 'but the poet should (either) invent or if he uses the traditional stories should use them in the correct way'. In either case Else's contention is valid—εὑρίσκειν must here be accorded its full meaning, 'to invent'. The opposite case is found at *A.P.* 119, 'aut famam sequere aut sibi convenientia finge'. The poet is told to use traditional stories or *if* he invents to invent in the correct manner, that is, with consistency. At *Poet.* 17, 1455*a*34, imaginary and traditional stories are juxtaposed: τούς τε λόγους καὶ τοὺς πεποιημένους δεῖ καὶ αὐτὸν (i.e. τὸν ποιητὴν) ποιοῦντα ἐκτίθεσθαι καθόλου.

probability or necessity, not what did happen.[1] Nor are the logical categories of probability or necessity attached to the concept of the universal.

Nevertheless the Aristotelian concepts are not jettisoned. They are adapted to the purposes of a writer and literary critic. This is the tendency which has been observed throughout this analysis and which lends probability to the assumption that we are in fact here dealing with Neoptolemus. Earlier on I suggested that the sense of the terms καθόλου and καθ' ἕκαστον is expressed by *communia* and *proprie* (*dicere*) at line 128, *difficile est proprie communia dicere*, 'it is hard to lend individual features to general concepts'. Though discarded as a definition of poetry, the notion of the universal can still do duty to describe a new concept in a poet's mind—'the *kind* of thing which (Aristotle said) a certain *kind* of person may say or do in accordance with probability or necessity'.[2] That is (Aristotle continued) what poetry aims at and then attaches individual names to the (abstract) concepts.[3] This individualizing process, for which the philosophers had no other terminology than 'the giving of names', has now been identified with Aristotle's 'particulars', τὰ καθ' ἕκαστον. So that the poet who invents a new plot goes through two stages as it were: he starts off with the abstract concept, καθόλου, and ends up with individual persons and actions, καθ' ἕκαστον. Horace (and perhaps Neoptolemus) may be thinking of the process of drafting a play which Aristotle (in a later passage)[4] suggested should be in three stages: (1) the sketching of the plot *in abstracto*, καθόλου, even when the story is traditional and therefore contains named characters; (2) the giving of names, ὑποθέντα ὀνόματα, whether or not previously known; and (3) the adding of episodes.

---

[1] Ar. *Poet.* 9, 1451*a*36, φανερὸν δὲ ἐκ τῶν εἰρημένων καὶ ὅτι οὐ τὰ γενόμενα λέγειν, τοῦτο ποιητοῦ ἔργον ἐστίν, ἀλλ' οἷα ἂν γένοιτο καὶ τὰ δυνατὰ κατὰ τὸ εἰκὸς ἢ τὸ ἀναγκαῖον.

[2] 1451*b*8, ἔστι δὲ καθόλου μέν, τῷ ποίῳ τὰ ποῖα ἄττα συμβαίνει λέγειν ἢ πράττειν κατὰ τὸ εἰκὸς ἢ ἀναγκαῖον.

[3] 1451*b*9, οὗ στοχάζεται ἡ ποίησις, ὀνόματα ἐπιτιθεμένη.

[4] 17, 1455*a*34.

Once this is agreed the context of the section helps to make a further identification. *Ars* 119 offers two possibilities to the novice: 'aut famam sequere aut sibi convenientia finge', 'either follow tradition or, if you invent, do so with consistency'. In the light of the later passage (128) which we have just discussed, *communia* (128) expresses the content of *finge* (119); fictional or new subjects are conceived by the poet as *communia*. But *proprie dicere* (128) was not expressed in the first passage (119). The philosopher made light of the process of individualizing; for him it consisted merely in the attaching of names, ὀνόματα ἐπιτιθεμένη. The literary critic is concerned with workmanship and finds much difficulty in Aristotle's way of describing the process of poetic creation. The difficulty he finds is so great that it moves him to warn against subjects which make it necessary to instil individual life into new general concepts. He therefore looks at new poetic subjects twice over. First, at 119, he only contrasts legendary and personal subjects as regards the consistency of the finished article. The legends have their own consistency. All the user of legendary subjects needs to do is to use them as they are: Medea *ferox invictaque*, and so forth. But if he invents his stories, he needs to create the consistency which in the case of myths tradition had created for him: *sibi convenientia finge* (119) and *sibi constet* (127). Secondly, at 128, he returns to the invention of new subjects. He points to the difficulty of inventing new subjects in a consistent manner. The difficulty lies in the process of individualizing an abstract conception: 'difficile est *proprie communia* dicere' (128). His vocabulary does not contain words for abstract, concrete, and individual. He deals with the matter by employing Aristotelian ideas, although not apparently a literal rendering of καθόλου and καθ' ἕκαστον.

These considerations give us an easy, uninterrupted run from *Ars* 119 to 152. The passage now makes sense—which it has not always made. The sense is not Aristotelian. On the other hand it is not far removed from Aristotle either. The doctrine is Aristotelianism adapted to the purposes of a

literary critic; this is what we have now learnt to expect from
Neoptolemus. The train of thought may be summed up as
follows. At 119 Horace offers a choice between traditional
and imaginative subjects, *aut famam sequere aut sibi convenientia
finge*. Only for the latter is consistency required; for the
former it must be thought to be immanent in the myth. For
120–4 exemplify traditional subjects by putting forward
instances of (consistent) character drawing in the received
poetic myths (Achilles, Medea, Ino, etc.; individuals that fit
certain myths), whereas 125–7 simply expand the peremptory
command of line 119, *sibi convenientia finge*. Up to this point
the choice was open and undecided. At 128 the novice's (and
the reader's) mind is made up for him. Since it is hard to
create new plots, the poet is told to stick to old ones (128–30).
And yet imitative verse is not commended. There are a creative and an imitative manner of accepting tradition. The
writer of the common, 'cyclic', epic follows tradition in an
imitative way, 131–9. Homer reshaped the *fama* of the Trojan
War and followed it creatively; he added imaginative episodes; he achieved unity as well as variety, 140–52.[1]

The passage on subject-matter began with a demand for
unity—explicitly as a condition for invented plots and by
implication as a thing realized in traditional plots. Unity and
consistency were remembered throughout this passage. And
again at the end, the exemplary poet, Homer, is praised for
achieving unity and consistency in spite of the rich variety of
his episodes, *primo ne medium, medio ne discrepet imum* (152).
Although nothing could be more Aristotelian than to describe
the appropriate way of shaping poetic subject-matter as
unified or consistent, it is rather the Aristotle of chapters 7
and 8 of the *Poetics* who comes to mind than the Aristotle of
chapter 9. Now it has been seen that the ideas of universality,
καθόλου, and of possibility, οἷα ἂν γένοιτο, were no longer
felt to be descriptive of poetry as such but only of the

[1] Cf. *Poet.* 23, 1459a35. The Aristotelian sequence, *Poet.* 17, 1455a34, allows for
the main plot (and its unity) as well as for the episodes (and their variety).

initial stage in the conception of a plot. Consequently the demands for unity and consistency acquire a more literary ring; they are no longer closely connected with the generality of poetic thought and no longer contrasted with the particulars of history or chronicle, which are said to lack such a unity. This may go some way towards explaining why the ἓν καὶ ὅλον of *Poetics*, chapters 7–8, are present throughout the Horatian section on subject-matter, which otherwise is based chiefly on the general ideas of chapter 9.

The basis of criticism has been broadened by bringing into the section on subject-matter certain observations on the narrative art of Homer, derived mainly from the final chapters of the *Poetics*. With their stress on variety and unity, on the faults of the cyclic poets and the virtues of Homer, Aristotelian observations required little or no adaptation to fit the new context.[1] Two points however deserve notice. Whilst the content of this part of the section is largely Aristotelian, its placing is not. As before, it needs to be noted that the large heading of 'subject-matter' involves a rearrangement of Aristotle's *Poetics*. The two literary genres, tragic and epic, which appeared in two diverse sections of the *Poetics* are here employed in the same part of the discussion to exemplify the teachings on poetic subject-matter. And there is another nuance which does not strike one as Aristotelian. I mean the interest in refinement for its own sake, a patent delight in slanging the vulgar and their well-trodden high road—which, very properly, has put readers in mind of Callimachus rather than of Aristotle.[2]

---

[1] *Scriptor cyclicus*, *A.P.* 136, cf. Ar. *Poet.* chs. 8 and 23; Homer, *A.P.* 140, cf. Ar. chs. 8, 23, 24; *speciosa miracula* in Homer, *A.P.* 144 does not however recall τὸ θαυμαστόν, discussed at Ar. *Poet.* ch. 24.

[2] Hor. *A.P.* 131–5, 'publica materies privati iuris erit, si | non circa *vilem patulumque* moraberis *orbem*', etc. The standard commentaries rightly refer to Callimachus, *Epigram* 28, ἐχθαίρω τὸ ποίημα τὸ κυκλικὸν οὐδὲ κελεύθῳ | χαίρω τίς πολλοὺς ὧδε καὶ ὧδε φέρει | ... σικχαίνω πάντα τὰ δημόσια. Also, Apollo's command, *Aetia*, I, fr. I, 25, τὰ μὴ πατέουσιν ἅμαξαι | τὰ στείβειν, ἑτέρων ἴχνια μὴ καθ' ὁμά | δίφρον ἐλᾶν μηδ' οἷμον ἀνὰ πλατύν, ἀλλὰ κελεύθους | ἀτρίπτους εἰ καὶ στεινοτέρην ἐλάσεις. For the metaphors, see W. Wimmel, *H*, Einzelschr. xvi

The remaining Aristotelian chapters on the tragic plot can be dealt with briefly. The detailed discussion of simple and complex plots in the next two chapters (10–11) has been discarded. So has the brief catalogue of the quantitative parts of tragedy (chapter 12). It is more remarkable that chapters 13, on the outcome of tragic plots, and 14, on tragic emotions, have also left virtually[1] no trace in the *Ars*. This may be explained by saying that the present section, *A.P.* 119–52, discourses on subject-matter in general; tragic drama and epic are brought in only by way of examples. The explanation is correct as far as it goes. But there was another opportunity to discuss the details of plot-construction when rules for the making of tragedies are rehearsed from line 179 onward—and again the opportunity was not taken. Here our evidence is insufficient. Neoptolemus may or may not have jettisoned this part of the *Poetics*. He may well have jettisoned it because he was more interested in subject-matter and the consistency of its poetic treatment than in the Aristotelian profundities of plot-construction.

The *Poetics* next deals with character, ἦθος, the second of Aristotle's elements of tragic drama. Horace, too, continues with *mores* (*A.P.* 153–78). The bulk—twenty-six lines—may cause some surprise if the thirty-four lines of a larger subject, the plot, are recalled (119–52). It is not unreasonable to assume that Horace elaborated this piece because he liked *ethologia*. Yet for this there may be good Aristotelian precedent. Character comes second in importance in the hierarchy of the *Poetics*, preceded only by the 'soul of tragedy', the plot.[2]

(1960), 103–11, and below, p. 182. Alexandrian scholars inherited Aristotle's and Callimachus' views on the cyclic epic, and may have expressed them according to preference either in the Aristotelian or the Callimachean fashion. The Alexandrian colouring of *A.P.* 131–2 may well have been the colouring also of Neoptolemus' treatise. This does not however exclude a further, Horatian, criticism of the Latin versions of the *fidus interpres*. But there are Alexandrian touches again in *speciosa miracula, A.P.* 144, and *nitescere*, 150.

[1] I say 'virtually' because there may be one trace of the theory of tragic emotions at *A.P.* 185, cf. *Poet.* 14, 1453*b*8. For emotional speech see *A.P.* 101.

[2] Ar. *Poet.* 6, 1450*a*38, cf. *a*20, οὔκουν ὅπως τὰ ἤθη μιμήσωνται πράττουσιν, ἀλλὰ τὰ ἤθη συμπεριλαμβάνουσι διὰ τὰς πράξεις· ὥστε τὰ πράγματα καὶ ὁ μῦθος τέλος τῆς τραγῳδίας, τὸ δὲ τέλος μέγιστον ἁπάντων.

Judging from what we hear about *mores* in the *Ars*, we may conclude that Neoptolemus felt them to be even more important.[1] Now Aristotle reminded his readers that tragedies in his own time could do without character, were ἀήθεις.[2] And since he reports the procedure of 'most of the recent tragic poets',[3] perhaps it is true that a majority of them were more interested in plot than in character, and ethos was not a *forte* of contemporary drama. How little that is likely to have remained true also for the time of Neoptolemus, perhaps two or three generations later, during the ascendancy of the New Comedy—that is an open question. To the question we have no answer so far as tragedy is concerned. But the point has been rightly made that in this portion of the *Ars* discussion has not yet been narrowed down to tragedy only[4]—and the same may apply to Neoptolemus' work.

Aristotle offers his treatment of character at *Poetics*, chapter 15. The criterion is the same as in the elaboration of the plot—one must aim at what is probable or necessary. The words or actions of a person—so Aristotle says, led by his axiom rather than by the practice of Greek tragedy—should be the outcome of what he is. He lays down four rules to which character-drawing should conform. He is here brief to a fault, and commentators are hard put to it to make sense.[5] One of the postulates is however clear enough—I mean the second, τὰ ἁρμόττοντα, appropriateness. This in particular attracted Horace, and, to judge from his leanings so far observed, Neoptolemus also. But it is well-known that what

---

[1] In the technical section of the *Ars* alone there are three passages on character: 114–18, 120–7, and 153–78 (discussed in the text above); there is a fourth in the final section, 312–18. Their placing in different contexts of Horace's (and perhaps Neoptolemus') work and their relation to Aristotle's teaching are discussed below, pp. 139–40, 251–2.

[2] *Poet.* 6, 1450a23, ἔτι ἄνευ μὲν πράξεως οὐκ ἂν γένοιτο τραγῳδία, ἄνευ δὲ ἠθῶν γένοιτ' ἄν.

[3] *Poet.* 6, 1450a25, αἱ γὰρ τῶν νέων τῶν πλείστων ἀήθεις τραγῳδίαι εἰσίν, καὶ ὅλως ποιηταὶ πολλοὶ τοιοῦτοι, οἷον καὶ τῶν γραφέων Ζεῦξις πρὸς Πολύγνωτον πέπονθεν κτλ.

[4] Rostagni's note on *A.P.* 153–219; O. Immisch, *op. cit.* p. 121.

[5] Cf. below, pp. 139–40.

Horace here gives us is not a logical analysis, like *Poetics*, chapter 15, but a descriptive sketch of the four ages of man. The demand is that the *mores* of every age should be marked;[1] changing characters and years should be depicted appropriately, 'mobilibusque *decor* naturis *dandus* et annis'.[2] What follows is the only borrowing from the *Rhetoric*, in this section of the poem, which is not concerned with style. The passage is ultimately derived from *Rhet.* II, 12–14, where in the treatment of *inventio* a rich store of moral qualities is provided for the orator who is proposing to make his speeches 'characteristic', ἠθικούς. The different ages stand out as a feat of descriptive virtuosity.[3] The parallel has often been noted although the borrowing has been doubted. Bentley knew better: 'principio illud pro comperto habendum est, in his aetatum characteribus ut Aristotelem Naturae, ita Nostrum Aristotelis vestigiis institisse'. Nature apart, this seems to me not less true because Horace was so good at these pen-portraits that he is thought not to require a source, or because he describes four ages whereas Aristotle was content with three, or finally because this kind of *ethologia* may be a common Hellenistic heritage. Other considerations are more relevant. One

---

[1] Hor. *A.P.* 156, *aetatis cuiusque notandi sunt tibi mores*. *Notare*, as Immisch, *op. cit.* p. 123, says, denotes a rhetorical character-sketch, χαρακτηρισμός. He cites *Ad Her.* IV, 63, 'notatio est cum alicuius natura certis describitur signis quae ⟨sunt⟩ sicuti notae quae naturae sunt attributa'. The censorious *notare* of *Sat.* I, 4 differs however, cf. below, p. 157. The poet sets down traits of character, the satirist foibles or obnoxious traits.

[2] *Decor* refers to the appropriateness of a given character—τὰ ἁρμόττοντα in the passage of the *Poetics* cited above in the text.

[3] The passage closely resembles the description of moral qualities in the *Nicomachean Ethics*. It may be noted that in the *Ethics* as well as in the *Rhetoric* the underlying logical scheme of a mean between two extremes provides a framework for the wealth of descriptive detail. Horace's pen-portraits resemble Aristotle's in that they are built up from single qualities juxtaposed (like the case-histories of the Hippocratic doctors), the Roman poet being even briefer and more impressionistic than the Greek philosopher: *difficilis, querulus, laudator temporis acti*: καὶ δυσέλπιδες διὰ τὴν ἐμπειρίαν· τὰ γὰρ πλείω τῶν γιγνομένων φαῦλά ἐστιν· ἀποβαίνει γὰρ τὰ πολλὰ ἐπὶ τὸ χεῖρον· καὶ ἔτι διὰ τὴν δειλίαν. But there is no logical scheme to temper descriptive detail in Horace. That already is the way of Theophrastus' characters. And if Neoptolemus was the intermediary between Aristotle and Horace, as I think he was, he resembled in this regard Theophrastus rather than Aristotle.

is, that the section on character comes at the very *place* where the *Poetics* leads the reader to expect it, but that, nevertheless, the abstract *argument* of the *Poetics* is not employed. Another is, that Horace differs from the argument of the *Poetics* precisely in the point in which the *Rhetoric* passage differs from the *Poetics*—in its descriptive detail. A third is, that this borrowing from the *Rhetoric*, if Neoptolemus was the borrower, would correspond to others noted earlier on: the *Rhetoric* proved in many ways a useful book to Neoptolemus. A final point is the tendency of the borrowing. It bespeaks the writer. It recalls the occasions where a practical interest in his literary craft seems to have prompted Neoptolemus to choose and arrange his materials. The Hellenistic propensity to *ethologia*, so far from being an instance to the contrary, surely fits this case well enough. Why indeed should not an Alexandrian writer have preferred Aristotle's character-sketches to the same authority's abstract arguments?

After dealing with the plot of tragedy and with its characters,[1] Aristotle puts together some miscellaneous matters in chapters 17–18 before going on to 'thought' and diction. These matters largely deal with the practical business of laying out a tragedy. Editors still differ as to the sequence of thought in these chapters, or indeed as to whether there is such a sequence. Practical and miscellaneous rules also follow at *Ars* 179. The vista is that of drama—*in scaenis*, 179. This recalls the general reference to the theatre, at 153. But in fact the examples for some time to come concern tragic drama. It will be seen later at what point Horace finds his way to other literary genres.

These miscellaneous rules then recall the *Poetics* both by their general purport and by their placing. Aristotelian placing has so far been used as a tentative criterion for Horace's borrowings from Neoptolemus, and should be so

---

[1] Ar. *Poet.* chs. 6–14 on the plot of tragedy, ch. 15 on its characters. I have not commented on ch. 16, which is generally agreed to disturb the context in its present place; its true context is that of ch. 11.

used here. The unconnected sequence of these rules recalls similar sections of ζητήματα or προβλήματα καὶ λύσεις, in Aristotle and other Peripatetic writers. But the rules themselves have few parallels in Aristotle. There are five of them. The first (179–88) forbids horrors enacted, not reported, on the stage. *Incredulus odi* (178) hints at two reasons: suspension of belief and revulsion. Aristotle certainly talked of physical representations of horrors, but he contrasted their external and realistic aspect with the logic of tragic events that is inherent in the plot.[1] This indicates a different scope for his remarks; *incredulus odi* is not Aristotle's reaction in the *Poetics*, whether or no he shared Horace's (and probably Neoptolemus') sentiment. The second rule (189–90) propounds the five-act scheme. The topic of act-division recalls the remarks on the quantitative parts of tragedy, set loosely and unconvincingly in the context of the *Poetics* at chapter 12. But it is known that the five acts are not an Aristotelian postulate; they are however likely to be Hellenistic. The third rule (191–2) restricts the *deus ex machina* to cases where the *dénouement* requires divine intervention. This has been called a distorted reminiscence of Aristotle's demand that the μηχανή should not be employed except for matters outside the play.[2] I should be inclined to call it a different demand altogether, although it certainly agrees with Aristotle in restricting the device. The fourth rule (192) restricts the number of actors to three. A fourth should not trouble to speak, that is, he should remain a *muta persona*. Aristotle does not mention a fourth actor; three is the largest number implied in the historical context of *Poetics*, chapter 4.[3] The fifth rule (193–201) assigns to the chorus an actor's part. It opposes musical interludes between the acts of a play—a

[1] Ar. *Poet.* 14, 1453*b* 1–11. The words, οἵ τε ἐν τῷ φανερῷ θάνατοι καὶ αἱ περιωδυνίαι καὶ τρώσεις καὶ ὅσα τοιαῦτα, at *Poet.* 11, 1452*b* 12 (which I should find hard to translate 'deaths in the visible realm', etc., G. F. Else), do not object to the dramatic use of such happenings.

[2] Bywater on Ar. *Poet.* 15, 1454*b* 2, ἀλλὰ μηχανῇ χρηστέον ἐπὶ τὰ ἔξω τοῦ δράματος. The functions of the device allowed by Aristotle are those of certain Euripidean prologues and epilogues.

[3] *Ibid.* 4, 1449*a* 18, τρεῖς δὲ (ὑποκριτὰς) καὶ σκηνογραφίαν Σοφοκλῆς.

Hellenistic and Roman practice. This is the only precept which appears to rely on one of the miscellaneous chapters of the *Poetics*.[1] As in Aristotle the demand is that the chorus should be treated as an actor; it should be an integral part of the whole; so Aristotle, μόριον εἶναι τοῦ ὅλου, and so Horace, 'neu quid medios intercinat actus|quod non proposito conducat et haereat apte'. Theatrical convention in the Hellenistic age would lend actuality to Aristotle's implied criticism in the *Poetics*, and to his explicit condemnation of Agathon's *entr'actes*, ἐμβόλιμα. But the *Ars* goes beyond the *Poetics* in specifying the part the chorus should play. Its function is to act as a champion of sound morality—'ille bonis faveatque et consilietur amice'.

Music in the drama (202–19) is treated in a spirit different from these laconic and imperious precepts. Though connected with the foregoing passage through the contention that archaic music 'sufficed as an accompaniment of the chorus' (204), the new section is longer and more elaborate; and whereas the writer's preference for rural simplicity is unmistakeable, no 'rule' enjoining it is put forward. The *Poetics* offers nothing comparable upon μελοποιία—a subject treated with scant attention in that work. And yet there is in fact an Aristotelian basis to all this, in the eighth book of the *Politics*; but that, surprisingly, was not brought into the discussion until 1932.[2] The sequence that is said to lead from political aggrandisement to wealth and leisure, and ultimately to the development of the fine arts, is Aristotelian.[3] So is the descrip-

---

[1] *Ibid.* 18, 1456a25–32.

[2] O. Immisch, *Horazens Epistel über die Dichtkunst*, p. 134. Earlier A. Kiessling had referred to the Aristotelian passage in his note on Hor. *Ep.* ii, 1, 93, likewise R. Heinze in his editions of Kiessling's commentary. But the *Ars* is at least as relevant as the Epistle to Augustus.

[3] Ar. *Pol.* viii, 6, 1341a28, σχολαστικώτεροι γὰρ γενόμενοι διὰ τὰς εὐπορίας καὶ μεγαλοψυχότεροι πρὸς τὴν ἀρετήν, ἔτι τε πρότερον καὶ μετὰ τὰ Μηδικὰ φρονηματισθέντες ἐκ τῶν ἔργων, πάσης ἥπτοντο μαθήσεως, οὐδὲν διακρίνοντες ἀλλ᾿ ἐπιζητοῦντες. διὸ καὶ τὴν αὐλητικὴν ἤγαγον πρὸς τὰς μαθήσεις. Hor. *A.P.* 208, 'postquam coepit agros extendere victor et urbis | latior amplecti murus vinoque diurno | placari genius festis impune diebus, | accessit numerisque

tion in social terms of a degenerate type of music, specially associated with the flute,[1] and such concomitants as the unseemly swaying of the body.[2] Yet once more the revision of Aristotelian doctrines must not escape notice. The concentration on the practical, literary, side of the subject has been noted often in the course of this study; here it is noted again, for no echo of the educational and polemic context of *Politics*, Book VIII, can be heard. Nor is there a reminiscence of the crisp and sure conclusions of Aristotle. Instead there is resignation and nostalgia. The passing of the old type of music (and with it its simple instruments and the right kind of listener, *frugi castusque verecundusque*) is a fact that must be regretted but cannot be helped. From these simplifications it is a far cry to the expertise of the great *musicus* of the Aristotelian school, Aristoxenus. But it is not unlikely that he would have agreed with the sentiment.[3] That kind of sentiment in turn may account for the fact that the practical

---

modisque licentia maior'. Leisure after a victorious war is noted also at *Ep.* II, 1, 93, 'ut primum positis nugari Graecia bellis | coepit et in vitium fortuna labier aequa'; 162, 'et post Punica bella quietus quaerere coepit | quid Sophocles et Thespis et Aeschylus utile ferrent'.

[1] Ar. *Pol.* VIII, 7, 1341 b 15, ὁ γὰρ θεατὴς φορτικὸς ὢν μεταβάλλειν εἴωθε τὴν μουσικήν. 1342 a 18, ἐπεὶ δὲ ὁ θεατὴς διττός, ὁ μὲν ἐλεύθερος καὶ πεπαιδευμένος, ὁ δὲ φορτικὸς ἐκ βαναύσων καὶ θητῶν καὶ ἄλλων τοιούτων συγκείμενος, ἀποδοτέον ἀγῶνας καὶ θεωρίας καὶ τοῖς τοιούτοις πρὸς ἀνάπαυσιν κτλ. Hor. *A.P.* 212, 'indoctus quid enim saperet liberque laborum | rusticus urbano confusus, turpis honesto?'

[2] Ar. 1341 b 16, ὥστε (ὁ θεατὴς φορτικὸς ὢν) καὶ τοὺς τεχνίτας τοὺς πρὸς αὐτὸν μελετῶντας αὐτούς τε ποιούς τινας ποιεῖ καὶ τὰ σώματα διὰ τὰς κινήσεις. Cf. *Poet.* 26, 1461 b 29, ὡς γὰρ οὐκ αἰσθανομένων (τῶν θεατῶν) ἂν μὴ αὐτὸς προσθῇ, πολλὴν κίνησιν κινοῦνται, οἷον οἱ φαῦλοι αὐληταὶ κυλιόμενοι ἂν δίσκον δέῃ μιμεῖσθαι, καὶ ἕλκοντες τὸν κορυφαῖον ἂν Σκύλλαν αὐλῶσιν. Hor. *A.P.* 215, *traxitque vagus per pulpita vestem* (*tibicen*). Theophrastus reported that a Sicilian flute-player first combined music and pantomime—whence the word σικελίζειν for dancing (fr. 92, Wimmer, *ap.* Athen. I, 22 c, Bywater on *Poet.* 26, 1461 b 30).

[3] In his Σύμμικτα Συμποτικά Aristoxenus (*ap.* Athen. XIV, 632 a) told the story of the inhabitants of Paestum in the Tyrrhenian Gulf, now barbarian Etruscans, but formerly civilized Greeks. Once a year however they assemble for one of the old Greek festivals, and, remembering their Greek language and customs, they bewail their fate—and then depart. οὕτω δὴ οὖν, φ⟨η⟩σί, καὶ ἡμεῖς, ἐπειδὴ καὶ τὰ θέατρα ἐκβεβαρβάρωται καὶ εἰς μεγάλην διαφ⟨θ⟩ορὰν προελήλυθεν ἡ πάνδημος αὕτη μουσική, καθ᾽ αὑτοὺς γενόμενοι ὀλίγοι ἀναμιμνησκώμεθα οἵα ἦν ἡ μουσική.

advice,[1] invariable in the other parts of this section, is here wanting.

The five rules for tragic drama, and (up to a point) the remarks on music, share some characteristic features. Certainly the rules, and perhaps, by implication, the musical section as well, have a practical tinge. They tell the playwright how to set about his business and they are not burdened with much theoretical matter. The connexion with Aristotle is not entirely lost, however, since the section comes at precisely the place where the *Poetics* too has some miscellaneous chapters on the practical problems of framing a tragedy. Although the actual precepts of the *Ars* are not Aristotelian, and are in some cases more decidedly Hellenistic, there is yet, in one way or other, a link with problems debated in the *Poetics*. The precepts are Aristotelian with a difference, and on that score they fit the tentative sketch of Neoptolemus drawn in this chapter.

The difference from Aristotle, in this section, may be described more clearly. All the rules, and by implication also the passage on music, have a restrictive and moralizing bias which can scarcely be called Aristotelian. The rules are more negative than Aristotle would have made them. There must be *no* horrors on the stage; there must *not* be more acts than five; the *deus ex machina* must *not* be admitted except on stated conditions; the number of full-dress parts must *not* be more than three and a fourth actor must *not* be allowed to speak; choruses must *not* degenerate into mere interludes; and, to add a statement of fact to the precepts, music is *not* now what it was. It is only in two of the six cases that the novice is given reasons why so many doors are barred to him. *Nisi dignus vindice nodus*, in the case of divine intervention, probably has a purely aesthetic bearing. But in the case of the chorus the

---

[1] The same resignation is humorously embroidered in the anecdote at the beginning of Themistius' 33rd Oration. Aristoxenus was asked by one of his disciples what would happen to him if he adopted his advice and practised ancient music rather than its degenerate, modern, counterpart. The Master replied: 'You will sing less in the theatres.'

motive is twofold. One motive is aesthetic. Horace, like Aristotle, demands that the chorus should be an integral part of the play, not merely a musical interlude. This demand is close to the ideal of poetic unity, which seems to have inspired Neoptolemus. The other motive is moralistic; unlike the first it does not represent Aristotelian teaching. A strong moral bias is noticed also in Horace's discussion of music, ancient and modern, which has been considered earlier.

The portion of the *Poetics* dealing with tragedy (chiefly its plot and characters) and epic poetry constitutes the bulk of that work, chapters 6–18 and 23–6. In Horace's *Ars*, and by implication in the work of Alexandrian literary criticism that underlies it, at least a large portion is devoted to the same matters, lines 119–219, dealing with the content of poetry as a whole, of which drama and epic are considered the only genres fit for prolonged consideration. All this the Alexandrian critic subsumed under the head of ποίησις. What is left in the part of the *Poetics* now extant is the section comprising chapters 19–22, thought and diction. In Horace's (and by implication in Neoptolemus') work that section preceded the other, lines 46–118, with the brief passage on arrangement, 40–5. These stylistic matters the Alexandrian critic subsumed under the head of ποίημα. Finally, in the introductory portion of the *Ars*, up to line 40, the (Aristotelian) principle of unity or appropriateness is discussed. This principle underlies style as well as content, and its discussion reasonably precedes both in the *Ars Poetica*. It may be surmised, but cannot be proved, that it was similarly placed in the treatise of Neoptolemus.

The rest of the section on drama (*A.P.* 220–94) calls for little comment. Horace did not leave the tragic field when he passed from the topic of music to that of satyric drama, for satyric drama—in his discussion no less than in a Greek performance—is considered an adjunct of tragedy.[1] The trimeter is discussed next, and discussed for the same reason; it is the

[1] *A.P.* 220–50.

verse employed in the dialogue of tragedy.[1] Finally the rapid
survey of the history of drama, which concludes the section.
Metre is used as a transitional subject, paving the way from
the preceding topic.[2] But now comedy is joined with tragedy.
The vista is widened. The whole of Greek drama comes into
view—a large backcloth to set off Horace's magisterial advice
to the Roman heirs of this long and impressive tradition.
These are topics to which few parallels can be adduced from
the *Poetics*. Metre received a passing glance in the historical
context of the *Poetics* (ch. 4), but Aristotle's remarks are not
technical in the sense in which Horace's (and by implication
Neoptolemus') are; they purport to draw attention to the
'natural appropriateness' of certain metres to certain literary
genres, and resemble in this regard Horace's earlier section
on metre. The juxtaposition of tragedy and comedy in
chapters 4 and 5 of the *Poetics* and the 'comic' nature of τὸ
σατυρικόν indicate the point of departure for the historical
speculations and researches of Aristotle's successors—but they
indicate no more. Comedy appears to have been discussed in
the lost second book of the *Poetics*.[3] But even if the second book
were extant, we should not necessarily be better informed.
For the history of drama in the *Ars* differs materially from
Aristotle's observations. It has the affiliations—Peripatetic
and Alexandrian—which one might expect to find in Neoptolemus' case.[4] And this may be equally true for the section
on satyric drama.[5]

[1] *Ibid.* 251–74. The metre of Roman drama is brought in at line 258: Roman
tragedy, *ibid.*, Roman comedy 270.

[2] Note the criticisms of Roman metre particularly at 263, 270, 274.

[3] Above, p. 85, n. 1.

[4] Inquiry is stimulated by two papers specifically concerned with Hellenistic
and Roman theories on the origins of Greek drama, F. Solmsen, 'Eratosthenes'
Erigone', *TAPA*, LXXVIII (1947), 252–75, and K. Meuli, 'Altrömischer Maskenbrauch', *MH*, XII (1955), specially 209–12, 226–7.

[5] An Alexandrian background to Horace's account of satyric drama has been
convincingly suggested by K. Latte, 'Reste frühhellenistischer Poetik im Pisonenbrief des Horaz', *H*, LX (1925), 1. I add the caution however that this tells us
something about Horace's (presumed) authority, Neoptolemus; but it tells us
nothing about Horace's motive in adopting this account.

CHAPTER 4

NEOPTOLEMUS AND ARISTOTLE'S 'DE POETIS'

The long final section of the *Ars*, from line 295 all the way to the end, revives the quest for Neoptolemus' Aristotelian principles. *Ex hypothesi* the section corresponds to the chapter *de poeta*, περὶ ποιητοῦ, of Neoptolemus.[1] But what served as a clue for the technical portion of the poem will now serve no longer. For the *Rhetoric* and the *Poetics* indeed represent Aristotle's philosophy of literature; but the interest of the rhetorician in poetry is limited to a narrow aspect of style and the *Poetics* is primarily concerned with two or three exemplary genres. Now the final section of the *Ars* is devoted entirely to those general matters on which the *Rhetoric* is silent and the *Poetics* is brief and allusive. If there is anything in the contention that Neoptolemus' work had Aristotelian affiliations, the question needs to be raised afresh for the final section.

Here one of Aristotle's lost dialogues comes into play, the three books *De Poetis*, Περὶ ποιητῶν.[2] As in the case of the *Rhetoric* and the *Poetics*, it will be necessary to determine the relevance of the work for the present inquiry. But scholars find it hard to agree about the *Poetics* and *Rhetoric*, which are extant; it is not surprising that they find it even harder in the case of the *De Poetis*, which is lost. Discussion has been bedevilled by the tendency to assert either too much or too

---

[1] Above, p. 73.

[2] The number of books is attested by the lists of Aristotelian titles, above, p. 87, and the *Vita Marciana* of Aristotle declares it to have been a dialogue. The fragments of the dialogue were collected by V. Rose, 1st ed., with full notes, in *Aristoteles Pseudepigraphus* (1863), 3rd ed. (1886); they are now available in an Oxford text, W. D. Ross's *Aristotelis Fragmenta Selecta* (1955), pp. 67–72. Rose's meticulous presentation of the evidence is not superseded by the Oxford text, which offers little documentation.

little when what is required is a clear statement of the evidence.

The known evidence amounts to this: four fragments are transmitted with the numbers of the books: one from each of Books I and II, and two from Book III.[1] To the single fragment cited as belonging to Book I, five more may reasonably be added on internal grounds, two of them even without the title of the work.[2] These six fragments belong to the same context. The *Poetics* helps to trace it. In both works the essential nature of poetry was discussed, and defined as 'imitation', mimesis, in the specific, Aristotelian, sense known from the *Poetics*. In turn, the fragments of the first book of the dialogue help to fill certain gaps in the argument of the *Poetics*.[3] It is only when all indications are fully used that it becomes possible to reject the assertion that Aristotle was content merely to trace the early history of the dialogue form for its own sake.[4] But when all indications are so used there can be no doubt that Aristotle

---

[1] I am considering all the fragments printed by Ross, with the exception of the three neo-Platonic citations subsumed under fr. 5 and discussed below, p. 123. Book I is specified in fr. 3, Book II in fr. 6, and Book III in frs. 7 and 8. The five items belonging to Book I are printed as frs. 1–4 by Ross. Further evidence may still accrue from the papyri. F. Sbordone thought that he had discovered such evidence in the remains of the fourth book of Philodemus' *De Poematis*, cf. *Atti della Accad. Pontaniana*, Naples, n.s. IV (1954), 129–42, 217–25. But other explanations are equally plausible since the passages contain neither the name of the writer nor the title of the book.

[2] Frs. 2 and 4, Diog. Laert. VIII, 51 (cf. 74) and III, 37, only refer to 'Aristotle'. But the provenance of the citations is confirmed by the subject-matter.

[3] The 'semi-poetic' character of Plato's dialogues, fr. 4 and the (anonymous) genre to which mimesis in verse *or* prose belongs, *Poet.* I, 1447*b*9; metre *versus* mimesis as poetic essentials, frs. 3 and 4, *Poet.* I, 1447*b*, cf. 9, 1451*b*1; Plato's interest in the mimes of Sophron, alleged by Duris *ap.* Athen. XI, 504*b*, *FGH*, 76, fr. 72 Jac. (for the context see *CQ*, XL (1946), 25); the comparison of the mimes of Sophron and Xenarchus and 'the Socratic dialogues', fr. 3 and *Poet.* I, 1447*b*10; the chronology of Plato and Alexamenus as writers of dialogues, fr. 3; finally the discussion of Empedocles' poetic faculties, frs. 1–2, *Poet.* I, 1447*b*16–20. The alleged contradiction between the last two passages is discussed by G. F. Else, *op. cit.* pp. 50–1.

[4] If Athenaeus, XI, 505*c* (fr. 3*a*, Ross), had not reported more fully the passage which Diog. Laert. III, 48 (fr. 3, Ross) cites briefly, Aristotle's purpose in tracing Alexamenus would remain obscure. The textual crux in Athenaeus is irrelevant to this issue.

was concerned not only with literary research but with speculations on the essence of poetry, which he saw in mimesis, not
in the use of metre. Two conclusions have then been rightly
drawn: the speculative context of mimesis links the first book
of the *De Poetis* and the introductory section of the *Poetics*;[1]
also, the poetic character of Plato's own, mimetic, dialogues
was linked with the rebuttal of Plato's doctrines on the subject
of mimetic poetry.[2] It is no contribution to knowledge, therefore, if students of Aristotle are now told that the *De Poetis* was
une brillante histoire anecdotique et littéraire.[3] No doubt Aristotle
had collected some facts of literary history; but he employed
them for a speculative and apologetic purpose. He sought to
vindicate poetry against the strictures of Plato.[4]

Information on the second and third books of the *De Poetis*
is much more scanty. The *one* piece of evidence attested for the
second book is a critique of Euripides. In his *Meleager* the
poet is said to have slipped up on folklore and physiology at
the same time.[5] This passage too has been linked with the
Poetics. Euripides, commentators say, may well have been
criticized for an offence against 'the perceptions that neces-

---

[1] This connexion was first noted a century ago by J. Bernays in his book on *Die
Dialoge des Aristoteles*, 5–13. V. Rose (*Ar. Pseudepig.* 73) however and R. Hirzel
(*Der Dialog*, I, 1895, 288) tended to underestimate the historical features of the
dialogue, cf. F. Leo, *Die gr.-röm. Biogr.* (1901), p. 100. More recently A. Rostagni
has linked these matters with the wider context of ancient aesthetics; see specially
for this dialogue 'Il dialogo aristotelico Περὶ ποιητῶν', *RFIC*, IV (1926), 433–70; V
(1927), 145–73, repeated in *Scr. Min.* I (1955), 255–322. But it must also be said
that he has made many unfounded assertions and that his use of the evidence, particularly for this dialogue, has been reckless and unconvincing. See below, pp. 127–8.

[2] Rostagni, *loc. cit., Scr. Min.* I, 265–7.

[3] Thus D. de Montmollin, *La Poétique d'Aristote* (1951), pp. 202–3. This assertion
disregards important features of the evidence. Cf *Gnomon*, XXIV (1952), 380, and
Else's observations, *op. cit.* pp. 14, 41, 53, 501. H. Dahlmann too, *op. cit.* p. 93,
stresses chiefly the personal and historical character of the *De Poetis*.

[4] This vindication would involve Plato as a metaphysician, as a literary critic,
and as a writer; cf. *Proc. Cam. Phil. Soc.* n.s. VI (1960), 15. Moreover, since Plato's
notion of mimesis was based on the theory of Forms, whereas Aristotle's was based
on his own theory of universals, the two philosophies are likely to have clashed in
this dialogue.

[5] Fr. 6, from Macrob. *Sat.* v, 18, 9, 'ipsa Aristotelis verba ponam ex libro quem
de poetis secundo subscripsit'.

sarily belong to poetry' (τὰ παρὰ τὰς ἐξ ἀνάγκης ἀκολου-
θούσας αἰσθήσεις).[1] The poet did not perceive, αἰσθάνεσθαι,
sufficiently what he was describing. Aristotle makes him
responsible for this kind of offence, and took it seriously
enough to provide a reference to a full account in 'the published λόγοι', that is, most probably, the dialogue *De Poetis*.[2]
The ascription is possible, but hazardous in view of the ob-
scurity of the passage in the *Poetics*. The third book is represented by two fragments, one of them a longish extract from a
biography of Homer.[3] If we go by the interest of the later
litterati who cited details from Aristotle's account, then here
again would be a piece of literary history, or, in this case, of
literary legend. But several features of the Aristotelian
account, even in the garbled form in which it has come down
to us, suggest that there was much emphasis on the details of a
good and rather circumstantial tale, a μῦθος. Artistic as well as
antiquarian satisfaction must have been intended. Moreover
there is a miraculous element in the tale which must not escape
notice. The story is told that Homer had sprung from the mar-
riage of a daimon and a mortal woman, and the daimon is
described as 'a fellow-dancer of the Muses'.[4] The conviction
underlying this fairy-tale is expressed by the last two words of
the epitaph which is cited at the end of the extract—'divine
Homer'.[5] It chimes in with the degree of admiration for
Homer noticeable in various places of the *Poetics*, and
Aristotle's description of him as θεσπέσιος.[6]

There remains a group of three neo-Platonic texts, all

---

[1] *Poet.* 15, 1454*b* 15.

[2] *Loc. cit. b* 18, ἐν τοῖς ἐκδεδομένοις λόγοις. The relation to the *De Poetis* of this passage (at the end of ch. 15), and similar (but not identical) matters in ch. 17, are still debatable. Else, *op. cit.* pp. 487–502, gives a careful discussion.

[3] Fr. 8. The other, fr. 7, records critics and rivals of poets and philosophers; its bearing on the subject of the dialogue is still unknown.

[4] Fr. 8, κόρην τινὰ τῶν ἐπιχωρίων γενομένην ὑπό τινος δαίμονος τῶν συγχο-ρευτῶν ταῖς Μούσαις ἐγκύμονα.

[5] *Loc. cit.* θεῖον Ὅμηρον. G. F. Else (*op. cit.* p. 501) suggests that the tale might have come at the end of the dialogue, like certain Platonic myths.

[6] *Poet.* 23, 1459*a* 30.

obviously referring to the same passage of Aristotle, but not, unfortunately, citing the title of the work from which they are taken. Their subject resembles Aristotle's celebrated doctrine of catharsis. In the *Poetics* the term catharsis describes the effect of tragedy.[1] Yet the reader is not told what that catharsis is supposed to mean. In the *Politics* catharsis is set in a wider context—the social implications of music.[2] But again no definition of the term is provided. Instead the reader is referred to the *Poetics*—where however no such definition can be found.[3] So far as the *Poetics* is concerned, critics will deal with the embarrassment in accordance with their view of the (lost) second book of the work.[4] If they believe that such a book ever existed (as I do myself), they will be able to assume that Aristotle's promise was fulfilled in that place. If they do not, they must find another explanation, whatever it may be. But assume Aristotle's promise was made good in the second book of the *Poetics*: even so this can hardly be what the neo-Platonists have in mind. For they speak of an explicit Aristotelian criticism of Plato's aesthetic doctrines, and that is not found in the extant portion of the *Poetics* where Aristotle replaces Plato's philosophy of 'imitation' by his own: all criticism of Plato in that context is by implication; muffled, as it were, by the objective character of a treatise. The same is likely to apply to the topic of the passions aroused by drama— beside mimesis the most important object of Plato's attack. It appears therefore that Aristotle's defence of aesthetic emotion stood in the same relation to the *Poetics* as his defence of mimesis. Both were put forward in a different (and probably earlier) work explicitly opposing Plato; and both reappear in an objective, doctrinal, shape in the *Poetics*, where opposition to Plato is but implicit. The *De Poetis*, both on

---

[1] *Poetics* 6, 1449 *b* 27 (ἔστιν οὖν τραγῳδία μίμησις) δι' ἐλέου καὶ φόβου περαίνουσα τὴν τῶν τοιούτων παθημάτων κάθαρσιν.

[2] Ar. *Pol.* VIII, 7.   [3] Ar. *op. cit.* 1341 *b* 39.

[4] See above, p. 85, n. 1. Moreover there is no explanatory phrase like those attached to two other elements of the definition, 1449 *b* 28–31, nor is there a reference to the second book. G. F. Else's dating of this puzzling passage has been mentioned above, p. 85, n. 3.

account of its subject-matter and its tendency, is the most likely candidate for that part.[1] What cannot be guessed with any reasonable amount of probability is the book of the *De Poetis* in which aesthetic emotion was debated. The items that can be considered established are: the subject of imitation, with its Aristotelian corollaries, for Book I; perhaps the subject of the sense-perceptions that are inherent in the poet's art, for Book II; and the biographical legend of Homer, and perhaps Homer's poetic art and genius, for Book III.[2]

Is it reasonable to infer more, specially as regards the sequence of subjects in the *De Poetis*? And has the *Ars* any bearing on this question? If we are to believe Rostagni, much more can be inferred about the sequence of subjects, and the *Ars* is the very source from which the material for such inferences must be drawn.

To begin with the latter question. Rostagni, undeterred by other commentators, was strong-minded enough to follow Norden's lead in identifying Horace's own headings, at lines 306–8, with the subsequent sections of the poem.[3] The first heading is provided by 307: the sources of poetry and the formation of the poet. This Norden found discussed at lines 309–32, on the *scribendi principium et fons* and a theory of mimesis: *Socraticae chartae* (310), *exemplar vitae morumque* (317), *doctus imitator* (318). The second heading is to be found in the initial part of 308: *quid deceat, quid non,* the 'fitness' of poetry. What should a true poet aim at? This Norden recognized at lines 333–46, the aim or τέλος of poetry: moral instruction, or entertainment, or a judicious mixture of both. The third heading and last is in the latter part of 308, poetic perfection, *virtus,* and its obverse, *error.* This Norden found discussed in

---

[1] Thus rightly, so far as it goes, Rostagni's argument, *op. cit., Scr. Min.* I, 276–93.

[2] In addition there is one item ascribed to Book III; its bearing on the subject-matter of the dialogue is not now certain: see above, p. 123, n. 3.

[3] E. Norden, *H,* XL (1905), 497–507, *Agnostos Theos.* p. 108 n.; Rostagni, commentary on *A.P.* 306–7, and *Il dialogo aristotelico* Περὶ ποιητῶν, *Scr. Min.* I, 296–306. K. Barwick, *H,* LVII (1922), 50–2, has confused the matter by his insistence on certain rhetorical terms which do not here apply.

the rest of the poem, from 347 to the end. Critical doctrine in this final portion is crystallized above all in three passages: (*a*) 391–407 sketch the origins of the (social) setting of the desired kind of poetry; (*b*) 408–52 discuss the traditional problem of the schools, *natura...an arte*, φύσει–τέχνῃ; (*c*) 453–76 portray the *malus poeta*, caricatured as the *vesanus poeta* (455) who pretends to genius, *natura*.

Is this the true arrangement in the final portion of the *Ars* or has Rostagni used external criteria to foist an artificial order on the poem? The answer to this question will differ according to the purpose of the exercise. The subtle and flexible sequence of Horace's poetic thought is far from being recaptured by this rough and ready division into three sections. Norden however did not attempt to recapture Horace's poetic procedure, and Rostagni, who did attempt it, did not keep Horace sufficiently in view. If on the other hand inquiry purports to examine the traditional ideas that are fundamental to Horace's poem, then there seems to me little doubt that the three topics singled out by Norden and Rostagni correspond to that description. And it is the tradition influenced by Neoptolemus that is under discussion.

How then about the sequence of subjects in the *De Poetis*? Again if we are to believe Rostagni that sequence is known. It is simply the tripartite division that Norden's analytic operations have uncovered in the *Ars*. A qualified approval has just been given to that analysis. But assuming the tripartite division to be Neoptolemus', how are we to get back from the Alexandrian treatise to Aristotle's dialogue? I do not believe that the evidence is sufficient for an unequivocal judgement.

Rostagni makes two points in favour of his thesis. One of them may be justified; I do not think that the other is.

The argument that may have some substance is the following.[1] Titles of Hellenistic books on poetic criticism are divided between a type containing a word for poetry or poems

[1] Rostagni, *op. cit.*, *Scr. Min.* I, 258–62, and elsewhere.

in it, and another containing a word for poets, such as Περὶ ποιητικῆς or Περὶ ποιημάτων on the one hand, and Περὶ ποιητῶν or the like on the other. Heraclides of Pontus combined the two in the title Περὶ ποιητικῆς καὶ τῶν ποιητῶν.[1] Rostagni has observed that these correspond to the titles of Aristotle's two major writings on the subject, the former a treatise on the chief genres of poetry, the latter a dialogue on the making and makers of poetry. The content of the *Ars* suggests that Neoptolemus, too, may have combined these two diverse topics; and since Aristotelian influences have been observed in the technical part of the *Ars*, there is a presumption in favour of like influences in the second, general, part. The influences in the technical part may be traced to the *Poetics* and the *Rhetoric*. There would be a presumption that the influences in the general part may be traced to the *De Poetis*—if more could be known about that dialogue and if the plural *De Poetis* and the singular *De Poeta* could be easily equated.

Inspired by this possible (if unprovable) link between the *Ars* and the *De Poetis*, Rostagni went on to project the tripartite order from the final section of the *Ars* back to the *De Poetis*.[2] The only piece of evidence to go by is the topic of mimesis, which has been established for the first book of the *De Poetis* and likewise for the first part of the final section of the *Ars*. If the Homeric legend in *De Poetis*, Book III, was told as a myth concluding the more prosaic discussion on *natura an arte*, this would help to place this topic in the same book; it would there come last, as it does in the *Ars*.[3] However, seeing

---

[1] Diog. Laert. v, 88, cited as fr. 166 by F. Wehrli, *Herakleides Pontikos* (1953).

[2] Rostagni, *op. cit.*, *Scr. Min.* I, 293–307.

[3] Hor. *A.P.* 408–end. Else (*op. cit.* p. 502) suggests that poetic inspiration was not treated in Aristotle's *De Poetis* under the general heading 'art *vs.* inspiration', as it had been by Plato and was to be again in the Hellenistic and Roman period. It was rather (he thinks) discussed, as it is, briefly, in the *Poetics*, as an instance of the poetic gifts that are needed in the stage of the creative process where the poet's abstract conception, the σύστασις τοῦ μύθου, is translated into words. This is certainly so in the *Poetics*; whether it was equally so in the *De Poetis* seems to me still open to doubt.

that when it suited his purpose Neoptolemus adopted an order of contents which differs from that of the *Poetics* or the *Rhetoric*, it would be exceedingly imprudent to suggest that he would have made no changes in the order of the *De Poetis*— even if one could be quite sure what the order of the *De Poetis* was. There is no reason why the Horatian and the Aristotelian order of things should not have been very much alike. But there is too little evidence to prove that they were. In the present state of our knowledge it is expedient to rely on the fragments of the *De Poetis* and to elicit from them what little can be elicited as regards the arrangement of the topics. It would be foolish to 'reconstruct' the *Poetics* (if it were lost) from what survives of Neoptolemus' work in Horace and Philodemus. The same applies to the *De Poetis*, which is lost.

Having reduced the evidence from what we would like it to be to what (regrettably) it is, we can now resume our quest for Neoptolemus' revised Aristotelianism. Only one passage exists in this part of the *Ars* in which, by good luck, Horace can be confronted with both Neoptolemus and Aristotle— I mean, lines 333–46. Earlier on, Horace has demanded that poetic diction must have an emotional quality along with its artistic perfection.[1] In the present passage three ends of poetic endeavour are allowed: either moral utility, or entertainment, or indeed both.[2] The first prize is awarded to the third competitor who pleases as well as instructs.[3] Horace's assertion appears to be both traditional and trivial. It is certainly traditional; whether also trivial remains to be seen when Horace, not Neoptolemus, takes the centre of the stage. The immediate provenance of the proposition cannot be in doubt; Jensen discovered its source in Neoptolemus. 'To fulfil his function the perfect poet needs to entertain as well as benefit

[1] *A.P.* 99–100, 'non satis est pulchra esse poemata: dulcia sunto | et quocumque volent animum auditoris agunto'.

[2] *Ibid.* 333–4, 'aut prodesse volunt aut delectare poetae | aut simul et iucunda et idonea dicere vitae'.

[3] *Ibid.* 343–4, 'omne tulit punctum qui miscuit utile dulci | lectorem delectando pariterque monendo'.

and instruct.'[1] Horace's *animum auditoris agunto* recalls Neoptolemus' traditional term ψυχαγωγία, and *idonea dicere (vitae)* renders what seems to be the Greek critic's neologism, χρησιμολογεῖν. Aristotle's reaction to Neoptolemus' mixture of moral instruction and aesthetic enjoyment would doubtless have been sceptical. One thing is common to both, and only one: the defence and justification of poetry. For the rest, Neoptolemus disregards Aristotle's subtle and speculative theory of mimesis and catharsis. Instead he expresses the common Greek conviction that poetry must instruct as well as please.[2] He is commonsensical and down-to-earth about it all. No Aristotle was required to inspire this attitude. If Neoptolemus' Aristotelian leanings were not known from other evidence, no one could have inferred them from this. His Aristotelian leanings are however undeniable elsewhere and they reappear in the rest of the final part of the *Ars*, but they reappear in conjunction with more traditional sentiments.

The last paragraph of Horace's final section contains two points that call for notice. The traditional problem of the schools, whether talent or technique is more important to the poet, is solved by a truism: *natura* as well as *ars* is required.[3] The second point requires discussion, for here there is the same curious conjunction of Aristotelian and popular doctrine that has been noted above. Horace lays down the 'philosophy' from which the poet draws his subject-matter.[4] 'Knowing', *sapere*, is said to be the fountain-head, *principium et fons*, of poetry.[5] Socratic books will provide the novice with

---

[1] Neoptol., no. 10 (*De Poem.* v, col. xiii) cited above, p. 55, πρὸς ἀρε[τὴν δεῖν τ]ῶι τελείωι ποι[ητῆι μετὰ τ]ῆς ψυχαγω[γί]α[ς τοῦ τοὺς] ἀκούοντ[ας] ὠ[φελεῖ]ν καὶ χρησι[μο]λ[ογεῖ]ν.

[2] K. Ziegler, *R-E*, 'Tragoedia', 2054, is right to stress the prevalence of popular aesthetics in the early Hellenistic age.

[3] *A.P.* 408–11. One recalls Aristotle's refusal to decide the same question, *Poet.* 8, 1451 *a* 22, ὁ δ' Ὅμηρος... καὶ τοῦτ' ἔοικεν καλῶς ἰδεῖν, ἤτοι διὰ τέχνην ἢ διὰ φύσιν. Both the Sophistic and Platonic positions differed from Aristotle's in this regard.

[4] *Ibid.* 307, 'unde parentur opes, quid alat formetque poetam'.

[5] *Ibid.* 309, 'scribendi recte sapere est et principium et fons'.

subject-matter for his poems; the wording comes thereafter.[1]
Thus he will come to know the qualities appropriate to each
type of person.[2] Only then, after he has been told what the
philosophical matter consists of, is he instructed to turn to the
model of life and manners, and draw living words from it.[3]
He has learned, *didicit*, how to represent reality: he is a *doctus
imitator*[4]—a counterpart of the Hellenistic *doctus poeta* which
carries with it the mark of its provenance.

Aristotle maintained, in the ninth chapter of the *Poetics*,
that the reality apprehended by poets is more typical, or
universal—καθόλου—than particular, καθ' ἕκαστον. It is to
this universal character of poetry that the principles of
probability or necessity belong—οἷα ἂν γένοιτο rather than
τὰ γενόμενα.[5] But although it is said to be more philosophical
than history, which concentrates more on τὰ γενόμενα, poetry
is not said to be philosophy. There is no indication in the
Poetics that its author encouraged budding poets to take up
the study of philosophy. Nor indeed did he encourage
philosophers to consider themselves poets—unlike Plato who
thought that (true) poets *should* be philosophers,[6] and unlike
the Stoics who held that 'only the Wise Man *is* a good poet'.[7]
There are indications however which point to a change in the
attitude of the Lyceum, within one or two generations. This
would account for Neoptolemus' brand of Aristotelianism

[1] *A.P.* 310–11, 'rem tibi Socraticae poterunt ostendere chartae, | verbaque
provisam rem non invita sequentur'.

[2] *Ibid.* 316, 'reddere personae scit convenientia cuique'.

[3] *Ibid.* 317–18, 'respicere exemplar vitae morumque iubebo | doctum imitatorem
et vivas hinc ducere voces'.   [4] *Doctus*, 318, takes up *didicit*, 312.

[5] This is the Aristotelian doctrine of mimesis, adapted to its new purpose and
shifted from the technical to the general section of the discussion. Cf. above, p. 105.

[6] According to Plato's *Phaedrus*, 278 *b–e*, poets as well as other composers of
speeches, λόγοι, should be named 'philosophers' if they compose with a knowledge
of the truth (τὸ ἀληθές) and can both defend and challenge their own writings. If
on the other hand they have nothing of greater value (τιμιώτερον) than their
literary compositions, then they should be rightly named poets, or composers of
speeches, or composers of laws. Passages of the same purport are adduced from
other Platonic dialogues by J. Tate, *CQ*, xxii (1928), 23.

[7] Stob. *Ecl.* vol. ii, p. 67 (ed. Wachsmuth) μόνον δέ φασι τὸν σοφὸν καὶ μάντιν
ἀγαθὸν εἶναι καὶ ποιητὴν καὶ ῥήτορα κτλ., Plut. *Tranq. an.* 12, 472.

which I take to underlie this section of the *Ars*. There seems to have been a shift in emphasis that brought to the fore moral theory, character-study, literary criticism and rhetoric— courses in 'philosophy' that may have commended the Lyceum to young poets. One can see that a poet like Menander might benefit by Theophrastus' teaching; but one might also surmise that, on the showing of the *Poetics*, Aristotle would have doubted if that was the best, or indeed the only, way of teaching him.

That however is precisely what Neoptolemus appears to have thought philosophy could teach. The present passage tells the reader how he conceived the teaching. First then the moral qualities which will lend appropriateness to character-drawing. Philosophy will supply them, but it is a philosophy which is a guide to life rather than an intellectual discipline.[1] It offers a moral code of a simple and traditional kind.[2] It is more narrowly conceived than the earlier portions of the treatise in that only correct and dutiful attitudes are considered. *Poetic* characters must conform to a narrow interpretation of Aristotle's precept for *tragic* characters—which lays down first and foremost that they shall be good.[3] This adds a

---

[1] The philosophy is specified as *Socraticae...chartae*, *A.P.* 310: Plato's dialogues, according to F. Solmsen, *Zeit. für Aesth. u. Allgem. Kunstwiss.* XXVI (1932), 153; Xenophon and the minor Socratics, according to some commentators; Panaetius' Stoicism, according to others, see below, p. 136, n. 4. A reference to Lucilius, fr. 709 (Warmington, 788–9), *Socratici carti*, may be intended, but the context of the fragment is unknown. It may well be that no specific schools are in the poet's mind and *Socraticae chartae* stands for 'moral philosophy', as, I take it, is the case at *Odes*, III, 21, 9, 'non ille, quamquam *Socraticis* madet | *sermonibus*, te neglegit horridus' (*te* being the *pia testa*) and Petron. *Sat.* 5, 'mox et *Socratico* plenus *grege* mittat habenas'. But *Odes*, I, 29, 14, 'libros Panaeti *Socraticam* et *domum*', may be a different matter.

[2] The code recalls Lucilius' eloquent catalogue of *virtutes*, frs. 1326–38 (Warmington, 1196–1208); particularly at *A.P.* 312–13, 'patriae quid debeat et quid amicis, | quo sit amore parens, quo frater amandus et hospes', the last two lines of the Lucilian fragment may be compared, 'commoda praeterea patriai prima putare, | deinde parentum, tertia iam postremaque nostra'. Both Horace and Lucilius define traditional moral qualities. Horace's form of speech—'the poet who has learned what *he* owes to his country', etc.—does not, I believe, illustrate the Stoic paradox, cited p. 130, n. 7. Strabo, 1, 2, who does illustrate it, shows up the difference.

[3] Ar. *Poet.* 15, 1454 *a* 16, ἓν μὲν καὶ πρῶτον, ὅπως χρηστὰ ᾖ (τὰ ἤθη).

further interpretation of character, *mores*, to the others which punctuate the argument of the *Ars*.[1] At the same time it lends a moral bias to the 'universal' of Aristotle which the poet is to 'imitate'—'respicere exemplar *vitae morumque* iubebo'.[2]

In the conventional Greek view poetry had an educative and moral function. This is the view expressed in the section which has just been considered. It is given a great deal of emphasis in the section on archaic poetry.[3] The speculative writing of cultural history which is found here has a modest Aristotelian parallel in some brief remarks in the fourth chapter of the *Poetics*—modest because Aristotle does no more than speculate on two types of pre-Homeric poetry.[4] In the *Ars* much more is asserted than that. The oldest poets were also the earliest priests, civilizers, and law-givers. Such were Orpheus, Amphion, and others who had established the name and function of the divine *vates*. Next come the functions of the poetic genres: Homer's and Tyrtaeus' verse to arouse warriors, *carmina* and gnomic verse to give oracles and show the right 'way of life', lyric to gain the favour of kings, and drama for civic holidays. No need to demonstrate that these genres are apt to be useful to the body politic:[5] 'ne forte pudori | sit tibi Musa lyrae sollers et cantor Apollo' (406–7). The well-known likeness of a passage of Aristophanes' *Frogs* shows the traditional character of some of these assertions.[6] Accounts such as these must have been bandied about in the schools of the sophists and rhetoricians; this sort of teaching cannot have

---

[1] The passages are discussed below, pp. 140, n. 1; pp. 251–2.

[2] *A.P.* 317. Rostagni's reference to Aristotle's καθόλου, in his note on the passage, seems to me justified. Immisch's reference to Panaetius and Antiochus (*op. cit.* pp. 179–80) does not.   [3] *A.P.* 391–407.

[4] Ar. *Poet.* 4, 1448 *b* 24; one of them is said to be of serious intent, consisting first of hymns and *encomia*, the other less high-minded, consisting first of invectives. In Homer both strains are said to be united. After him they again divide, one issuing in tragedy, the other *via* iambics in comedy.

[5] The genres are not entirely identical with those rehearsed at *A.P.* 73–91, because here the kinds of poetry are selected which can be shown to have a social function. This is likely to explain also why the iambic genre is omitted in the present passage.

[6] Aristoph. *Frogs*, 1030–6.

been less current after the philosophers had established themselves. Aristophanes demonstrates the 'usefulness' of the
approved poets[1] by referring to Orpheus, Musaeus, Hesiod,
and Homer: Orpheus for his rites and his warnings against
bloodshed, Musaeus for medical incantations and oracles,
Hesiod for advice to farmers, and Homer for inspiring military
men. Horace's list is very similar but, details apart, it
differs in two respects. According to Aristophanes, Orpheus
was an ancient poet who revealed rites and taught men to
abstain from slaughter; Musaeus another poet whose speci-
alities were medical and oracular. Horace says that Orpheus
deterred men from slaughter and animal food, and Amphion
founded a city; and he adds that such is the meaning of the
tale about Orpheus taming tigers and lions and Amphion
moving stones by the sound of his lyre. Aristophanes then
purports to give a historical account whereas Horace tells a
mythical tale and allegorizes it.[2] The second difference from

---

[1] Aristoph., *op. cit.* 1030, σκέψαι γὰρ ἀπ' ἀρχῆς ὡς ὠφέλιμοι τῶν ποιητῶν οἱ
γενναῖοι γεγένηνται. H. Koller, *Die Mimesis in der Antike* (1954), p. 189, neglects
the passage of Aristophanes and overestimates the importance of Quintilian, *I.
O.* I, 10. Quintilian is commending the value of music for a rhetorical education.
He therefore relies on a musical propagandist and is not specifically relevant to
Horace. In his chapter on *Orpheus der Kulturbringer* (*op. cit.* pp. 185–92) Koller has
assembled some of the material. But, so far as accounts of archaic poetry are concerned, he overstates the musical nature of the archaic *vates*. The Orpheus of
Aristophanes and Horace is a poet and singer, not an 'instrumentalist'; Amphion's
magic relies on the words of his spell, *prece blanda*, as much as on the music of his
testudo. Koller (pp. 190–1) names Horace's account *Musikgeschichte*. But in con-
cluding, 'ne forte pudori | sit tibi Musa lyrae sollers et cantor Apollo', Horace wants
to assert what Aristophanes said in the passage cited above. And that is no less true
because Horace and Aristophanes fill the empty spaces of pre-Homeric *poetry* with
a legend or two on some early poets *and* singers, whereas Aristotle was critical
enough to leave these spaces blank, *Poet.* 4, 1448 *b* 28–9, and Bywater's note.

[2] F. Solmsen, *H*, LXVII (1932), 154, declares Horace's (and perhaps Neoptolemus') allegory to be Stoic. So it may well be. But allegory had been applied to
the ancient myths long before the Stoics and there is nothing specifically Stoic
about this allegory. Similar interpretations of Orpheus' musical magic are cited
from Stoic and other sources by Ziegler, *R-E*, 'Orpheus', 1308–11. Rationalistic
criticism of the Orphic legends may be traced back as far as the fourth century
B.C. or earlier, cf. I. M. Linforth, *The Arts of Orpheus* (Berkeley, 1941), ch. 1;
F. Jacoby, *FGH*, 324 (Androtion), F 54. But the early critics do not appear to
allegorize the Orphic legends in the Horatian manner.

Aristophanes is more telling. The list of the earliest poets in the *Frogs* is truly archaic: it closes with Homer. In Horace, and *ex hypothesi* in Neoptolemus, it neatly dovetails into the Peripatetic, or Alexandrian, account of literary genres that was set out above: Orpheus, Amphion, and the anonymous civilizers of mankind precede Homer, Tyrtaeus, and the anonymous founders of literary genres.

The last three passages of the *Ars* that have been considered show a similar pattern. Although only one of them is ascribed to Neoptolemus in an ancient source, it is noted that they all mix Aristotelian with traditional or popular features, and they all assign to poetry a civilizing, moral, and educative function. These resemblances encourage attribution to the same author, Neoptolemus. But they do not add to our information on Aristotle's *De Poetis*.

CHAPTER 5

ALEXANDRIAN CRITICISM AND NEOPTOLEMUS ON POETRY

It is time to sum up. What does Horace owe to Neoptolemus? What does he owe to Aristotle? What are the salient features of Neoptolemus' *ars poetica*?

The debt to the Hellenistic critic is indicated by Porphyrion's unequivocal statement that in the *Ars Poetica* Horace had brought together the most outstanding literary precepts of Neoptolemus. It is indicated too by the resemblances between the *Ars* and the remains of Neoptolemus' critical writings. The debt to Aristotle is indicated by the Aristotelian, or rather Peripatetic, character of Horace's teaching which is thus imputed to Neoptolemus. Now it may be argued on general grounds that Horace's poetic procedure was such as to make it impossible to trace these affiliations. This has been shown to be contradicted by the facts of the case. Starting from the known facts I have also attempted to trace the underlying Greek doctrines where certainty does not obtain. On the face of it, virtually everything in the *Ars* is Horatian and Roman. Yet matters demonstrably Horatian and Roman may be no more than a Horatian construction placed on Neoptolemus' teachings. For example, what could be more in Horace's vein than *qui miscuit utile dulci*? Nevertheless the evidence renders it certain that this doctrine was held by Neoptolemus as well as by Horace.[1] Again nothing could be more Horatian than the high spirits of the introduction of the poem. Nevertheless the general axiom, 'denique sit quidvis, *simplex* dumtaxat *et unum*', beside Aristotle's insistence on poetic unity and beside the relevant fragment of Neoptolemus, leaves little doubt that here Horace's epigrams rest on a

[1] *A.P.* 343; Neoptol., no. 10 (col. xiii), above, pp. 55, 57, 128–9.

foundation laid by the Alexandrian critic.[1] This applies in principle to all items of the Greek *technologia* on which Horace has put his own construction.

Although much play has been made with doctrines incompatible with or dated later than those of Neoptolemus, it is surprising how few of them there are and how hard it is to prove them so.[2] Two assertions in particular have tended to throw researchers off the scent. The first is the influence which the Academic school is said to have exercised on the *Ars*; but while a convincing proof of this assertion is far to seek there are many indications to the contrary.[3] The second is the pervasive presence of Panaetius and his theory of 'appropriateness', or τὸ πρέπον; but other men than Panaetius, above all Aristotle, had debated this topic. Specific resemblances with Panaetius' theories are lacking. What resemblances can be claimed are of a general kind: talk of the obligations that are laid on a citizen or a member of a profession.[4]

[1] *A.P.* 23; Neoptol., no. 9 (col. xiii), above, pp. 55, 56–7, 102–3.

[2] I have given reasons for doubting the Stoic origin of the allegorizing that is applied to two myths in the *Ars*; *A.P.* 393–4, above, p. 133, n. 2. The origin of two other passages has been thought to be early Hellenistic though not Peripatetic. Commentators find the allegedly Stoic theory of the λόγος ἐνδιάθετος and προφορικός at *A.P.* 108; they invoke Epicurean and other naturalistic theories to explain Horace's *usus* in language, 'quem penes arbitrium est et ius et norma loquendi', *A.P.* 71. Neither case is certain and neither affects the literary criticism of the *Ars*. The controversy as regards the origin of elegy, *A.P.* 78, does affect it since Horace describes it as undecided—'grammatici certant et adhuc sub iudice lis est'. Yet it may be no more than a humorous remark designed to bring older scholarship 'up to date'.

[3] Thus Jensen, *op. cit.* p. 125, and Immisch, *op. cit.* pp. 26–8 and elsewhere. In particular I cannot find a trace of 'the eclecticism of Antiochus of Ascalon'. The frequent similarities with Cicero which C. G. Fiske and Mary A. Grant have shown to exist (see above, p. 30, n. 4) do not prove Academic affiliation. Nor can I see much relevance in Immisch's reference to *Socraticae chartae*, *A.P.* 310, and none whatever in *Ep.* II, 2, 45: young Horace in Athens, proposing *inter silvas Academi quaerere verum*.

[4] Panaetius' moral theory was found in the *Ars* by Immisch, *op. cit.* p. 179; M. Pohlenz, Τὸ Πρέπον, etc., *NGG* (1933); L. Labowsky, *Die Ethik des Panaitios, Unters. zur Gesch. des Decorum bei Cicero und Horaz* (1934), and others. Above all the passage, *A.P.* 310 ff., is invoked to prove such dependence; cf. p. 131, n. 1. But that passage also lacks the specific marks of Panaetius' argument which are displayed in Cicero's *De Officiis*. For the more common notion of obligations, *officia*, at that time, cf. L. Edelstein, 'The Professional Ethics of the Greek Physician', *Bull. Hist. Med.* (1956), pp. 410–14.

These are interesting details but they are irrelevant to the main issue. For Horace's twofold debt involves not only details but the *Ars* as a whole. Neoptolemus' intermediate position between Aristotle and Horace suggests that the Greek doctrines underlying the *Ars* may be recovered when all the Horatian evidence has been submitted to the test of (indirect) Aristotelian provenance.

Very few assertions can be made with the backing of all the extant material. But there is one that can be so made and which offers the key to the whole of the work. I consider certain the arrangement of Neoptolemus' critical work because Horace's threefold division echoes Neoptolemus' triad of ποίημα–ποίησις–ποιητής, and the technical part of that triad is related to the divisions of Aristotle's *Rhetoric*.

Once this is agreed the second step may be made. The matters for which only two sources are extant may yet qualify as part of Neoptolemus' doctrine. Horace and Aristotle's *Poetics* and *Rhetoric* have been confronted. The results though not certain are yet probable: the rhetorical doctrine of poetry in the two technical sections of Horace amounts in fact to that revision of Aristotle's teaching which the fully documented material leads one to expect.

Finally the matters for which Horace is the only extant source. In this group stand out the introduction on unity and the last section on the function of the poet. As for the introduction, it is the placing of the demand for unity which cannot be proved; the demand itself is likely to be Neoptolemic,[1] and parallels in Aristotle and Horace suggest the same intermediate position between Aristotle and Horace for this doctrine as was observed for other doctrines of Neoptolemus. The section on the function of the poet displays a similar position for that mixture of *utile* and *dulce* which Philodemus ascribes to Neoptolemus.[2] Other arguments are not definitely ascribed to Neoptolemus but adapt Aristotelianism, like the passages whose provenance is more certain. But, again, the

---

[1] See above, p. 136, n. 1.   [2] See above, p. 135.

placing of these doctrines is uncertain since too little is known about the *De Poetis* which may have been adapted in this section of Neoptolemus.

The concurrence of the three witnesses may be schematized, thus:

Neoptolemus' fragments	—	ποίημα	ποίησις	ποιητής
Aristotle	*Poetics*, chs. 7–8	*Rhet.* III	*Poetics* (+*Rhet.* II, 12–14)	(? *De Poetis*)
Horace, *A.P.*	1–40	40–118	119–294	295–476

The new treatise is divided into a technical and a general portion. The Aristotelian axioms are shifted either to the general portion, at the close of the book, or else they are made the main pillars of the new technical order. What remains of the philosophy of poetic universality is placed either in the discussion of content or in the general concluding discussion. The essential 'parts' of tragedy—content or plot, character, thought and diction, music, the visual element—these *tragic* elements either become the mainstays of the discussion of *poetry* (thus, content and diction), or are dealt with specifically among the practical hints for the writing of *drama*, mainly *tragic* (thus, music, and perhaps the visual element).

What then happened to the axiomatic demand for poetic unity which in the *Poetics* is put forward near the beginning of the section on tragedy?[1] Or, for that matter, to the item of character which in the *Poetics* comes second among the 'parts' of tragedy?[2] Or, finally, to the principle of appropriateness, which is mentioned so frequently as a stylistic criterion in the *Rhetoric*?[3] This raises a larger question, suggested also by Neoptolemus' way of arranging his material under a few formal subject headings. Anyone adopting this arrangement, and yet wishing to draw attention to certain features of his subject which concern more than one of his headings, will have to recur to these features as occasion arises. He has then to consider the impact such repetition will make on the economy

---

[1] Ar. *Poet.* chs. 7–8.   [2] *Poet.* ch. 15.
[3] Ar. *Rhet.*, repeatedly in Book III, especially ch. 7.

of his material. These considerations scarcely arose for Aristotle since the argument of the extant part of the *Poetics* largely proceeds within the context of one, exemplary, kind of poetry; so that on the whole items needed to be repeated only because other genres had to be related to the paradigm of tragedy.[1] Neoptolemus, on the other hand, had divided his material according to three formal principles—style, content, and general questions of poetic theory. Since the principles of unity and appropriateness may apply to any or all of these divisions, there is at least a suspicion that, like Horace, Neoptolemus placed certain overriding demands such as the principle of unity at the beginning of his treatise, and later reiterated them whenever it was expedient to do so. A suspicion there is, even a probability, that in this regard, too, Horace followed Neoptolemus' lead. But the suggestion cannot be called certain because the evidence is insufficient for a proof.

Character is another item often discussed in the *Ars*. Unlike unity and appropriateness, it is not entirely unplaced in Neoptolemus' (hypothetical) scheme because it serves as a sub-heading of the section on subject-matter, and it duly appears at the place provided for it by the *Poetics*.[2] Aristotle distinguishes four conditions which the tragic poet must observe in dealing with it. Ethos must be good, appropriate, 'like', and consistent, or χρηστόν, ἁρμόττον, ὅμοιον, and ὁμαλόν. It so happens that Horace refers to character-drawing in four different contexts of the *Ars*; apart from the section just mentioned, they are: diction, subject-matter, and the moral theory prescribed for the schooling of the poet.[3] It is harder to assign each to its opposite number in the *Poetics*, partly because it has always been recognized how much the

---

[1] In the extant book of the *Poetics* epic has to be related to the paradigm of tragedy, and this occasions some repetition in the final chapters. Another kind of repetition is the reference to the introductory portion on mimesis in the relevant contexts of the main discussion; for example, discussing character at ch. 15, 1454 *b* 9, and mentioning portrait-painters and their sitters, Aristotle repeats ch. 2, 1448 *a* 5, where the same point is discussed as a case of mimesis.

[2] Ar. *Poet.* ch. 15, after discussion of the plot; *A.P.* 153, in a like position, cf. above, p. 110.   [3] *A.P.* 114–18, 120–7, 312–18.

Aristotelian conditions resemble each other, and partly because Horace (and probably Neoptolemus) used appropriateness as an essential feature for all four.[1] But there can be no doubt about a more important point: Horace simply expands Aristotle's precepts. This seems to have been Neoptolemus' procedure. Nor must another matter escape notice; the placing of the four items accords with the demarcations of Neoptolemus' treatise.

My argument is chiefly based on a comparison between Horace and Aristotle. The question has sometimes been asked whether it could not have been Horace himself who applied to Aristotle's *Poetics* what revision was called for, perhaps with an occasional glance at the work of Neoptolemus and other relevant authors that may have come to hand. And it must certainly be admitted that there is much in what I consider Neoptolemus' revised Aristotelianism that Horace could have set down unaided. In spite of that, my answer to this question is an unqualified 'no'. I know no evidence of any first-hand knowledge of Aristotle's *Poetics* in Horace's time.[2] No new evidence accrues from the *Ars*. But there are

[1] One of them only seems to me to be certain: lines 312–18 take up 'goodness' as an essential condition of character-drawing; cf. *Poet.* 15, 1454 *a* 16, ἓν μὲν καὶ πρῶτον, ὅπως χρηστὰ ᾖ (τὰ ἤθη), and above, p. 131. Tentatively I would assign the other three thus: lines 114–18 illustrate τὸ ἁρμόττον because Aristotle's example is the difference of sexes, which recurs in Horace's catalogue of types of character. Lines 156–78 illustrate τὸ ὅμοιον, 'likeness', because, in spite of Aristotle's failure to exemplify, a vivid sense of portrait likeness is the prevailing impression of these pen-sketches. The fact that 'age' also appears among the types of 114–18 should not make the reader overlook the difference of approach: the earlier passage simply demands that diction be commensurate with 'natural types', and then proceeds to list some of them; the latter is a vivid demonstration of how to draw figures that are types and yet true to life. Over the last item I find myself in disagreement with scholars expounding the *Poetics*. It seems to me that lines 125–7 illustrate Aristotle's fourth condition, τὸ ὁμαλόν, or consistency. As I argued above, p. 108, consistency is implicit in the traditional characters, and is not therefore specially stressed although it is brought out in the examples 120–4; but consistency is stressed for invented characters. This suggestion avoids the awkwardness of finding Aristotle's ὅμοιον in the passage 120–4; so for example Else (*op. cit.* p. 460), who renders it by 'faithfulness to the literary tradition', not an Aristotelian sense, as Else himself points out.

[2] G. F. Else, *op. cit.* p. 337, n. 125, 'can see little firm evidence of a knowledge of *our Poetics* at any time between Theophrastus and the fourth century A.D.' There

many internal indications to the contrary. The analysis of the poem, and a comparison, section by section, with Aristotle, suggest that there is another mind interposed between Horace and Aristotle. Suppose Porphyrion had not told us that Horace had brought together the most outstanding precepts of Neoptolemus of Parium on the art of poetry. Even then, I suggest, an unbiased and careful analysis would have come to the conclusion that a Greek critic with a mind of his own, though hardly a great mind, not far removed in time from Aristotle, had abridged and revised all the available Aristotelian teaching on poetry, or used such a revision; had brought it up to date in the light of opinion partly Peripatetic, partly Alexandrian; and had put it in the form of an *ars poetica*, τέχνη ποιητική, which more than two centuries later Horace had freely adapted in the poetic letter to the Pisos. Then there would be much raising of eyebrows: reviewers would fulminate against unfounded hypotheses and lovers of Horace would denounce analyses that do not help them to enjoy the poetry of the poet. Nevertheless *et ratio et res ipsa* point that way. But by good luck we have Porphyrion's information, and can put a name to the face that has now emerged.

Much of the preceding discussion has shown Neoptolemus at work on the basis of two, or possibly even three, works of Aristotle. The question must now at last be raised whether Neoptolemus himself rearranged the Aristotelian material or whether, in the same way as he has to be interposed between Horace and Aristotle, so others acted as intermediaries between Aristotle and Neoptolemus. Apart from many points of detail, two decisive changes account for the main features of Neoptolemus' literary criticism. One is the substitution of the large, formal, headings of the *Rhetoric* for the literary genres of the *Poetics*. The other is the generalizing process which adapted the rhetorical headings of diction and content

is no such evidence as regards Horace, and what Rostagni says about it in his edition of the *A.P.* Introd. LIX–LX does not provide it. Whether the same is true for Neoptolemus is quite another question.

to the field of poetry, in the form of ποίημα and ποίησις.[1] The question can then be asked again in a different way: did Neoptolemus himself rearrange the Aristotelian headings, and did he first use the triad which so impressed later critics? The question can be asked, but it cannot at present be answered with any degree of certainty. It has been tentatively suggested that this scheme was borrowed either from Aristotle's dialogue *De Poetis*[2] or from the Περὶ ποιητικῆς καὶ τῶν ποιητῶν of Heraclides of Pontus.[3] Both works have been discussed above.[4] What is known about the former does not accommodate anything like Neoptolemus' triad and nothing at all is known about the latter. A more popular choice has been Aristotle's successor, Theophrastus. Again, evidence is sadly lacking: the proof that has been given proves nothing.[5] Tangible likenesses with Theophrastus' stylistic doctrine would have been expected, but have not in fact emerged.[6]

[1] R. S. Crane and his colleagues have contrasted Aristotle's *Poetics*, which examines the nature of certain distinct types of poems, with rhetorical poetics, which reflects on poetry *generaliter* as one of the verbal arts; cf. R. S. Crane, *The Language of Criticism and the Structure of Poetry* (Univ. of Toronto Press, 1953), and *Critics and Criticism: Ancient and Modern*, ed. R. S. Crane (Chicago, 1952). But the distinction between words and content that governs 'rhetorical poetics' also has some standing in Aristotle's poetic criticism. And thus, *per contra*, I here set forth the difference between two ways of applying to poetry some rhetorical concepts, that of Aristotle and that of Neoptolemus. I have attempted to read the *Poetics* as a Hellenistic reader might have read it. This serves to bring out certain features of the *Poetics* which are not so brought out in the studies mentioned in this note.

[2] G. F. Else, *op. cit.* p. 43, n. 162.

[3] C. Jensen, *Philodemos*, etc., p. 102; *Herakleides*, etc., *SBPA* (1936), pp. 292–320; K. Barwick, *H*, LVII (1922), 40, 52.   [4] Above, pp. 126–7.

[5] F. Marx, *C. Lucilii Carminum Rel.* II, 130; Rostagni, *Aristotele e Aristotelismo*, etc., ch. v, *Scr. Min.* I, 188–233; *Appendice, Il Proemio Suetoniano De Poetis*, etc., ibid. pp. 238–54. Ardizzoni, *op. cit.* pp. 112–13, Dahlmann, *op. cit.* p. 126, and others consider the ascription probable but not provable. Antonietta Dosi seems to find it hard to decide whether she is contending for Theophrastean authorship or early Peripatetic origin. Cf. 'Sulle tracce della poetica di Teofrastro', *Rend. Istituto Lomb., Cl. di Lett.*, etc., Milan, XCIIII (1960), 618, for the former proposition, and *ibid.* 626 and 660 ff., for the latter.

[6] In particular there are no definite traces of Theophrastus' four 'virtues' of style. But even that is not fully conclusive since little is known about Theophrastus' poetics, apart from his *De elocutione*. Cf. O. Regenbogen, *R-E*, Supp. VII, col. 1532. Neither Rostagni nor A. Dosi, in the paper cited in the last note, sets out clearly what little can be known.

I believe then that without new information no useful assertions can be made. Instead of unfounded conclusions however a further question is prompted by the nature of the
material. Neoptolemus' treatise presupposes the rearrangement on a large scale of two or three Aristotelian works. It
appears that the professional teaching of the Lyceum was
based on these, or similar subsequent, works.[1] The question
may be asked whether a rearrangement on this scale is not
likely to be the result of the work of more than one teacher
over a prolonged period of teaching in the Lyceum. Men of
greater standing in the school than Neoptolemus are likely to
be involved. It seems more prudent therefore to consider the
problem as open until the time when more information comes
to hand. In the meanwhile the scale of these changes should
be noted. This, I think, makes it premature to ascribe to one
man what is not likely to be one man's work. It remains
convenient however to consider these changes in the setting
of Neoptolemus' treatise.

Comparison of Neoptolemus' work (so far as it can be considered to be known) and Aristotle's *Poetics* and *Rhetoric* has
revealed extensive changes in the fabric of the poetic treatise.
The Aristotelian order—literary genres prefaced by an
analysis of mimesis, and a speculative history of poetry—has
yielded to a simpler and more straightforward arrangement
by large, formal, subject headings and perhaps a preface on
the principles of unity and appropriateness. The impression
is that the *Rhetoric* was used to make a textbook out of an
Aristotelian treatise. The new approach to poetic subjects
greatly clarifies the involved Aristotelian procedure. But the
didactic gain involves a greater loss: the metaphysics of

---

[1] One Andromenides, apparently a literary critic and grammarian, propounded
the same triad, *poema–poesis–poeta*, if Jensen's plausible supplements in the papyri
of Philodemus are correct. Philodemus seems to set his doctrines beside those of
Crates (of Mallos). There are some traces of Peripatetic teaching. But the evidence
is too scanty for conclusions as to Andromenides' date and affiliations, particularly
in relation to Neoptolemus. Cf. Jensen, *op. cit.* p. 152; Rostagni, *Scr. Min.* I,
410–13; Dahlmann, *op. cit.* p. 125.

mimesis no longer disturbs literary criticism—but neither does it stimulate philosophical inquiry. There is a didactic gain also in Neoptolemus' tidy way of dealing with the exemplary character of tragedy. In the *Poetics* some of the qualities that Aristotle considered fundamental to poetry at large are discussed as qualities of tragedy, not of poetry.[1] Neoptolemus no longer makes tragedy the topic of the largest and most comprehensive section of his book. Style and content in poetry, or ποίημα and ποίησις, form the large and comprehensive divisions. Yet the gain must not be overstated, for (to judge from our evidence, which may be distorted) little fresh light is in fact shed on any poetry that is not dramatic or epic. The two large genres, and drama even more than epic, are still considered the chief kinds of poetry; literary criticism is largely based on them.[2]

Neoptolemus' approach is primarily practical and literary. This is borne out not only by the large number of precepts on style and subject-matter, but by the literary and unphilosophical tenor of the remains of his work. As a writer he is much concerned with the skill of writing. The domain of style comes into its own. It is made one of the two pillars of the system: ποίημα. The section on style is much enlarged. And it takes pride of place at the beginning of the technical portion of the book.

The study of character was traditional in the Lyceum—a field where 'ethics', in Aristotle's sense, impinges on poetics. This field is much extended by Neoptolemus. It suits the outlook of the man of letters. It has an immediate, practical, role to play for the novice. The Aristotelian provenance of ethos in poetical theory, its suitability for the writer, the use of the *Rhetoric* to supply character studies, the Hellenistic interest in ethos—all these are arguments in favour of the assumption that the importance assigned to character throughout the *Ars* was in fact a feature of Neoptolemus' work.

Very much the same is true for another Aristotelian sub-

[1] Above, pp. 86 ff.   [2] For the two exceptions in the *Ars*, see p. 146, n. 1.

ject—the history of literature. Here again the origins can be seen in the *Poetics*,[1] and teaching in the Lyceum must have stimulated the growth of that most fashionable of scholarly interests in Alexandria. Neoptolemus himself was not only a poet but also a grammarian in the Alexandrian sense of the word, a literary scholar. He was known as the author of works on epigrams, on witty sayings, on the vocabulary of the Phrygian language, and on glosses.[2] There are no fragments putting on record the same interest for his work on literary criticism. But there is enough comparative material to show that the passages in the *Ars* on Greek literary history reasonably assigned to Neoptolemus are in the Peripatetic and Alexandrian tradition.

In my last chapter I came to the conclusion that if the labels 'Alexandrian' and 'Aristotelian' are to be employed at all, then the character of his learned verse, his scholarship, and the stylistic refinement which he demands for poems small and large would make Neoptolemus an 'Alexandrian'; but his belief in poetry on a large scale, and in the organic unity of a large composition,[3] would make him an 'Aristotelian'. The present chapter has added more Alexandrian features and, on the other hand, has linked his literary criticism with Aristotle's *Poetics*. Neoptolemus' critical work, as far as it can be known, differed from the *Poetics* in scope and arrangement. Yet the literary critic appears to have accepted the philosopher's teachings on the large genres and the principle of unity. Judging from the kinds of poetry to which he attaches importance, one can only conclude that his use of the new poetic triad of ποίημα, ποίησις and ποιητής turns out to be a matter of presentation, not of substance. His literary criticism reasserted the Aristotelian pre-eminence of drama and epic against influential tendencies of his own day. It is true, he seems to have paid more attention to the smaller genres than Aristotle; but if Horace may be called in evidence again,

---

[1] Above, p. 132.   [2] Above, pp. 44, 47.
[3] Above, p. 74.

Neoptolemus found no room for them in the central portion of his book.[1]

Like Aristotle he offers an *apologia* for poetry. But whilst Aristotle desired to set the philosopher's mind at rest, Neoptolemus was less complicated and altogether more traditional. He addresses himself to a less discriminating audience— probably also a larger audience. The mixture of ψυχαγωγία and χρησιμολογεῖν which he prescribes is shown up as a moral commonplace beside Aristotle's theory.[2] There is perhaps one saving grace. Fashionable opinion in Neoptolemus' time was not wedded to χρησιμολογεῖν. What may seem a truism in the classical, Attic, setting, and even in the Aristotelian setting, was a controversial statement in the Hellenistic world. This sense of controversy is too easily forgotten.

Elsewhere in the final portion of the *Ars*, there is no such proof for Neoptolemic provenance as there is in the case of Horace's *miscuit utile dulci*. But the revised Aristotelianism which has been the distinctive mark in passages ascribed with certainty to Neoptolemus constitutes at any rate a tolerable case for the same ascription in other cases. Most matters that transcend the technical discussion seem to have been shifted to the section on the 'poet', the receptacle of generalities. If the intellectual tone does not seem to rise above a somewhat conventional moralizing, the tenor of contemporary literary output in the third century should be remembered. It must have imparted a certain oppositional force to anyone who tried to argue that the great literary forms of the classical past should still be attempted and that poetry should still make its traditional social impact.

Neoptolemus seems to have retained Aristotle's suggestion that a poet practised mimesis. But Aristotle held that the chief object of mimesis was καθόλου, the universal features of life. It is hard to tell how much of this notion survived in Neoptolemus' literary theory. Horace is here our only source;

---

[1] The *Ars* adds other genres to epic and drama in the section on style, 75–85, and in the historical context, 391–7. [2] Above, pp. 57, 129.

and when he enjoins *respicere exemplar vitae*, 'to scan the model of life',[1] he is commending no realism. But if Horace fairly restates Neoptolemus' position, the Hellenistic critic explained his demand in moralistic fashion as poetic teaching through ethical commonplaces and character drawing. This teaching will make the poet into a *doctus imitator*[2]—the counterpart of the *doctus poeta* of the Alexandrians, whose syllabus presumably dispensed with the *Socraticae chartae*.

This may well seem a conventional and moralistic attitude. But behind it lies an admirable if romantic ideal of the worth of poetry. This is revealed by the literary 'history' of the same, final, portion of Horace's poem; its ascription to Neoptolemus is at any rate not improbable.[3] There was a time in the earliest history of man when poetry revealed its true nature and fulfilled its true function. The ancient poets were the civilizers of mankind, the earliest priests, moral teachers, lawgivers, founders of cities. They were divine seers, *divini vates*.[4] And those who came after them still fulfilled a function in the life of the community: the verses of Homer and Tyrtaeus sharpened the courage of warriors, the didactic poets taught the right way of life, oracles were given in the form of verse, lyric poetry celebrated the exploits of the kings, and the playwrights entertained the rustic community during their holidays, after the long toil and exertion of their work. The simplicity and innocence of ancient music (we hear elsewhere) was sufficient to accompany the choruses of ancient drama and was in harmony with their severe style.[5] This charming picture of a golden, romantic, past of poetry and music projects into ancient history the desires of modern poets, whose audience was no longer the community at large and who would not have accepted that audience if it could have been

---

[1] *A.P.* 317; see above, p. 130; cf. pp. 103 ff. for other traces of Aristotle's notion of poetic universality.

[2] *Ibid.* 318; see above, p. 130.

[3] *Ibid.* 391–407; see above, pp. 132–4.   [4] *Ibid.* 400.

[5] *Ibid.* 202–19; it will be seen that the same bias colours the section on ancient music and that on ancient poetry.

theirs in their time. These complaints were first heard in the fifth century when poetry had begun to lose its traditional place in the life of the community.[1] The protests continued with renewed vigour when that process had advanced much further in the early Hellenistic age. The narrow and conventional features of this view of the matter cannot escape notice. But if the view was traditionalist, the tradition at any rate was that of the great Greek classics; and there can be no doubt that the classical forms of poetry no longer fulfilled the function which they had when they were produced, whilst the new, Hellenistic, forms appealed on different grounds to a much smaller audience of *conoscenti*. Accordingly there was some sense in the contention that the case for poetry on the large, classical, scale could not easily be divorced from the moral and social conditions of a more archaic civilization. Hence the moral and social implications when the writer wishes to broaden the basis of contemporary poetry, and demands a larger canvas for his *doctus imitator* than the *poetae docti* were willing to use. Hence, too, the somewhat restrictive and conventional atmosphere that now comes to surround the freer Aristotelian principles, notably in the precepts designed to preserve the purity of classical drama.[2]

In the last two chapters various aspects of Neoptolemus' literary work have been discussed. Much consideration has been given to the revised form of Aristotle's teaching which must have appeared in his poetics. For us he represents the only survey of the whole field of Peripatetic literary criticism after Aristotle which is, albeit indirectly and partially, preserved. In this however he may only have summed up the work of one or two generations of Aristotelian philosophers. He is perhaps more remarkable for combining the Peripatetic approach to literary criticism with the Alexandrian pursuits of scholarship and the writing of learned verse. This, as the

[1] The passage from Aristophanes' *Frogs* cited above, p. 132, is a characteristic example.
[2] *A.P.* 179 ff., above, p. 117.

last chapter has shown, adds a new item to our map of the Alexandrian literary scene. But easily the most outstanding feature of his work is that it raised the controversial issue of classical poetry in the Hellenistic world.

There is a temptation to magnify Neoptolemus' importance simply because he represents a point of view which, according to our scanty information, is not much represented in the literary setting of the third century. It seems no small matter that a poet who produced learned poems of the Alexandrian type and professed Alexandrian scholarship should yet have maintained that the function of poetry had not changed, that poets should be the teachers of their cities, and that the classical forms of drama and epic should not only be admired but were the ποίησις still worth attempting. This would probably be overstating his importance. No drama of that time survives that would bear out these claims. But it is known that at any rate in the early third century new playwrights received much acclaim and enjoyed the royal patronage of the new monarchy. The poets of the 'Pleiad' under Ptolemy Philadelphus must have shown just the same contradictory features which are now noticed in Neoptolemus. Lycophron and Alexander Aetolus were known as authors of celebrated tragedies, but equally professed the most learned scholarship of the Alexandrian Museum.[1] Attic New Comedy was still contemporary poetry. There was enough interest in Satyric drama to encourage experiment: the activities of Sositheus may well show some of the realities even behind what seems mere theory in the *Ars*.[2] Probably then Neoptolemus was rather one of many who had not seen so clearly as Callimachus[3] that the ethos of classical poetry was not to be

---

[1] Wilamowitz, *Hellenist. Dich.*, I, 166–9.

[2] This has, I believe, been established by K. Latte's paper on 'Frühhellenistische Spuren im Pisonenbrief', *H*, LX (1925), 1–13; see above, p. 119, n. 5.

[3] I have argued above, pp. 45, 52, that Neoptolemus' precise date is unknown. It may now be added that his classical taste well suits the time of the Alexandrian Pleiad. His link with the Lyceum also suits the period of the first two Ptolemies when the Aristotelian school exerted some influence: *CQ*, XL (1946), 11; Wilamowitz, *Hellenist. Dicht.*, I, 160 ff.

had for the asking. Such is the Alexandrianism which he represents and which we cannot find so fully represented anywhere else. It is a fair guess that more than two centuries later, in the Augustan setting, for all its differences, Horace had some use both for his Alexandrian refinements and the ideals of his Aristotelian criticism. For Horace paid him a compliment that is worth remembering: *congessit praecepta Neoptolemi* τοῦ Παριανοῦ *de arte poetica, non quidem omnia sed eminentissima.*

PART III

HORACE AS A LITERARY CRITIC:
THE LITERARY SATIRES AND
EPISTLES

CHAPTER I

PRELIMINARIES AND THE LITERARY SATIRES

PRELIMINARIES

The label 'literary critic' conceals an ambiguity. For there are two types of critic so different that all they have in common is talk about literature or poetry. One type is expert as a critic but (to bring the matter down to poetry) not a poet. He writes upon poetry, but the 'making' of verse is not his chosen activity. Aristotle is the exemplar of a philosopher who philosophized on poetry although, in the happy phrase of an eighteenth-century critic, he never (or rarely) meddled with it.[1] Philosophers are joined by scholars and rhetoricians, essayists and men of letters—some of them poets *manqués*. The other type is the poet-critic, who is expert as a poet but not primarily as a critic. He is the poet pronouncing on poetry, in the sense of Byron's saying, 'Every poet his own Longinus'. Callimachus and Horace are ancient examples. Many later poet-critics come to mind—Boileau, Dryden, Pope, Schiller, Coleridge, Matthew Arnold, not to mention our contemporaries.

The Aristotelian view is the external view—external, that is, to the poet. The critic describes the impression made by poetry; hence his criticism has a certain wholeness and impartiality. On the other hand being poetically unprofessional it may be mistaken on technical matters. It is essentially the reader's or listener's view, writ large and systematized. Since poetry is not only made but read or listened to, the critic's view is justified on these grounds. Contrariwise when the poet

---

[1] John Dennis, *Reflections Critical and Satyrical*, etc. (1711), 'There have been Criticks, who have been approved by all the World, who never meddled with poetry'.

becomes a critic he is likely to be a partisan, for he tends to commend the poets and poems that have stimulated his own writing, just as he tends to dispraise those poets and poems that have failed to stimulate it. His view is internal and professional; it reveals his own creative and one-sided nature. Its value and justification lies in its professional one-sidedness.

At times however even poets feel moved to critical thought that is more objective and coherent. Such poets approach the vista of the professional critics on the other side of the divide. Coleridge's *Biographia Literaria*, for example, although clearly the autobiographical work of a poet has some measure of the systematic aim of professional criticism. These distinctions have an obvious bearing on Horace's literary criticism. Any writer on the *Ars Poetica* will ignore them at his peril. The failure to observe them has proved the undoing of many.

Horace had been a poet-critic almost as long as he had been writing as a poet. His criticism was fragmentary, *critique d'occasion*. It was prompted by his experience as a craftsman, and limited by the restricted aims of each of his critical writings. At one point of his career however he produced a work with a larger critical purpose. The work was the *Ars Poetica*, and its purpose was to present a view of the whole of what he considered great poetry. This was a large subject, and to deal with it a framework of thought was needed. When Coleridge decided to formulate his theory of poetic imagination he employed neo-Platonic philosophy as a framework. When Horace decided to present his view of great poetry he too employed a philosophical framework. In his case it was not Platonic but Aristotelian. He took it where he found it ready-made, in the poetics of Neoptolemus of Parium, and adapted it to his own sentiments and opinions. The *Ars Poetica* agrees with the literary *Satires* and *Epistles* in its personal and contemporary complexion; in spite of the Aristotelian and Neoptolemic provenance of its basic thought, no one but Horace could have written the work: it is unmistakably personal. But it differs from the literary *Satires* and *Epistles* in one regard. In the *Ars* Horace is not only looking at some select aspects of poetry as he is in the other works, but he is bringing his personal opinions to bear on a consistent, and in a sense systematic, critical philosophy. A just assessment of the *Ars* is not therefore promoted by the observation that the purpose of that work is 'practical'.[1] The label 'practical' here describes the species 'poet-critic'; it does not describe the particular work of the poet-critic Horace, known as *Ars Poetica*. For this work shares the practical character with the literary criticism of Horace and other poet-critics; but in addition the *Ars* has a 'theoretical' purpose and layout to which there is no analogy whatever in the rest of Horace's critical work.

I have asserted that the *Ars* combines two qualities which are still too often dissociated—personal and traditional. Horace's *exemplaria* were Greek and were ancient. So far from detracting from his personal contribution, a Greek and an ancient form seems to have been felt to lend to it the weight and dignity of a great tradition. Like other ancient writers, and in fact more than most, he chooses to put in a traditional form what he feels most strongly about. That feature is specially marked in the *Ars*. This poem calls for elucidation twice over: the reader must be made aware of the personal growing-point of Horace's thought; but he must also be made aware of the traditional cloak in which the poet clothes his ideas.[2]

---

[1] In the course of an instructive appraisal of the literary criticism produced by Roman poets, E. Fraenkel (*Horace*, p. 125), has the following remarks about Horace. 'But whether late or early, all his writings on problems of poetics, while drawing on a large store of theories, served an eminently practical purpose.' There is a footnote: 'This fact is often misunderstood, and in particular the *Epistula ad Pisones*, misnamed *De arte poetica*, has had to suffer from this misunderstanding.' The *Ars* may have had to suffer from this misunderstanding half a century ago. The misunderstanding nowadays current is precisely the opposite—a tendency to underestimate its theoretical purpose and character.

[2] 'What he does is to express his own thought in the form and phrase of his predecessors; so that to his teaching may therefore be attached a personal and an original value.' Thus J. W. H. Atkins, *Lit. Crit. in Antiquity*, ii, 98, as regards Horace.

Hence the temptation to stress unduly either the one side or the other. In spite of the Greek provenance of most of the doctrines of the *Ars*, there are few in which the Roman, the contemporary, and the personal aspects are not equally obvious.[1] Indeed, considering how little is known about the by-paths of the Augustan literary scene, it would be exceedingly hazardous to infer too much to the contrary if in a few cases the material is insufficient to prove a contemporary application.[2] With this proviso I propose to examine both the personal and systematic *motifs* of the *Ars*, and relate them to Horace's poetic criticism elsewhere. It should then appear whether I have justly asserted that the *Ars* differs in its critical purpose from the rest of his literary essays.[3]

THE FIRST LITERARY SATIRE

Apart from the *Ars*, and apart from occasional pronouncements in the *Odes* and elsewhere, three of Horace's satires and three of his epistles are devoted to poetic criticism. *Satires*, I, 4, I, 10, and II, 1, poems of the thirties B.C., contain his early criticism. His subject, the nature of satire, is restricted in purpose. But by implication he deals with larger questions and it is striking how much of his mature criticism is foreshadowed in these early works.

In his first literary essay, *Sat.* I, 4, he raises two subjects with which every poet-critic is likely to deal: What constitutes a good poem? How do the poet, his contemporaries, and his predecessors, measure up to that standard? The poem presupposes that certain satires of Horace had attracted notice and, in some critical quarters, notoriety. They had been attacked for both their form and their content, and Horace

---

[1] It was O. Immisch who particularly attempted to elucidate these two aspects in his book on *Horazens Epistel über die Dichtkunst* (1932).

[2] For satyric drama, the most controversial of these cases, see pp. 119, n. 5, 228.

[3] This however is not how the difference is commonly described; note for example D. M. Pippidi, *Rev. Clasica*, XI–XII (1939–40), 132, A. Ardizzoni, *op. cit.*, L. Ferrero, *La 'Poetica' e le Poetiche di Orazio*, Turin, 1953.

defends them against both charges.[1] Neither the charges nor the case for the defence are put forward in pedestrian fashion. In the imaginative manner which he favours, Horace makes straight for what literary doctrine taught was the ultimate model of Roman satire—old Attic comedy. We may feel that there is little point in that doctrine.[2] It was based on three assumed similarities. Both satire and old comedy were humorous, both were in verse, and both censured human frailty or vice by pointing to real persons by name, *notare* being the Latin word for the activities of the censor, ὀνομαστὶ κωμῳδεῖν the Greek term for the activities of the old comic poets of Athens:

> Eupolis atque Cratinus Aristophanesque poetae
> atque alii quorum comoedia prisca virorumst. (*Sat.* I, 4, 1–2)

Next comes their subject: moral censure levelled freely, and by name, at known persons:

> siquis erat dignus describi quod malus ac fur
> quod moechus foret aut sicarius aut alioqui
> famosus, multa cum libertate notabant.   (3–5)

Lucilius entirely depended on the Greek model; he is said to have changed only the metre.

---

[1] I reject then G. L. Hendrickson's contention that this poem is not a defence on his own behalf in order to establish the milder tenor of his own satire, but a protest against the harsh personal satirizing practised by Lucilius, cf. *AJP*, xxi (1900), 121–41. I accept the view that Horace is here offering a defence against literary attacks. This view is commonly held, but the contrary arguments still prevented an unbiased reading of the poem, and deserved to be as fully exploded as N. Rudd has done in *AJP*, lxxvi (1955), 165–75, and in *CQ*, xlix (1955), 142–56. I should not however go so far as to say that the poem needs to be studied primarily in terms of contemporary feuds (Rudd, *CQ*, *loc. cit.* 148–9). It needs to be studied equally in terms of the poet's own aspirations.

[2] The Romans however assented: *mire autem per haec origo saturae ostenditur*, remarks Porphyrion, commenting on *Sat.* I, 4, 1. Varro felt likewise—and perhaps it was he who established the link between Roman satire and Old Attic comedy; for the evidence see the paper cited below, p. 193, n. 4. Lucilius himself may have said that his *notare* resembled that of the old Attic writers of comedy, but Rudd rightly notes that the remains of Lucilius' work do not bear this out, cf. *Mnemos.* ser. iv, x (1957), 320.

What then is the point in recalling this doctrine? To the older critics the (partly assumed) similarity would suggest a Greek poetic form successfully transplanted to Rome by Lucilius. Thus they would assert a literary tradition. Horace too asserts that tradition, for Lucilius as much as for himself; and he makes use of it for his own, defensive, purposes. But he also dissociates Lucilius from the tradition. In his humour and his unerring eye for moral faults Lucilius evinces the qualities of the genre. But in his style he does not; he is a harsh composer:

> facetus,
> emunctae naris, durus componere versus.[1] (7–8)

Horace then had another reason for recalling the doctrine of the critics. It allowed him to distinguish Lucilius from his (assumed) exemplars. In Lucilian satire content and style were not sufficiently on a par. And that hints at the poetic stature of the old Greek masters from whom he is anxious to dissociate the stylist Lucilius. It also hints at potentialities of the satiric genre that were not as yet realized.[2]

Note too the manner in which the stylistic problem is raised. It is not raised in general terms but by way of 'practical criticism'; a poet, Lucilius, is censured for his formal inadequacy. Nevertheless the satirical wording scarcely conceals a personal conviction of some generality and width.

[1] H. Rackham suggested that *durus componere versus* applied equally to the old Attic masters as to Lucilius (*CR*, xxx (1916), 224)—'*and* (not *but*) harsh in his composition'. This suggestion was happily forgotten until Rudd resuscitated it, though in rather gingerly fashion, *CQ*, n.s. v (1955), 156. *Durus componere versus* would call for a counterpart in lines 1–2, just as *facetus* and *emunctae naris* have such counterparts in 1–5. The counterpart is clearly *poetae* (1), which corresponds to *componere versus* (8); *durus* cannot be so paralleled. To make it parallel, Rackham must give the phrase a gratuitous twist: Lucilius, he maintains, carried the (supposed) Attic roughness of versification *to excess*—which is not what Horace is saying. On the other hand an unnecessary emphasis has often been placed on *poetae* (1) as though it meant 'true poets'. This is not the case: cf. Rudd, *op. cit.* pp. 154–6. In this poem at any rate the exemplary character of Attic style is only implied; it is made explicit in the tenth satire.

[2] This is about as far as a contemporary reader of the fourth satire could have got, even without knowing the (later) tenth satire. It is not necessary 'to read the tenth into the fourth satire' in order to take Horace's hints in the fourth.

nam fuit hoc vitiosus: in hora saepe ducentos,
ut magnum, versus dictabat stans pede in uno;
cum flueret lutulentus, erat quod tollere velles;
garrulus atque piger scribendi ferre laborem,
scribendi recte; nam ut multum nil moror.[1]   (9–13)

The conviction giving rise to this criticism has been obvious
to many readers. Horace is censuring Lucilius because he
himself approves of a strenuous poetic technique—*scribendi
ferre laborem,* | *scribendi recte.* Redundancy and slipshod
writing are poetic failings, *vitia.*[2] They are taken seriously
enough to nullify Lucilius' claim to the full poetic honours to
which the humour and the content of his satires entitled him.
Labor scribendi recte is an Alexandrian ideal although others
than Alexandrians may profess it. That the Alexandrian ideal
is in Horace's mind is rendered likely by his using a metaphor
which Callimachus had applied to poetic style. Commentators rightly note that the criticism of Lucilius' 'muddy style',

cum flueret lutulentus, erat quod tollere velles,

recalls the Alexandrian master's skit on the style of a large
epic composition: 'Large is the current of the Assyrian river,
but on its waters it drags along many bits of earth and much
refuse.'[3]

It may be of some significance that Horace expresses himself in a manner reminiscent of Callimachus. However there

---

[1] The phrase *ut magnum* may, as Heinze remarked, point to this kind of claim
on the part of Lucilius.

[2] *Vitiosus* indicates technical shortcomings. The term is opposed to *virtus*,
technical sufficiency; it was used in this sense in rhetoric and literary criticism, for
example *Ad Her.* i, 11, 'nunc ne quando vitioso exordio utamur, quae vitia
vitanda sint docebo'; Cic. *De Or.* iii, 103, 'vitiosissimus orator'. Poetic *error* is
contrasted with *virtus* at *A.P.* 308, 'quo virtus, quo ferat error'.

[3] Callimachus, *Hymn to Apollo*, 108. At iii f. Callimachus contrasts and
commends the purity of a small spring. For the metaphors see W. Wimmel, *H*,
Einzelschr. xvi (1960), 222–33. The metaphor of the stream recurs in various
ways at *Sat.* i, 1, 59 and at i, 10, 62, but also at *Ep.* ii, 2, 120 (below, p. 188, n. 4),
and at *Odes*, iv, 2, 5, where its tenor is laudatory. Horace's criticism of Lucilius'
lutulentum was controversial in his own time, as *Satires* 4 and 10 show. That it was still
controversial a century later may be gathered from Quintilian's judicious rejection
of Horace's phrase, *I.O.* x, 1, 94.

is no trace of Callimachus when Horace deals with criticisms of the content of satire, Lucilian or Horatian. He assumes that the subject-matter of satiric verse is moral. In a very engaging passage he claims to satirize the world not from malice but as a consequence of his father's moral teaching.

> liberius si
> dixero quid, si forte iocosius, hoc mihi iuris
> cum venia dabis: insuevit pater optimus hoc me,
> ut fugerem exemplis vitiorum quaeque notando.   (103–6)

His father's naïve 'exemplifying' was *notare* practised by the light of nature: that, Horace is saying humorously, put him on the way to the artistic *notare* of satire which Lucilius had practised before him.

Satire needs to attack moral faults; satire needs to aspire to a high degree of formal finish. This combination is sufficiently unusual in the Hellenistic and Roman scene to require some comment. That the poet's main business should be with words and their elaboration seems common sense. Yet it was of interest to practitioners rather than to their critics. The demand is not found in Aristotle's *Poetics*, where formal features are assigned a lowish place.[1] Although this may have changed in the subsequent history of the Lyceum, it was the Alexandria of Callimachus that insisted on formal elaboration to the exclusion of other demands. The setting in which Callimachus placed this demand was that of the small, highly-wrought poem; and with it there goes a rejection of the large form, and the heroic tone and serious content, of the traditional epic as a vehicle for modern poetic effort.[2] The intimate connexion between a modern poetic technique and 'small' poetic forms persisted when the views of Callimachus came to inspire the young Roman poets of the mid-century before our era. Nothing is known for certain about Horace's views on Catullus, Calvus, and their friends. Horace's, and indeed Virgil's, use of certain Catullan phrases caused some critics

[1] Above, pp. 86, 144.
[2] Cf. 'Callimachus and Aristotle', etc., *CQ*, XL (1946), 11–26.

half-a-century or so ago to deny the older assumption of an
antagonism between the two generations of poets. This has
been contradicted, not without justification.[1] For the impression which Catullan phrases made on Horace or Virgil is one
thing; the aims and aspirations of two groups of poets, belonging to two successive generations, are quite another. The
evidence of Horace's first literary satire is limited but clear-
cut. The Callimachean principle of painstaking poetic workmanship is no longer tied to the advocacy of the small
Alexandrian forms. Satire is not viewed as a small poetic
genre whose form is all-important but whose content does not
matter. For better or worse, poetry is assigned an ulterior
purpose; satire has a moral mission. The Callimachean ideal
of poetic technique was to exercise Horace for the whole of his
career as a poet and critic. The first literary satire shows it
severed from its Alexandrian context and linked with moral
and poetic aspirations which would have been as distasteful
to its first advocates as to the poets of the preceding generation. The subsequent satires and epistles will tell a similar
story.

The reader of the *Ars Poetica* will be impressed not only by
what the first literary satire claims but by what it disclaims.
The attack on satiric *poets* gives Horace a chance to pronounce
not only on the virtues of satiric verse but on *poetry*—which,
to him, is a different matter. It appears that he distinguishes
between good verse and great verse: the latter he names
poetry. To himself he begrudges the name of poet.

> primum ego me illorum, dederim quibus esse poetis,
> excerpam numero. (*Sat.* I, 4, 39–40)

He begrudges it as long as he writes satires, *sermones*, talk in
verse.
> neque si qui scribat uti nos
> sermoni propiora, putes hunc esse poetam. (41–2)

---

[1] Cf. Brooks Otis, 'Horace and the Elegists', *TAPA*, LXXVI (1945), 177, citing the
earlier literature.

If here he denies himself what some of his lyric verse shows
him to care for most—poetic grandeur, the part of the bard
and the priest of the Muses—then clearly there is a larger
conception of poetry in his mind.

> neque enim concludere versum
> dixeris esse satis. (40-1)

The dignity of the name of poet, *nominis huius honorem* (44),
should be granted only to the writer of verse who has a certain
cast of mind and whose language attains a certain level of
style. The sort of mind that is required he describes variously
as genius, *ingenium*; inspired mind, *mens divinior* (43), passionate
spirit, *acer spiritus*, and force (*vis*) (46). Truly poetic utterance
is said to come from a mouth that will speak forth great things,
os magna sonaturum (43-4); words and matter, *verba* and *res*, will
then have the force which critics found wanting in certain
kinds of verse (45-8).[1]

These lines put in the language of ancient literary criticism
certain critical notions of the poet Horace. They show that
even at the time of this early satire he envisaged a wider field
of poetic production and a larger poetic purpose. They show,
too, that he employs critical doctrines when they bear out his
own aims. The Aristotelian school of criticism taught that
metre does not make a poet but that other qualities are
fundamental.[2] Some Greek critics held that comedy was not
a poetic genre because of its proximity to colloquial speech.
In a passage of Cicero this opinion is coupled with the
Peripatetic view as regards metre: the prose of a Plato or
Democritus may be called poetic on account of its inspiration
and the splendour of its style whereas the verse of comedy is
less worthy of that name on account of its flat and colloquial

---

[1] This defines in the first place the poet's endowments, as J. F. D'Alton, *Roman
Lit. Theory*, p. 387, n. 2, remarks. But *magna*, for an ancient critic, involves doubtless *l'épopée, la tragédie et la haute lyrique* (Lejay, on line 44)—the 'genres' in which
such poetic endowments could find adequate expression.

[2] Ar. *Poet.* 1, 1447*b* 15; 9, 1451*b* 27. Cf. above, p. 121, n. 3.

speech.[1] Horace the satirist too refuses to be called a poet, and he links that refusal with the debates among certain critics (*quidam*, 45) who doubted the truly poetic character of comedy on account of its colloquial speech (*sermo merus*, 48). The matter is illustrated by a comparison between the speech of an angry father in a comedy and a lofty passage from Ennius' *Annals*. The former, however emotional, would be prose but for its metre; the latter may be turned into prose and yet retain *disiecti membra poetae* (62). By the same token satire must be judged pedestrian.

Horace clearly attaches much importance to this disquisition. His subject is satire and on a narrow interpretation this subject does not call for a lengthy discussion of 'poetry'. A narrow interpretation however would be a false interpretation. This discussion does help to illustrate the nature of satire, by showing what it is not. Thus the discussion defines more clearly the limits that should be placed on the criticism of Lucilius, and on the potentialities of Horace's own genre.

These remarks on the nature of poetry call for a further observation. They are instructive because they are extreme and one-sided—a characteristic which they share with many such pronouncements of Horace and other poet-critics.[2] His definition of *poetry* as impassioned and elevated utterance is open to certain objections. It applies to *some kinds of poetry* more than to others and might exclude some of the most 'poetic' odes of Horace which are neither impassioned nor elevated. It would be misleading if it were accepted without the qualification of other pronouncements equally partial. It has a polemic point directed against certain sets and

---

[1] Cic. *Or.* 67, cited by Lejay, *op. cit.* p. 102, and Kiessling and Heinze, in their notes on the passage of Horace. The doctrine suits the Lyceum but its originator is unknown. Wilamowitz makes a guess at Theophrastus.

[2] J. F. D'Alton's remarks on Wordsworth's theory of poetic language are a case in point: *op. cit.* p. 387. He censures Wordsworth for overstatements, 'theories born of reaction' and 'carried to excess'. But he does not notice that Horace's theory of poetry shows similar features.

coteries which thought poetry to be playing with words in verse, but suspected such a concept as poetic greatness.

Horace takes great pains not to seem to commit himself unduly to these views. He reports judgements that deny the poetic nature of comedy and satire; yet in the end he leaves the question open and does not fully accept the strictures.[1] He defines the nature of great poetry; yet the writer of pedestrian *sermones* does not aspire to that honourable title.[2] He defines the moral and educative function of satire; yet he is not willing to exercise it. Why should he slander his fellows, and publish libellous satires? He is not writing for publication:[3] at most he will read his work to some friends.[4] Such at any rate is the fiction of this early satire. When there is leisure he passes the time scribbling away for his own amusement—

> haec ego mecum
> conpressis agito labris: ubi quid datur oti
> inludo chartis.
> (137–9)

Thus the argument is resolved into uncommitted irony. Cheerfulness breaks in and the sting is taken out of the possible charge that the writer of satire also lays down its laws, or that the same Horace is on the bench and in the dock.

The first literary satire lays the foundation for all of Horace's literary criticism. It is remarkable for the inventiveness and flexibility which enabled the poet to bring together so many critical themes into the (somewhat tightly packed) poetic unity of a *sermo* of some 140 lines. The remaining two literary satires were written a few years later. The critical basis remains but the purpose is more specific in each case. Only the points that amplify the earlier position here call for comment.

---

[1] *Sat.* I, 4, 63, *alias iustum sit necne poema.*
[2] *Ibid.* 42.   [3] *Ibid.* 71.
[4] *Ibid.* 73.

Preliminaries and the Literary Satires

THE SECOND LITERARY SATIRE

The tenth Satire pronounces on the stylistic problems that the earlier poem raised but scarcely discussed. It offers a reply to those critics who had attacked the new satires and had defended Lucilius against what they considered Horace's aspersions.[1] It also introduces a concept that dominates the Hellenistic and Roman literary setting—I mean the concept of imitation. The wider subject is the sufficiency of satiric style, the narrower contrasts the 'imitator' (Horace) with the 'inventor' (Lucilius). In the economy of the poem the two subjects are closely related.

The narrower argument fills the central portion. Horace is blamed for carping at the founder of his own genre. The reply is that working in an established genre the younger poet is *inventore minor*;[2] but this judgement does not involve the quality of his writing. Lucilius is more polished than 'the crew of archaic poets',[3] yet he requires the 'file'. He has established the genre but has not grasped its potentialities.

The poem leads off with the wider topic of technical sufficiency. Condone the quality of Lucilius' verse and you might as well admire Laberius' mimes as *pulchra poemata*. A list of technical demands is then presented[4] in which

---

[1] The literary controversy has been frequently discussed; cf. the bibliography. N. Rudd reviews the contributions of Hendrickson and others, *Mnemos.* ser. iv, x (1957), 319–36; his own paper concentrates (a little too much, I think) on the terms *libertas* and *facetus*.

[2] *Sat.* i, 10, 48.

[3] *Ibid.* 67, *poetarum seniorum turba*. The archaic poets need not be identical with the *rudis et Graecis intacti carminis auctor*, indicated in the preceding line, cf. Leo, *Gesch. Röm. Lit.* i, 424, n. 1, and Fraenkel, *op. cit.* p. 131, n. 3, who cites an explanation of line 66 that accommodates the theorizing of *Satires* 4 and 10—I mean K. L. Nipperdey's *Opuscula* (1877), p. 508. Lucilius is an *inventor*, but what he achieved was to Romanize a (supposedly) Greek genre. H. Wagenvoort, *Donum natal. Schrijnen* (1929), pp. 749–50, suggests that Horace himself had been attacked as *rudis et Graecis intacti carminis auctor*. If so, that is not implied in the context.

[4] Lucilian satire lacks the variety of qualities that distinguish Old Attic comedy. Horace demands that variety. His list is based on the assumed resemblance between the two genres and it could not be recognized for what it was until scholars paid attention to ancient Greek opinion on Greek comedy. This was done by Leo,

Horace defines the style as much as the attitude of the satirist.[1] The Greek model is named which the fourth satire had introduced. But what remained an implication in the earlier satire is made explicit in the later: old Attic comedy represents poetic perfection so far as it is attainable in this genre.[2] Lucilius did not attain these standards. Some modern poets attempt to attain them. If Lucilius lived now he would perfect his craftsmanship.[3]

At this point discussion turns to the modern standards of poetry. The opponents whom he ridicules are lay figures. But what he says about them seems to hint that they were contemporary followers of Catullus and Calvus—modernists after yesterday's fashion. If these men were among the defenders of Lucilius it would be instructive to find the latter-day modernists taking up the cudgels for an archaic

H, xxiv (1889), 67 ff. (*Ausgew. Kl. Schr.* i, 283 ff.), with regard to *Sat.* i, 4, and by Hendrickson, *AJP*, xxi (1900), 125, n. 1, and *Studies...Gildersleeve* (1902), p. 153, n. 2, with regard to both satires. The ancient theories are set out in G. Kaibel's *Com. Gr. Frag.* (1899), 1 ff.; some extracts are printed in Heinze's commentary.

[1] The meaning of lines 7–15 is not easily seized. Horace is applying the traditional theories mentioned in the last note, but he is applying them in a personal manner. Rudd, *Mnemos., loc. cit.* p. 334, abandons the topic of style after line 10—too soon, I believe. Lines 11 ff. do concern the 'spirit' of satire; but that surely does not exclude attention to the way in which a 'satiric attitude' is expressed; cf. Fraenkel, *op. cit.* p. 129. Prolixity was one of Lucilius' faults; hence *brevitas* (always a Horatian ideal) is enjoined with especial emphasis and with regard to all the types of satiric speech. Like some of the older editors, for example Orelli, I take 'the parts of the rhetor and poet' (12) to pick up the *sermo tristis* of 11, and 'the part of the civil man' (13) to pick up the *sermo iocosus* of 11. The restricted territory assigned to 'the poet' is in keeping with the satirist's renunciation of full poetic honours at *Sat.* i, 4, 42; satire is a mixed genre. In sum, the demand is for a shifting and flexible mean between serious and humorous criticism, which well describes Horatian satire.

[2] *Sat.* i, 10, 16–17, '*illi scripta quibus comoedia prisca viris est* | hoc stabant, hoc sunt imitandi'. Commentators have no doubt that this passage echoes the first literary satire, i, 4, 2, *atque alii quorum comoedia prisca virorum est.* Yet Lejay and (if I understand him rightly) Heinze accept Porphyrion's erroneous explanation: the old playwrights are brought in here because their example showed that humour has often a greater force than sharp opposition (14–15). Fraenkel (*op. cit.* p. 129) is surely more convincing: 'they fulfil the stylistic demands which have just been formulated'.

[3] *Ibid.* 67–71, in particular 68, *hoc nostrum...in aevum.* The stylistic requirements of the poet's own time are a new feature of the poem. They remain a feature of Horace's literary criticism.

satirist. Horace objects not to their tastes but to their narrow tastes. Old Attic comedy provides the sound standard of workmanship for satirists; but these defenders of Lucilius have not read the old masters; they can only recite Catullus and Calvus.[1]

If the standards of these men do not then suit 'our age', *nostrum aevum,* what are the standards that do? Horace now appeals to the group of poets who share his views. The same ideals which inspire Fundanius, Pollio, Varius, and Virgil also inspire Horace (40–9); he is attempting 'to write better' than others who have taken up Lucilius' genre.[2] The exacting standards of the new poets require a discriminating and critical public. Who is to judge perfection? The question occurs time and again in Horace's critical writing. His answer, given at the close of the poem, by way of a parting shot, is twofold. He rejects as readers the *soi-disant* 'moderns' —Hermogenes and his friends—whom he describes as fashion-mongers and devoid of judgement.[3] Their approval would bring easy popularity. Rather he would be content with the approval of a few readers who can judge what they read. The list contains three of the four poets whom he had mentioned earlier—Pollio, Varius, and Virgil. It also contains Maecenas and Messalla, and other men whose connexion with the circles of Pollio, Messalla, and Maecenas is either

---

[1] *Ibid.* 17–19, 'quos [the old Attic writers of comedy] neque pulcher | Hermogenes unquam legit neque simius iste | nil praeter Calvum et doctus cantare Catullum'. Whether we are entitled to make use of the much-discussed eight lines that two groups of codices prefix to the beginning of this satire depends on one's assessment of the evidence. I regard the passage as spurious but contemporary; for its style, see Fraenkel, *H*, LXVIII (1933), 392–9. It shows a major *littérateur* of the time, Valerius Cato (*summum grammaticum, summum poetam,* as Furius Bibaculus called him), to have had some part in this dispute. But Horace prefers to thrust at some of the minor figures. The conjunction of archaic and (outmoded) modernistic tastes does not however depend on these spurious lines but on the genuine part of the poem. With this proviso the conclusions of Hendrickson, at *CP*, XI (1916) and XII (1917), may retain some validity also for those who like myself are not persuaded by his case for the Horatian origin of *Lucili quam sis mendosus.*

[2] *Ibid.* 46–8, 'hoc erat, experto frustra Varrone Atacino | atque quibusdam aliis, *melius quod scribere possem,* | inventore minor'.

[3] *Ibid.* 78–80, 90–1, cf. 17–19.

certain or likely.[1] The group of the true *conoscenti* therefore overlaps with the group of the true poets; what links them in Horace's mind is their high poetic standards.

Lucilius put on record the kind of readers he wished for. He wanted them to be neither wholly inexpert nor unduly expert: *Persium non curo legere, Laelium Decumum volo.* Cicero who cites the line explains that the latter was a gentleman of some literary erudition but much beneath the level of the learned C. Persius.[2] Lucilius then claims to write for what might be called the *homme moyen lettré*, and that implies the expectation of a large reading public.[3] Horace pitches his demand both higher and lower. He still maintains he is not writing for publication.[4] A good poet must be content with a few readers.[5] But they must be the right readers—*doctos...et amicos*.[6] From his list it appears that they are so to say the Persiuses and Scipios of his age. There are many features in the *poetae docti* of the last generation which Horace condemned. *Doctrina* however he did not condemn; he demanded it. Now it is probable that in drawing up lists of desirable and undesirable readers, in a poem concerned with Lucilius, Horace was deliberately adapting a Lucilian procedure.[7] If this be so, what is the point of the adaptation? Horace (it has been suggested) is 'paying an elegant compliment to the same Lucilius whose shortcomings he has just been criti-

---

[1] *Sat.* I, 10, 81–90.

[2] Cic. *De Or.* II, 25; Lucilius, fr. 593 (Marx). In what is likely to be a different passage Lucilius even claimed to write for readers whose Latinity was as dubious as that of the people of Tarentum, Consentia, and Sicily, rather than for Scipio Africanus or Rutilius Rufus; so Cic. *De Fin.* I, 7, *quorum* [i.e. Scipionis et Rutili] *ille iudicium reformidans Tarentinis ait se et Consentinis et Siculis scribere* and the notes of Madvig *ad l.* and Marx, fr. 594. It is still unknown how a similar, third, passage, fr. 595 (Marx), is related to 593.

[3] Lejay justly contrasts the Lucilian and Horatian attitudes, *op. cit.* p. 101. He refrained however from employing the phrase used above in the text.

[4] *Sat.* I, 10, 37–9, cf. above, p. 164.   [5] 74.

[6] 87; the claim is that the strenuous elaboration, the *stilum vertere* (72), which Lucilius dispensed with is practised by the poets of Horace's circle.

[7] This was suggested by Hendrickson, *Horace and Lucilius, Studies in honor of Basil Gildersleeve* (1902), p. 161. F. Marx, *C. Lucilii carminum fragmenta* (1905), II, 221, listed the Horatian passage, along with Persius, I, 2, as 'imitations'.

cizing'.[1] Another explanation strikes me as more convincing. The very satire which has found fault with Lucilius' poetic standards ends by demanding a more discriminating type of reader than Lucilius did. Surely then the younger poet is confounding the older by dexterously reversing his pronouncement.[2] That is certainly elegant. But it is not a compliment.

In this satire the attitude of non-committal poetic play seems to clash strangely with the high standards and the strenuous workmanship demanded with so much conviction. This is more noticeable here than it is in the first literary satire (I, 4), where the same standards were merely implied in the criticism of Lucilius' slovenly technique. There the problem did not fully arise; Horace was content to write off the whole genre as insufficiently poetic. His words are *inludo chartis*[3] and they well describe the 'paper game' which he there claims he is playing. The words do not much differ from *haec ego ludo* in the present poem.[4] The setting differs however. For now so much stress is laid on the seriousness and intricacy of the game that it is hard to believe in its light-hearted spirit. *Haec ego ludo* now fails to convince. Horace seems to be striking two attitudes. He pronounces that poetry is an intricate and serious art: this is one attitude. He also pronounces that poetry is a game which he likes playing: this is another attitude.

The non-committal attitude had become familiar in the large societies of the Hellenistic age ever since the poets had moved to the circumference of the body politic. No longer were their subjects large enough to be the concern of society as a whole. Nor could the poets themselves feel that they were taken as seriously as they were in the days of the small close-knit city states. They had to regain the sympathy they

---

[1] Fraenkel, *op. cit.* p. 131.
[2] Hendrickson (in the paper cited at p. 168, n. 7) makes a similar point, if I understand him rightly.
[3] *Sat.* I, 4, 139.
[4] *Sat.* I, 10, 37.

had lost and thus came to rely on the enlightened patronage, or the self-interest, of the ruling monarchs or grandees. Yet the best of the poets claimed personal, artistic, independence, however dependent they may have been otherwise. So Callimachus readily declines all large and monumental subjects, including (perhaps expressly, perhaps only by implication) those that were of great concern to his own age.[1] Enjoying the support of the powers that be, he is allowed to stand outside the body politic and indulge a fanciful imagination which will hurt no one, though it may give pleasure to readers sophisticated enough to understand (as Catullus was to say some centuries later) *aliquid esse meas nugas*. Hence a playful refusal to attempt 'serious themes' and 'matters of great concern' became the Hellenistic poet's defence of his vital, artistic, independence. A like problem arises in the Augustan age when poets once more come to rely on political protection and enlightened patronage. But their task is harder, their attitude more contradictory, for some of them craved matters of great concern—if only they could satisfy their craving in their own way. Thus the individualistic refusal to embark on large poetic enterprises acquired a new significance—and a new depth. Horace is saying precisely what he feels when he declines the responsibility of an author[2] and jealously guards his freedom of 'play'. But he is not less sincere when he proclaims the high standards and the strenuous workmanship of the new poets. In each case

---

[1] R. Pfeiffer, *H*, LXIII (1928), 322, noticed that Callimachus preceded the Augustans in employing this playful if rather laboured manner of declining large topics. Some scholars use the word *recusatio* to denote the same refusal. A large book on this subject has been published by W. Wimmel, 'Kallimachos in Rom: Die Nachfolge seines apologetischen Dichtens in der Augusteerzeit', *H*, Einzelschr. XVI (1960), 344 pp. Owing to the fragmentary character of what survives of Callimachus' verse, the details of this refusal are still obscure. For example, that Callimachus declined heroic subjects and the lofty manner is obvious. What is not yet obvious is whether he explicitly declined to celebrate in his verse the deeds of his unconquered king as Horace declined *Caesaris invicti res dicere*.

[2] *Sat.* I, 10, 37–9, 'haec ego ludo, | quae neque in aede sonent certantia iudice Tarpa, | nec redeant iterum atque iterum spectanda theatris'.

Horace speaks as a different *persona*. Each *persona* is true and revealing, but neither *persona* represents the whole of Horace the critic, let alone the poet.

THE THIRD LITERARY SATIRE

These attitudes lend an especial zest to the third of the literary pieces, *Satires*, II, I. Now the poet refuses the 'important themes' suggested to him, and this refusal is made to convey, adroitly and amusingly, the nature of personal poetry. Horace's satires have been censured for being savage attacks or slipshod compositions. What is the poet to do? He calls on a celebrated lawyer, Trebatius, for a mock-serious consultation. The adviser suggests simple remedies: let him stop writing; or if write he must, let him compose an epic on the wars of Caesar the Unconquered (thus meeting both criticisms), or else use *satura* to *praise* Caesar's achievements (thus meeting the first criticism). The proposals are refused tactfully but firmly. An epic requires the *stile eroico* which transcends the poet's powers; this *apologia*, in what appears to be a set form, is here employed for the first time in Horace.[1] To panegyric he will turn some time when occasion offers; the great man must not be importuned. Compliments paid by way of *apologia*, the poet is well on the way to saying what in fact makes him write, and write satire. He writes satire because it pleases him. Others enjoy dancing or riding or boxing. *Chacun à son goût.* Horace's *goût* is the writing of satire. It is as simple as that. *Me pedibus delectat claudere verba | Lucili ritu, nostrum melioris utroque.*[2] But whereas he said earlier *inludo chartis* and *haec ego ludo*, he now continues:[3] 'Lucilius entrusted his secrets to his books as to loyal friends,

---

[1] *Sat.* II, I, 10–23. The writer of *sermones* used it again, many years later, to apologize in higher quarters (*Ep.* II, 1 *fin.*). In his lyrics he employed a like *apologia* at *Odes*, I, 6, but *Odes*, II, 12 refuses a lyric subject. For this apologetic attitude, see above, pp. 169–70, for the manner of his *apologia*, see p. 170, n. 1.

[2] *Sat.* II, I, 28–9.   [3] *Ibid.* 30–4.

turning nowhere else whether things went badly with him or well. Hence it is that the whole life of the man in his old age stands open to view as though it were painted on a votive tablet.'

When Horace eschews the grand impersonal epic, here is his own choice—a form of verse in which he can express himself as a person, the satire or *sermo* as personal poetry. This is as close as Horace the literary critic comes to formulating the modern concept of personal poetry. Lucilius' *sermones*, and Horace's, are described as poems in which their authors unburden their minds. By that token they resemble the modern verse of confession and self-revelation.[1] But Horace is not individualist enough to think in terms of *méditation, réflexion, expression des sentiments*, or of *Empfindung*. It is true, on occasion the poet speaks in his own person and about himself. Yet he is not reflecting by himself; the personal aspect as he sees it is limited. It is a sharing of personal secrets with friends; and his writings take the place of friends—*velut fidis arcana sodalibus olim | credebat libris*. Personal poetry was cast in the small genres, Archaic, Hellenistic and Roman. Satire, or rather *sermo*, was one of them; the grand and impersonal genres of epic and drama were not. Whether it was Horace who first formulated this concept of *sermo* is unknown. But for what it is worth it should be remembered that it was a Greek philosopher of the Aristotelian persuasion, Aristoxenus, who represented Sappho, Alcaeus, and Anacreon, as 'having their writings (*libris*) in the place of friends'.[2] This may not be a just estimate of the personal poetry of the early lyric writers. Yet in view of the social conventions of archaic lyric verse, the intrusion into his poetry of the poet's person is not perhaps unreasonably

---

[1] Readers may wish to compare Fraenkel's divergent discussion of this topic, *op. cit.* p. 153.

[2] Porphyrion, on *Sat.* ii, 1, 30, mentions Sappho and Alcaeus, pseudo-Acro mentions Anacreon and Alcaeus. Both cite Aristoxenus, but do not record the placing of the fragment. C. Müller, for no good reason, assigned it to the Πραξιδα-μάντια, the contents of which are unknown (*Hist. Gr. Fr.* ii, 285, fr. 52); F. Wehrli, for an undisclosed reason, to the Περὶ μουσικῆς (Aristoxenos, fr. 71).

described in the social terms familiar to the Greeks.[1] Horace may have borrowed the metaphor in order to express his own experience as a writer of *sermones*.[2] He may also have thought in similar terms of the personal elements of his lyrics. But whatever the origin of the imagery, its purpose here is to denote the personal character of Horace's and Lucilius' *sermones*. His language is uncompromising. This sort of writing Horace considers his natural bent; and he will follow his bent whatever his circumstances: 'I shall write whatever the colour of my life.'[3]

What is the conclusion that all this talk of personal poetry seems to be inviting? Is the refusal to write a grand epic to order prompted by the desire to write personal *sermones* rather than polemical satires? Is Horace preparing his readers for the *Epistles* which are to be *sermones* though they are not satires? Indeed this satire has been described as Horace's final account of how satire ought to be written.[4] The proposition is attractive. Yet there are serious flaws in it and I do not think it can stand. It has recently been questioned on the grounds that then the poet would be describing his own satires as what so many of them—some early and some late— are not: *sermones* without the attack of satire.[5]

Like doubts are raised by the literary criticism which is offered in this poem. Horace describes Lucilius' satire as a painting in which *omnis vita senis* is displayed. The suggestion is that in comparison with this view Horace's former description of Lucilius 'looks like a caricature or at any rate a fragmentary sketch'.[6] But does it? The present description of a varied and complex phenomenon is surely as fragmentary as all

---

[1] As late as the fourth century the process of thinking was described by Plato as a conversation of the soul with itself (*Soph.* 263*e*, 264*a*, *Theaet.* 189*e*). Here again a social metaphor was used to seize the concept of 'personal reflection'.

[2] The metaphor may have occurred in Lucilius, although pseudo-Acro's comment, on Hor. *Sat.* II, 1, 30, is too vague to inspire confidence: 'hoc Lucilius ex Anacreonte Graeco traxit et Alcaeo lyricis quos ait Aristoxenus libris propriis vice amicorum usos esse'.   [3] *Sat.* II, 1, 60.   [4] Fraenkel, *op. cit.* pp. 147–8.

[5] Thus N. Rudd, *CQ*, n.s. x (1960), 175, 177.

[6] Fraenkel, *op. cit.* p. 152.

the rest. Even on the showing of the scanty remains of Lucilius' *saturae*, this account applies to some but not to others.

With this stipulation return to the first satire of Book II. The scales of its literary criticism will then be seen not to be wholly tilted in favour of self-portraiture. The celebrated passage about autobiographical *sermones* must not be considered apart from the rest of what Horace has to say about his own satire. First the setting of the whole poem. It depicts the poet consulting the lawyer Trebatius on two hostile criticisms of his satiric verse. Both criticisms appeal to 'the law';[1] both reject Horace's satires. The lawyer's final 'Opinion' is legal, but the verdict is connected with the literary question through a pun —Horace's, not Trebonius'.[2] *Mala carmina*, be they libels or bad poems, are mentioned, but the risk of violating the law of the land is dismissed as hurriedly as it is introduced.[3] The poet may continue the writing of satire.

Moreover, Horace is not defending himself by reminding Trebatius that Lucilius was autobiographical and not satirical. Lucilius figures in the poet's defence because, like Horace, he could not help writing, and writing honestly. Hence his life is in his writings. But in each case it is the life of a fighter. The poet belongs to a pugnacious border-race, *Lucanus an Appulus anceps*.[4] He wishes for peace; but let anyone disturb him—'then I shout, "better not touch me"':[5] 'at ille | qui me commorit—melius non tangere clamo— | flebit et insignis tota cantabitur urbe'. And warned by the lawyer that the warmth with which his powerful friends now receive him

---

[1] *Sat.* II, 1–3, 'sunt quibus in satura videar nimis acer et *ultra* | *legem tendere opus*; sine nervis altera quidquid | composui pars esse putat', etc. The *lex* must in the first place be the *lex saturae*, like the *lex operis*, *A.P.* 135; that is shown by the criticisms. But there is also likely to be a sidelong glance at the law of the land as there is in the *double entendre* at the close of the poem. And a lawyer is being consulted. The identity of the law has been discussed judiciously by R. E. Smith, 'The law of libel at Rome', *CQ*, n.s. 1 (1951), 169–79.

[2] *Ibid.* 83.

[3] *Ibid.* 80–6; for *mala* (instead of *famosa*) *carmina*, see E. Fraenkel's enlightening remarks, *Gnomon*, 1 (1925), 195, R. E. Smith, *op. cit.* 177, n. 6.

[4] *Ibid.* 34–9.   [5] *Ibid.* 44–6.

may well cool off if he does not mend his ways, his rejoinder is worthy of note. He reminds Trebatius of Lucilius the fighter (not the painter of self-portraits) who would reveal his contemporaries' depravity by stripping off the moral cloak which covered a multitude of sins—and yet he was not deprived of Scipio's friendship.[1]

Finally the purpose of this poem. The probability that this is the last satire Horace ever wrote may easily make us forget that its writer does not say so. The purpose of the poem is unequivocal—it introduces a second book of satires. And it carries out that purpose. A new aspect of satire is noticed. But the other aspects are not forgotten. The concept of moral improvement by means of satirizing is not abandoned. If this is Horace's last satire his final word is not an apology to his readers that the satires are not epistles.

Such is Horace's literary criticism at this early stage. It is the work of a poet-critic who clarifies the nature of the genre in which he himself is productive. His criticism paves the way for his new satire and for the new school of poetry in general. Each time he attacks the subject his point of view differs to accord with the purpose of each poem. Yet there is something more settled and comprehensive at the back of his mind. It would be misleading to call it systematic criticism. But he seems to rely on a rational (even a rationalistic) manner of looking at poetic matters that are only partly rational. This is shown by his use of critical concepts.

Three of these concepts require notice. In the first place Horace relies on the rhetorical distinction between style and matter which was enshrined in the teachings of the Aristotelians, the Stoics, and most of the professional critics and grammarians. The opposition to this view must have been well known to him. Οὐκ ὀρθῶς ἔδοξε τὴν σύνθεσιν τῆς λέξεως τῶν διανοημάτων χωρίζειν: this was Philodemus' criticism of Neoptolemus and it applied to many others besides. If Horace adopted that distinction nevertheless, there

---

[1] *Ibid.* 60–79.

must have been good reasons for it. Talk of words, their selection and arrangement is, or seems, close to the poet's workshop. Horace was taking workmanship seriously. It may have seemed to him less vague and more enlightening than the more sophisticated talk of Philodemus and others. And it is kept in its place. It provides a convenient tool for the workaday business of literary critique when, for example, he considers the stylistic weaknesses of Lucilius[1] or the poetic potentialities of comedy.[2] The words may be weak; so the matter may be; or the words do not sufficiently 'fit' the matter, according to the traditional doctrine of the 'fitting style'. But once the critic goes beyond such technicalities he recognizes that the distinction is valid no longer. Form and matter then seem to become *one*. Moreover, the union of style and content is proclaimed by Horace's own verse when he writes criticism. For his critical poems attempt to recreate in poetic form the qualities which are the substance of his criticism.

Another traditional distinction is adopted by Horace in the field of the literary 'genres'—I mean the distinction between major and minor poetry. Callimachus and his followers in Greece and Rome alike had fought hard in order to achieve recognition for the small and personal forms of verse in which they excelled. Much discussion on the merits of major and minor poetry was heard. Horace cannot have been unaware that, in a sense, that distinction was unreal because the essence of all true poetry was alike. There was rather a distinction between good poets and bad than between the large forms of epic and drama on the one hand and the smaller forms on the other. Horace adopted the traditional distinction presumably because even at this early stage it allowed him to hint at poetic potentialities which were not realized in the small form of the satire.[3] So long as different levels of

---

[1] So in *Satires*, I, 4 and I, 10.

[2] *Sat.* I, 4, 46–7, 'quod acer spiritus ac vis | nec *verbis* nec *rebus* inest'.

[3] *Sat.* I, 4, 39–62 hint at larger promises not fulfilled by the satiric genre. See above, p. 162.

style were felt to be naturally expressive of different literary
subjects and genres it is arguable that more was gained by
using than by discarding this terminology.[1]

Finally there is Horace's moral nomenclature in describing
the aim of satire. Progressive opinion in literary coteries had
long since dissented from the ancient Greek view that poetry
and the moral standards of a community were connected by
way of cause and effect. Philodemus held, not unreasonably,
that the moral effect of poetry, if it had one, was not an
essential outcome of its aesthetic nature.[2] This is the kind of
view that Horace grew up with. There is no evidence that he
ever accepted it. At a later stage he held that poetry was
nothing if it could not reach the whole personality of his
readers, their feelings and minds as well as their *mores*. He
expressed that traditionally by saying that poetry must
delight as well as instruct. When he wrote satire he similarly
juxtaposed the aesthetic and moral aims of his verse.

Literary criticism in the *Satires* is both prompted and
limited by the genre Horace was writing and criticizing. It is
prompted by it, for he thought that satire had been brought
into existence but had not been brought to perfection. If the
yardstick of perfection is a type of verse in which the words so
closely fit the matter that the two are indivisible, then the
founder of the genre falls short of this demand. As a poet
Horace is striving to attain the potentialities satire could
attain; as a critic he demonstrates its potentialities, those
attained and those not attained. But his criticism is also
limited by his subject, for he believed that satire was in-
capable of accommodating poetry at full stretch. There is a
glimpse of a wider vista but no more. His criticism remains
limited until he comes to face the genres which he believed
could accommodate such poetry.

---

[1] The references to satire, comedy, and epic, show how the poetic potentialities
are thought to be tied to certain genres and their styles.

[2] Philod. *De Poem.* v, col. xxix, 17, καὶ διότι κᾶν ὠφελῇ, καθὸ ποήματ᾽ οὐκ ὠφελεῖ.
Cf. *ibid.* fr. 2, 29 (Jensen, p. 7).

CHAPTER 2

THE SHORTER LITERARY EPISTLES

In the setting of the *Satires* Horace had, not unnaturally, concealed that he sensed in himself the imaginative power which transcends mere *sermones*.[1] *Odes*, I–III, appeared in 23 B.C., about seven years after the second book of the *Satires*. Here the *os magna sonaturum* could be heard and Horace took the part of the priest-poet, *vates*. He speaks as *Musarum sacerdos* in the Roman Odes, foretells his immortality in *exegi monumentum aere perennius*, claims to have transposed Aeolian song into Italic strains, to feel the inspiration of the Muse, to experience Dionysiac frenzy, and to tell nothing small, lowly or mortal.[2] These moods do not accord with the ironical and conversational graces of the *sermo*, whether satire or epistle. And even in the *Odes* they are deliberately and carefully restricted to the propitious moments of the highest poetic intent. Without warning, urbanity and reticence may put in their appearance, and lighten what might otherwise be heavy and solemn:

> sed ne relictis Musa procax iocis
> Ceae retractes munera neniae,
> mecum Dionaeo sub antro
> quaere modos leviore plectro.   (*Odes*, II, 1, 37–40)

Or again, after the majestic oration of Juno,

> non haec iocosae conveniet lyrae:
> quo Musa tendis? desine pervicax
> referre sermones deorum et
> magna modis tenuare parvis.   (*Odes*, III, 3, 69–72)

---

[1] *Sat.* I, 4, 39–44, where he declines the title of poet with its *ingenium, mens divinior,* and *os magna sonaturum.*

[2] Thus *Odes*, III, 1, 3; 30, 6 and 13; II, 16, 38; III, 25, 1 and 17.

Or indeed such urbanity may provide the contrast for a whole *carmen* as it does in the odes of 'refusal', I, 6 and II, 12, where the underlying contrast reaches the surface in the sharp antitheses of *tenues grandia,* or of *me dulcis dominae Musa Licymniae | cantus...dicere (voluit),* after the heavy weather of the *longa bella.*[1] These self-portraits are variable and apt to change. No likeness of the poet can convince if it fails to display a similar variety and flexibility. And even then it is not likely that the whole poet emerges. A writer on the 'image of Horace' in Alexander Pope's poetry has done well to remind us of this very matter. 'There is scarcely any poet who has revealed himself more fully as a writer and person than Horace, and yet the result is to make us feel how elusive his... personality is.'[2] The poetic claims in the *Odes* are scarcely 'literary criticism'. But no one writing on this topic can disregard with impunity their bearing on the criticism of the literary *Satires* and *Epistles.*

EPISTLES, I, 19

The first literary discussion after the *Satires* and *Odes* was published as part of the first book of the *Epistles* in December of 20 B.C., about three years after *Odes,* I–III. In the nineteenth letter Horace defends himself against charges of imitativeness. The letter is outspoken and harsh—an invective. But it is not more outspoken than some of the satires. And were it not for its form it could be called a satire, in the sense envisaged at *Satires,* II, 1: Horace has been attacked; he fights back. But unlike *Satires,* I, 4 or 10, this poem no longer names any

---

[1] *Ibid.* I, 6, 9; II, 12, 1 and 13–14.

[2] R. A. Brower, *Alexander Pope; the Poetry of Allusion* (1959), p. 165. It is a pity that he has spoilt his observation, adding the words *or any* between *his* and *personality.* The point surely is that the degree of Horace's self-revelation and self-concealment is not easily paralleled anywhere. Facile psychologizing on the basis of a few self-revealing remarks can only mislead writers and readers, as I believe it has done in G. Highet's chapter on Horace in *Poets in a Landscape* (1957).

179

adversaries.[1] It is an epistle. Its addressee is one who understands, Maecenas, and Horace is ostensibly answering his question why his poems are eagerly read and admired in private but traduced in public.[2] The target however is the slavish flock of imitators who impute their own failings to Horace: *o imitatores, servum pecus.*[3]

The centre of the short piece lies in lines 21–34.[4] Readers, among them critics and poets, had denied one aspect of the *Odes* which was surely above criticism—the striking originality of these poems. Horace's defence turns on the question of originality; its antecedents lie in the assessment of Lucilius in the *Satires* and the self-assessment of Horace in the *Odes*. In the *Satires* he acknowledged Lucilius' originality but blamed him for slipshod work. He himself was *inventore minor*, though striving to raise the quality of the semi-poetic genre of satire. Now here is a like argument, but it is on a higher plane. The *Odes* are 'poetry' without the pedestrian element which he felt was inherent in the genus *sermo*. His lyric verse prompts the question of poetic greatness as well as that of poetic perfection. For Latin *carmina* Horace is what Lucilius was for Latin satire—the originator of a new Latin genre. But he is still the same poet who demanded a high degree of technical finish and who criticized Lucilius for his slipshod work. Thus a problem of literary criticism arises: the self-assessment of Horace as regards both his originality and (by implication) his craftsmanship in the *Odes*.

It is well known that the central passage of the letter restates the terms of the *Odes* in which he had claimed primacy

---

[1] E. Courbaud, *Horace—Sa vie et sa pénsee à l'époque des épîtres* (1914), p. 318, felt reminded of *Sat.* 1, 4 and 1, 10. Also see Fraenkel, *op. cit.* p. 340, and, for the naming of adversaries, Rudd, *CQ*, n.s. x (1960), 161.

[2] Hor. *Ep.* 1, 19, 35–6.   [3] *Ibid.* 19.

[4] Fraenkel has convincingly shown the imaginative progress of thought in this as in many other poems of Horace, see *op. cit.* p. 341 for *Ep.* 1, 19. These remarks will show however why I cannot accept Fraenkel's contention (p. 350) that this is the only thoroughly bitter document which we have from Horace's pen. This is not a 'bitter document' but a satirical defence of Horace's position as a lyric poet. And the poem has its share of lighter moments.

in the fields of Latin lyric and iambic verse—*princeps* (21), *dux* (23), *primus* (23), *non prius* (32), *immemorata* (33). But the restatement is in the fashion befitting a *sermo*. Horace explains in what sense a poet working within a great literary tradition can justly claim originality. It is not the sense of the word familiar from the nineteenth century. On the contrary, the claim of originality is based on a family tree of literary affiliations: from Archilochus to Sappho and Alcaeus, from Archilochus to Horace's *Epodes*, and from Alcaeus to Horace's *Odes*.[1] Moreover the claim is set forth in the traditional language of literary criticism, derived ultimately from the professional critics of the Aristotelian type and from the poet-critics of the Callimachean type. To the former he owes the distinction between rhythm and mood on the one hand and matter and words on the other (*numeri animique* and *res et verba*), or between verse on the one hand and subject and arrangement on the other (*modi* and *res et ordo*).[2] These distinctions enable him to speak of both the tradition which he has continued and the difference which he has made to the tradition: his indebtedness and his originality. To the latter, the poet-critics of the Callimachean type, he owes the language of the pioneer,

> libera per vacuum posui vestigia princeps,
> non aliena meo pressi pede. qui sibi fidet,
> dux reget examen. (21–3)

But the language is tempered by Roman legalism. The new lyric ground was unoccupied, *vacuum*; Horace refrained from trespassing on ground occupied by others, *aliena*.[3] The *Ars*

---

[1] I can be brief on this passage because Fraenkel has gone into the major problems of interpretation (*op. cit.* pp. 339–48).

[2] The pair 'subject–style' was used already in the *Satires* to good purpose. *Ordo*, arrangement, belongs to the same technical context; see above, pp. 81–2, 99. That *ordo*, next to subject, style, and metre, must have its technical connotation was seen by R. Heinze, 'Die lyr. Verse des Horaz', *BVSA* (1918), p. 30. The 1957 reprint of Heinze's commentary of 1914 still perpetuates Kiessling's erroneous explanation.

[3] Lejay and some of the older commentators have noted the legal imagery, see Fraenkel, *op. cit.* p. 341, n. 2. Horace at any rate held that in spite of Catullus and his friends the ground was still 'unoccupied'.

Poetica shows how this sort of language could help to unravel an even more complicated problem—individual treatment of traditional material—

> *publica* materies privati iuris erit si
> non circa *vilem patulumque* moraberis *orbem*
> nec verbum verbo curabis reddere fidus
> *interpres* nec desilias *imitator* in artum
> unde pedem proferre pudor vetet aut operis lex.[1]

(A.P. 131–5)

The agreement between *Epistle* 19 and the *Odes* is, then, very close. So close is it that a significant disagreement has remained unnoticed—I mean that between the letter and the rest of Horace's *sermones*. Epistle 19 is unique in that it alone among the literary satires and letters reiterates Horace's claim to be the Latin *fidicen*. Such a claim was impossible in the *Satires* simply because they precede the lyric poetry of the *Odes* and Horace is content to proclaim that the *Satires* are not poetry. Nor did it normally suit the deprecating and ironical attitude of the *Epistles*. Nor, finally, did it accord with the sentiment which the *Epistles* display towards 'the game of poetry'. The sentiment, often noticed, is expressed with much emphasis near the beginning of the book—'now I put aside lyric verse and other toys; truth and goodness are my concern; to them I am wholly dedicated'.[2] Biographers may hunt for the motives that brought about this change of mood. Exhaustion after the strenuous poetic discipline of the *Odes* is certain to be among them. So is disappointment with the reception of his lyric verse. There may be other motives. The style of the *sermo* alone cannot account for it. For *Epistle* 19 demonstrates that this personal mood could have been accommodated by way of satirical defence, or in other ways.

To this there is a corollary which is essential for a just

---

[1] This passage likewise combines Callimachean with Roman legal language; for Callimachus, see above, p. 109, n. 2.

[2] *Ep.* 1, 1, 10–11, 'nunc itaque et versus et cetera ludicra pono; | quid verum atque decens curo et rogo, et omnis in hoc sum'.

appreciation of the literary epistles. It was only when Horace's status as a poet had been established by the *Odes* and when his lyric inspiration seemed to have ceased that he felt free to look at poetry as a whole. Hence the curious (but for a poet-critic not perhaps anomalous) position that his best criticism was written when he felt constrained to say 'poet no more' and 'no poet I' (as in the *Epistle to Florus* and in the *Ars*)[1] or 'poet against better judgement' (as in the *Epistle to Augustus* when he had resumed the writing of lyric verse).[2] Only in *Epistles*, Book II, and in the *Ars* does he turn magisterial, undisturbed by the lyric poetry he himself was writing. And because he is ostensibly no longer involved he speaks freely and in more general fashion.

THE LETTER TO FLORUS

Epistles, II, 2, also known as the *Letter to Florus*, is addressed to one of the young men of the circle of Tiberius, with a taste and perhaps an aptitude for poetry.[3] The recipients of Horace's moral criticism in the first book of the *Epistles* frequently belong to the same circle.[4] The young audience fits the mood of the middle-aged poet[5] who says he has turned

---

[1] *Ep.* II, 2, particularly 143–4, 'ac non verba sequi fidibus modulanda Latinis, | sed verae numerosque modosque ediscere vitae'; *A.P.* 306, 'munus et officium, nil scribens ipse, docebo'.

[2] *Ep.* II, 1, 111–13, 'ipse ego qui nullos me adfirmo scribere versus | invenior Parthis mendacior et prius orto | sole vigil calamum et chartas et scrinia posco'.

[3] P. Lejay drew attention to the retinue of the young Tiberius as a setting for Horace's writings after 20 B.C., *Rev. de L'Instruc. pub. en Belgique*, LXVI (1903), 173. Tiberius himself was aged 22 in the year 20. *Ep.* I, 3, also addressed to Florus, gives more information about these men and their interests.

[4] Nor is the criticism directed only to ethics. *Ep.* I, 1, addressed to Maecenas, tells of Horace's turn from (lyric) poetry to philosophy. *Ep.* I, 19, again addressed to Maecenas, deals with the reception of *Odes*, I–III. The subject of I, 2 is poetry as moral instruction.

[5] For the writer of the *Epistles* teaching the young, see *Ep.* I, 2, 67–71, 'nunc adbibe puro | pectore verba puer, nunc te melioribus offer. | quo semel est imbuta recens, servabit odorem | testa diu. quodsi cessas aut strenuus anteis, | nec tardum opperior nec praecedentibus insto'.

critic and teacher, although in fact his *Epistles* are a new form of personal poetry. The date of the letter is not quite certain. But part of the case for what is reasonably regarded as the most probable date is the close similarity to the first book of the *Epistles*.[1]

In the epistles of Book I the poet is turning from the writing of lyric poems (which he rejects as mere 'play') to moral philosophizing (which *per contra* is a worthier activity).[2] In the present letter lyric verse and moral theory are confronted, with the same outcome.[3] How does this attitude square with the concern for poetic standards exhibited in the same letter? The answer seems to me to be that his strictures on Roman poetry and his demands for poetic standards would still be valid if they were not part of an apology for his failure to continue the writing of lyric verse. Conversely his strictures and his demands derive much force from the personal setting in which they appear.

The letter to Florus is not a literary treatise. It is a poetic epistle and it has the structure of a Horatian poem.[4] Horace has gone back on his promise to send Florus some new lyric poems (*carmina*, 25) and he explains why he has defaulted and

---

[1] The letter to Florus strongly expresses the poet's refusal to write any more lyric verse, and his leanings towards moral theory. Both recall *Ep.* I, 1, 10–11, paraphrased above, p. 182, 'nunc itaque et versus et cetera ludicra pono; | quid verum atque decens curo et rogo, et omnis in hoc sum'. These sentiments could have been expressed at any time between the publication of *Odes*, I–III, in 23 B.C., and the *Carmen Saeculare*, of 17 B.C., but particularly during the triennium after the publication of *Epistles*, Book I, in 20 B.C. Cf. E. C. Wickham, *The Works of Horace* (1891), II, 330. Neglect of these indications caused P. Lejay and others to date the letter to *c.* 12 B.C., after the *Epistle to Augustus*: *op. cit.* (above, p. 183, n. 3), p. 170, n. 1. External data, specially the military movements of Tiberius to whose suite Florus was attached, are not equally clear but do not much matter since the choice lies only between two years, 19 and 18 B.C., with an unlikely extension to 17, the year of the *Secular Hymn*. Mommsen's argument in favour of 19 is made in *Die Literaturbriefe des Horaz* of 1880 (*Ges. Schr.* VII, pp. 182–5). It dispenses with the special pleading of J. Vahlen (1878, *Ges. phil. Schr.* II, 58 f.) and the assumption of R. Heinze (in his introduction to the letter) that Tiberius received the praetorian ornaments *in absentia*.

[2] Above, p. 182.

[3] *Ep.* II, 2, 141–4, cf. above, p. 183, n. 1.

[4] M. J. McGann, *RM*, n.s. XCVII (1954), 343–58.

proposes further to default. Hence the resemblance to certain features of the 'poems of refusal' that were discussed earlier.[1] The literary criticism of the letter is fitted into this psychological setting with great skill. The malaise of Roman poetry and the demand for new standards are part of Horace's present disenchantment. It is this personal emotion which causes him to make his critical points.

This surely explains why so much room is given to the setting and so little (by comparison) to the strictly literary subject of the letter. The tone of personal dissatisfaction is set by way of wryly humorous story-telling and argument. Horace writes no lyric verse because he has now got enough money (26–54), because he is ageing (55–7), because too many diverse demands are made upon him (58–64) and because Rome is too noisy (65–86). That, with the personal introduction, amounts to more than two-fifths of the poem. The final portion is not much shorter (141–216). It leads the reader away from poetry to 'philosophy': a grown man needs to philosophize and leave fun and games, poetry included, to the young. What is left may be called literary criticism (say, 87–140). Although comparatively brief, it comes with much emphasis right in the centre of the poem and its bearing on poetry is clearly greater than the scope of the letter would lead one to expect.[2]

In the restricted ambit of the *Satires* Horace set up the poetic ideal of old Attic comedy, or he appealed to the standards of the new school of poets to which he himself belonged. In the letter to Florus he goes much farther. Personal approval is not enough. Rome is full of poets who insure their own

---

[1] Above, pp. 170–1. But it is not a 'poem of refusal' in the sense that Horace is here writing the poetry which he avowedly refuses to write, as was suggested by H. Lucas, *Festsch. J. Vahlen* (1900), pp. 322 f. Cf. McGann, *op. cit.* p. 346, n. 10. The *Musa pedestris* of the *sermo* does not sing *carmina*.

[2] This apparent incongruity may help to explain why the central portion yet seems to be reduced to 'a kind of digression' within the framework of the poem— a problem which puzzled McGann (*op. cit.* p. 354). The structure of the poem only provides for literary criticism incidentally, before transition is made from the lack of poetic *savoir* (*sapere et ringi*, 128) to the philosophic *savoir vivre* (*sapere*, 141).

status by paying homage to rivals and receiving their homage in turn.

> discedo Alcaeus puncto illius; ille meo quis?
> quis nisi Callimachus? si plus adposcere visus,
> fit Mimnermus et optivo cognomine crescit.[1]

> > (*Ep.* ii, 2, 99–101)

Horace no longer competes; so he no longer listens in order to be listened to.

> multa fero ut placem genus inritabile vatum
> cum scribo et supplex populi suffragia capto;
> idem finitis studiis et mente recepta
> obturem patulas impune legentibus auris.

> > (*Ibid.* 102–5)

For a poet or a critic here the awkward problem of poetic standards arises. Horace professing to look at Roman poetry from outside raises the problem. If neither mutual approval among poets nor self-approval of poets nor popular success settles that problem, what does? Horace's answer presupposes the existence of a traditional poetic art. He believes— reasonably, in view of the Greek and Roman traditions—that there is such an art and that it makes sense to speak of a 'poem devised in accordance with the laws of the art', *legitimum poema* (109). He believes too that since there are standards to which a poem must conform to be 'legitimate', there must also be persons judging such claims. The poet who seeks to produce a *legitimum poema* must also sit in judgement on his own work and acquire the spirit of an unbiased critic, *animum censoris sumet honesti* (110).

The laws or rules which Horace then proceeds to enunciate cut right across the two fields which would now be called 'poetic' and 'rhetorical'. The assumption that it is expedient or reasonable to formulate a body of axioms or rules applying

---

[1] The contrast between a Roman Alcaeus on the one side and a Roman Callimachus–Mimnermus on the other is probably too telling not to qualify for the common identification with Horace and Propertius if its due weight is given to line 91, *carmina compono, hic elegos.*

partly to verse, partly to prose, and partly to both, is not now held, and would be rightly censured as a rhetorical chimera. The assumption, however, that a good poet does much to enrich and purify the language would be felt by many to be justified. Horace does not make this distinction. He can turn to rhetorical theories without violating poetic taste or being censured by his contemporaries for violating it. Such theories had for long been applied to poetic criticism and they provide him with a scale of values and an agreed critical vocabulary.

Horace does no more than allude to literary theories, but the allusions were probably sufficient to remind his readers of the critical background which he, and most of them, could take for granted. He would thus avoid the vagueness which so easily besets literary criticism. On the other hand, Horace is careful not to obtrude prosaic technicalities. He moves from the choice of words to their connexion in a piece of verse.[1] At the bottom of this is the rhetorical distinction between *delectus verborum* and *compositio*, ἐκλογὴ καὶ σύνθεσις ὀνομάτων, on which the tradition of ancient literary criticism is based. But whereas his observations just touch on these traditional distinctions, the scope of his observations is strictly personal and contemporary.

In the *Satires* he had set forth the poetic ideals that inspired him as a writer of satiric verse. The aspiration was to make satire worthy to be ranked with the writings of the new poets —Fundanius' comedies, Pollio's tragedies, Varius' epic poetry and Virgil's eclogues. Now Horace puts a general interpretation on the ideals that had inspired him and his friends. The letter to Florus shows once again that his standards are those of living art. A vocabulary which is merely archaizing, or which is stationary, is dead art. Language as he sees it is a thing in motion. The poet keeps it alive and moving. It is he who must have enough courage to remove 'words that have grown dull and have lost weight and

[1] *Ep.* II, 2, 111–21, on choice of words, 122–3, on composition and ornament.

standing'.[1] The opposite case is not less true. There are old words that have all that requisite splendour which many modern words have lost, but they are now forgotten and dust has settled on them: these the poets will bring back into the light of day.[2] And finally it is the poet who will annex new words to the language of poetry when they are needed.[3] This is the wealth of language with which he will quicken and enrich Latium.[4]

Doubtless such talk recalls the distinctions of the professional critics, rhetoricians, and grammarians.[5] It resembles Ciceronian and Peripatetic theory. But the impression is that of a mere family likeness. Horace freely omits what does not suit his hand. Of the three traditional items—*aut inusitatum verbum aut novatum aut translatum*[6]—he jettisons the third usage

---

[1] *Ep.* II, 2, 111–13, 'audebit quaecumque parum splendoris habebunt | et sine pondere erunt et honore indigna ferentur | verba movere loco', etc.

[2] *Ibid.* 115–18, 'obscurata diu populo bonus eruet atque | proferet in lucem speciosa vocabula rerum | quae priscis memorata Catonibus atque Cethegis | nunc situs informis premit et deserta vetustas'.

[3] *Ibid.* 119, 'adsciscet nova quae genitor produxerit *usus*'. This is a naturalistic explanation of the origin of new words which closely resembles Lucretius' Epicurean account of the origin of language, cf. Lucr. v, 1029 '*utilitas* expressit nomina rerum'. The passage, *A.P.* 70–2, resembles it but its precise explanation is still controversial, cf. Solmsen, *H*, LXVI (1931), 246, n. 2; W. Steidle, *Studien zur A.P. des Horaz* (1939), p. 39.

[4] *Ibid.* 120–1, 'vehemens et liquidus puroque simillimus amni | fundet opes Latiumque beabit divite lingua'. The poet's language, or rather the poet himself, is compared to a river—the Callimachean metaphor discussed above, p. 159, n. 3. But the poetic attributes that answer to the *purus amnis* are *vehemens* and *liquidus*. M. J. McGann, *op. cit.* p. 353, n. 31, may well be right in saying that *vehemens* introduces an independent nuance. As in other cases, this would serve to add a Horatian note to a borrowed phrase. The Callimachean purity of a clear stream is indeed desirable, but the stream must also have a strong current. The imagery at *Odes*, IV, 2, 5, is similar, but W. Wimmel, *op. cit.* (above, p. 159, n. 3), stresses the resemblance more strongly than I should care to do.

[5] R. Heinze in his notes on lines 111, 115, and 122, cites Cicero's rhetorical and Varro's grammatical theory; Cic. *De Or.* III, 150 ff., Varro, *De ling. Lat.* IX, 16 ff. (cf. Dahlmann, *op. cit.* p. 145). He does not say that Horace 'took' these doctrines from Cicero or Varro, although no doubt the poet knew them both. Heinze is likely to be right. Rhetorical and poetic vocabularies had been compared for centuries and there is nothing specifically Ciceronian or Varronian in Horace's doctrines.

[6] Cicero, *De Or.* III, 152, noted by Heinze. This *technologia* goes back to Aristotle and beyond. E.g., *Poet.* 22, 1459 *a* 5 and 9, διπλᾶ ὀνόματα, γλῶτται, μεταφοραί, may be compared with Cicero's *novatum, inusitatum, translatum*. For the post-

188

(that of the metaphor) because it does not chime in with his telling antithesis, old *versus* new. And he so turns the other two items that they lose their confined, technical, character and can express what he is wishing to express—the balance of old and new in a poetic language which has both strength and purity.

The style of the poem comes next. Horace's precepts deal with revision rather than with drafting. In two lines an ideal of stylistic balance is sketched out. Three faults need to be corrected in a piece of verse: immoderate ornament, immoderate ruggedness of composition, and, finally, a style that lacks force (*virtus*).[1] Horace has been anxious to avoid technicalities and he is concise in the extreme. Hence the difficulty of clearing up the technical implications.[2] But enough is said to leave the impression of balance without weakness—a major problem in writing and a Horatian problem at that.

These lines make valid critical points. They describe the principles guiding Horace's own style and presumably that of the new poets. But they demand more than what any single poet, even a Horace or Virgil, could achieve. They enunciate an ideal of poetic style. Cicero did more than describe his own oratorical style in the *Brutus*, or indeed the style of Demosthenes in the *Orator*. As a consummate practitioner he knew the difficulties of his craft and he was able to bring to the notice of his contemporaries (many of whom were and had to be

---

Aristotelian doctrine on ἐκλογὴ ὀνομάτων see the hints of F. Solmsen, *H*, LXVI (1931), 246–8.

[1] *Ep.* II, 2, 122–3, 'luxuriantia conpescet, nimis aspera sano | levabit cultu, virtute carentia tollet'. For the same subject, treated in greater detail, see the activities of the true critic at *A.P.* 438–52, particularly 445–9. The critic is called *vir bonus et prudens* at *A.P.* 445, and *censor honestus* in the present letter where he is identified with the true poet.

[2] Since Horace did not care to be specific, details are dubious and should perhaps be allowed to remain so. The only definite indication is that extremes of style are deprecated; this has a Peripatetic note. Moreover, it is likely that the present passage and the longer list, *A.P.* 445 ff., help to explain each other. For *luxuriantia conpescet*, see *A.P.* 447–8, *ambitiosa recidet | ornamenta* (so Heinze, *ad loc.*); for *nimis aspera sano | levabit cultu*, see *A.P.* 446, *culpabit duros*; and for *virtute carentia tollet*, see *A.P.* 445 *versus reprendet inertis*, 446–7, *incomptis adlinet atrum | ...signum*.

orators) what oratory at its best might be: 'atque ego in summo oratore fingendo talem informabo *qualis fortasse nemo fuit.* non enim quaero quis fuerit sed quid sit *illud quo nihil esse possit praestantius*'.[1] Versifying was a fashionable pursuit in Horace's time and fashions thrive on the well-meant and ill-conceived efforts of the amateur. Horace, unlike Cicero, has no need to import Platonic Forms[2] in order to clarify the ideal and optimal nature of *his* demands. As a poet-critic he conveys it by the setting of his criticism.

To the attentive reader the letter to Florus brings home the stringency of the technical demands which the true poet has to satisfy. A *legitimum poema* demands mastership; it demands art that has become second nature,

> *ludentis* speciem dabit *et torquebitur* ut qui
> nunc satyrum nunc agrestem Cyclopa movetur.

(Ep. II, 2, 124–5)

Nothing could be more telling than Horace's own reactions to the 'torture' of the poetic 'game'. 'So long as my botching pleases me, or at any rate deceives me, I would rather be a dilettante with a craze than know—and growl.'[3] This, he asserts, is one of the reasons why he has given up lyric verse. The emotional temperature of the poem reveals some of the essential conditions of the poetic process as Horace saw it. From the writers of the textbooks he takes what they have to teach about the technicalities of *delectus verborum* and *compositio* and he applies the 'rules' to his own purpose. But he is not writing a *technologia*. He is writing a poem on the problems facing a maker of poems. His larger subject is, 'Why I, Horace, do not write lyric verse'. By setting the *technologia* in the context of a personal *apologia* he tackles in his own way what modern critics tackle in theirs when they write about poetic imagination.

---

[1] Cic. *Or.* 7. The sequel of the Ciceronian passage, to 10 *fin.*, is also relevant to the point I am making.

[2] *Ibid.* 10, has rerum formas appellet ἰδέας... *Plato.*

[3] *Ibid.* 126–8, 'praetulerim scriptor delirus inersque videri, | dum mea delectent mala me vel denique fallant, | quam sapere et ringi'.

The Shorter Literary Epistles

The *Letter to Augustus*, *Epistles*, II, 1, lacks the psychological subtlety of the *Letter to Florus*. The poet's mood is different; certainly his conditions are different. The letter was composed four or five years after that to Florus,[1] when Horace had brought together (or was busy bringing together and completing) the fourth Book of the *Odes*. This book shows him more deeply involved with the régime, or (as he saw it) with his society, than *Odes*, I–III.[2] The letter to Augustus well fits this setting. It is a command performance[3] executed with great candour and skill. It is also a personal poem designed to give voice to some of Horace's most cherished convictions as to the relation of poetry and society. The two features are not mutually exclusive.

Having returned to lyric poetry, Horace cannot any longer plead either inability, or else lack of inclination, to write such verse. But he can, ironically, minimize his return *ad Musas*. With a change of front as amusing as it is unexpected, he now pretends to have joined the ranks of the amateurs whom he is so anxious to discredit, in this poem and elsewhere. He who a few years ago had renounced the writing of lyric verse has

---

[1] The letter was dated to 14 or 13 B.C. respectively by Vahlen (1878), *Ges. Phil. Schr.* II, 46–54, and Mommsen (1880), *Ges. Schr.* VII, 175–82. E. C. Wickham, *op. cit.* II, 328, gives a summary of the evidence.

[2] Of the fifteen poems of *Odes*, Book IV, five are concerned with Augustus and his family, and another four with the official performance of the *Carmen Saeculare*, which marks Horace's return to lyric verse, or with poetry as the remembrancer of great public deeds.

[3] Augustus' celebrated remarks from a letter to Horace suggest just that: 'irasci me tibi scito quod non in plerisque eius modi scriptis mecum potissimum loquaris; an vereris ne apud posteros infame tibi sit quod videaris familiaris nobis esse?' Suetonius concludes his citation by saying, *expressitque eclogam ad se cuius initium est*; there follows the beginning of the letter to Augustus. For Suetonius' remarks see below, p. 241. The verb *exprimo* as well as *cogo* and *iniungo* used elsewhere in Suetonius' account are not so far off the mark as Fraenkel's observations (*op. cit.* p. 383) might suggest. *Cogo* was apparently the *mot juste* for official encouragement. Thus Horace, lines 226–8 of this very letter to Augustus, 'ut simul atque | carmina rescieris nos fingere, commodus ultro | arcessas et egere vetes et *scribere cogas*'. And Suetonius' *expressit* is not ill chosen to describe Horace's reluctance and Augustus' insistence.

now caught the general passion for writing.[1] This *volte face* helps to re-establish his earlier procedure. In a *sermo*, satire and epistle alike, he looks at poetry as it were from outside: when he writes poetic criticism he claims to write it as a critic who is not involved as a poet. The writing of poetry and writing on poetry are two diverse activities and the poet is anxious to see their diversity recognized.

Horace has chosen a subject which is as Augustan as it is Horatian: the position of poet and poetry in contemporary Rome. Clearly the politician and the man of the Muses must have looked at it with different eyes. It is significant however that there is some ground common to both. Otherwise this letter could not have been written.[2] The function of poetry (to give it a modern name) was a topic widely discussed in ancient philosophy and literary criticism. True to the procedure adopted in all his writings on poetry, Horace moulds his own thought so that it may be expressed in the traditional language of criticism. This has the advantage that his readers could know what he was talking about; it has the disadvantage that superficial readers might take the traditional surface for the personal substance.

In the long final section of the poem two important types of contemporary poetry are scrutinized—drama and epic.[3] For obvious, personal, reasons Horace has found a different place for his own genre, lyric poetry.[4] Other motives must account for the omission of other genres. The argument that precedes the literary criticism of the last section supplies the

[1] *Ep.* II, I, 111–13, 'ipse ego qui nullos me adfirmo scribere versus | invenior Parthis mendacior, et prius orto | sole vigil calamum et chartas et scrinia posco'; 117, 'scribimus indocti doctique poemata passim'.

[2] Indeed the letter is equally remarkable for its outspoken criticism of popular fallacies (some of them known to be shared by the emperor) and the consistently high level of its thought and presentation. Cf. Fraenkel's apt comments (*op. cit.* p. 395), and the following observation of R. A. Brower (*Alexander Pope: The Poetry of Allusion*, 1959, p. 183): 'Whatever Augustus may have thought of this performance, we can only admire. An age in which the leading poet could honour the chief of state with a piece of literary criticism seems to us fairly agreeable.'

[3] Drama, *Ep.* II, I, 139–213; epic, 214–70.

[4] Lyric verse is noticed in the section on the poet who is *utilis urbi*, at 132–8.

reasons for his procedure. The scope of the argument is wholly Horatian. Horace believes that in the Augustan setting poetry can regain, and partly has regained, some of the 'public ground' which it occupied, with low standards of taste, in archaic Rome, and with high artistic standards, in the social setting of classical Greece. But he is also a self-conscious and sophisticated artist, concerned with the high standards set by the new poets. To him the function of poetry means the function of modern and sophisticated poetry. There are three apparently divergent topics that make up the unity of the preparatory argument—old *versus* new, Greek *versus* Roman, and poet *versus* society. That the divergence of the topics is only apparent will be seen as the poem progresses. The three subjects are all brought together in the last section. Horace is debating whether Augustan Rome can create modern poetry which has a measure of the public status of archaic poetry and which can match the artistic standards of ancient Greece.[1]

The first part of the poem[2] establishes a critical basis for Augustan poetry. The popular equation old = good is quickly exposed. 'Old' is a relative term; it may be reduced to nought by the logical device of the 'falling heap'.[3] But current critical doctrine is little better. *Ut critici dicunt* (51) marks the adversaries; the plural is justified; that Horace is thinking of more than one is probably borne out by *ambigitur* (55). There is some evidence to show that Varro's, pre-Augustan, criticism exhibited the tendencies that are here censured.[4] But Horace is poking fun at the archaic tendencies which still pervade Roman education and the Roman literary scene.

---

[1] The *Letter to Augustus* has been fully discussed twice in the last few years, by F. Klingner, 'Horazens Brief an Augustus', *SBBA*, v (1950), 1–32, and Fraenkel, *Horace* (1957), pp. 383–99. I am chiefly concerned with Horace's literary criticism and raise questions of poetic style and arrangement only inasmuch as they obtrude on the subject-matter of this poem.

[2] *Ep.* II, 1, 18–89 (92).

[3] *Ruens acervus, ibid.* 47; the whole, general, argument, 18–49.

[4] The evidence for Varro and the Varronians has been discussed recently by Dahlmann, *op. cit.* p. 147, and Fraenkel, *op. cit.* p. 387, n. 4. I hope to review it in the forthcoming *Entretiens* of the Fondation Hardt.

He finds fault with both the procedure of the *critici* and the standard of the poetry which their theories are made to fit.

Their procedure Horace describes as a technique of labelling. This technique is known from Greek literary criticism. It applies to writers sensory qualities such as 'sweet' or 'astringent', or else qualities supposed to illustrate characteristic features of their work such as 'learned', 'serious', and so forth. Varro appears to have employed this technique. Horace gives some well-chosen examples—Pacuvius is *doctus*, Accius *altus* (56), Caecilius excels *gravitate*, Terence *arte* (59). The procedure persisted in Roman literary and rhetorical theory, as may be seen from the tenth book of Quintilian's *Institutions* and later works of criticism.[1] These labels, the argument seems to be, were used in order to establish the supposed status of archaic Roman poets by comparison with their Greek counterparts equally labelled. Horace mentions the great figures in the two pre-eminent genres of epic and drama: Ennius attached to Homer—*alter Homerus | ut critici dicunt*—Naevius, Pacuvius and Accius, Afranius attached to Menander, Plautus to Epicharmus, Caecilius, Terence, and even Livius Andronicus.[2]

Horace disallows both arguments. The claims implied by the labels of the connoisseurs are not even rejected; the ironical manner of the poet's report calls for no further comment. Nor is the facile identification of Greek and Roman writers here overtly opposed. This identification seems to imply a perversion of critical judgement. It causes Horace in this poem, as it had done in the satires and the letter to Florus, to raise the problem of poetic criteria. If age does not cause a poem to be 'good', what does?

[1] In view of the popularity and persistence of this critical technique Klingner must be mistaken in describing it as 'out of date' in the time of Horace (*op. cit.* p. 11).

[2] *Ep.* II, 1, 50–62. Since Horace restricts himself to only two poetic genres and yet mentions most of the great names, H. Dahlmann, *loc. cit.*, is right to be doubtful if conclusions as to contemporary theories of literary genres such as he considers himself are here legitimate.

In the criticism of the satires and the letter to Florus the contemporary note was unmistakable. A high degree of poetic workmanship was the hallmark of the new verse.[1] The wording in this poem indicates that this criterion still is in his mind: *emendata videri | pulchraque et exactis minimum distantia* (71–2). One might expect some mention of the *poetae novi* of the last generation who had shown a similar preoccupation with contemporary workmanship. However it is well known that Horace makes no such mention, here or elsewhere. Since he fails to tell us, we are reduced to guessing the motive for his omission. But it is not unduly hard to guess. The motive is likely to lie in his, and his friends', disagreement with the aspirations of the preceding generation and of their partisans among contemporaries.[2] He argues with them not by name but by implication. This procedure is a (dubious) way of eschewing controversy. It allows him to join the principle of technical finish (the 'file'), of which they would have approved, with the Augustan principles of elevated poetry, of which they would have (and, in the case of his contemporaries, probably had) disapproved.

In dealing with Callimachus his procedure is not entirely different. It is true, he allows himself an occasional indirect reference to a telling phrase or two by which the Alexandrian master voiced his demands for *tenui deducta poemata filo*. But that is all. More than that would imply an agreement with Alexandrian principles with which Horace was in flagrant disagreement.[3] The Callimachean principle of cultivated writing becomes part of the larger principle of Augustan poetry.

---

[1] Cf. above, p. 159 on *Sat.* I, 4, 9–13; p. 167 on *Sat.* I, 10; pp. 187 ff. on *Ep.* II, 2, 119–28. [2] Above, pp. 166–7, and below, p. 214.

[3] F. Klingner, however, *op. cit.* p. 29, is sure of Horace's Callimachean principles. 'Nimmt man dieses Bekenntnis mit anderen verwandten in Satiren und Episteln bis zur ars poetica zusammen, so wird man eines einheitlichen Kunstglaubens inne. Das Kallimacheische Fundament, wie es eben genannt wurde, tritt offen zutage.' This position seems to be somewhat modified in a later pronouncement (*Kunst und Kunstgesinnung des Horaz*, in *Der altsprachliche Unterricht*, 1951, no. 2, pp. 28–9). Cf. below, p. 219.

By now the categories of old and new, based on chronology, have been pushed out of the way to make room for the categories of good and bad writing, based on poetic quality. The road is clear for the second of the three subjects of this poem—poetry and the arts in the societies of Greece and Rome. This topic was inherent already in his first section, for it will be remembered that Horace combats a theory which based the poetic worth of archaic Latin literature on a similarity between Roman and Greek poets, which was partly assumed and partly real. The fallacy of such reasoning so far as poetry is concerned is revealed early in this letter. In Greek poetry perfection had come early; the praise accorded to the old Roman poets assumes the same thing for Rome. If that were true, no long argument would be called for.

> si quia Graiorum sunt antiquissima quaeque
> scripta vel optima, Romani pensantur eadem
> scriptores trutina, non est quod multa loquamur.
>
> (*Ep.* II, 1, 28–30)

But Horace is not a Callimachus looking back with a wistful mixture of inferiority and superiority on the glory that was Homer. Hence there is much to add, as the argument from age and quality issues into the section on Greeks and Romans[1] which it was designed to foreshadow from the beginning.

The disquisition on national psychology and the arts stands midway between the preceding argument, which is chronological and literary, and the subsequent one, which is political and literary. The middle section shares with the preceding the interest in 'old and new' and in poetry (as one of the arts); with the subsequent one the conviction that poetry concerns the community as a whole.

The arts like the rest of civilization are creatures of leisure. They may flourish when societies acquire a modicum of external security and freedom from internal oppression, some political stability and economic well-being. So it seems Aristotle had taught in the Τεχνῶν συναγωγή in order to

---

[1] *Ep.* II, 1, 93 ff.

explain the rise of rhetoric, and Cicero had expressed agreement.[1] In his *Politics* Aristotle had made use of a like argument when he wanted to explain how the Athenians came to change their minds in a weighty educational matter.[2] His explanation lies in the sudden emergence of entertainments and 'cultural pursuits' in the favourable circumstances of Athens after the Persian Wars once greater wealth gave rise to greater leisure, σχολαστικώτεροι γενόμενοι διὰ τὰς εὐπορίας. The note of sarcasm is unmistakable when Aristotle notes their high-minded craving for excellence, μεγαλοψυχότεροι πρὸς ἀρετήν; their getting above themselves because they had done well, φρονηματισθέντες ἐκ τῶν ἔργων; their omnivorous appetite for every kind of skill, πάσης ἥπτοντο μαθήσεως; and above all their indiscriminate zeal for discovering new pursuits, οὐδὲν διακρίνοντες ἀλλ᾽ ἐπιζητοῦντες. Commentators refer to this passage as a notable illustration of Horace's views in the present letter.[3] Whether the Roman poet is directly or only indirectly indebted to the Greek philosopher I do not know.[4] That there is a debt, however, both in this letter and in the *Ars Poetica*, seems to me very likely.[5]

Horace here wants to describe the volatile nature of the artistic temperament, so he magnifies Aristotle's sarcasm and

---

[1] Cic. *Brutus*, 45, citing Aristotle. V. Rose, *Aristotelis Fragmenta*, 3rd ed., starts his fr.137 at *Brutus*, 46, where indeed the words *ait Aristoteles* occur. However the passage of Aristotle's *Politics* noticed in the text above, the coherence of the context at *Brutus*, 45–6, and Cicero's wording '*itaque* ait Aristoteles', render it likely that *Brutus*, 45, too is part of Aristotle's doctrine. L. Spengel's Τεχνῶν συναγωγή (1828), 23, n. 39, adds one further sentence instead of two; L. Radermacher, 'Artium Scriptores', *SBÖA* (1951), 12–13, follows suit.

[2] Ar. *Pol.* viii, 6, 1341 *a* 28–32. The educational matter concerns the introduction of the flute πρὸς τὰς μαθήσεις.

[3] Kiessling and Heinze, and Wickham, in their notes on Horace, *Ep.* ii, 1, 93.

[4] Marie Delcourt, *Mél. Paul Thomas* (1930), pp. 187–200, says that she does know.

[5] I have mentioned the passage in an earlier chapter, p. 115, in connexion with *A.P.* 208 f., where new-fangled music, rhythms, and instruments (the flute included), are the subject under discussion. The point made in the letter to Augustus, 93–101, is different, but the similarity to Aristotle is striking. The flute-players are mentioned at line 98.

mercilessly caricatures fifth-century Athens. *Positis bellis* (93) and *hoc paces habuere bonae ventique secundi* (101) mark the beginning and end of the passage on post-war Athens. *Nugari* (93), *in vitium labier* (94), and the childish changeability of a *puella infans* (99–100)—these are the key-notes of his description. The Athenians tried everything and stuck to nothing: πάσης ἥπτοντο μαθήσεως οὐδὲν διακρίνοντες ἀλλ' ἐπιζη- τοῦντες, said Aristotle; 'quod cupide petiit mature plena reliquit', says Horace. Thus they changed from one entertain- ment to another, admiring in turn, athletics, horse-racing, sculptures in marble, ivory or bronze, and paintings, flute- playing, and the acting of tragedies.

Some of the sins which Romans liked to lay at the door of *Graeculi* do appear in Horace's caricature. Hence the tempta- tion to discover a chauvinistic note in Horace's philhellenism.[1] I think the temptation should be resisted. The rest of the sec- tion surely dispels the suspicion of chauvinism. If anything so crude is in the poet's mind at all, it is more likely to be the opposite: to show up such notions for what they are—carica- tures.[2] For the companion piece to the picture of the ever- childish Greeks is that of the ever-mature Romans, who felt so little the weight of chance-desires that for years on end they actually enjoyed the long business hours of the *patronus*.

> Romae dulce diu fuit et sollemne reclusa
> mane domo vigilare, clienti promere iura,
> cautos nominibus rectis expendere nummos,
> maiores audire, minori dicere, per quae
> crescere res posset, minui damnosa libido. (*Ep.* II, I, 102–6)

Finally the two caricatures of Greek *otium* and Roman *negotium* are capped by a third, the New Roman. Of a sudden the Romans have shown after all that they can change their minds. They all, talented or no, have taken to writing verse—

[1] Thus Fraenkel, *op. cit.* p. 390.

[2] It might be remembered that, at *A.P.* 323–32, a similar antithesis is sharply turned against Roman materialism. Such a conclusion is alien to the spirit of this portion of the letter to Augustus, although the figure of the unworldly poet puts in a brief appearance at 119–25. Also the *gloria* and *laus* at lines 177–80 may be compared.

so much so that even Horace has caught the fever and, breaking his word, has become a lyric poet once again;[1] *scribimus indocti doctique poemata passim.*[2]

At this stage of the letter Horace has given short shrift to the contention that mastery in Latin verse was an archaic matter, established centuries ago and therefore finished and done with; short shrift, too, through an elaborate show of irony and caricature, to the contention that the Romans are a people without poetic sensibility. Can his belief in Augustan poetry be established without political propaganda, that is, without the absurdity which he had censured in the first part of the letter?

> venimus ad summum fortunae: pingimus atque
> psallimus et luctamur Achivis doctius unctis.
>
> (*Ep.* ii, i, 32–3)

What Horace says next, with much emphasis, seems to serve as a link between the preceding context, on the artistic sensibility of the Greeks and Romans, and the subsequent context, on the beginnings of Roman drama.[3] It brings the idea of the poet as the conscience of the state into the central position of the poem. But Horace shuns solemnity. As so often when his personal convictions are engaged his demeanour is humorous.[4] The true poet's temper, *vatis animus* (119–20), is quite unlike that of the good Roman householder of the foregoing passage.[5] The *vates* laughs at financial losses,

---

[1] *Ep.* ii, i, 108–17.   [2] *Ibid.* 117, cf. above, p. 192.

[3] *Ibid.* 118–38. The place of the passage in Horace's scheme may be variously judged. Though connected with the previous context through the mock-serious defence of the poet's position, it is clearly not part of that context. Again though connected with the subsequent passage on another poet's genre, that of drama, the mention of lyric verse is closely linked with the educational claims for the poet who is *utilis urbi*. These indications make against F. Klingner's suggestion, *op. cit.* p. 19, that 93–133 should be regarded as a *Teil der Epistel*.

[4] To this passage of Horace certainly applies what R. A. Brower, *op. cit.* (above, p. 192), n. 2, p. 162, enunciates, I think, too generally: 'Pope, like Horace, can be convincingly serious only when it is certain that no one will take him seriously.'

[5] The tone is both humorous and naïvely innocent. This makes me wonder if E. Fraenkel's way of combining this passage with the preceding caricatures of the Greeks and Romans is not a little bit too pat. According to him the implied thought is this. 'Yet it is possible to have the best of both these worlds and combine the moral and political virtues of a Roman with the best gifts of the Greek Muse'

runaway slaves, incendiary damage to property. His only interest is verses. He is poor and he leads the simple life. He makes a bad soldier. But if he is of no account in the activities which the *urbs* takes seriously—economic, political, military— he is innocent also of the failings that debase these activities. He is free of *avaritia* (119). Because of his very uselessness he is useful to the city—ὠφελεῖ τῇ πόλει, as the Greeks would have said—

utilis urbi

si das hoc, parvis quoque rebus magna iuvari.

(*Ep.* II, 1, 124–5)

To see a highly skilled manipulator with words and rhythms thus claim the moral efficacy of verse must have brought a smile to the lips of many a sophisticated colleague or reader. For in spite of all assurances to the contrary on the part of philosophical theorists, poetry had travelled a long way from the romantic universality which the old Greek poets were thought to have displayed. The parts of the moralist, the philosopher, the rhetorician, and the teacher, had long since been claimed by other professions. Readers or audiences no longer expected to be taught how to live the good life. Nevertheless the claim is here made with great charm and modesty. And, after all, the conviction that poetry is nothing if not moral has been a feature of Horace's poetic creed in *Satires*, *Odes*, and *Epistles* alike.

At 126 he begins to make good the claim. Through his verse the poet is the educator of the young. And since in Roman as in Greek education early teaching was based on verse, there was nothing unrealistic about this claim although philosophers and rhetoricians would have disagreed as to the aim and manner of this education.[1] Horace first claims that the poet 'sets' (*figurat*) the tender and lisping mouth of the

(*op. cit.* 392). I see no 'combination' in this passage. It is precisely because the poet has no political virtues but is a 'good man' that he can be of use to the city with its attention to material interests.

[1] Plutarch's *praeparatio poetica* to the study of philosophy, *Quomodo adolescens poetas audire debeat*, is a case in point. But we have still to learn how to read Horace's letter in the light of this educational tradition.

child. He then moves inward as it were—from the enunciation of words and verses to the avoidance of *obscaeni sermones*,
and finally to the shaping of the emotions and the mind.[1]
The poet guides the child from the moment when he starts
speaking. Horace marks the stages of the *institutio poetica*: *os
tenerum* (126), *iam nunc* (127), *mox etiam* (128).[2] Through verse
read and learned early each generation goes to school with
the poets. Like many before and after him, Horace wants it
to be a good school. It is worth finding out how he conceives
of that school. The claim that he makes for poetry is large, for
verse thus written and thus taught will stay with the pupil
thereafter. But it is *paideia* with a small *p*, παιδεία for παῖδες.[3]

Horace has commented on the stages in the schooling of a
young Roman rather than on the types of verse employed at
each stage.[4] He thus contributed to the large Graeco-Roman

[1] Cf. E. C. Wickham's note on 127–8.

[2] Likewise marked are the stages in the eaglet's education, *Odes*, IV, 4, 5 ff., *iam,
mox, nunc* (Wickham, *loc. cit.*), and the adultress' progress, *Odes*, III, 6, 21 ff., *iam
nunc, mox* (Heinze, *ad loc.*). Cf. Petronius' educational poem, *Sat.* 5, *primos annos,
mox, hinc, interdum.*

[3] On this assumption there would be one sequence of thought from 118 to 138.
Horace would not then abandon the context 'the poet and the young' at 130 and
return to it at 132. Doubts are caused by lines 130–1, *recte facta refert, orientia
tempora notis | instruit exemplis, inopem solatur et aegrum.* But *orientia tempora instruit*, etc.,
may well mean 'he furnishes the rising years with...'; for *tempora*, 'age', see *Odes*,
IV, 13, 25, cited by Lucian Mueller, *ad loc.* This gives a clearer sense to *orientia*
than in the now current rendering as 'future generations', or 'each future genera-
tion'. As for *inops* and *aeger*, *Ep.* II, 2, 49, 'unde simul primum me dimisere Philippi, |
decisis humilem pennis *inopemque paterni | et laris et fundi*', etc., envisages just that
sort of situation in the poet's early twenties; *Ep.* I, 8, 8 shows how easily *aeger* passes
from being 'out of sorts' physically to being 'out of humour', and there is no lower
age limit for that. Several of the correspondents in *Ep.* Book I still would qualify
for education under *orientia tempora*, witness *Ep.* I, 2, 68 in particular.

[4] The instruction obviously begins with short metrical 'ditties', at 126. 127 is
indistinct. Gnomic verse may be indicated at 128–9. But the *recte facta*, 130, and
exempla and consolations, 131, again may refer to a number of genres. For *recte
facta* commentators point to the moralistic interpretation of Homer practised in
Ep. I, 2. Heinze, *ad loc.*, and Fraenkel, *op. cit.* p. 391, think that Horace may have
in mind above all the *Aeneid*. So he may. But since he does not go into the matter
it is perhaps safe to infer that he is not indicating poetic genres or individual poems
but making a general point. When he wanted to be precise he defined literary
genres succinctly, as at *A.P.* 73–85 and 401–6 or indeed in the final portion of this
letter. What is clearly indicated is the character of the relevant verse.

literature on education. The verse employed first should be cautionary and rich in maxims and precepts. It should teach how to control manner and emotion. Having accompanied the child to the stage of adolescence, Horace does mention two subjects. *Recte facta* and *exempla nota* (130–1) refer to admired deeds, but they do not state the kind of poem reporting them. One kind of verse however is mentioned and that is lyric. This is a subtle way of dissociating lyric from the subsequent discussion of the large genres. It is a subtle way, too, of displaying the most public function lyric verse, and Horace's own lyric verse, may fulfil—the function of providing the hymn in religious ritual. Some hymns, ancient and modern, have poetic merit; many have not. The allusion to Horace's own *Carmen Saeculare*, and the reflections of that hymn in the fourth book of the *Odes*,[1] show what he has in mind: it is the function of such a hymn when it has poetic qualities.

In discussing the poet who is *utilis urbi* Horace has largely spoken of educational matters. The philosophers' strictures upon poetry have been rejected by implication. But while delimiting the field of poetry he has also moralized it. In the utopian setting of the *Republic* Plato had restricted poetry to hymns to the gods and songs of praise of heroes.[2] In the educational context of this part of the poem the same two topics have been admitted, religious *carmina* and poems commemorating *recte facta*, and nothing besides that has any moral connotation. Had Horace been pressed hard to give examples of poems on *recte facta*, the resemblance to Plato's theory might have been less impressive. Plato legislated for a

---

[1] *Ep.* ii, 1, 132–3, 'castis cum pueris ignara puella mariti | disceret unde preces, vatem ni Musa dedisset', cf. *Carm. Saec.* 6, 71, 75; *Odes*, iv, 6, 29–32, 43–4; *Ep.* ii, 1, 136, *avertit morbos, metuenda pericula pellit* and 137, *locupletem frugibus annum*, cf. *Carm. Saec.* 29–32, 59–60; *Odes*, iv, 6, 39; *Ep.* ii, 1, 137 *impetrat et pacem*, cf. *Carm. Saec.* 46, 57.

[2] For example, Plato, *Rep.* x, 607 a, ὅσον μόνον ὕμνους θεοῖς καὶ ἐγκώμια τοῖς ἀγαθοῖς ποιήσεως παραδεκτέον εἰς πόλιν. The hymns and *encomia* play an important part in the tradition of literary criticism, cf. Ar. *Poet.* 4, 1448 *b* 27, and other passages discussed, though too narrowly, by H. Koller, *Die Mimesis in der Antike* (1954), pp. 177–92.

utopian community at large. Horace sought to show how poetry touched the moral fibre of the young. There is no evidence that he accepted Plato's strictures once the discussion turns away from the educational context. The discussion of the literary genres that now follows shows him sympathizing with other views. He selects drama and epic for comment and this selectivity is in agreement with the Aristotelian tradition in literary criticism.

Aristotle had placed tragic drama in the centre of his *Poetics*, with epic poetry in a supporting part. Comedy seems to have followed in the second book now lost.[1] This procedure suited some of the great literature to which he looked back with profound admiration, that is, Homer and the Attic dramatists. It did not suit the smaller genres; and the philosophy on which it rested—the doctrines of imitation and large-scale poetic unity—did not make it possible even to relate the small genres to the large. In spite of the flourishing poetic output at Alexandria and elsewhere, third-century aesthetics failed to take stock of the new, Hellenistic, situation. The system of the post-Aristotelian Lyceum certainly did not remain unchallenged. But our scanty information on Callimachus' position[2] suggests that the combined weight of the epic and dramatic tradition and the intellectual coherence of Aristotle's philosophy of poetry were too strong for Alexandrian aesthetics to prevail. Of the two great Hellenistic schools of philosophy, the Epicureans were reticent in matters of φιλολογία while the Stoics readily accepted the pre-eminence of the large poetic forms and moreover regarded the right kind of poetry as an adjunct to Stoic philosophy. Hence the continuing influence of Aristotle's judgements in matters of epic and drama.[3] The Aristotelian and Stoic positions were

---

[1] Above, p. 85, n. 1. [2] Above, p. 74.

[3] Later attempts to theorize on kinds of verse other than epic and drama are preserved in the Greek and Latin compilations of the Roman era such as the London Scholia to Dionysius Thrax or Diomedes' *Ars Grammatica*, Book III. But their underlying schematism shows them in fact to be highly traditional in the Peripatetic vein.

powerfully strengthened when the great Augustans derived new inspiration from the pre-Hellenistic types of Greek literature. In the letter to Augustus the scale of treatment with regard to the poetic genres noticed by Horace is in fact Aristotelian.[1]

Horace shared the belief common among Greeks and Romans that the manner of poetic expression was related to certain contents and genres. He held therefore that full poetic expression resided in some kinds of verse but not in others. In *Satires*, I, 4, he had withheld the name of poet from the writers of *sermones*.

> ingenium cui sit, cui mens divinior atque os
> magna sonaturum, des nominis huius honorem.[2]
>
> (*Sat.* I, 4, 43–4)

That the two forms of epic and tragedy fall in the category of 'great poetry' is easily seen.[3] Horace's habit of refusing the title of poet when he does not write lyric verse,[4] and also of claiming the bardic honours in the *Odes*, suggests that he places this genre in the same class. There remains comedy, whose poetic quality he had questioned at an early stage. But even at that stage the critics' strictures do not seem to have been accepted[5] and in the letter to Augustus comedy is discussed, alongside epic and tragedy, as one of the poetic forms that are the concern of the Roman *urbs*.

In considering what Horace says about the select genres of poetry, his reluctance (apart from the *Ars Poetica*) to go into

---

[1] In the economy of the poem, drama, tragic and comic, gets the lion's share, 75 lines, *Ep.* II, 1, 139–213; epic gets 57 lines, 214–70, lyric verse and the *carmina* mentioned at 132–8 half-a-dozen or so lines.

[2] Above, pp. 161–2.

[3] Ennius' *Annals* are cited for their truly poetic style, *Sat.* I, 4, 60–2. Grand epic too is the genre to which he asserts in certain odes and *sermones* he cannot rise, thus for example at the end of this letter, 250–9. As for tragedy, set *Ep.* II, 1, 165–6, 'et placuit sibi, natura sublimis et acer; | nam spirat tragicum satis et feliciter audet', beside *Sat.* I, 4, 46–7, 'quod acer spiritus ac vis | nec verbis nec rebus inest', etc., and compare Heinze's commentary.

[4] Thus *Sat.* I, 4, 39–42; *Ep.* I, 1, 10; II, 1, 111; II, 2, 57, 141–4; *A.P.* 306, etc.

[5] *Sat.* I, 4, 45 ff.; 63; I, 10, 16–17.

the niceties of professional criticism must be remembered. He is writing a poetic letter, not a treatise. This may account for the fact that the reasoning which would be required to establish his selection of genres is absent from his account. He has dealt with lyric verse in a different connexion. The smaller genres, above all elegiac verse, are conspicuously absent. Presumably they did not qualify as πολιτικόν under his definition. His silence may well point to deliberate censure.[1]

Drama, which now follows,[2] has an established place in the life of the city and the country-side. The traditional character of Roman drama is demonstrated by an account of its origins. The underlying theory is Greek; it may be traced back to Peripatetic and Alexandrian researches.[3] Varro seems to have applied it to Roman conditions. It certainly attracted the Augustans, though for different reasons.[4] Virgil, Livy, and Horace himself, give accounts of the beginnings of Roman drama which in spite of differences of detail have certain important features in common. The three writers believe that Roman drama was preceded by rustic jollifications on the occasion of religious festivals. Horace stresses two points. One is the traditional character of these early performances; the other is their rusticity.

On the former point Horace is brief. Drama is part of the Roman scene. He notes admiringly how his emotions are engaged by tragedy.[5] The emotional impact of drama from which Plato derived some of his charges does not move him to attempt a justification. He takes the justification of

---

[1] Cf. T. F. Higham, *CR*, xlviii (1934), 110; Brooks Otis, 'Horace and the Elegists', *TAPA*, lxxvi (1945), 177–90.

[2] *Ep.* ii, 1, 139–213, with a 'gliding transition' from the preceding context; Klingner, *op. cit.* p. 22; Fraenkel, *op. cit.* p. 393.

[3] Above, p. 119, n. 4.

[4] Cf. Virgil, *G.* ii, 380, Livy, vii, 2. The matter has been frequently debated. I hope to present a discussion of the evidence for Varro and the Augustans in the paper cited above, p. 193, n. 4.

[5] *Ep.* ii, 1, 210–13; his wording recalls what the philosophers had to say about the nature of dramatic illusion, but he makes no attempt to argue the matter.

drama for granted. He acknowledges, moreover, the Roman dramatist has a truly tragic bent, is

> natura sublimis et acer;
> nam spirat tragicum satis et feliciter audet.[1]

(Ep. ii, 1, 165–6)

On this score he holds that Augustan tragedy is both possible and by implication desirable. His doubts arise from the poetic demerits of Roman drama, tragedy and comedy. It is here that the second feature of the learned tradition is taken to explain present shortcomings.

At a late stage in Roman history, 'in the peace and quiet after the Punic Wars', writers of tragedy first felt encouraged to submit themselves to the influence of ancient Greek drama[2]— so Horace argues with an obvious reference to his earlier, Aristotelian, statement about the Athenians after the Persian Wars.[3] The Romans are late beginners who have (so to say) missed too many of the early lessons and have not quite caught up.[4] The elements of rusticity have clung not only to the earlier history of Roman tragedy but still remain in current writing—*hodieque manent vestigia ruris* (160).

Thus subtly the burden of the earlier sections reappears in this context; old and new, good writing and bad, the subjects of the first section, are closely related to the subject of the second, Greeks and Romans, and applied to the criticism of contemporary drama. It is seen therefore that the complaints of the literary satires and the letter to Florus still remain valid, at any rate as far as drama is concerned. Although social and political conditions are now felt to be auspicious, the writer of tragic drama suffers from an insufficiency of artistic principle—*sed turpem putat inscite metuitque lituram* (167).

---

[1] For the resemblance to *Sat.* i, 4, 46, see above, p. 204, n. 3.

[2] *Ep.* ii, 1, 161–3, 'Graecis admovit acumina chartis', etc.

[3] *Ibid.* 161 *serus*, and 162 *post Punica bella quietus*; this recalls 93, *positis bellis*. Cf. above, pp. 196–8.

[4] *Serus*, 161, hints at ὀψιμαθία, late learning and hence insufficient learning. Cf. *Sat.* i, 10, 21, *o seri studiorum*, addressed to ignoramuses.

Comedy stands condemned by the same token.[1] Motives are readily imputed. Plautus was more interested in the box-office than in the quality of his comedies. His *nonchalance* in the past and the present vagaries of public approval tell the same story.[2]

Now the second large genre remains to be scrutinized. It is the only genre in this letter on which Horace puts a wholly favourable construction, apart of course from the earlier mention of lyrics, which was on a different footing—and had to be since the poet's own verse was implicated. Epic verse is placed with much emphasis at the end of the survey, and of the poem. It was the only genre (apart again from lyrics) which by Horace's scale of judgement fully represented the new, Augustan, approach.

Epic was the oldest of the large Greek genres, Homer's genre. Owing to its subject-matter and its style it is one of the great 'public' genres. All poetry commemorates. Epic poetry does so *par excellence*. Its subject is heroes and heroic deeds.

> vixere fortes ante Agamemnona
> multi; sed omnes illacrimabiles
>   urgentur ignotique longa
>   nocte, carent quia vate sacro.   (*Odes*, IV, 9, 25–8)

Thus the fourth book of the *Odes*.[3] Thus too the letter to Augustus, if in a more pedestrian strain befitting the *sermo*. That epic verse had found a new public subject in the *res gestae* of the *princeps*, whether military or political, this Horace had remarked many a time, from the *Satires* and *Odes* to the present letter.

---

[1] *Ep.* II, 1, 168–76.

[2] Old Attic comedy was an approved genre in the literary satires. Here no Greek 'models' are indicated which can be taken as standards of excellence as the Greek tragedians are at line 163. The mention of Plautus would point to New Comedy. Horace's criticism of the *fabula palliata* may have gone counter to Augustus' predilection, cf. Suet. *Aug.* 89, 1, and Fraenkel's comments, *op. cit.* p. 396, n. 1.

[3] Cf. *donarem pateras*, IV, 8 and elsewhere.

Here once more the subject and quality of the new verse are brought into the discussion of one particular genre. The transition from the last section raises the topic of poetic quality in the distractions of public performances and entertainments.[1] The conclusion is that however strong its emotional impact may be, drama is a show that suffers from the disdain of the *spectator superbus*.[2] Poetry that is written for reading does not so suffer. It is more likely to be worthily received. In the case of drama the last word was that it may well rise to the heights. Epic verse has risen to the heights.

Poetic adequacy and inadequacy are contrasted in two patrons of the arts. Alexander, great king though he was, could not perceive poetic mediocrity when he saw it. He thought only Apelles and Lysippus competent to paint and model his features; but the second-rate Choerilus became the herald of his deeds. Augustus on the other hand will live in the epics of Virgil and Varius.[3] What Horace says about their portraiture of the hero of the new age must be set beside the verses cited above from the *Odes*:

> nec magis expressi voltus per aenea signa
> quam per vatis opus mores animique virorum
> clarorum apparent.   (*Ep.* II, 1, 248–50)

Horace does not spare criticism so long as he scrutinizes earlier Roman poets and contemporary Roman drama. The absence of all critical strictures on contemporary epic renders it more than likely that the survey of Augustan poetry is meant to culminate in these implied references to the *Aeneid* and the epic writing of Varius.

If that be true, Horace has here *post eventum* rewritten his early survey of the new poetry.[4] The genres there considered

---

[1] *Ep.* II, 1, 177–81, 182–213, specially 185–6, 'si discordet eques media inter carmina poscunt | aut ursum aut pugiles: his nam plebecula gaudet'. That it was not only the *plebecula* that enjoyed such items is rendered likely by Suet. *Aug.* 45, cited by Kiessling and Heinze, *ad loc*.   [2] *Ibid.* 215.

[3] *Ibid.* 245–7, 'at neque dedecorant tua de se iudicia atque | munera quae multa dantis cum laude tulerunt | dilecti tibi Vergilius Variusque poetae', and contrast 232–4.   [4] *Sat.* I, 10, 40 ff.

were: comedy, tragedy, epic, bucolic, and satire; elegy and small lyric verse did not qualify, but were perhaps depreciated by the mention of some contemporary nonentities.[1] The genres now considered are Aristotelian: drama, tragic or comic, and epic; lyric is mentioned at a remove as it were; bucolic and satire no longer qualify and there is still no mention of elegy or less elevated lyric verse. The poets there named (apart from Horace himself) were Fundanius, Pollio, Varius, and Virgil. Of these only three seem to have reached Augustan status—Virgil, Varius, and Horace. Writing as a judge he ruled himself out of court and placed his lyric verse outside the large and elevated genres, though within the ambit of *vates* who are *utiles urbi*. The epics of Virgil and Varius on the other hand fulfil the demands made in the letter to Augustus. They belong to the weighty Greek genre, they have public themes, and they have the new poetic qualities which may perhaps be taken to displace the *alter Homerus* satirized in a previous part of this letter.

[1] *Ibid.* 17–19.

PART IV

THE 'ARS POETICA' AS LITERARY CRITICISM AND AS A POEM

CHAPTER I

THE PRINCIPLES OF LITERARY CRITICISM IN THE 'ARS POETICA'

Literary criticism in the *Satires* and *Epistles*—apart from the *Ars Poetica*—has called for a lengthy and discursive treatment. For Horace has expressed the literary content of these essays in the imaginative form of poems; so that the content can be usefully approached only as it were *in situ*. Discussion however has shown that there are certain recurring features of thought and opinion in all of the critical poems. It will be expedient to tabulate the most outstanding.

(1) Horace's literary criticism is that of a poet-critic. By this I mean that it is not set forth by way of a critical 'system'; rather it selects, affirms, clarifies certain features of his own verse; it describes the character of his verse and it marks his agreement, or else disagreement, with other poets.

(2) Horace tends to present his most cherished personal convictions in the traditional garb of rationalistic Graeco-Roman criticism. The traditional character of its presentation and terminology must not make us ignore its personal content.

(3) Many qualities of poetry, and of Horatian poetry at that, do not come within the purview of this kind of criticism. It needs to be remembered therefore that the imaginative and poetic form of his literary essays supplies some of the gaps left by the critical content. To inquire whether the lyric verse of the poet Horace satisfies the claims made by the critic is beyond the scope of this book.

(4) Among the topics of his literary criticism two stand out. With many critics, before and after him, Horace shares the desire to describe qualities that are thought to be essential to poetry. Many modern critics make a distinction between

(mere) 'verse' and 'poetry'. Horace makes a comparable though by no means identical distinction between the technique of writing in verse and the qualities which he considers poetic. Technique, *ars*, is a *condicio sine qua non*, which however he finds rarely fulfilled. But poetry calls for more than that—intensity of spirit and great subjects. By these subjects he denotes matters of common concern, personal, moral, political. Unlike modern critics he believed great subjects to be allied to certain genres, and thus to certain styles: either to the large forms and monumental styles of drama and epic, or to the corresponding scale and tone in his own smaller genre, that of 'high lyric'. At the stage of the *Satires* he affirms his technical and moral demands and he hints at the larger aspirations that could not be realized in this genre. At the stage of the *Epistles* he reaffirms the technical demands and he specifies the larger poetic aims or achievements. Second only to the great poetry itself, it is the literary satires and epistles that gave voice to the Augustan spirit in poetry.

(5) Horace's polemic appears to be directed against two diverse tendencies in contemporary criticism. These may be superficially described as archaistic and modernistic. Just enough is known of the Roman literary scene to show that these tendencies must not be equated with literary groups: there is a suspicion that some of the modernists commended Lucilius, whom Horace censures for his archaic want of style.[1] To speak of two, let alone of two opposed, camps would be an over-simplification. Nevertheless, Horace has no use either for the critics who made great claims for the archaic writers of Latin drama, epic, and satire, or for those whose view was bounded by the sophisticated small poems of the preceding generation. Against the former he urges their lack of technical sophistication; against the latter the narrowness of their poetic world. Against both he urges the qualities of ancient Greek poetry.

Discussion now must show how far the *Ars Poetica* agrees,

---

[1] Above, pp. 166–7.

or else disagrees, with Horace's smaller literary essays. As I said at the beginning of the last section, I propose to make a case for the view that the *Ars* contains all the personal features of the poet-critic, but in addition takes a more comprehensive and 'systematic' view of poetry.[1] How is the *Ars* related in date and purpose, content and form, to the rest of Horace's literary essays?

It will be seen at once that the *Ars* conforms to the pro-cedure—in part fiction, in part reality—of almost all the literary essays.[2] Here, as nearly always, Horace maintains that in writing poetic criticism he is looking at poetry from with-out, not as an active poet from within. 'I will then perform the function of a whetstone, which can sharpen iron but itself has no cutting edge. Though writing no poetry myself, I will teach the poet's job and profession.'[3] In the *Satires* too Horace declined poetic honours because the doctrine of genres made it possible for him to understate the poetic merit of the genre *sermo*.[4] The first book of the *Epistles* renounces lyric verse, and the letter to Florus calls in literary criticism to explain that decision.[5] The letter to Augustus playfully disguises the poet's return to lyric verse.[6] The sentiment of the *Ars* is expressed by *nil scribens ipse*. Does this sentiment fit the *Satires*, or the first book of the *Epistles*, the letter to Florus, or the letter to Augustus? I do not think it does. For the poet who has decided to write (lyric) poetry no longer but teach *munus et officium* (*poetae*) could not speak in these terms if his reputation were not established; but at the stage of the *Satires* this reputation (in the emphatic sense in which he used the word) was not established. Nor does the sentiment of *nil scribens ipse* fit the first book of the *Epistles*, or the letter to Florus, because it is free from the feeling of chagrin, the dis-content with the creation of poetry, there displayed. Nor

---

[1] Above, pp. 153–5. [2] Above, p. 183.
[3] *A.P.* 304–6, 'ergo fungar vice cotis, acutum | reddere quae ferrum valet, *exsors ipsa secandi*; | munus et officium, *nil scribens ipse*, docebo'.
[4] Above, pp. 161–2. [5] Above, pp. 183–5.
[6] Above, pp. 191–2.

finally does it fit the mood of the letter to Augustus, or of any period in which he wrote lyric verse, because *nil scribens ipse* by definition excludes the writing of lyrics, although in Horatian language it does not so exclude the writing of 'pedestrian' talks or letters. In sum, then, the procedure whereby in the *Ars* the critic and teacher Horace keeps the creative poet at bay resembles that of the other critical writings. On the other hand the mood in which the job of criticism is performed has no parallel in any of the other writings. It makes sense only at a time subsequent to the composition of *Odes*, I–III; at a time too when the poet was no longer swayed by the contradictory emotions of *Epistles*, Book I, and the letter to Florus.

If this is a just observation it may help to fix the time when the *Ars* was composed. The date of the *Ars* is unknown. By that I do not mean that there are no scholars who think they know it. I do mean that there is not a single piece of evidence, nor a combination of such pieces, from which the date can be indubitably inferred. Since this is a controversial statement, and since moreover the facts of the case are complicated and require sifting, I have given my reading of the evidence in a note appended to this chapter.[1] This position does not absolve the writer on the *Ars* from using such indications as there may be.

If there is no unequivocal, external, evidence (such for example as the date furnished by Horace at the end of *Epistles*, Book I) it is still open to anyone to urge the force of internal evidence. Being contingent on personal interpretation, such hints and signs are liable to distortion.[2] It is possible

---

[1] Below, pp. 239–43.

[2] A case from contemporary writing will enforce my point. It comes from the little world of the animal fable which Horace enjoyed. The late Miss Beatrix Potter's last book has features which encouraged Mr Graham Greene to describe it in Shakespearian terms. She had (he thought) gone from the comedies to the near-tragedies and now had reached her *Tempest*. 'Miss Potter too had reached her island, the escape from tragedy, the final surrender of imagination to safe serene fancy' (*The Lost Childhood*, 1951, p. 110). So far the internal evidence and Mr Greene's interpretation of it. The external evidence was provided by Miss

that the interpretation I have placed on the *tone* of the *Ars*, and in particular of *nil scribens ipse*, is distorted. But that these indications need to be accounted for I have no doubt. If a four-square fact turned up, assigning the *Ars* to one of the periods from which I am proposing to remove it, a different interpretation of the *tone* of the *Ars*, and of the passage in question, would have to be found. Being unaware of such a fact, and noting that the external evidence does not *exclude* a late date, I interpret the indication as best I may. I suggest therefore that the divergence of *nil scribens ipse* from passages otherwise resembling it points to a date for the *Ars* after the publication of the fourth book of the *Odes* and the letter to Augustus, that is, after the years 14–13 B.C.

A late date would well suit other internal indications, specially the mature and comprehensive nature of the criticism—although these qualities taken on their own would be insufficient to exclude a somewhat earlier date. It would also have the advantage of endorsing Porphyrion's information as regards the letter *ad Pisones*. His much-maligned information is that it was addressed to L. Piso, subsequently city prefect, and his two sons—a family with known interests in the arts. Nothing is known of such interests in the case of Cn. Piso, or his family, who alone would seem to fit an earlier date.

The *Ars Poetica* not only sets as much store by poetic craftsmanship and sophistication as any of the smaller critical writings, but it allows technical considerations more space and greater importance in the 'teaching' of poetry. The *Ars* is nearly as long as the two longest critical letters put together, 476 lines as against the 486 (270 and 216) of *Epistles*, II, 1

Potter, who wrote to say that the book in question although published last was in fact the first written (p. 111). She deprecated sharply 'the Freudian school of criticism'. But Mr Greene's *débâcle* has nothing to do with Freud. It is a mistake in reasoning. He put *one* interpretation on a piece of imaginative writing which was capable of a number of rival explanations and he thought he was covered by the external evidence, the date of publication. Just so the 'character' of the *Ars* (which is not even covered by a date of publication) may be accounted for in various ways.

and 2. About a quarter of this, the initial 118 lines, is given over to the technical discussion of style and metre. Nor is that all. Wherever an opportunity offers, Horace returns to the topic of technique, and inculcates its vital importance. Discussing the content of poems he again brings craftsmanship to the fore. How can a poet make an old subject new?[1] How can he make a multiplicity of incidents into a unity?[2] Next comes the framing of 'characters'; here a celebrated passage shows how ethos is in fact depicted.[3] The following section on drama has always been recognized as what it is— a series of technical precepts.[4] The topic of drama again offers a chance of advising on metre. And the chance is taken. Unobtrusively and swiftly advancing from elementary beginnings, Horace is again propounding the puzzle of poetic workmanship before the reader is aware of it.

> non quivis videt immodulata poemata iudex
> et data Romanis venia est indigna poetis. (*A.P.* 263–4)

This is his old and deep-seated conviction as to the artistic sufficiency of the Greeks and the amateurishness of the Romans. Attention to the *exemplaria Graeca* and the *limae labor* and *mora* must be inculcated.[5] And there is more to follow. For no one doubts that craftsmanship, *ars*, is one of the underlying themes of the whole of the final portion.[6] Here the concept of verbal artistry is much deepened by other considerations. But the last of his traditional themes is '*natura* fieret laudabile carmen an *arte*, | *quaesitum est*'.[7] The question is answered in the balanced, Peripatetic, fashion: they are both required. But it is art not nature that remains in view, and the poem closes with a reminiscence of the stylistic criticisms of Quintilius Varus[8] and the sketch of the

---

[1] *A.P.* 128 ff.   [2] *Ibid.* 136 ff.   [3] *Ibid.* 153 ff.
[4] *Ibid.* 179 ff.   [5] *Ibid.* 268, 291.   [6] *Ibid.* 295 ff.
[7] *Ibid.* 408–9.

[8] *Ibid.* 438 ff. The passage recalls the censure of Lucilius in *Sat.* I, 10, and the work of the poet who proposes to write a *legitimum poema* and who takes, along with his writing tablets, *animum censoris honesti*, *Ep.* II, 2, 110.

insanus poeta, whose untutored *ingenium* proves both his undoing and a peril to his fellow men.[1]

Horace had often, if unobtrusively (for he did not mention his name), paid a tribute to Callimachus by speaking in the meticulous accents of the Alexandrian master in order to voice his own preoccupation with poetic elaboration.[2] So he does in the *Ars*. Wanting to demonstrate how a poet can make a traditional subject his own he advises him not to tarry within the common round of mere imitation—

> non circa vilem patulumque moraberis orbem.   (*A.P.* 132)

That wording recalls, and is meant to recall, Callimachus' fastidious rejection of the high road of versifiers; this has been observed by Horatian scholars and I have noted it before in the course of my analysis of the *Ars*.[3] But scholars are bound to come to grief if they would make Horace an Alexandrian on the strength of this and like passages.[4] Here as elsewhere Horace is careful to follow Callimachus so far but not farther. Here as elsewhere the context leaves no doubt that a reference to Callimachus also serves to score a point against Callimachus. Nothing could be more telling than the context of the *Ars* which gives rise to this reference. Horace is talking of the two large genres, drama and epic, and is demanding the care and brilliance of workmanship which will render the epic and dramatic *publica materies* the poet's private property. But epic was precisely the genre against which Callimachus warned the modern craftsman, however much Homer may have excelled in it. And the other genre, drama, shared with epic poetry the artistic awkwardness of its bulky frame and impassioned utterance. According to the *Ars* then there is everything to be said for formal artistry so long as you do not restrict it to the genres which the Alexandrian poet and his successors had said could not carry it under modern conditions. The *Ars* argues throughout for the cultivation of

[1] *A.P.* 453 ff.   [2] Above, p. 159.
[3] Above, pp. 109, 181–2.   [4] For example, see above, p. 195.

style while denying its Alexandrian corollary—insistence on the small and highly wrought forms. Virgil, Horace, and doubtless other Augustans, had long since shown by their verse that the monumental types of poetry and a high degree of technical polish were not mutually exclusive. The letter to Augustus and the *Ars Poetica* free the postulate of formal finesse from its 'Alexandrian' restrictions, whether Greek or Roman. Formal finesse must be a quality of any poetry, and above all of great poetry.

Strong convictions with regard to the formal qualities of verse thus link the *Ars* and the rest of the critical writings. There is a second axiom which the *Ars* equally shares with the literary satires and epistles—I mean the outstanding position assigned to certain literary genres. It is true, the interests of one of the addressees have sometimes been adduced as accounting for the pre-eminence of drama in the scheme of the *Ars*. Now the other letters certainly show that the subject in each case has some relation to the interests of each addressee. But in each case, too, the poet is offering to the world what *he* has to offer. So it is in the letter to the Pisos. The concern of the Pisos with poetry cannot well be doubted—as readers and perhaps more than readers; in the case of the elder son probably as one attempting to write it.[1] Biographical detail eludes us, and biographical detail may add colour to various features of the poem. Yet it is equally true that Horace is speaking to a larger audience than 'the father and the sons worthy of the father'.[2] I have still to find the features of the poem which do not come to life without such extraneous information. Whatever the interests of the Pisos may have been, the agreement between the *Ars* and the other critical writings shows that Horace is enunciating *his* sentiments with regard to the hierarchy of poetic genres.

---

[1] Porphyrion on *A.P.* 1 (on the assumption that he knew what he was talking about), *nam et ipse Piso poeta fuit et studiorum liberalium antistes*; as for the elder son, see *A.P.* 366 ff., 385 ff.

[2] *A.P.* 24; J. Vahlen (1906), *Ges. Phil. Schr.* II, 754 ff.

The Principles of Literary Criticism in the 'Ars Poetica'

In various ways the literary satires had pointed beyond the restricted sphere of those poems.[1] The letter to Augustus focuses discussion on the two large genres, first drama and next to it epic, and their commensurate subjects and styles; the lyric of the *vates* is given a place on account of its religious and moral implications.[2] In the *Ars* too various ways are found for noticing the smaller genres, and again lyrics are emphatically mentioned;[3] but the two kinds of poetry that receive full critical consideration are, as in the letter to Augustus, in the first place drama, and in the second epic.

In an earlier chapter I have made the point that even the section on poetic style turns, towards its end, to drama, tragic and comic, for illustration.[4] And certainly, once the content of verse comes to the fore, Horace's true concern is the poetic forms in which a large subject has to be organized, drama and to a lesser degree epic. That at first the two are conflated[5] is easily understood on account of their affiliations and re-semblances. But having traversed the area in which epic and drama meet, Horace moves on to drama[6] and remains in that field for the whole of this central section, letting pass in review first the drawing of character, then various matters concerning the staging and layout of a play and its chorus and music, and finally, the three types of drama, tragic, satyric, and comic, Greek and Roman.[7]

Nor are the political and moral implications of poetry judged differently in the *Ars* and in the smaller critical writings. Satire concerns itself with society. Its originator at Rome, Lucilius, is praised 'quod sale multo | urbem defricuit'.[8] For all the artistic demands Horace makes, satire has, and should have, a moral effect. No trace here of the serviceable distinction of Philodemus—asking whether poetry was educative

---

[1] Above, p. 177.   [2] Above, p. 202.
[3] *A.P.* 73–85, on account of their style and nature; 391–407, on account of their importance to society. In both passages drama and epic are noted as well.
[4] Above, p. 98, on *A.P.* 89 ff.   [5] *Ibid.* 128 ff.
[6] *Ibid.* 153.   [7] *Ibid.* 153–294.
[8] *Sat.* I, 10, 3–4.

qua poetry.[1] Enough, satire belongs to the life of man in society. The larger, and according to Horace more 'poetic', genres are not less but more involved with morals and men. The poet reads Homer and he finds that

> quid sit pulchrum, quid turpe, quid utile, quid non,
> planius ac melius Chrysippo et Crantore dicit.   (*Ep.* 1, 2, 3–4)

From such reading, and writing, it is not a long way to the decision of the first epistle,

> nunc itaque et versus et cetera ludicra pono;
> quid verum atque decens curo et rogo et omnis in hoc sum.
> (*Ep.* 1, 1, 10–11)

But conversely it is not a long way back to the 'philosophy' in verse which the letter to Augustus and the *Ars* profess. The *carmina* of the *vates*—so the letter to Augustus observes—are both poetic and religious.[2] The poet thus writing is *utilis urbi*.[3] Drama is an entertainment for the city at large and the thorny problem of politics enters into the patriotic genre of epic verse.[4] A critic holding such views will place poetry squarely in the centre of society, giving to verse large subjects and thereby exposing it to the large dangers of political servility or equivocation.

The *Ars* offers similar views, save that its writer does not recommend public themes, as he did in the letter to Augustus. Nor indeed does he refuse (as he did in the same letter)—

> res componere gestas
> terrarumque situs et flumina dicere et arces
> montibus impositas et barbara regna *tuisque*
> *auspiciis* totum confecta duella per orbem
> claustraque custodem pacis cohibentia Ianum
> et formidatam Parthis *te principe* Romam
> si quantum cuperem possem quoque.[5]   (*Ep.* II, 1, 251–7)

---

[1] Above, p. 177.   [2] *Ep.* II, 1, 126 ff.; above, p. 202.
[3] *Ibid.* 124; above, p. 200.   [4] Above, pp. 207–8.
[5] In the *Ars* the *res gestae* are noticed first in connexion with the metre and style of Homer, 73–4, but later also as part of a course in the drawing of character-

But if the aim of the *Ars* excludes political application there is certainly an appeal to moral 'values' and the social efficacy of poetry.

The poet must carry in his mind the values and categories taught by the philosophers. He must 'know' before he can start writing as he ought,

> scribendi recte *sapere* est et principium et fons. (*A.P.* 309)

These values and categories are his true subjects, *res*, and moral philosophy is called in to provide them,

> *rem* tibi *Socraticae* poterunt ostendere *chartae*.[1] (*A.P.* 310)

The lessons are briefly illustrated. They amount to a moral code of a traditional kind.[2] In view of what is said about patriotic subjects in the letter to Augustus it may be noted that duty to one's country—*patriae quid debeat*—opens the list.[3] This teaching lends a moral ethos to the disciple and to his poetic experiments. It is a companion piece to the early education through poetry envisaged in the letter to Augustus.[4] The poet has been trained to represent life and manners; he is a *doctus imitator*.[5] His matter has been provided (*provisa res*) and he may turn to the job of composition,

> verbaque provisam rem non invita sequentur. (*A.P.* 311)

A person who has been thus taught will be predisposed to temper 'poetic sweetness' with 'moral principle', like the ideal poet

> qui miscuit utile dulci
> lectorem delectando pariterque monendo. (*A.P.* 343–4)

---

sketches: 'quod sit conscripti, quod iudicis officium, quae | partes in bellum missi ducis', etc., 314–15; doubtless *res gestae* are also the burden of the verses with which 'insignis Homerus | ...animos in Martia bella | ...exacuit', 401–3.

[1] For the meaning of *Socraticae chartae* see above, p. 131, n. 1.
[2] Above, p. 131.
[3] *A.P.* 312.
[4] *Ep.* II, 1, 126 ff.; above, pp. 200 ff.
[5] *A.P.* 317–18.

This description may fit equally the Divine Comedy and a cautionary tale which is devoid of poetic virtue. Just as before the problem of political interest, so here the equally thorny problem of moralizing enters into the argument because the moralistic purpose may nullify the poetry. Horace however writes at a high level of poetic intent; so the earlier part of the *Ars* has shown. In the second piece of *Epistles*, Book I, it was Homer whom he thought to illustrate more fully than the moral philosophers 'what is noble or base, expedient or not'.[1] In the letter to Augustus he adduced Virgil and Varius as epic writers who had dealt successfully with great patriotic themes. How Varius solved the problem no one can tell. But that the *Aeneid* satisfies Horace's moral point as much as the patriotic I do not doubt. A leader in war who in a clash of claims sets aside inclination for duty surely illustrates not only *patriae quid debeat et quid amicis*[2] but *quae partes in bellum missi ducis*.[3] It may also be noted that Horace's principles accommodate Homer as much as Virgil. In this regard too the letter on Homer (*Epistles*, I, 2) illuminates certain passages of the *Ars* where Horace has taken his own advice to heart—*quidquid praecipies, esto brevis*.[4]

Having laid down the principles of the craft, as he said, mock-seriously, he would,[5] he turns to ancient myth and history for corroboration.[6] He assembles on one large canvas many of the beneficial 'public uses' of verse and song which were possible in more primitive social settings when *sapientia* had not as yet been sorted out into religion, morals, law, government, philosophy, personal poetry, music, and entertainment, courtly, rural, and civic. Once again Horace puts his own strongly held views in a traditional manner. He is concerned with the impact poets have made on society. His narrative begins as a myth and leads into a historical account

---

[1] *Ep.* I, 2, 3–4; cf. above, p. 222.
[2] *A.P.* 312.   [3] *Ibid.* 314–15.
[4] *Ibid.* 335, and the brevity of the precepts, *Ep.* I, 2, 55 ff.
[5] *Ibid.* 306–8, *munus et officium...docebo*, etc.
[6] *Ibid.* 391–407.

of the relevant poetic genres.[1] Such accounts had been drawn up for centuries by men of letters, 'sophists', philosophers, poets, rhetoricians, and musicians. They were drawn up in order to show the various arts as agents of progress in a simpler social setting which preceded the ages of specialization.[2] The narrative is historical; it does not depict the face of poetry at a time when man had departmentalized various human activities. Nevertheless it offers too many resemblances with Horace's own view of poetry—both in the *Ars* and the letter to Augustus—not to be taken as an exemplary tale and a tract for the times. Dealing with the past, partly mythical and partly historical, the *Ars* can make larger claims than the letter to Augustus. But both works alike assert the concern of poetry with human affairs at large.[3]

Four articles of Horace's poetic faith are now seen to be present not only in the smaller writings but in the *Ars* as well: the conviction that artistry is at the root of the art of poetry; the conviction that poetry aims at the 'whole man', not only at 'aesthetic man', and therefore has a function in society; the conviction that some kinds of verse can fulfil this function better than others; and finally the conviction that the Greek temperament, or else their sense of values, was more apt to generate that kind of poetry than the Roman.

[1] Relevance to man as a social being determines the genres selected at *A.P.* 401 ff. Elsewhere Horace's view is not so determined. That is the reason why the selection at *A.P.* 73 ff. differs in some respects; for there he seeks to determine the relation between poetic forms and their style and metre. Archilochus' iambics are omitted in the later passage but noted in the earlier. Elegiacs qualify in the later passage as a martial genre, but in the earlier do so as a vehicle for laments and votive epigrams. As T. F. Higham observes, *CR*, XLVIII (1934), 110, 'one might conclude from lines 401–3 that the martial strains of Tyrtaeus were almost the only kind of elegy worth considering'.

[2] The accounts vary greatly in tendency and substance. The progressive tendency in the writing of them dates back to the Sophists of the fifth century B.C. The role of Orpheus had been variously rationalized; the present passage has striking resemblances to the chorus of Aristophanes discussed above, pp. 132–4.

[3] The *Ars* is also more outspoken on national failings. Whereas the letter to Augustus keeps the two national psychologies, Roman and Greek, in a humorous balance (cf. above, p. 198), the *Ars* roundly condemns Roman materialism, and draws an idealized picture of the Greeks as a nation of poets, *A.P.* 323–32.

There is no point in accumulating further evidence (of which there is plenty) for a simple observation: the *Ars* re-affirms, in some ways strengthens, the views of the smaller literary writings. Now if this were all it should be possible to explain the *Ars* on the basis of the smaller *sermones*. But that is precisely what students of the *Ars* have been unable to do, however hard they have tried.[1] The *Ars* offers something larger and more comprehensive. Unlike the smaller critical writings, it rests on a set of abstract notions. What are these notions and how are they used in the *Ars*?

I have suggested in an earlier chapter that Horace employed Aristotelian and Alexandrian notions to define the critical territory of the *Ars*. I have also suggested at the beginning of my last section that Horace turned to Aristotelian teaching (as Coleridge turned to neo-Platonic) because he required a more comprehensive framework for his criticism.[2]

The first of these systematic notions is the triad 'wording (and arrangement)–content–general criticism' which under-lies the technical portion of the *Ars*.[3] The cut-and-dried division of the creative process into content and style (and arrangement) clearly commended itself to Horace throughout his career as a critic.[4] But with one exception no single essay of his makes this division the mainstay of his literary criticism. The one exception is the *Ars*, for these notions provide the framework for whatever else Horace may wish to say.

Such is the systematic order of subjects which Horace

---

[1] I am thinking of such studies as F. Klingner's 'Horazens Brief an die Pisonen', *BVSA* 88, no. 3 (1936), and such nineteenth-century studies as O. Weissenfels' 'Aes-thetisch-kritische Analyse der Ep. ad Pis. von Horaz', *Neues Lausitzisches Magazin*, xxvi (1880), 118–200. Also cf. above, p. 155, n. 1.   [2] Above, pp. 153–5.

[3] For the traditional notions of his general criticism in the section on 'the poet', see above, pp. 125 ff.

[4] The passage starting at *Ep.* 1, 19, 21 offers as good an example as any. Horace puts in the language of literary criticism what he had said more simply and poetically at *Odes*, III, 30, 13–14, 'princeps Aeolium carmen ad Italos | deduxisse modos', and elsewhere. Now a distinction is made between *numeri animique* and *res et verba* and between agreement in *modi* and *carminis ars* and disagreement *rebus et ordine*; see above, p. 181. However illuminating in this context, these abstract notions are incidental to the poem as a whole.

adopted from an Alexandrian adherent of the Aristotelian school. The order is unobtrusive, rarely brought to the surface (as at lines 41 and 306), and used with enough flexibility to give room to less pedantic procedures. If it had been more obtrusive, then the interminable discussions as to the order of the *Ars* could have been avoided; there would have been no need for them. What Horace has done is to make an intellectual framework out of ideas which present themselves incidentally everywhere in his smaller writings. So far from objecting to them he actually sought them out. But he did not allow them to dominate his poem. There is nothing incongruous in this procedure. The Aristotelian order of things may have been rationalistic and rhetorical. But, particularly in its later shape in which he found it, it had the great advantage of offering a framework for his literary criticism.

Nor is this all. In his critical writings, early and late alike, Horace displays an enthusiasm for drama and epic which would be surprising in a lyric poet and satirist, were it not for two motives: the actualities of the contemporary poetic scene, and the bearing (partly assumed, partly real) of the large genres on his own lyric verse.[1] Thus in adopting Aristotle's valuation of the large genres (adopted by Neoptolemus himself) he clearly expresses a cherished personal conviction in traditional terms. In that respect the *Ars* does not differ from his literary satires or from the letter to Augustus. It differs however in the manner in which the large genres are made an integral part of a comprehensive literary theory, Horatian as much as Aristotelian and Neoptolemic. As in Aristotle's *Poetics*, drama, in the first place, and epic, in the second, are considered the exemplary kinds of poetry. In the *Ars* they are in sole possession of the central section,[2] and in addition receive much attention in the section on style. As for satyric drama I would append only this caution. Seeing that Horace's outlook is as personal as it is Aristotelian, and as contemporary as it is traditional, I should hesitate to

---

[1] Above, p. 214.   [2] *A.P.* 119–294.

pronounce too confidently on this particular dramatic genre.
All that can safely be said today is that the genre was Attic
and Alexandrian, not Roman;[1] but the actuality of all his
traditional precepts renders it probable that Horace had an
actual purpose in mind. Our evidence is insufficient to establish the personal nature of that purpose. But I doubt if he
would have spoken as he did if he had not considered satyric
drama a viable genre, at any rate for recitation.

The Horatian *sermo*, whether satire or epistle, is not noticed
at all. I have discussed earlier why it does not fully qualify.
Lyric verse, Horace's own genre, does qualify. It is here accommodated in the same way as in the letter to Augustus.[2]
Not being one of the large, Aristotelian, genres, it finds no
place in the central doctrines about the 'content' of poetry
and the exemplary 'kinds'. Though disqualified by size it
qualifies by its character, the elevation and intensity of its best
representatives, its noble ancestry, and the moral and social
impact of its *carmina*. Hence a brief appearance is warranted
along with drama and epic, and some of the smaller genres, in
the weighty passage on the social origins of poetry.[3] The
smaller genres likewise appear in the stylistic section of the
Ars.[4]

In dissociating style and content, Greek and Roman critics
of poetry tended to put asunder what in the nature of poetry
is joined together. Their doctrine of the 'appropriate style',
τὸ πρέπον, serves to join the two once again. The Greek term
in this context denotes the right relation between two entities;
this is expressed also by the Latin words used by Horace and
Cicero, as *decorum, decor, decens, aptum, conveniens*, and the like.
The doctrine had undergone many modifications since the
fifth century B.C. when it first acquired some importance.[5]
Philosophers as well as men of letters paid much attention to

[1] Above, pp. 119, n. 5, 149.   [2] Above, p. 202.
[3] *A.P.* 391–407.   [4] *Ibid.* 73–85.
[5] M. Pohlenz was the first to provide a comprehensive account of τὸ πρέπον,
NGG (1933); also see W. Süss, *Ethos* (1910); J. F. D'Alton, *Roman Literary Theory
and Criticism* (1931), pp. 423 ff., 480; L. Labowsky, *Die Ethik des Panaitios*, etc. (1934).

it and formulated various theories. Horace must have known a number of them. But here as everywhere he is careful not to become unduly involved with the details of specific philosophical theories. The *Ars* serves to show however that its author favoured some theories more than others. For the Aristotelian and, presumably, the Neoptolemic varieties loom very large, perhaps because they were more apt for a poet and man of letters than those of other philosophers.[1]

Among the basic axioms of the *Ars*, *decorum* ranks second in importance only to the basic distinction between style (and arrangement) and content, to which in fact it provides an essential complement. Horace recurs to it so persistently that one can sympathize with scholars who take *decorum* to be the chief subject, and the connecting link of the manifold topics, in the *Ars*.[2] This suggestion has not however commended itself to many critics[3] and I myself find it hard to accept. In fact, I am not aware of any single item of the *Ars* to which this suggestion could be reasonably applied. But Horace would not have referred so frequently to *decorum*, *aptum*, and the like, had he not found it profitable so to do.

Decorum, or appropriateness, is the common term of reference between style and content, style and emotion, and style and character. Aristotle taught in the *Rhetoric*,[4] and presumably Neoptolemus restated in discussing the topic of ποίημα,[5] that style must appropriately express the subject and the emotions and the ethos involved in speech. Likewise *decorum* is employed by Horace as the essential condition which the poet must fulfil in bringing style in line with his subject and the emotion and the ethos of a piece of poetry.[6]

---

[1] For the theories of other schools cf. above, pp. 96, n. 1, 136, below, p. 230, n. 4.

[2] Above, p. 35, n. 1.

[3] It is rejected for example by J. F. D'Alton, *op. cit.* p. 480, n. 7, and J. Tate, *CR*, LIII (1939), 191–2.

[4] Above, p. 97, on Ar. *Rhet.* III, 7.   [5] Above, pp. 96, 138–9.

[6] See above, pp. 98 ff., for *A.P.* 89–98, on style, subject, and genre; 99–113, on style and the emotions; and 114–18, on style and types of character. The references to appropriate diction, in the narrow sense of the term, are somewhat different. New coinages in vocabulary must be made *pudenter*, *A.P.* 51, and *parce*, 53. This may be

Subsequent uses of the principle in the *Ars* may be related to the first but are not identical. As *decor* it is the measuring rod for the consistency of character drawing (an Aristotelian topic),[1] and this in turn impinges on the shaping of plot and character in drama or narrative[2] and on certain precepts on the construction of drama.[3]

Another application of the principle of appropriateness is made in the general portion of the *Ars* (from 295 onwards). The modern accounts of its functions vary.[4] But it is certain that at any rate a similar word, *decet*, is used to express the ideals a poet should aim at; 308, *quid deceat quid non*, probably refers to the balanced, Peripatetic, aim of *miscuit utile dulci* (343). Moreover when the principles of character drawing are resumed, at 312, 'reddere personae...*convenientia* cuique' is made dependent on the study of moral theory (316).

The axiom of unity may here follow on. It is clearly related in thought to the subtle discussions on how to preserve appropriateness, and although it may have similar historical roots,[5] it is not merged with its counterpart by Aristotle, or indeed by Horace himself, who largely depends on Aristotelian theory.[6] He demands twice in the *Ars*, with much emphasis,

the μέτρ⟨ι⟩ον recommended for such matters in Aristotle's *Poetics*, 22, 1458*b* 12, and explained as the avoidance of ἀπρεπές and ἐπίτηδες ἐπὶ τὰ γελοῖα; cf. above, p. 96, n. 2. A sense of the right mean is enjoined at *A.P.* 24 ff., and elsewhere in this work. Again the alignment of metres and genres at *A.P.* 73–85 may be explained in terms of *decorum* of style and content; the transitional passage, 86–8, gives some substance to this assumption.

[1] *A.P.* 156–7 thus introduce the section on characterization: 'aetatis cuiusque notandi sunt tibi mores | mobilibusque *decor* naturis dandus et annis'.

[2] The incidents of a new plot must be consistent, *sibi convenientia*, 119; and similarly about a new personage, 126–7.

[3] Choral odes must be related, *apte*, to the causal nexus of incidents, 195 (see above, p. 115, for its Aristotelian provenance); compare the restriction placed on the *deus ex machina*, 191.

[4] I find myself unable to discover in Horace's account any such Stoic elements of Panaetius' theory of τὸ πρέπον as have been asserted specially by L. Labowsky, *op. cit.* (see above, p. 136, n. 4).

[5] Cf. the remarks of M. Pohlenz, *op. cit.* p. 54, on Gorgias and Isocrates. Appropriateness and unity are complementary terms in Plato's discussion, *Phaedrus*, 264*c*, 286*d*.

[6] J. F. D'Alton, *op. cit.* pp. 482–3; above, pp. 138–9.

that a work of poetry must exhibit unity. The first demand comes near the beginning, the second later in the central section of the poem.

The whole of the introductory portion aims at this very point: 'denique sit quidvis, *simplex* dumtaxat *et unum*'.[1] There is some likelihood, but no certainty, that the axiom was placed in this position by Neoptolemus.[2] Whether or not Horace was the first to place it in this conspicuous position, he did not adopt its Aristotelian placing within the context of tragedy. Where it now stands it has pride of place as the first large axiom enunciated in the *Ars*. It is also likely that the Alexandrian controversialists employed this term; Neoptolemus perhaps argued in favour of the large genres on this very basis.[3] Horace is both more general and more controversial in this section than is Aristotle in chapters 7 and 8 of the *Poetics*, where he introduces unity as a fundamental principle but applies it primarily to tragedy and in the second place to epic. What seems to interest Horace is the maximum of allowable variety within the overall unity of a poetic conception—an eminently Roman and Horatian problem, as the odes and hexameter poems suggest.

When the concept of unity reappears it is linked with drama and epic; that is precisely the context in which Aristotle sets it in the *Poetics*. The postulate of consistency in the shaping of a plot or a narrative, and of its characters, has been noticed already. Horace returns to the demand of unity a few lines later, at 131. Like Aristotle he contrasts the cyclic poets with Homer; the author of the *Odyssey* is commended for making a unity out of the diverse elements of his narrative. Horace's wording is deliberate and to the point. As was noted earlier, he uses the language of Callimachus when he argues that a poet may be original while using traditional material.[4] But

[1] *A.P.* 23; *quidvis*, Bentley.
[2] Above, pp. 102–3, 139.
[3] Above, p. 102.
[4] Above, p. 109, n. 2, on 131–5, 'publica materies privati iuris erit si | non circa vilem patulumque moraberis orbem', etc.

as in other places where Callimachus comes into the picture, praise is readily turned into dispraise. For Homeric unity is enjoined along with a large Homeric subject—not a Callimachean injunction. Again Homer's 'brilliance' is celebrated in two phrases which Callimachus might have endorsed: *speciosa miracula*, 144, and *nitescere*, 150. But they are capped by the resounding reference to the Aristotelian ἓν καὶ ὅλον which concludes the discussion—

> primo ne medium, medio ne discrepet imum.   (*A.P.* 153)

The concurrence with the letter to Augustus and earlier writings suggests the contemporary, Augustan, tendencies on which I have frequently commented. But the *Ars* again stands apart for an important reason. Horace now speaks almost like a professional, philosophical, critic. The principle of unity is here preserved in a large semi-Aristotelian context. At the outset, unity is established as a valid principle for all of the technical disquisition that follows. And in the central portion, the same principle once more is assigned its Aristotelian role; it is to relate the diverse elements of a long narrative or drama, and bring them together into a single large structure.

The evidence is now before the reader. My inference from it is this. The *Ars* resembles the smaller literary writings in that it puts forward the personal and contemporary notions of the poet and critic, Horace. It also resembles the systematic expositions of Aristotle and the professional literary critics in that it makes use of a framework of such abstract notions as style, content, and the like. It follows that it differs from the smaller literary writings chiefly through the use of such a framework, that it differs from the works of professional criticism in balancing the claims of coherent and rigorous exposition with other claims. In fact the systematic order that underlies the *Ars* is concealed and diversified by poetic artistry. It is only rarely that a glimpse of the framework can be caught, as at lines 40–1 and 306–8. But though in the background this framework is not useless. Without it, the *Ars* would fall apart into an unrelated sequence of fleeting impressions,

> cuius velut aegri somnia vanae
> fingentur species, ut nec pes nec caput uni
> reddatur formae.   (*A.P.* 7–9)

With it, the *Ars* turns out to be the work of a poet and critic who for once aspired to the objective canons and rigorous principles of the philosophers while yet insisting on his rights as a poet.

In writing the *Ars*, Horace's purpose was larger than the piecemeal criticism in the other satires and letters. He was presenting his view of the whole field of what he considered great poetry. For this purpose he required at any rate the skeleton of a critical 'system'. He also had to adopt a most selective sort of treatment. Whether he named his poem *Epistula ad Pisones de arte poetica*—or just *Epistula ad Pisones*—the original title had been ousted by a nickname, *De arte poetica*, or *Ars Poetica*, in the time of Quintilian, about three generations after the poet's death,[1] and perhaps earlier. The nicknames remained in the place of the original title in almost all of the ancient and the whole of the medieval tradition.[2] *Ars poetica*, τέχνη ποιητική, is certainly a misnomer if you demand from an *ars* the exhaustive and rigorous treatment of a treatise or textbook. But not all ancient *artes* were exhaustive textbooks (Aristotle's *Poetics* for one is not), and their degree of rigour varies considerably. The nicknames have their uses however because they draw attention to the wholeness of a large subject

---

[1] Quint. *I.O.*, *Ep. ad Tryph.* 2, *Horati consilio qui in arte poetica suadet*, and VIII, 3, 60, *Horatius in prima parte libri de arte poetica*, referring to lines 1–2.

[2] The only possible exceptions at present known from the ancient tradition are two probably incomplete forms of citation of the *Ars* by the fourth-century grammarian Charisius, *Horatius epistularum* (ed. Barwick, 263, 9; 265, 1; Keil, *Gram. Lat.* I, 202, 26; 204, 5).

and the consistency of the critical philosophy underlying it.[1] It is these qualities that partly account for the remarkable fact that the *Ars*, together with Aristotle's *Poetics*, could provide the foundations for Western literary criticism from the sixteenth century to the nineteenth, when the traditional link snapped.

There are three different features of Horace's *Art of Poetry* which merit attention in an assessment of his literary criticism —the *Ars* as a body of general axioms, conclusions, and 'rules'; the *Ars* in its contemporary and Augustan aspects; and finally the bearing of its poetic form on its literary criticism.

As a body of general axioms, conclusions, and rules, the *Ars* has been of great historical importance; but the history of criticism has also shown up its vulnerability. As a piece of critical reasoning the *Ars* cannot lay claim to the virtues of its ultimate model, Aristotle's *Poetics*, although it suffers from some of its weaknesses. It lacks the Aristotelian coherence and punch, and on the other hand it is open to the same objections as the axiomatic conclusions of the *Poetics*; for it is liable to lose its validity when the axioms underlying its reasoning are no longer acceptable. It is however relevant to distinguish its 'rules', in the narrow sense of the term (such as the post-Aristotelian five-act scheme), from its wider aspects (such as the concept of unity). For rules, in the narrow sense, are based on authority and convention, and are likely to be disregarded when authority and convention come to be disregarded. The wider aspects reveal the practical turn of mind of a poet or writer dealing with the practices of his craft. There is, for example, little that puts the reader in mind of the intricate Aristotelian problems of plot-construction. But the relation between the parts of a poetic or literary structure may be usefully considered apart from the immediate relevance of classical and neo-classical drama or epic.

J. W. H. Atkins' opinion, *Lit. Crit. in Antiquity*, II, 74–5, should have been taken to heart.

But however they are employed, the principles underlying the *Ars* are rationalistic in character. *Sapientia*, explained as moral theory, is said to lie at the root of the poet's education. Horace assures us that once the content has been so provided for the poet, 'words will follow it not unwillingly'. Form and content thus remain distinct in Horace's theory of poetry, just as they were distinct in Aristotle's; much reflection on *decorum* is thereafter needed to bring the two together again. While this divorce of style and matter allows of a clarity of statement about either which cannot easily be matched in modern critical writing, its artificial character has often been deplored.

The question then arises why Horace, who cannot be said to have been insensitive to the nature of poetic expression, should have turned to a philosophy which purveyed such unreal distinctions. Why, it is asked, did not he turn to the more flexible and less cumbersome procedure of a Philodemus, which was doubtless known to him? The following reflections will be relevant. It may be conjectured (for conjecture is still required with regard to his critical doctrines) that Philodemus, in spite of his objections to Aristotelian principles, employed the traditional, Aristotelian, procedure for the workaday discussion of the problems of style. So that in drawing on the criticism of Neoptolemus of Parium Horace would have done no more than approach an earlier and perhaps better exponent of the Aristotelian doctrine of style. Moreover the study of style was among the great achievements of the Aristotelian school and it may well be the case that the craftsman in Horace preferred the gain in drawing on its stores to less tangible doctrinal considerations. However that may be, there is a further important motive which is not likely to have been purely literary or aesthetic. Throughout his career as a critic Horace steadily pleaded for professional poetic standards; but he pleaded no less steadily against the divorce of poetry from the activities of the *civis Romanus*, the *vir bonus*, the *vir sapiens*. The Aristotelian philosophy of poetry, restated by an Alexandrian poet, seems to have provided the intellectual foundation and the balance of aspirations, intellectual, moral, social, and poetic, which he required. Here he found poetics as part of a larger philosophy without the Stoic paradoxes; the large genres (the realm of *poesis*), but an equal preoccupation with style (the realm of *poema*); and finally the proximity of the moral and political worlds which still hinted at the function of poetry in the close-knit political scene of the Greek city state. It is doubtful whether any other literary theory could have supplied these needs.

The contemporary aspects of the work must next be considered. The *Ars* is not a mechanical restatement of classical rules and regulations. Nor was Horace's position as a critic comparable to that of Aristotle. The Greek philosopher determined with prophetic hindsight the canons of a select number of past poetic genres. Horace, Roman and poet, was twice removed from Aristotle. He reiterated the principles of a large and generous concept of poetry for present and future endeavour. Greek poetry entered into his criticism as a stimulant of Roman creativeness, just as Alcaeus and Sappho had stimulated the imagination of the *Latinus fidicen*. If my assessment of Neoptolemus should prove acceptable,[1] the Aristotelian concept had been earlier restated in the less propitious Alexandrian setting. In the Italian Renaissance and thereafter the *Ars* was called upon to play a decisive part as a source-book of classical standards in poetry and the fine arts. Thus a premium was put on the static and normative features of its criticism; on the other hand the dynamic features were easily ignored. When Horace's *Ars* is commended as an expression of classicism, 'even though his classicism falls short of the genuine classical ideal',[2] the reader should recall its contemporary role. Both the *Ars* and the letter to Augustus opposed a type of classicism which was then current at Rome.

[1] Above, pp. 149–50.
[2] J. W. H. Atkins, *op. cit.* II, 101; cf. the chapter in J. F. D'Alton's *Roman Lit. Theory*, entitled 'Horace and the classical creed'.

The Principles of Literary Criticism in the 'Ars Poetica'

For the contemporary archaists Roman poetic achievement lay in the past; Rome's archaic poets had recaptured the spirit of the old Greek masters in the native tongue.[1] It may also be remembered that Horace was equally opposed to another type of classicism—I mean, what he considered the narrow tastes of the admirers of Calvus and Catullus which he ridicules in the tenth satire of Book I.[2] His reticence with regard to contemporary Roman elegists, and his double-edged compliments to Callimachus, may equally bespeak his desire to widen the contemporary poetic effort. Horace's judgement may or may not have been at fault. But the dynamic character which the *Ars* displayed in that historical context must be set against its later, static, image as an upholder of the classical proprieties. Since therefore various kinds of 'classicism' are involved, I have here avoided the use of the ambiguous term 'classical' in order to combat confusion.[3]

Finally there is the poetic aspect of the *Ars*. There have been plenty of poets to write literary criticism out of their poetic experience. They usually take on another *persona* when they reach for the critical pen. Horace remained what he was. In his critical poems he was not content to superadd metre and a few graces of style to the doctrines of literary criticism. He attempted to cast such subjects in the form of poems that evince the critical attitudes and doctrines which he was putting forward. That has rarely been done in the long history of literary criticism, and when it was done (as by Boileau and Pope) it was in the succession of Horace.

Complaints are often heard that Horace the literary critic tells us little or nothing about the matters which he knew better than most; that his criticism is doctrinaire and un-

---

[1] Above, pp. 193–4. [2] Above, pp. 166–7.

[3] The late A. Y. Campbell could scarcely have been charged with blindness to the classical features of Horace's poetry. But he rightly remarked, in discussing the letter to Augustus (*Horace*, 287), 'we see, then, that the standpoint *vulgarly* known as classical is that which Horace is opposing'. This is true enough even if the Edwardianism *vulgarly* is replaced by *commonly*.

237

inspired by the poetry which he himself had written.[1] Such complaints would be reasonable only if it were true that the whole of his critical doctrine could be abstracted from poems which are both less and more than the self-contained theories of the professional critics. The poems are less than critical theory because they do not profess to argue a subject in the manner of a treatise or textbook. They are more because they do profess to capture not the letter so much as the spirit of a poetic creed. Anyone writing on Horace's critical *sermones*, and above all on the *Ars*, must address himself therefore to their poetic form as much as to their critical content. It is possible to restate in prose the argument of prose; it is only possible to point to certain devices of composition and style if that argument has undergone an imaginative reshuffling in a poet's mind. My concluding chapter will point to some such devices of composition and style in the *Ars*. Thus at the same time it will consider the bearing of Horace's poetic form on the content of his literary criticism.

[1] Thus for example W. Wili, *Horaz* (1948), p. 317, summing up what he misses in the *Ars*, 'hierbei bewahrt der Dichter seinen Altersblick auf das Drama, berührt die Probleme des Epos kaum, schweigt fast ganz über die Lyrik und verzichtet darauf, zur eigenen Kunstübung, sowie zur hohen epischen seiner Freunde Vergil und Varius Stellung zu nehmen'.

APPENDIX III

CAN THE 'ARS POETICA' BE DATED?

The purpose of this note is wholly negative.

I have tried hard but in vain to determine the date of the *Ars*. No external criterion comes to hand which indubitably settles the matter. Scholars persist in disregarding the state of the evidence; with a few honourable exceptions they write as though they knew of such a criterion. What are the facts of the case?

Up to the beginning of the nineteenth century most scholars thought they knew. Without much reasoning they assigned to the *Ars* the last place in the chronology of the poems, often, one suspects, because H. Stephanus had assigned to it the last place in the sequence of the poems. The apparent lack of arrangement suggested to some critics posthumous publication of bits and pieces, composed at various times but not completed or published by the poet.

The first to cast a critical glance on the evidence was a young Dutch scholar, J. H. van Reenen.[1] A. Michaelis added a little material; he knew of van Reenen's arguments, but only at second hand.[2] Van Reenen, just as later on Michaelis, argued that the evidence of the poem does not square with what we are told about the identity of the addressees, and (by implication) the date. They therefore rejected the only ancient piece of evidence that identifies the Pisos. Porphyrion reported that the poem is addressed to Lucius Piso, later *custos urbis*, himself a poet and champion of the arts, and his sons.[3] Their dates were too late to fit what they thought was the evidence of the poem and they proposed another Pisonian family, Cn. Piso and his sons.[4] Their choice of persons may be wrong. But they were right in seeking to fit the Pisos to the evidence of the poem (such as it is), and not the evidence of the poem to the Pisos. Even now epigraphic evidence is insufficient to assign the Horatian

---

[1] J. H. van Reenen, *Disputatio philologico-critica de Q. Horatii Flacci Epistula ad Pisones* (thesis, Amsterdam, 1806).

[2] A. Michaelis, *Die Horazischen Pisonen, Commentationes...Mommsen* (1877), pp. 420–32.

[3] Porph. on *A.P.* 1, 'hunc librum...ad Lucium Pisonem, qui postea urbis custos fuit, eiusque liberos misit; nam et ipse Piso poeta fuit et studiorum liberalium antistes'. Cf. C. Cichorius, *Röm. Stud.* (1922), pp. 325–7, 338–41; E. Groag, *PIR²*, C 289 (1936).

[4] Groag, *PIR²*, C 286, Cn. Calpurnius Piso, consul with Augustus in 28 B.C.

honours to any contestant. For Cn. Piso was not apparently *artium antistes* whatever else he was. On the other hand it is now clearly seen that so far there is no record of the sons of L. Piso.[1] Nor does the Horatian corpus exhibit any other dedication to the Pisos that might assist inquiry. A recent and judicious survey of the historical evidence has rightly reached a sceptical conclusion. So far at any rate as the Pisos are concerned—'the perplexity subsists'.[2]

Van Reenen cited four personal references from the *Ars*; three he thought incompatible with a date after 19 B.C., and hence with L. Piso. He was mistaken;[3] only one reference may be incompatible, and its explanation remains doubtful.[4]

The *Ars* cannot therefore be dated by its references to persons; this claim must be disallowed. Van Reenen was successful however in raising the concomitant and still unsolved problem of the addressees— who were the *pater et iuvenes patre digni*? A. Michaelis went hunting over much the same ground; he brought home no larger bag. He did indeed search for other criteria as well. Little if anything can be

---

[1] Two great scholars thought otherwise, cf. Borghesi, *Œuvres*, v, 312; Mommsen, *Eph. Epig.* I (1872), 144–5, repr. *Ges. Schr.* VIII, 247–8. The absence of any record of the sons is now recognized: the only possible candidate is too young: see n. 2. Mommsen himself expressed doubts a few years later, cf. *Ges. Schr.* VII, 185.

[2] R. Syme, *JRS*, L (1960), 20. Cf. Groag, *loc. cit.* (*PIR²*, C 289 (1936), p. 66), 'si Horatium sumimus L. Pisonem pontificem et filios eius adloqui, hi filii videntur aliunde ignoti'. A later L. Piso, supposed to be one of the sons, is ruled out as too young; see Groag and Syme on the praetorian legate of that name, assassinated in Spain in A.D. 25.

[3] Quintilius Varus, at *A.P.* 438, can be eliminated from the list. According to St Jerome he died in 24–3; which serves only to put the *Ars* after that year. Confirmation of that fact however will be required by few. Aulus Cascellius, the celebrated lawyer, born apparently before 100 B.C., is mentioned along with Messalla Corvinus, Horace's contemporary, at *A.P.* 371. He would have been in his nineties after 20 B.C. The contingency may be considered too seriously. *Nec scit quantum Cascellius Aulus* may but need not mean more than 'no great lawyer'. Nor finally does the mention of Virgil and Varius, at *A.P.* 55, imply that they must have been alive at the time of writing. I agree with J. Vahlen, *Ges. Phil. Schr.* II, 59, and Wickham, *General Introd. to the Lit. Epistles*, in his edition of Horace, vol. II, p. 334, that the difference between this and the like passage in the Letter to Florus (*Ep.* II, 2, 115 ff.) has been overstated. And the Letter to Florus is certainly dated after 19 B.C., the year of Virgil's death.

[4] The critic Sp. Maecius Tarpa is dated, within fairly wide limits, by Cicero's mention of his activities as a selector of plays as early as 55 B.C., *Ep. Fam.* VII, 1, 1. A person of about 30 in 55 B.C. would be in his early seventies after 14 B.C. Whether Horace could refer to a person of that age in the terms of *A.P.* 387 is anyone's guess. Doubts remain, but I find it hard to eliminate the difficulty by assuming (as does Bentley) that Maecius' name is here used generically. In this regard the context of *A.P.* 387 differs from that of 371, discussed in the last note.

made of his stylistic and metrical observations; and so he himself recognized.[1] He also considered the *regis opus* of *A.P.* 65. This would be relevant if we could be sure that Horace was hinting at the operations of contemporary engineers. Michaelis reasonably rejected suggestions of this kind.[2] Others were not deflected from basing a date for the *Ars* on an unexplained or controversial passage.[3] This is a topsy-turvy procedure, and to be discounted.[4]

Two other pieces of evidence escaped van Reenen and Michaelis, but have attracted attention more recently. In his *Life of Horace* Suetonius cited a letter of Augustus in which the emperor, playfully but unmistakably, requests the dedication to himself of Horatian poems: 'irasci me tibi scito quod non in plerisque eius modi scriptis mecum potissimum loquaris; an vereris ne apud posteros infame tibi sit quod videaris familiaris nobis esse?' Suetonius finds this request met by the letter to Augustus: 'post sermones vero quosdam lectos nullam sui mentionem habitam ita sit questus...; expressitque eclogam ad se cuius initium est, *cum tot sustineas*', etc.[5] There was no point in relating Suetonius' information to the *Ars* so long as the literary epistles were undated. But when probable dates for the letters to Augustus and Florus were put forward, the possible relation to the *Ars* was bound to be considered. It was so considered in the same paper of J. Vahlen's in which he suggested 18 and 14 B.C. as the dates of the letters to Florus and Augustus.[6] Vahlen convinced himself of the equation *sermones quosdam lectos* = *Letter to Florus* and *Ars Poetica*. Hence both would have been written at a time before work on the *Carmen Saeculare* brought lyric verse once more into the poet's purview. The suggestion is attractive and is still often repeated.[7] But it neglects the difference between two writers—Suetonius who reports and Augustus who is reported. The crucial difference was soon noted: the biographer talks of a mention of the emperor; the emperor himself talks of poems addressed to him.[8] There are other

---

[1] Michaelis, *op. cit.* pp. 427–9.

[2] *Ibid.* pp. 425–7, discussing the theories of L. Preller, *P*, II (1847), 483 (repeated *Ausgew. Aufs.* 1864, pp. 515 ff.); *Ber. Sächs. Ges.* II (1849), 138 ff.

[3] Notably P. Lejay, *Rev. de l'instr. publ. en Belgique*, XLV (1902), 375–81; J. Carcopino, *Virgile et les origines d'Ostie* (1919), p. 732.

[4] Cf. R. Meiggs's just criticism of Carcopino, in *Roman Ostia* (1960), Appendix II, p. 486.   [5] See above, p. 191, n. 3.

[6] J. Vahlen, *Über Zeit und Abfolge der Literaturbriefe des Horaz* (1878); *Ges. Phil. Schr.* II, 46–61.

[7] It was repeated as recently as 1957, in Fraenkel's *Horace*, p. 383.

[8] Noted for example by M. Friedrich, *Q. Horatius Flaccus* (1894), p. 223, and P. Lejay, *Rev. de l'instr. publ. en Belg.* XLVI (1903), 167, n. 1; more recently by O. A. W. Dilke, *Bull. London Inst. Cl. St.* V (1958), 50.

differences between the two texts that shake one's confidence in Suetonius' reporting. Augustus' words are not necessarily incompatible with the letters to Florus and to the Pisos: what Augustus meant by *eius modi* is after all unknown.[1] On the other hand his words, unlike those of Suetonius, could well apply to *Epistles*, Book I.[2]

One item now remains—the most important of all; and yet by no means conclusive. In the letter to the Pisos, Horace describes himself as teaching but not writing, *nil scribens ipse*.[3] In accordance with the nomenclature of his literary criticism Horace's 'writing' applies to poetry but not to the quasi-poetry of his satires or epistles. So far as Horace is concerned (not so far as others are concerned) *scribere* then applies to his lyric verse, his incursion into poetry proper. In the chronology of his *œuvre*, *nil scribens ipse* relates to any *period* (not, I suggest, any *occasion*) in which he was not predominantly engaged upon lyric verse: thus it may relate to (*a*) the time up to the writing of the *Odes*, (*b*) the *intervallum lyricum*, 23–c. 18 B.C., (*c*) the time between the publication of *Odes*, Book IV, and the end of his life, *c.* 14–8 B.C. The first contingency should be excluded on other grounds. For there is no indication that Horace saw himself as a teacher of the art at any time before he became *Latinus fidicen*.[4] The choice, therefore, still lies between the *intervallum lyricum* and the period after the publication of *Odes*, Book IV. But the supply of external criteria is now exhausted.

The upshot of this lengthy discussion is as follows. The *Ars Poetica* was composed either during the *intervallum lyricum* or after *Odes*, Book IV. I see no unexceptionable proof on external criteria that one of the two periods must be preferred to the other.[5] A com-

---

[1] A. Kiessling, *Phil. Unt.* (ed. Kiessling and Wilamowitz-Moellendorff), II (1881), 58, thinks it is plausible that *eius modi* refers to the (literary) content of these writings. It *is* plausible. But Suetonius' *sermones* may suggest that *in eius modi scriptis* denotes the stylistic genre, not the content.

[2] This conjecture was hazarded by Mommsen, *Die Litteraturbriefe des Horaz* (1880), *Ges. Schr.* VII, 177–8, and indeed by others. Mommsen attempted at the same time to account for the interval that then lies between the publication of *Ep.* I, in 20 B.C., and the letter of Augustus, complimenting Horace on poems published four or five years earlier. Mommsen's mention of only 'one such poem (*eius modi scriptum*)' is however a slip. [3] Hor. *A.P.* 306.

[4] This would seem to exclude any such attempt as that of J. Elmore, *CP*, xxx (1935), 1, to date the *Ars* early in the twenties B.C.

[5] This applies to the earlier as much as to the later period. O. A. W. Dilke, *op. cit.*, suggests 'that a late date should be accepted' (p. 49); he concludes 'that the work was written in 10, 9, or 8 B.C.' (p. 55). But this conclusion does not follow from the evidence which he presents. At best he proves that a late date cannot be excluded—which is a different matter.

promise between the two, assuming some early and some late work, is what I have just called it, an assumption: two uncertainties do not add up to one certainty.[1] So far as external criteria for the *Ars* are concerned, no certainty can be reached. Something can be known about the probable dates of the letters to Augustus and Florus; but for the *Ars* a variation of Bentley's pronouncement in his preface still describes the position—*Ars Poetica anno incerto*.[2]

Here a literary historian could stop; he has assessed the external evidence. A student of Horace should attempt to go further. He may plead that the two periods are so close in time as not to matter. They are close in time; but the choice between them does matter. There is a divergence of outlook between the letters to Florus and to the Pisos.[3] This divergence may be the difference between the two periods in question. The argument must then turn to the internal evidence—the imponderables of the foregoing chapter.[4]

---

[1] W. K. Smith, *CP*, xxi (1936), 163, suggests such a compromise.

[2] He does however say *postremo* as well, and in his note on *A.P.* 387 implies that 15 B.C. is the date of the work; but he does not say why.

[3] J. Vahlen, *op. cit.*, *Ges. Phil. Schr.* ii, 56, 60, is not aware of this difference.

[4] The *Ars*, as has often been remarked, is not attached to the *Epistles* in our manuscript tradition, but rather, in various ways, to the corpus of the *Odes* and *Epodes*. Separate and late publication has been inferred from that. In discussing the date I have disregarded this matter because the nature of textual transmission is rarely such as to take us back close to an ancient author's copy. In this case we penetrate no farther than the copies used by Porphyrion (third century A.D.) and Servius (fourth century), neither of which attached the *Ars* to the letters. There are however possible traces of a different order; cf. Charisius citing the *Ars*, *c.* 400 A.D., as *Horatius epistularum* (above, p. 233, n. 2); and perhaps the commentary of Q. Terentius Scaurus, compiled under Hadrian and mentioned by Charisius in the former passage. The earliest citations of all, however (those of Quintilian, above, p. 233, n. 1), firmly refer to the *Ars Poetica* by that title, and not as one of the letters.

CHAPTER 2

POETIC PATTERNS IN THE 'ARS POETICA'

The books that stimulate a poet's work are one thing; what he makes of them is quite another. That is seen to be so when, for once, a whole poem happens to be preserved which stimulated more than an occasional detail in one of Horace's own compositions.[1] The reading of any amount of literary criticism did not persuade the poet simply to versify a treatise. Yet I have sought to demonstrate in the foregoing chapter that the *Ars* differs from the rest of Horace's writings on poetry in that it allows some importance to the layout of professional criticism. The contention therefore that the poem proffers either a 'system of literary criticism' or a 'chatty discourse' cannot stand up to examination.[2] The question is not whether there are some focal points of this kind, but what they are and how they are placed.[3] Horace deals with technicalities not for their own sakes but with an ulterior purpose. He uses some systematic thought patterns,

[1] I feel persuaded by the arguments of W. Christ, *Metrik der Gr. und Römer*, 2nd ed. (1879), p. 654, and Fraenkel, *op. cit.* pp. 291 ff., suggesting that the whole structure as well as details of *Odes*, 1, 12, *quem virum aut heroa*, are reminiscent of Pindar's second Olympic ode. Yet the difference is even more impressive than the likeness. How much more must that be so when a poem stands over against a prose treatise, the *Ars* over against Neoptolemus' poetics.

[2] This is the contention of F. Klingner (1950), citing F. Klingner (1937); cf. 'Horazens Brief an Augustus', *SBBA* (1950), p. 1, 'Zwar den Gedanken an eine "ars", d. h. eine systematische Lehre, wonach man beim Hervorbringen verfahren könnte,...hat man längst fallen lassen; man weiss dass diese Epistel wie die anderen sermo ist, d. h. lockeres, plauderndes Gespräch (F. Klingner, *Horazens Brief an die Pisonen*, Leipzig, 1937, etc.)'. Similar contentions are discussed above, pp. 34-5.

[3] That a poetic presentation and some systematic thought patterns need not be incompatible has been reasonably argued by H. L. Tracy, *TAPA*, LXXVII (1946), 342, *GR*, XVII (1948), 104-15. But agreement is not so easy to obtain when this maxim is applied to the peculiar difficulties of the *Ars*.

but their use is limited; their importance can easily be over-stated..[1]

Once it is agreed that the *Ars* conforms to some principles of arrangement which the professional literary critics would have recognized as their own, then the textbook, and all it stands for, is not unduly important. There are few textbook headings and they are largely pushed out of sight—a traditional system of reference in the intricate diversity of the poem. The poet's contemporaries were conversant with rhetorical theory. Hence without much prompting they would recognize that the *Ars* applies the rhetorical triad of matter–wording–arrangement to poetry. They would sense some order behind the poetic convolutions; which is precisely what many modern readers find so hard to do since they are not used to rhetorical conventions.

The poem shows that Horace did not want to give prominence to the headings of a textbook. Students of the *Ars* have frequently noted what he does not do. He does not begin at the beginning of the textbook. The headings are not mentioned until forty lines have gone by and even then the table of contents is not given for the whole poem and it is not rehearsed plainly. The headings, *res–facundia–ordo*, or matter–style–arrangement (40–1), do not cover more than the technical portion of the poem. And they cover it only if the initial forty lines[2] are understood as introductory, not as a discussion of 'subject-matter'. The table of contents is not set out plainly. It comes in almost by the way, incidental to a warning against poetic plans which the would-be author cannot carry out *in toto*. In its turn this warning forms the link between two portions of the poem. One portion is introductory; it deals with the ideas of unity and wholeness. The other, line 42, deals chiefly with the technicalities of literary criticism—order, style, subject-matter, and the large forms of epic and particularly of drama.

[1] Cf. above, pp. 3–4, on Cicero and Horace.
[2] Or 37 if the link passage is discounted.

The textbook presumably put a clear dividing line between the discussions of style and subject-matter. Again Horace proceeds otherwise. He makes an abrupt break after 118, where the discussion of style ends. At 119 he suddenly talks of subject-matter (*aut famam sequere*, etc.). But as I argued in my first chapter, the break is mitigated by links on both sides of the divide: the gulf is bridged by the secondary topic of 'character'. On the other hand the transition to the specific discussion of drama is made more obvious by three introductory lines (153–5); the would-be author is promised an audience that will stay the course of a play if he submits to the 'rules' now to be laid down. Thus a simpler scheme is superimposed on that of the literary critics. The lines of the technical division are not blocked out. But they are overlaid by another division in which unity, style, and content are gathered together into one large section, from the beginning of the poem to line 152; and this section in turn is followed by another, 153–294, which deals with drama, tragic, satyric, and comic, Greek as well as Roman. The new section too is linked in various ways with the preceding.

The third part of Neoptolemus' triad, 'the poet', is the only one to be introduced with a certain *aplomb*: *munus et officium, nil scribens ipse, docebo* (306). The subjects of the teaching are stated succinctly in the following two lines. Yet Horace has made it hard for his readers to identify these subjects in the final portion of the poem; some students altogether deny that the subjects are in fact taken up one by one as they are announced. Another relevant point has not escaped notice. The lecturer's announcement is part of a larger passage that begins at line 295 and is itself not unconnected with the close of the preceding portion of the poem. Here too a slow and deliberate transition is the characteristic feature of the poem. If *munus et officium* are the underlying subjects of the final portion of the *Ars* (as I think they are), they too are brought into the poetic context with the same circumspection as the preceding topics.

Horace rarely chooses to remind his readers that he knows the jargon of the literary critics. His use of such words as *poema* and *poesis* is not 'technical'. His wording does not recall Neoptolemus' triad, *poema*, *poesis*, and *poeta*, although his discussion does so recall it.[1] From his failure to employ these terms it can hardly be concluded that he was unaware of Neoptolemus' terminology; nor indeed is this an argument against his use of Neoptolemus' poetics.[2] What can be concluded is simple. Here as elsewhere in his literary *sermones* Horace steers clear of tediousness and technicality. He avoids the language of the schools (except for emphasis, or for the purposes of parody) and he makes sure that the framework of literary criticism does not disturb the flow of the poem.

It follows that the *Ars* contains several and diverse principles of arrangement. The astringent schema of the textbook belongs to Neoptolemus, not to Horace. Yet it is not wholly discarded. It has its uses and I have indicated what I think these uses may have been. But its importance has been severely restricted. The triad of *poema–poesis–poeta* has been pushed into the background, where it serves to remind the reader of the technical motifs in a poem on literary criticism which is not by any means all technical. It indicates a division, mitigated by various types of transition, into (1) lines 40–118, (2) 119–294, and (3) 295–476. An unbiased reader will readily find other principles of division. I have just drawn attention to two more which may still be related to Neoptolemus' original layout. Horace has stressed the subject of the final section more strongly than that of the second. Hence a case may be made for a bipartite division into a section concerned with the

---

[1] A. Ardizzoni, *op. cit.* (1953), pp. 31–40, rightly notes that Horace's use of these words differs from that of Neoptolemus. But he, as others before him, is mistaken in replacing one set of terms by another: *poemata*, at *A.P.* 99, 263, 276, 303, 342, 416, and 'ut pictura *poesis*', at *A.P.* 361, conform to ordinary Graeco-Roman usage; they do not recall the idiom of literary theory.

[2] So, for example, if I understand him rightly, N. A. Greenberg, *HS*, lxv (1961), 266.

details of the craft, and another not so concerned (1–294 and 295–476 respectively). This is still pretty close to the *ars poetica* of the professional critics. It is in fact the division which provided the point of departure for modern analysis. But no one can tell how clearly Neoptolemus indicated this boundary line, or indeed whether he brought together in this manner the first two of his three subjects. Moreover, Horace has given some prominence to a third schema. This is more balanced than the other two. It divides the poem into three somewhat symmetrical portions: lines 1–152 deal with style and content, after an introduction on the principle of unity, 153–294 deal with the chief kinds of drama in Greece and Rome, and 295–476 deal with some general aspects of poetic theory. The sections thus divided contain 152, 142, and 182 lines respectively.

This conclusion should give pause to controversialists. Any poem that is sizeable and supple enough to relate various themes in a large design is bound to have various principles of design and, consequently, different 'unities'. This is particularly true of classical and neo-classical works. Large Augustan poems have a multiplicity of patterns. Students should not therefore be surprised that if they ask different questions of such a work the answers will differ in accordance with their questions. As long as readers conceived of the *Ars* as a textbook on poetics versified, they looked for an arrangement that would fit a textbook—and they found such an arrangement. Others conceived of the *Ars* as a conversation, *sermo*, or a medley of unrelated literary topics, so they looked for unobtrusive transitions and similar devices, and they found such devices. Others again conceived of the *Ars* as a piece of poetry—and they found elements of a poetic design that differed from the principles of the textbook and the *sermo*. These three answers add up to a controversy only if any two of them must needs be mistaken. In fact there is no controversy. For the answers are not mutually exclusive. But different principles fit different aspects of the work.

This proviso will have to be borne in mind when I now turn to the matters which Horace seems to have repeated so gratuitously throughout this work. The defenders of law and order in the *Ars* found it hard to account for these intruders and said surprisingly little about them. The dissenters protested, not unreasonably, that a book can scarcely be said to have a self-respecting arrangement, whether twofold or threefold, if topics are indiscriminately repeated in each of the assumed sections. Anyone therefore asserting the presence of a plan in the poem must account for these repetitions. What are they and what, if anything, are they meant to achieve?

Horace is one of the most deliberate composers among poets. On the face of it the recurrence of topics in the *Ars* is uneconomical. My reading of the poem has led me to the opposite conclusion. Topics are repeated economically and for a purpose. I have discussed some of the poet's attempts to mitigate the hard and fast distinctions of the textbook. His repeats need to be considered as serving the same purpose. Suppose Horace discusses a stylistic problem, first under the heading of style and later among the generalities of the final section. This can be explained in two ways. One explanation is that Horace could not or would not adhere to his plan, which assigns stylistic matters to the first and general matters to the last part of the poem. Since nothing would have been easier than to adhere to his plan, the alternative motive should be considered. He meant to bring the teachings of one of his sections to bear on another—in the language of Neoptolemus, the teachings of *poema* on *poeta*, and *vice versa*. Thus he would again play down the artificial distinctions between the two 'sections', without losing what he apparently considered the advantage of having such distinctions. The final section would still have the function of dealing with the generalities of literary criticism, but at the same time he would bring out some of the connexions with the preceding parts of the poem. I propose to review the outstanding topics that are so repeated in the poem. At the same time, if I make my point, this review will demonstrate yet further how the textbook is modified by the flexible methods of the poet.

Repetitions in the *Ars* are not all alike. It is probable that some derive from Neoptolemus; it is equally probable that others do not. Neoptolemus (provided my account of his teachings is correct) may have repeated certain items in his book, for two good reasons. He may have repeated them, perhaps because he found them important, but more plausibly because he was paying the price for the large and convenient subject headings imported from the field of rhetoric into that of poetics. Aristotle largely refrains from discussing identical items in various contexts, at any rate in the *Poetics*, because his procedure in that work does not encourage restatement.[1] Not so in the *Rhetoric*. The procedure of the third book is foreshadowed in the first two in that emotion and character have a *locus standi* in the discussion of *inventio* in Books I and II and in the discussion of *elocutio* in Book III. Neoptolemus is likely to have proceeded in the same manner. If style and content divide the whole field of poetry, and if either the circumstances of the plot, or the emotions or characters of the persons involved, equally apply to style and content, then some or all of these headings will equally appear in the context of style and in that of subject-matter. We must therefore reckon with the possibility (I should even say, probability) that Neoptolemus employed this secondary principle of grouping, or stressing, his topics. Horace certainly recalls Aristotle's procedure in the *Rhetoric*. The quality of 'ethos', or character, may usefully be placed first. For it so happens that this quality particularly took Horace's fancy. It now remains to be discussed how he makes a poetic virtue of what probably was a traditional arrangement of topics, by finding different nuances for each context in which ethos is mentioned. The nuances differ, yet each time the reader is made to feel that he encounters only another nuance of the same relevant quality.

[1] Above, p. 139.

Mores are discussed under style, under content, under drama, and finally in the section on the poet's training.[1] First of all, character is one of the qualities that should govern the poet's style. Here, as one would expect, character means type of character—god or hero, age, sex, social standing, nationality. Types of character also are supposed to regulate the style of speaking in Aristotle's *Rhetoric*; it is known that the tradition on which Horace draws is indebted to the Aristotelian chapter that I have just mentioned.[2]

Types of character would not fit the next topic, the content of a poem. For this topic demands individuals, the *personae* enacting the story of an epic or the plot of a drama. Hence Horace concentrates on individual traits. The characters of the legend must be what they are known to be: Achilles, 'impiger iracundus inexorabilis acer',[3] and so forth. The legend apparently has established the desired consistency. Invented characters must be made consistent. The two passages on character, the types and the individuals, link the two large contexts of style and matter. Thus Horace brings out the importance that he attaches to this quality, not only in each of its manifestations, as typical or individual, but as something which should always colour the poet's work. Reasoning divides the poet's *œuvre* into style and content. But the two coincide in the demand for ethos. In its form or in its substance, a poem must 'characterize'.

Mores, exemplified by a descriptive sketch of the four ages of man, introduce the specific precepts for the playwright. The ultimate model is again Aristotle's *Rhetoric*.[4] In the first of the four passages on character the demand was that the age of a speaker should determine his diction. Here the

---

[1] The passages are the following: *A.P.* 114–18, 120–27, 156–78, and 312–18; cf. above, pp. 139–40. The nature of the apparent doublet, 114 ff. ~ 156 ff., was rightly judged by Norden, *op. cit.* p. 496: the subject is not just 'repeated' but argued in different contexts for different purposes.

[2] Ar. *Rhet.* III, 7; see above, p. 94 ff.   [3] *A.P.* 121 in the context of 119–24.

[4] *Ibid.* 156–78 recall Ar. *Rhet.* II, 12–14; see above, p. 112. But the placing of the rules recalls the *Poetics*, see above, p. 111.

writer's point is different. The *dramatis personae* should have the right features; they should act in a manner that befits their natures. Aristotle speaks of 'appropriate features'; Horace says,

> aetatis cuiusque notandi sunt tibi mores,
> mobilibusque decor naturis dandus et annis. (*A.P.* 156–7)

Mores are noticed finally in the last part of the poem. Here they illustrate the uses that the poet is said to draw from his training in moral philosophy. He will learn to assign the appropriate qualities to each personage that he represents.[1] The reader is clearly meant to notice first how this context differs from anything that has been earlier said about character. But he will notice too that the renewed mention of this feature links this passage with the foregoing sections. In each case the context, and in each case the repeated topic, contribute to the literary criticism and to the economy of the poem.

I am not aware of a reader who has entered the claims of 'character' as the chief principle of the poem's design. Such a claim has however been made on behalf of another principle, *decorum* or appropriateness.[2] There is more sense in that, if only on quantitative grounds. For whereas character appears only in four key passages of the *Ars*, there are few places where 'appropriateness' is not invoked. Does the unity of the *Ars* then rest on this important concept? Against this suggestion it has been urged that appropriateness can carry any number of meanings; the concept is too vague to fulfil the function imputed to it.[3] I agree that the claim should be disallowed, but for another reason. The very large number of references to *decorum*, *aptum*, and the like is surely sufficient to show Horace's concern with this idea. But what *decorum* does not do is to establish dominion undisputed. As before, it

---

[1] *A.P.* 316, 'reddere personae scit convenientia cuique'.
[2] Above, p. 35, n. 1, 229.
[3] Above, p. 229, n. 3

should be remembered that the number of such claims is too large and diverse for critics to judge priorities.

My argument has been that the Greek counterpart of Horace's *decorum* was one of the items variously repeated in the different parts of Neoptolemus' textbook.[1] But whatever Neoptolemus has done or failed to do, the *Ars* can be set over against Aristotle's *Rhetoric* and the likeness between Horace's and Aristotle's arguments can scarcely be denied.

Horace's section on *facundia* is governed by the principle that style cannot be divorced from certain genres, metres, subjects, emotions, and types of character; style must be appropriate to them.[2] Most of these demands are transferred to the wider setting of the *Ars* from the confined setting of one chapter of Aristotle's *Rhetoric*, Book III (chapter 7). The section on content is governed by a like principle. The plot is largely considered through the medium of its characters, *personae*. And again it is the close relation between the activities of the *personae* and their *mores* which is inculcated, whether the plot is traditional or freely invented.[3] The *decor*, or appropriateness, in assigning activities to people in the following section on characters on the stage, is of the same order of thought.[4] Horace then has widened the scope of this principle. By referring repeatedly to the same idea of appropriateness he has made it into a connecting link between various parts of the poem. The unpoetic distinction between style and content is thus weakened, and *decorum* is established as a leading principle in all poetry. In spite of the importance that Aristotle allowed it, its Greek counterpart τὸ πρέπον has no such scope in the *Rhetoric* or *Poetics*. Moreover the final part of the *Ars* brings appropriateness into the philosophic training of the poet. This too serves to widen its scope and to continue the line of thought thus traced to this section of the poem.

Moreover attention may be directed to the introductory portion, and the organic unity which it enjoins. Unity, as

---

[1] Above, pp. 138–9. [2] *A.P.* 73–118; above, pp. 94 ff..
[3] *Ibid.* 119. [4] *Ibid.* 156–7.

Horace interpreted it *more Aristotelico,* consisted in a master design that makes all parts of a poetic conception appropriate to each other and to the whole. So that a large and diverse poem is yet *simplex et unum.*[1] This cannot fail to recall later passages: *servetur ad imum | qualis ab incepto processerit et sibi constet,*[2] or *primo ne medium, medio ne discrepet imum,*[3] and any injunctions so far noted under the heading of 'appropriateness'. The principles of unity and appropriateness are derived from different contexts of the writings of Aristotle. It is likely that they were brought into closer contact by Neoptolemus and others. Horace certainly brings them into close contact. But he does so less by argument than by poetic means such as the use of similar turns of phrase or the placing of items. Thus he brings the principle of 'appropriateness' right to the beginning of the poem.

It is doubtful whether other passages containing related terms such as *aptum* and the like here qualify for inclusion.[4] The use of similar terms suggests that Horace meant to qualify them for inclusion. But let them be disregarded. The passages on appropriateness and unity alone reveal the poet's purpose. Horace has placed these passages in key positions in the various sections and thus puts various contexts in a relationship which may not have been brought out in the tradition of literary criticism. He makes manifest by poetic means what he discusses on the level of critical argument—*simplex dumtaxat et unum.* I should describe this procedure as an attempt on his part to recreate poetically the intellectual subjects of his *sermo.* His precepts enjoin upon the poet that he should relate style to matter, just as his poetry relates the two by pointing to the same principle of appropriateness in both sections. His precepts enjoin diversity and unity. Diversity is the one principle on which every student of the *Ars*

[1] *A.P.* 23. The brief and misleadingly trite precept on *ordo* may also be recalled, *ibid.* 42–4.

[2] *Ibid.* 126–7. [3] *Ibid.* 152.

[4] I have noted some of them, above, pp. 228 ff. They come from different contexts of the relevant Aristotelian works.

readily agrees. As for unity no such agreement obtains. My contention is that so far from betraying a lack of arrangement, certain subjects, or principles, are repeated with due deliberation. They direct attention to a limited number of recurring items in the diversity of the poem. Their function appears to be to act as principles of design. But they are more flexible and poetic than the large headings of the textbook which are kept so discreetly in the background.

Character, appropriateness, and unity are the most outstanding among a larger number of recurring topics. These are likely to reflect certain features of the critical tradition on which Horace has drawn. Yet other matters tend to recur of which this cannot be said. They too are given prominence, and thus influence the design of the poem, because Horace believed them to be important. But unlike the others they recall personal preoccupations on Horace's part, without the Aristotelian or Neoptolemic precedents which have been noted. Among these perhaps the most impressive is the value attached to poetic craftsmanship. Concern with *studium* versus untutored *ingenium* will be recalled from the smaller critical writings.

There seems to be no precedent in Aristotle's *Poetics* or *Rhetoric* for the extraordinary importance which Horace attaches to the poet's craft. Presumably Aristotle took for granted the importance of what he called τέχνη. Technique is not taken for granted in Alexandrian poetics. For Callimachus, technique was not a preliminary to what a poet may achieve but all he can achieve.[1] Neoptolemus did not restrict poetry to highly wrought but small poems (or to a collection of them) in which 'art' was thought to display itself unalloyed. The artistry which he demanded for large poems as well as small may have rendered it desirable to enjoin technical sufficiency. He could have enjoined it in his section on 'the poet', if he, like Horace, had posed the traditional conundrum, '*natura* fieret laudabile carmen *an arte*', which in the *Ars* is

---

[1] Cf. R. Pfeiffer discussing Callimachus, *H*, LXIII (1928), 317–18, 341, 'dass es nämlich in der Kunst nur auf die "Kunst" ankomme'.

'solved' in the balanced, Peripatetic, fashion.[1] But no guesses are needed in order to determine Horace's own views. In almost all his criticism weak craftsmanship is said to be the besetting sin of Roman poetry, however great poems may be otherwise. This perhaps accounts for the poet's procedure. For in the *Ars* the need for *studium* is not one of the set topics of the critical discourse. Rather the topic weaves its way in and out of the whole discourse unceasingly. It is present almost everywhere. For ubiquity it beats 'appropriateness' by a large margin.

Three times in the last section of the poem, in contexts earlier singled out as traditional,[2] Horace has balanced the claims of *ars* against other claims. But he has done it in a fashion which makes the need for artistry an essential requisite for all great poetry.

Moral philosophy is thought to provide the essential substance for a poet.[3] Yet a play which has this essential substance, being *speciosa locis morataque recte*, may still be at fault when it is *nullius veneris, sine pondere et arte*.[4] Horace's version of old Cato's *rem tene, verba sequentur*,[5] and *orator (poeta) vir bonus dicendi peritus*,[6] must not then be taken too literally. It is true, the listeners who are willing to sit through the performance of this kind of play may have a sound instinct.[7] They demand *res* and *mores*. They may feel that *versus inopes rerum nugaeque canorae*[8] lack that substance. The antithesis, sound but inartistic substance *versus* empty formalism, calls for two comments. It is possible only in the traditional type of criticism which Horace has chosen as a vehicle for his ideas on poetry. It perpetuates the distinction *res–verba*. In the second place the resemblance to the smaller critical writings needs to be noted. *Speciosa locis*

---

[1] *A.P.* 408.
[2] Above, pp. 125–6.
[3] *A.P.* 309–16.
[4] *Ibid.* 319–20.
[5] *Ibid.* 311.
[6] *Ibid.* 312 ff.
[7] Such I take to be the meaning *ibid.* 321–2. The unprofessional judgement of Roman audiences is also given some prominence in the earlier portions of the *Ars*. This will be discussed presently.
[8] *Ibid.* 322.

morataque recte; that is how Horace views in the letter to
Augustus and elsewhere the best of early Roman poetry. And
it may be guessed (for Horace does not say so) that he thought
the verse of the Roman Callimacheans described by the
second limb of the antithesis, *versus inopes rerum nugaeque
canorae*. The antithesis is resolved in the idealized description
of the Greek poets that follows—*ingenium, ore rotundo loqui,
praeter laudem nullius avaris*. In its turn it gives rise to the un-
favourable description of Roman education to which I have
made reference before.[1]

The second of the traditional contexts in the final section of
the *Ars* concerns the aims of poetry.[2] Horace is concerned to
resolve another unreal antithesis. He believed that (in the
language of the schools) poetry aimed neither at moral benefit
alone nor at pleasure alone. To say, poets want *simul et iucunda
et idonea dicere vitae*, as Philodemus tells us Neoptolemus had
done in his Hellenistic terminology,[3] is adequate for the controversies of the schools. And in these terms Horace restates
Neoptolemus' compromise. But the practitioner of the art
wants more than that. He wants to be told *how* to 'mix' moral
benefit with poetic delight. That again is an artistic problem
and Horace attempts to give advice.[4] But the topic does not
detain him. The sequel will show that he has better things to
offer when he gets away from the textbook.

Finally the traditional problem of 'talent *versus* training'.
A practitioner of Horace's poetic stature could not well
believe that great poetry might be written without *ingenium*.
The burden of *Epistles*, i, 19, let alone his lyric expressions of
poetic inspiration, should not be minimized. Here is another
antithesis of the schools. On the debating level Horace puts
forward a compromise when, once more, he gives a balanced,
'Peripatetic', answer. The answer is that of Neoptolemus.[5]
Horace too demands both *natura* and *ars*[6]—or the truism may

---

[1] Above, p. 198, n. 2. [2] *A.P.* 333–46. [3] Above, pp. 57, 128–9.
[4] *A.P.* 335–40, with Rostagni's notes.
[5] Above, p. 58, δύναμις and τέχνη are required. [6] *A.P.* 408–11.

imply that he for one cannot see the problem. But whenever he really grapples with the problem the stress is always on *studium*. *Ingenium*, here as at the beginning of the *Ars*, is but a condition; without talent you cannot get down to work, *studium*.[1] He puts it no higher because he is speaking as a teacher. A pupil can be taught how to use his gifts, but no one can be told how to become gifted. Here again the topic does not detain him. He marks the point where his argument coincides with traditional teaching. If the reader wants more than brusque common sense he must attend to the large context of which this problem forms but a small portion.

Discussion so far has shown that each of the three traditional antitheses has been reduced to a non-committal *et–et*. Talent must enable artistry to do its work, and the work consists in fusing *sapere* and *venustas*, *docere* and *delectare*, *res* and *verba* into the organic unity of a great poem. Poetry thus conceived is the subject of the third part of his final section, from 347 onward. It consists of a long and difficult series of contexts with little connexion on the surface.[2] The connexion, partly of thought and partly of sentiment, is perhaps best traced when the topics are schematically juxtaposed. The subject throughout is poetic perfection.

(1) The occasional 'faults' of Homer contrasted with the persistent faults of Choerilus. In a long poem the former are venial and therefore irrelevant, the latter are not. (347–60)

(2) Certain poems, like certain paintings, are so well made that they satisfy repeated inspection and delight more than once. (361–5)

(3) In the utilitarian arts and crafts even mediocre performances have their value; in poetry, as in other non-utilitarian arts that aim to please, only the best is good enough. (366–78)

(4) In poetry, as in games, performers cannot do without

---

[1] Note the conditional way in which he talks of talent, *A.P.* 39–40, *quid ferre recusent,* | *quid valeant umeri*, cf. 40–1, 385, *invita...Minerva*, 412 ff.

[2] This is the kind of Horatian sequence discussed above, pp. 27–8.

training and talent; even if these conditions are met, poetry must be subjected to informed criticism. (379–90)

(5) Poetry has civilized humanity. (391–407)

(6) The antithesis 'talent *or* training' is false. (408–11)

(7) The craftsman is contrasted with the amateur; the bearing of criticism on the craft. (412–52)

(8) Untutored genius is caricatured. (453–76)

All of these eight points are superficially unconnected. But with the exception of the fifth,[1] they all contribute something to the airing of one problem—the nature of the craftsmanship that gives rise to great and enduring poetry. Horace does not however present a connected argument. He adopts a poetic, not an analytic, expedient. He sketches different aspects of one problem in the most varied forms, without attempting either to argue them fully or to fuse the several aspects which he has noted into a single piece of coherent reasoning. Such apparently disjointed pieces, here or anywhere in Horace's work, whether *sermo* or lyric, give the impression that they have in fact an inherent, poetic, unity. But the difficulty, as in some modern poetry, lies in their recalcitrance when they are forced into a continuous argument that can be stated in prose. Some readers see only unconnected pieces; others think that the pieces can be brought easily into the continuous argument of prose. Both are equally at fault. This constitutes the specific problem that faces the reader of Horace. Often the pieces do not fall into place until they are scanned from the end of the poem. Often, again, repeated words or images, or the areas in which two or more strands meet together,

---

[1] This passage praises the mythical *vates* for promoting early human civilization, and selects the later poetic genres in accordance with their impact on society; see above, p. 225. At the end of the passage the conclusion is drawn: there is nothing to be ashamed of in the activity of the Muse and Apollo the singer. Horace's intention in placing the piece here may perhaps be gathered from the preceding address to the elder son of Piso, 366, 383 ff. The social implication in the advice to the young nobleman is echoed by the social implication of the following sketch: *honor et nomen divinis vatibus atque | carminibus venit* (400–1). Moreover anyone wanting to write such poetry requires craftsmanship. The strenuous training demanded of the disciple prepares him for poetry of this description.

indicate Horace's intentions. The recurrence of the idea of poetic technique may be a pointer to one of the links connecting this part of the poem.

If the Horatian concept of *ars* has some of this importance in the final portion of the poem, there may here be a point of vantage from which to look back in order to discover the bearing of this concept on the more technical sections. Until about half way through the poem the general concept of technique is naturally subservient to Horace's specific teaching. But it is used to reinforce the argument, and marks important transitions.[1]

The concept however grows in importance and emphasis when Horace reaches Roman drama and its versification. For the time being he has moved out of traditional territory. A very Horatian concern for his art makes itself felt. The faulty metre of Accius and Ennius and the claims of artistic sufficiency are at first debated together. The neglected iambus, in accents reminiscent of the early satires,

> versus
> aut operae celeris nimium curaque carentis
> aut ignoratae premit artis crimine turpi. (*A.P.* 260–2)

Now the problem of poetic standards can be raised in a general indictment of archaic Roman drama.

> non quivis videt immodulata poemata iudex
> et data Romanis venia est indigna poetis.[2] (263–4)

---

[1] In the introductory section, at 31, unity is made dependent on craftsmanship: 'in vitium ducit culpae fuga *si caret arte*.' At 87–8 the *colores* of style and genre are likewise made dependent on mastering the styles and genres: 'cur ego *si nequeo ignoroque* poeta salutor? | cur *nescire* pudens prave quam *discere* malo?' Here the reminder serves at the same time to link two passages, to both of which it applies equally. In a less general way it is used to link two contexts, at 112–13, and moreover Horace now makes the audience the source of informed judgement: 'si dicentis erunt *fortunis absona* dicta, | Romani tollent equites peditesque cachinnum.' (The realistic appraisal of theatrical audiences in the letter to Augustus perhaps suggests educational intent in this passage.) The section on content and the genres is shot through with references to workmanship. Reference to the taste of the audience is made again, and used as an introductory item, at 153–5; note, in particular, 'quid ego et populus mecum desideret audi', 153.

[2] Cf. 265–8.

Greek poetic workmanship is contrasted with Roman negligence, and the *exemplaria Graeca* are assigned the place Horace considers rightful.[1] Then the opposite way is taken, which leads to the same conclusion.[2] The Greek theatre and its history are examined first, and next the Romans are brought in, competing with the masters of the art, but *limae labor et mora* are still seen to be disdained.[3] Now the demand for artistic sufficiency makes the link between two large sections of the poem. Concern with Roman drama recedes; the antithesis skill *versus* talent comes to the fore, and sets the tone of the last section of the *Ars*.

The most prominent of the recurring subjects have now been scrutinized. I have noted the great deliberation and deftness with which they are fitted into the standard scheme. I have drawn attention to the poetic diversity which they help to create. One important consequence follows from Horace's procedure. Such concepts as character, appropriateness, unity, poetry as the mastery of an art—these concepts and others continually cut across the boundary lines of the standard scheme. They diversify what otherwise might have been a staid and unpoetic argument by providing various additional patterns. Nor can their number be easily determined. Diverse topics that repeatedly appear in different contexts have not here been discussed. Such are the large genres, the social impact of great poetry, the ideal of moderation or balance, and the contrast of Greek and Roman psychology.

Horace's procedure has brought the charge of incoherence against an imaginative maker of poetic patterns. It may be expedient therefore to examine one or two items which seem to contradict the main division of style–matter–poet.

As Horace himself observed, he was by nature brief of speech, *animi raro et perpauca loquentis*.[4] Terseness attracted him.[5] It is not known if Neoptolemus was among the critics who

---

[1] *A.P.* 268 ff.   [2] *Ibid.* 275 ff.   [3] *Ibid.* 291.
[4] Hor. *Sat.* I, 4, 18.   [5] Hor. *Sat.* I, 10, 9.

canonized brevity as a 'virtue of style'.[1] Aristotle and Theophrastus were not. *Brevitas* is noticed with approval in different portions of the *Ars*. On a literal interpretation of the standard scheme it had no place apart from the technical section. As a stylistic feature it could be discussed under the heading of style; as a selective principle of subject-matter under the headings of unity, order, or content. What has happened in fact is different and the student of Horace should be prepared for it now. It has been seen that by attaching an item to various contexts, Horace illuminates both the contexts and the item thus attached. This is what he has done with the principle of *brevitas*.

First it appears in the introductory section on unity where Horace exemplifies from content, style, and order. Brevity is the first of some instances of style designed to illustrate the maxim *decipimur specie recti*, and its final application to diversity and unity.[2] As so often when Horace debates a subject of literary criticism, he portrays in his diction the subject he is debating. He wishes to express the following thought: 'in trying to avoid one fault, verbosity, we become liable to the opposite fault, excessive brevity, that is, obscurity.' And, with exemplary precision, he says, *brevis esse laboro, | obscurus fio*.[3] This proposition illustrates the larger context in which it is set; conversely the larger context gives it a wider application.

Horace returns to the matter twice more. Once in his discussion of content, where Homer is admired for his art of skipping subject-matter which he cannot make 'shine'.[4] That

---

[1] The Lyceum after Theophrastus may possibly have assigned a place to *brevitas* in a discussion of style. But Demetrius, *De interpret.* (103, 137, 253), who is sometimes cited as a witness, does not provide sufficient evidence for a decision. Neoptolemus' opinion is simply unknown. Rostagni's note on *A.P.* 25 is doubly misleading. He speaks of *brevitas* as a principle in the selection of subject-matter; but *A.P.* 25-8 seem to be concerned with style. And he imputes the principle to Neoptolemus, on the strength of a section in Philodemus for which Neoptolemic provenance is neither proven nor likely, *De Poem.* v, col. iii. For the teachings on *brevitas* of Isocrates, the Peripatetics, and Stoics, see J. Stroux, *De Theophrasti virt. dic.* (1912), ch. iv.

[2] *A.P.* 25, on *species recti*, and 29-30, for its application to the problem of unity.

[3] *Ibid.* 25-6. [4] *Ibid.* 149-50.

is *brevitas in rebus*. But Horace also mentions brevity in the final section on 'the poet'. Having told the poet to instruct as well as delight, he hastens to apply his teaching to the actual performance. Instruction must be brief if it is to be retained by the reader.

> quidquid praecipies esto brevis, ut cito dicta
> percipiant animi dociles teneantque fideles. (*A.P.* 335–6)

This is one of many cases in the final section where Horace breaks through the narrow bounds of the standard scheme, as indeed one of his predecessors might have done. To tell a poet to benefit as well as please, that is one thing and it can be done in general terms. But it is quite another, and much more specific, thing if these benefits and pleasures are identified with the teaching of lessons and the plausibility of his fiction respectively.[1] And it is a third thing, still more specific, if the poet is told how to set about this task. For then the matter cannot be put fully without bringing the topic of diction into the general argument. Horace clearly did not hesitate to do this, either here or in similar cases.

This procedure has been described as 'a trespass of *ars* on *artifex*'.[2] But is it? How strongly marked are the boundary lines which would make an intrusion unwarrantable? They are not strongly marked. The poet's procedure shows that he regarded the standard divisions as neither invariable nor exclusive. He has kept them sufficiently out of sight to be able to establish principles of arrangement which are more flexible. Hence a reference to the topic of style in the final section cannot well throw doubt on the presence of this or any plan in the poem.[3] When it suits the poet's purpose he links any part of the large field with any other part. But that does not mean that the field has no divisions.

---

[1] For the underlying doctrine of *verum–verisimile–falsum*, see Rostagni's notes and my paper in *Proc. Cam. Phil. Soc.* n.s. VI (1960), 17.

[2] L. P. Wilkinson, *Horace and his Lyric Poetry*, 2nd ed. (1951), p. 97, n. 4.

[3] L. P. Wilkinson, *loc. cit.*

He discusses style several times in contexts other than that ostensibly devoted to it. The case just discussed is not then an exception. In the introductory section on unity he naturally glances at style as well as subject-matter and arrangement of topics. I have mentioned that the axiom *decipimur specie recti* is illustrated by the risks which brevity of diction entails. This is followed by another illustration which recalls the stylistic teachings of the Aristotelian school.[1] Here then are specific doctrines of style employed to illustrate the introductory topic of unity.

After the section expressly devoted to style, Horace considers content and next the dramatic genres. These genres are considered *in toto*, that is, with regard to their language as well as to their content and structure.[2] To satyric drama in particular a style is assigned which is to keep an Aristotelian mean between the elevation of tragedy and the bathos of comedy. Horace employs a terminology that belongs to the doctrine of style[3] and he alludes to his earlier discussion of the power which resides in a clever combination of ordinary words. That discussion is found in the section on style.[4]

Tragedy and comedy are next considered. Horace sets out from the topic of metre. He thus dexterously fills a gap, for so

---

[1] *A.P.* 26–8, where two doctrines may be distinguished. Both are otherwise known from rhetorical and literary theory. Vahlen, *Ges. Phil. Schr.* I, 445–6, was mistaken in denying the rhetorical affiliation although some of his criticisms of L. Spengel (who had made the point) are justified. One of the theories in question is that of the 'types of style'; Horace notes three, the grand, smooth, and plain types. The other is the theory of the 'adjacent faults' which defines a fault as a virtue overdone. Horace connects this theory with the types of style. The two are likewise connected in Cicero's rhetorical writings, and earlier by the writer *Ad Herennium*, IV, 11 and 15. The theories also occur in Greek writings on rhetoric and literary criticism; they are certainly Greek in origin and have strong Peripatetic characteristics. But their precise provenance is still obscure. Cf. W. Kroll, *R-E*, Supp. VII, cols. 1074–5; H. Caplan, *Ad Herennium*, Loeb ed. (1954), pp. 252–3.

[2] Cf. above, p. 10.

[3] *A.P.* 234–5, *inornata et dominantia nomina solum | verbaque*. For the terminology see Rostagni's notes. *Dominantia* translates Greek κύρια; it is not found before this passage of Horace.

[4] *Ibid.* 240, 'ex noto fictum carmen sequar'; 242–3, 'tantum series iuncturaque pollet, | tantum de medio sumptis accedit honoris', cf. 47–8, 'notum si callida verbum | reddiderit iunctura novum'.

far metre has only entered as an agent of the appropriateness of style.[1] His observations seem to be on a footing both technical and elementary.[2] But this is a snare and a delusion. For it is precisely ignorance of some of the elementary, but fundamental, facts of metrical structure—the need for pure iambics which Horace asserts—that gives rise to his withering indictment of Roman poetic practice.[3]

The last part of the poem announces, and largely propounds, generalizations. But it readily turns to stylistic examples whenever there seems a call for them. The telling illustration of *prodesse* and *delectare* has been mentioned earlier.[4] The most impressive case comes near the end. It concerns the critic who is to subject the poet's work to scrupulous examination. Horace is specific, and spends five lines on the *emendatio* of diction and style.[5] He thus not only gives substance to an exhortation addressed to the poet—*ars* substantiating not trespassing on *artifex*—but conversely imparts some of the urgency of his exhortation to the technicalities—*artifex* to *ars*.

These are the motifs that appear so frequently. Such others as Greek and Roman psychology, poetry as a social phenomenon, the poetic genres, are not repeated but placed in conspicuous positions in the argument. Many of these had engaged Horace's attention in his earlier critical writings. They still engaged his attention when he wrote the *Ars*. Their position is so prominent that the reader cannot help noticing them. It is ironical that it should be the recurring motifs that have earned Horace the reproach, or compliment, of being a chatty and inconsequential composer. Closer reading suggests

---

[1] *Ibid.* 73–85.
[2] *Ibid.* 251, 'syllaba longa brevi subiecta vocatur iambus', etc.
[3] *Ibid.* 258 ff., cf. above, pp. 119, 218.
[4] Above, p. 263, on *A.P.* 335–6.
[5] *Ibid.* 445–9. These are technicalities that are best explained by the precepts on style propounded by the professional critics. Cf. *A.P.* 26–8, 46 ff., *Ep.* ii, 2, 122–3. The critic's work is very much also the poet's work; the approach is that of the craftsman in both cases. In the passage from the letter to Florus which has just been cited the poet and the critic are one and the same person, the poet criticizing his own work. Also *Ep.* ii, 2, 126–8 may be contrasted with *A.P.* 439–44.

that both their recurrence and their placing are deliberate. The conversational graces are certainly there. But they do not prevent Horace from employing these topics, almost like repeated musical motifs, as an additional and more personal means of arranging his subject-matter. They are assigned a function in the structure of the poem.

What Horace has attempted in the *Ars* is very simple when one sees it done by a great poet. It is not simple otherwise. He has introduced his personal criticism into the traditional, Hellenistic, *ars poetica*. The poem offers Horace's personal criticism, in the traditional form to which he was accustomed; it also offers a traditional *ars poetica*, adapted to fit in with his personal sentiments. Modern discontents with the *Ars* are largely explained by the complications of this procedure. Analysis is faced with two results instead of one because the *Ars* comprises both the headings of a traditional *ars poetica*, and others that express Horace's 'personal' criticism. Nothing is wrong with these results unless they are considered mutually exclusive. Horace did not so consider them. There is no reason why we should.

Horace established the unity of the *Ars* by keeping in the background a few large and not very profound concepts of a technical nature. They provide a system of reference. In front of them he placed a large number of competing poetic principles. It is idle to want to adjudge precedence between them. Craftsmanship, appropriateness, and character, certainly come very high in the list. But scan the poem from a different angle—and it will acquire a different complexion. This surely is a reason why the *Ars* does not easily pall. It encourages a large number of approaches. But being poetry it does not allow of a final assessment of claims. If it did, the poem would not easily please thereafter. In fact, *decies repetita placebit*.[1]

Modern writers complain that the literary criticism of the *Ars* lacks the freshness and humour which his best poetry so

[1] *A.P.* 365.

conspicuously exhibits. They are looking for the right thing but they are looking in the wrong place. Horace did not pronounce on imagination, poetic freshness, and humour because he had good reasons for adopting a framework of thought that had little room for these qualities. It is the poetic form of his criticism that must here be taken into account.

It has often been remarked that Horace has an engaging habit of portraying in his style the features which he is discussing on the critical level.[1] This habit pervades the whole of the *Ars*, from euphonic devices such as alliteration all the way to the larger ventures that influence the structure of the work.

Such writing may be described as an attempt to harmonize expression and content. The doctrines of appropriateness and unity express the same desire on the level of theory. How much Horace relied on these postulates can be gathered from his discourse on style, which is wholly governed by them: matter and genre must be proportionate, so must be matter and metre, matter and subject, matter and character, matter and emotion. And earlier on he had reiterated the Aristotelian demand that every part of a poetic composition must be in balance with every other.

Although he was not writing in one of the genres that are the chief concern of his literary criticism, he appears to have tried to live up to his own teaching in laying out the pattern of the *Ars*. Editors have been notoriously slow in paragraphing a poem that needs to be broken up into sections in order to make sense. The standard scheme and its parts provide an underlying plan. But Horace's poetic transitions—at times misleadingly unobtrusive, at other times misleadingly abrupt —either understate or else overstate what might otherwise

---

[1] For *A.P.* 25–6, *brevis esse laboro,* | *obscurus fio,* see above, p. 262. Not all instances are equally certain. To many scholars *A.P.* 87 and 263 have seemed to portray (perhaps humorously) Horace's subject in these passages—metrical deficiency; for a central caesura is there overlaid by a compound or elided word. Judgement is contingent on such passages as *A.P.* 377, to which this explanation does not apply.

be obvious partitioning. So do the many topics which recur in the various sections, and remind the reader of the many threads that bind together the diverse parts of a large poem. Moreover, Horace has made use of a prologue and an epilogue, two dramatic sketches which serve as a kind of frame for the whole work.

Neoptolemus perhaps started his book with an introductory section on unity and then went to work on his tripartite scheme. Or else he developed his triad without ado and proceeded to his first item, *poema*. Horace spurns such a procedure.[1] Many of his hexameter poems show that the Homeric lesson, developed in the *Ars* as a guide for narrative and plot, also guides him as a writer of *sermones*.[2] So he hurries to the event; the problem of unity is approached by way of a caricature without any unity: he describes a painting which is all variety and daring. *Descriptio* was known as a fashionable device of Hellenistic and neo-Hellenistic literature, relieving uniformity. But, as Horace is to argue presently, this device may disturb instead of relieving the unity of design. The caricature then has two functions. It offers a *descriptio* which is to the point; and it plunges straight into the dispute over unity. But even now there is no coherent argument; rather a rapid little dialogue in which artists and poets are made to claim the romantic right of genius to dare. But Horace draws a line at an inorganic combination of elements that will not combine. Here then some of the recurrent subjects are first mooted: unity and diversity; *ingenium* and its limitation. These are like musical themes on a first hearing. Their potentialities cannot as yet be sensed. But the reader has been

---

[1] Horace's imaginative opening has been considered an instance against his use of Neoptolemus' textbook, cf. N. A. Greenberg, *HS*, LXV (1961), 266–7. The argument seems to be that the 'shock-value' and the position of the first line cannot derive from a Hellenistic model. The Hellenistic critic may or may not have used a similar imagery. But I have still to meet the scholar who is literal-minded enough to hold that Horace rendered Neoptolemus line by line, *fidus interpres* (*A.P.* 133–4).

[2] *Ibid.* 148–50, 'semper ad eventum festinat et in medias res | non secus ac notas auditorem rapit, et quae | desperat tractata nitescere posse relinquit'.

drawn into the atmosphere of a work whose essential themes will be *simplex et unum, ingenium et ars*.

Occasionally it has been noted that a caricature comes at the close of the work as it does at its beginning. *Ingenium* is there ignominiously dismissed if it lacks the control of craftsmanship. 'Pictoribus atque poetis | quidlibet audendi semper fuit aequa potestas'—thus the doctrine traduced at the beginning.[1] 'Sit ius liceatque perire poetis'—thus the doctrine satirized at the end.[2] A poet must be allowed to indulge his 'death-wish' lest he destroy others, 'non missura cutem nisi plena cruoris hirudo'.[3] The first caricature introduces a scrutiny of the work done by the poet. The second caricature is an epilogue to the scrutiny of the maker. Such is the imaginative level of humour to which the poet raises the two largest divisions of the traditional *ars poetica*—poetry and poet, *ars* and *artifex*.[4] The two caricatures serve to link the beginning and the end. This is another touch lending unity to the poem.

Now unity and diversity are principles which Horace's critical procedure allowed him to argue about. They are also principles which could be shown in the pattern of a poem which in spite of its great diversity is all of a piece. Other poetic qualities however are brought out only in the poem but not in its argument. The two caricatures that open and close the poem are masterpieces of Horatian humour and wit. There are many like touches in this and many other works. The *Ars* nowhere theorizes upon them. Many years earlier the poet got nearer to the quality of his own writing when he laid down the needs of the new Satire. He demanded a style that could ring the changes between serious criticism and urbane wit.[5] Even then he was using the language of traditional theory. Teaching that would have fitted the conditions observed in the *Ars* was at hand, had Horace wished for it. But apparently he did not so wish. He did not pronounce on

[1] *Ibid.* 9–10.
[2] *Ibid.* 466.
[3] *Ibid.* 476, the last line of the poem.
[4] Above, pp. 247–8.
[5] *Sat.* I, 10, 7–15, and above, p. 166, n. 1.

these Horatian qualities of poetry. All the more should it be remembered therefore that the manner of the poem may supply part of the critical argument.

Perhaps this observation should be extended so as to comprise the whole of Horace's poetic manner in this *sermo*. The *Ars* shares many features with the rest of Horace's poetry. It should be read as a piece of Horatian poetry. I say this not so much because occasion may arise when he uses a key-word suddenly to raise the level of language to poetic intensity.[1] This has at times been noticed, as indeed has the great variability in the levels of language employed in this and other *sermones*. I have in mind rather the poetic structure and pattern of the *Ars*. Many of Horace's hexameter poems resemble his lyrics in that the constituent parts are juxtaposed, contrasted, and related with much flexibility and force. This poetic quality is more important than the conversational graces of the *sermo*.

Among the hexameter poems the *Ars* occupies an especial place. The underlying pattern of the standard scheme is very simple. It does not obtrude but it keeps discussion on the even keel of a few large topics. The simplicity of this scheme enables Horace to indulge to the full his Augustan desire for pattern-making. He can now move freely. He can introduce, and interweave, a large number of further topics. Many of these are known from his other critical writings. Their inherent interest is greater than that of the standard scheme. But they are set against the background of the traditional *ars poetica*. The multiplicity of such a design accounts for both the complication and the attraction of the pattern.

These are qualities which no literary criticism can assess; but a poet can realize them in his poetry; and that is what

---

[1] Note the 'lyric' intensity of *A.P.* 60, *ut silvae foliis pronos mutantur in annos*, 63 *debemur morti nos nostraque*, 68 *mortalia facta peribunt*. The key-word here is *mors*. This is the kind of thing he may have in mind when he allows poetic 'tone' to the serious criticism of *satura* at *Sat.* I, 10, 12. It goes without saying that there are also passages that fit the activities of the *rhetor* mentioned in the same passage of *Sat.* I, 10.

Horace has done. The design of the *Ars Poetica* brings into one large structure not only the traditional theory of poetry but features which lie beyond the reach of Horace's rationalistic criticism. Such a close-knit structure must have presented difficulties even to ancient readers who could take for granted at any rate a tradition of literary theory; it presents greater difficulties to many modern readers who cannot. To assist such readers this book has been written.

BIBLIOGRAPHY

This bibliography comprises a selection of titles up to 1961.

Of the four writers discussed in this book, only Neoptolemus of Parium is fully represented. Titles on Philodemus are selected chiefly with regard to the *De poematis*. Aristotelian literature on the *Poetics* and *Rhetoric* has been almost entirely omitted: had it not, the list would be twice as long. As for Horace himself, I have not recorded any plain texts of the poet. I have omitted all explanatory editions that do not deal with the topics discussed in this book. Moreover, I have freely jettisoned the titles of literary histories and of handbooks (including those on Roman Satire) even if they touch on these topics. But numerous titles have been listed to which no reference is made in my book and some relevant studies are included although they are not primarily devoted to Horace. Less selective lists may be found in the standard bibliographies and in E. Burck's *Nachwort und bibliographische Nachträge*.

ARDIZZONI, A. 'La problema della satira in Orazio', *RFIC*, n.s. xxvii (1949), 161–76.

—— 'ΠΟΙΗΜΑ: Ricerche sulla teoria del linguaggio poetico nell'antichità', ΜΟΥΣΙΚΑΙ ΔΙΑΛΕΚΤΟΙ, Supp., serie v, 4. Bari, 1953, pp. 129.

ATKINS, J. W. H. *Literary Criticism in Antiquity, a Sketch of its Development*. Cambridge, 1934 (repr. London, 1952), 2 vols., pp. 199, 363.

BARWICK, K. 'Die Gliederung der rhetorischen τέχνη und die horazische Epistola ad Pisones', *H*, lvii (1922), 1–62.

ΒΑΣΗΣ, Σ. 'Περὶ τοῦ χρόνου καθ' ὃν ἐποιήθη ἡ τοῦ Ὁρατίου ποιητικὴ τέχνη', Ἀθηνᾶ, xxii (1910), 92–4.

BECKER, C. Review of Fraenkel's *Horace*, *Gnomon*, xxxi (1959), 592–612.

BENVENGA, C. 'Per la critica e l'estetica di Filodemo', *Rendiconti della Accad. di Archeologia*, etc. Napoli, n.s. xxvi (1951), 192–252.

BIRT, T. 'Über den Aufbau der Ars Poetica des Horaz' (appendix in A. Dieterich, *Pulcinella*, 1897, pp. 279–301).

—— *Kritik und Hermeneutik* (1913), pp. 83, 378.

BO, D. Q. Orazio Flacco, *Satire, Epistole, Arte Poetica*, ed. crit. e traduz. (Ist. Edit. Ital.), Milano, 1956.

Bibliography

BOISSIER, G. 'L'Art Poétique d'Horace et la tragédie romaine', *RP*, XXII (1898), 1–17.

BOLAFFI, E. 'Probabili influssi platonici su Orazio', *Athenaeum*, n.s. XI (1933), 122–7.

BORGHESI, B. *Œuvres complètes*, t. V (1869), 312–14.

BÖRNER, J. *De Quintiliani institutionis oratoriae dispositione* [Thesis], Leipzig, 1911, pp. 72.

BOYANCÉ, P. 'Néoptolème et l'Art poétique d'Horace' [Summary], *Actes, Congrès de Nice* (1935), pp. 82–3.

—— 'À propos de l'Art poétique d'Horace', *RP*, 3e série, X (1936), 20–36.

BRINK, C. O. 'Callimachus and Aristotle, an enquiry into Callimachus' Πρὸς Πραξιφάνην', *CQ*, XL (1946), 11–26.

—— 'Horace and Aristotle. Second thoughts on the Ars Poetica', Summary, *Proc. Class. Ass.* LVI (1959), 26–7.

—— 'Tragic history and Aristotle's School', *Proc. Cam. Phil. Soc.* n.s. VI (1960), 14–19.

BÜCHNER, K. 'Horaz: Bericht über das Schrifttum der Jahre 1929–36', *Bursians Jahresber.* CCLXVII, Supp. (1939), pp. 179 [also contains list of earlier summaries in the *Jahresberichte*].

—— 'Humanitas Horatiana, *A.P.* 1–37', *Studia Classica*, Cape Town, I (1958), 64–71.

—— and HOFMANN, J. B. *Lateinische Lit. und Spr. in des Forschung seit 1937* (1951), pp. 127–43.

BURCK, E. 'Nachwort und bibliographische Nachträge', in Q. Horatius Flaccus, *Briefe*, erklärt von A. Kiessling, bearbeitet von R. Heinze, Sechste Auflage, 1959, pp. 381–437; *Satiren*, Siebente Auflage, 1959, pp. 353–414.

CAJETAN, G. 'De compositione Horatii Epistulae ad Pisones', *Živa Antika*, IV (1954), 277.

CALOGERO, G. Review of Rostagni's *Arte Poetica di Orazio*, *Arch. Gesch. Philos.* XL (1931), 297–300.

CAMPBELL, A. Y. *Horace. A New Interpretation.* London, 1924, pp. xii + 303.

CARCOPINO, J. *Virgile et les origines d'Ostie.* Paris, 1919, pp. 731–9.

CARTAULT, A. *Étude sur les Satires d'Horace.* Paris, 1899, pp. 370.

CAUER, P. 'Zur Abgrenzung und Verbindung der Theile in Horazens Ars Poetica', *RM*, LXI (1906), 232–43.

CICHORIUS, C. *Römische Studien*, etc. Leipzig, 1922, pp. 325–31, 337–41.

COURBAUD, E. *Horace, Sa vie et sa pensée à l'époque des Épîtres.* Paris, 1914, pp. viii + 368.

Bibliography

CRANE, R. S. (ed.). *Critics and Criticism: Ancient and Modern*. Chicago, 1952, pp. v+647.

—— *The Language of Criticism and the Structure of Poetry* (The Alexander Lectures). University of Toronto Press, 1953, pp. xxi+214.

CUPAIUOLO, E. *L'epistola di Orazio ai Pisoni*. Napoli, 1941, pp. 117.

—— 'L'epistola ad Pisones, Studi e pubblicazioni recenti', *Paideia*, v (1950), 234–41.

DAHLMANN, H. 'Varros Schrift De Poematis und die hellenistisch-römische Poetik', *AAM* (1953), no. 3, pp. 72.

D'ALTON, J. F. *Horace and his Age*, London, 1917, ch. VII, 'Literary criticism', pp. 250–91.

—— *Roman Literary Theory and Criticism. A Study in Tendencies*. London, 1931, pp. viii+608.

D'ANNA, G. 'Oraziani i primi versi della dec. sat.?', *Maia*, VII (1950), 26–42.

—— 'Contrib. alla cronol. dei poeti Lat. arcaici', (II) 'La prima rappr. di una *fabula* di Livio Andronico', *Rend. dell'Ist. Lomb.* LXXXVII (1954), 117–28.

DELCOURT, MARIE. 'L'esthétique d'Horace et les lettres grecques', *Mél. Paul Thomas*. Bruges, 1930, pp. 187–200.

D'ELIA, S. 'Properzio e Orazio.' *Ann. Fac. di Lettere di Napoli*, II (1952), 45–77.

DEWITT, N. W. 'Parresiastic poems of Horace', *CP*, XXX (1935), 312–19.

DILKE, O. A. W. 'When was the Ars Poetica written?' *Bull. Inst. Cl. St.* V (London, 1958), 49–57.

ELMORE, J. 'A new dating of Horace's Ars Poetica', *CP*, XXX (1935), 1–9.

ENGLMAIER, E. *Was ist in des Horaz Satiren und Episteln auf griechischen Einfluss zurückzuführen?* [Thesis], Erlangen, 1913, pp. 125.

FAIRCLOUGH, H. R. 'Horace's view of relations between satire and comedy', *AJP*, XXXIV (1913), 183–93.

—— Horace, *Satires, Epistles, Ars Poetica*, with an Eng. trans. (Loeb Class. Library), rev. ed. 1929 (repr. 1955).

FERGUSON, J. 'Catullus and Horace', *AJP*, LXXVII (1956), 1–18.

FERRERO, L. *La 'Poetica' e le poetiche di Orazio*. Univ. di Torino Publ., 1953, pp. 91.

FISKE, G. C. 'Lucilius, the Ars Poetica of Horace, and Persius', [Summary], *TAPA*, XLII (1911), xxiii–xxiv.

—— 'Lucilius, the Ars Poetica of Horace, and Persius', *HS*, XXIV (1913), 1–36.

FISKE, G. C. 'The plain style in the Scipionic circle', *Univ. of Wisconsin St.*, III (1919), 62–105.

—— 'Lucilius and Horace, a study in the classical theory of imitation', *ibid.* VII, 1920, pp. 524.

—— with Grant, Mary A. 'Cicero's *Orator* and Horace's *Ars Poetica*', *HS*, XXXV (1924), 1–74.

—— 'Cicero's *De Oratore* and Horace's *Ars Poetica*', *Univ. of Wisconsin St.* XXVIII (1929), pp. 152.

—— *See also* GRANT, MARY A.

FLICKINGER, R. C. 'When could Horace have become acquainted with Aristotle's Poetics?' [Summary], *TAPA* (1939), XXXIII–XXXV.

FOSSATARO, P. 'Neottolemo e Orazio. A proposito d'un saggio sull'opera Περὶ ποιημάτων di Filodemo', *RFIC*, XLIX (1921), 230–52.

FRAENKEL, E. 'Das Pindargedicht des Horaz', *SBA Heidelberg* (1932–3), no. 2, pp. 27.

—— 'Das Reifen der horazischen Satire', *Festschrift...R. Reitzenstein*, 1932, pp. 119–36.

—— 'Lucili quam sis mendosus', *H*, LXVIII (1933), 392–9.

—— *Horace.* Oxford, 1957, pp. 464.

FRANK, TENNEY. 'Horace on contemporary poetry', *CJ*, XIII (1917–18), 550–64.

—— 'Horace's description of a scene in Lucilius', *AJP*, XLVI (1925), 72–4.

—— 'On Augustus' references to Horace', *CP*, XX (1925), 26–30.

—— *Catullus and Horace. Two Poets in their Environment.* Oxford, 1928, pp. 291.

—— 'Horace's definition of poetry', *CJ*, XXXI (1935–6), 167–74.

—— 'On Horace's controversies with the new poets', *Class. St. presented to E. Capps.* Princeton, 1936, pp. 159–67.

FRIEDRICH, G. *Horatius Flaccus: Phil. Unt.* Leipzig, 1894, 'Abfassungszeit der Litteraturbriefe', pp. 213–32.

FRITZSCHE, T. 'Die Komposition von Horaz Ars Poetica', *P*, XLIV (1885), 88–105.

GALLI, U. 'A proposito di Aristotele e di Filodemo', *Atene e Roma*, II (1921), 175–88.

GETTY, R. J. 'Recent work on Horace, 1945–57', *CW*, LII (1959), 167–88, 246–7.

GIGANTE, M. Σημαντικὸν ποίημα, *Parola del Passato*, XVI (1961), 40–53.

GIRI, G. *La poetica di Q. Orazio Flacco, Studi.* Torino, 1890, pp. 161.

Bibliography

GIUFFRIDA, P. *L'epicureismo nella letteratura latina nel I seculo* (Pubblic. ... Univ. di Torino): vol. I, *Esame e ricostruz. delle fonti*: Torino, 1940, pp. 191; vol. II, *Lucrezio e Catullo*, 1950, pp. 317.

—— *Horat. Epist. II. 1. 118–138: Elogio o parodia? Studi in onore di Gino Funaioli*, 1955, pp. 98–119.

GOMOLL, H. 'Herakleodoros und die κριτικοί bei Philodem', *P*, XCI (1936), 373–84.

GRANT, MARY A. and FISKE, G. C. 'Cicero's *Orator* and Horace's *Ars Poetica*', [Summary], *TAPA*, IV (1923), xvii–xviii.

GREENBERG, N. A. 'The poetic theory of Philodemus', *HS*, LXII (1957), 146–8.

—— 'The use of *Poiema* and *Poiesis*', *HS*, LXV (1961), 263–89.

GROAG, E. *PIR²*, Pars II, 1936, Cn. Calpurnius Piso, pp. 57–8; L. Calpurnius Piso, pp. 61–7.

GUEUNING, L. 'La leçon d'Horace ou le métier du poète', *Humanisme*, II, Bruxelles, 1933, pp. 68.

—— 'Horace et la poésie', *EC*, IV (1935), 52–73.

HACK, R. K. 'The doctrine of literary forms', *HS*, XXVII (1916), 1–65.

HAERINGEN, J. H. VAN. 'Zur Frage des Pisonerbriefes', *P*, XXX (1925), 192–9.

HAIGHT, ELIZABETH H. 'The lyre and the whetstone: Horace redivivus', *CP*, XLI (1946), 135–42.

—— 'Menander at the Sabine Farm, Exemplar vitae', *CP*, XLII (1947), 147–55.

—— 'Horace on art, *ut pictura poesis*', *CJ*, XLVII (1952), 157–62, 201–3.

HAUSRATH, A. 'Philodemi Περὶ ποιημάτων libri secundi quae videntur fragmenta', *Ja. Phil.* Supp., XVII (1889), 211–76.

HEINZE, R. *See* KIESSLING, A.

HENDRICKSON, G. L. 'The dramatic *satura* and the old comedy at Rome', *AJP*, XV (1894), 1–30.

—— 'Are the letters of Horace satires?' *AJP*, XVIII (1897), 313–24.

—— 'A pre-Varronian chapter of Roman literary history', *AJP*, XIX (1898), 285–311.

—— 'Horace, *Serm.* i. 4: A protest and a programme', *AJP*, XXI (1900), 121–42.

—— 'Horace and Lucilius: A study of Horace, *Serm.* i. 10', *Studies in honor of Basil L. Gildersleeve*, 1902, pp. 151–68.

—— '*Satura*—the genesis of a literary form', *CP*, VI (1911), 129–43.

—— 'Horace and Valerius Cato', *CP*, XI (1916), 249–69; XII (1917), 77–92, 329–50.

HENEN, P. Horace, *Art Poétique*, annoté, Coll. Labègue, Brussels, 1941, pp. 84.

HERRICK, M. T. 'The fusion of Horatian and Aristotelian literary criticism, 1531–1555', *Univ. of Illinois St. in Lang. and Lit.* xxxii, 1 (1946), pp. 117.

HERRMANN, L. 'Horace adversaire de Properce', *REA*, xxxv (1933), 281–92.

—— Horace, *Art poétique*, éd. et trad., Coll. Latomus, vii, Bruxelles, 1951, pp. 48.

HIGHAM, T. F. 'Ovid, some aspects of his character and aims', *CR*, xlviii (1934), 105–16.

HOWALD, E. *Das Wesen der lateinischen Dichtung*. Zürich, 1948, pp. 98.

HUPPERTH, W. *Horaz über die scaenicae origines der Römer (epist. 2. 1, 139 ff.*) [Thesis, Köln], Düsseldorf, 1961, pp. 85.

IMMISCH, O. 'Horazens Epistel über die Dichtkunst', *P*, Supp. xxiv, 3 (1932), pp. 217.

JACKSON, C. F. '*Molle atque facetum*, Horace, Satire 1. 10. 44', *HS*, xxv (1914), 117–37.

JENSEN, C. 'Neoptolemos und Horaz', *APA* (1918), no. 14 (1919), pp. 48.

—— *Philodemos über die Gedichte, Fünftes Buch* (1923), pp. x + 178.

——'Aristoteles in der Auge des Machon', *RM*, N.F. lxxxiii (1934), 193–200.

—— 'Herakleides von Pontos bei Philodem und Horaz', *SBPA*, xxiii (1936), 292–320.

KIESSLING, A. *Zu Augusteischen Dichtern*, Phil. Unt., ed. Kiessling and von Wilamowitz-Moellendorff, ii. Berlin, 1881, pp. 57–9.

—— Quintus Horatius Flaccus, *Briefe*, erklärt, 1889.

—— Quintus Horatius Flaccus, *Satiren*, erklärt, 1886.

—— and HEINZE, R. *Briefe*, Vierte Auflage, 1914.

—— *Satiren*, Fünfte Auflage, 1921. *See also* BURCK, E.

KIRCHNER, C. *Quaestiones Horatianae*. Naumburg, 1834, pp. 41.

KLINGNER, F. 'Horazerklärungen', *P*, xc (1935), 277–93, 461–8.

—— 'Horazens Brief an die Pisonen', *BVSA*, lxxxviii, 3 (1937), pp. 68.

—— 'Horazens Brief an Augustus', *SBBA* (1950), no. 5, pp. 32.

—— 'Kunst und Kunstgesinnung des Horaz', *Der altsprachliche Unterricht*. Stuttgart, 1951, no. 2, pp. 18–42.

—— Also the papers repr. in *Röm. Geisteswelt*, Vierte Auflage, 1961, 327 ff., 353 ff.

Bibliography

KNAPP, C. 'Horace, Epistles, II, 1, 139 ff. and Livy, VII, 2', *TAPA*, XLIII (1912), 125–42.

—— 'The sceptical assault on the Roman tradition concerning the dramatic *satura*', *AJP*, XXXIII (1912), 125–48.

KNOCHE, U. 'Betrachtungen über Horazens Kunst der satirischen Gesprächsführung', *P*, XC (1935), 372–90, 469–82.

KOLLER, H. 'Die Mimesis in der Antike', etc., *Diss. Bern.* Ser. I, Fasc. 5 (1954), pp. 235.

KÖRTE, A. 'Augusteer bei Philodem', *RM*, N.F. XLV (1890), 172–7.

KROLL, W. 'Die historische Stellung von Horazens Ars poetica', *Sokrates, Zeit. für das Gymnasialwesen*, N.F. VI (1918), 81–98.

LABOWSKY, LOTTE. *Die Ethik des Panaitios: Untersuchungen zur Geschichte des Decorum bei Cicero und Horaz*. Leipzig, 1934, pp. 124.

LA DRIÈRE, C. 'Horace and the theory of imitation', *AJP*, LX (1939), 288–300.

LA PENNA, A. 'Orazio e la questione del teatro latino', *Annali della Scuola Normale Sup. di Pisa*, XIX (1950), 143–54.

—— 'Due note sulla cultura filosofica delle epistole oraziane', *SI*, XXVII–XXVIII (1956), 192–201.

LATTE, K. 'Reste frühhellenistischer Poetik im Pisonenbrief des Horaz', *H*, LX (1925), 1–13.

LEJAY, P. 'La date et le but de l'Art Poétique d'Horace', *Revue de l'inst. pub. en Belgique*, XLV (1902), 361–86; XLVI (1903), 153–85.

—— Q. Horati Flacci *Satirae*, texte latin avec un commentaire, etc. Paris, 1911. *See also* PLESSIS, F.

LEO, F. 'Varro und die Satire', *H*, XXIV (1889), 67–84; repr. *Ausgew. Kl. Schr.* I (1960), 283–300.

—— 'Livius und Horaz über die Vorgeschichte des römischen Dramas', *H*, XXXIX (1904), 63–77.

LUCAS, H. 'Recusatio', *Festschrift J. Vahlen*, etc. 1900, pp. 319–33.

LUCOT, R. 'Vertumne et Mécène', *Pallas* (*Annales, Fac. de lettres*, Toulouse), I (1953), 65–80.

—— 'Propertiana, I, Horace inspirateur de Properce', *Pallas*, II (1954), 97–102.

—— 'Mécène et Properce', *REL*, XXXV (1957), 195–204.

McGANN, M. J. 'Horace's epistle to Florus', *RM*, XCVII (1954), 343–58.

—— *Some structural devices in the Satires and Epistles of Horace* [Thesis, typescript], Oxford, 1954.

MARX, F. 'Römische Volkslieder', *RM*, LXXVIII (1929), 398–426.

Bibliography

MEERWALDT, J. D. 'Adnotationes in Epistulam ad Pisones ad picturam praesertim collatam pertinentes', *Mnem.* 3rd ser. IV (1936), 151–63.

MEIGGS, R. *Roman Ostia*, Oxford, 1960, Appendix II, pp. 483–7.

METTE, H. J. 'Neoptolemos von Parion', *R-E*, XVI, 2 (1935), cols. 2465–70.

MEULI, K. 'Altrömischer Maskenbrauch', *MH*, XII (1955), 206–35.

MICHAELIS, A. 'Dissertatio de auctoribus quos Horatius in libro de Arte Poetica secutus esse videatur', *Kiliae* (1857), pp. 35.

—— 'Die horazischen Pisonen', *Comm. phil. in hon. T. Mommseni*, etc. Berlin, 1877, pp. 420–32.

MICHELS, AGNES KIRSOPP. 'ΠΑΡΡΗΣΙΑ and the Satire of Horace', *CP*, XXXIX (1944), 173–7.

MOMMSEN, T. 'Titulus Atticus Frugi et Pisonis', *Eph. Epig.* I (1872), 143–50; repr. *Ges. Schr.* VIII, 246–54.

—— 'Die Literaturbriefe des Horaz', *H*, XV (1880), 103–15; repr. *Ges. Schr.* VII, 175–86.

MORRIS, E. P. Horace, *Satires and Epistles*. New York, 1909.

—— 'The form of the epistle in Horace', *YCS*, II (1931), 79–114.

MOSCA, B. *La satira filosofica-sociale in Orazio*. Chieti, 1926, pp. 95.

MUELLER, L. *Satiren und Episteln des Horaz. Mit Anmerkungen*, vol. II (1893).

NETTLESHIP, H. 'The original form of the Roman *Satura*' (1878); repr. *Lectures and Essays*, 2nd ser. (1895), pp. 24–43.

—— 'Horace, (2) The De Arte Poetica', *JP*, XII (1883), 43–61; repr. *Lectures and Essays* (1885), pp. 168–87.

—— 'Literary criticism in Latin Antiquity', *JP*, XVIII (1890), 225–70; repr. *Lectures and Essays*, 2nd ser. (1895), pp. 44–92.

NICOLINI, F. *Per la data dell'Epistola d'Orazio ad Pisones*. Monteleone, 1901, pp. 29.

NORDEN, E. 'Die Composition und Litteraturgattung der Horazischen Epistula ad Pisones', *H*, XL (1905), 481–528.

OGLE, M. B. 'Molle atque facetum', *AJP*, XXXVII (1916), 327–32.

—— 'Horace an Atticist', *CP*, XI (1916), 156–68.

ORELLI, J. G. and BAITER, J. G. Q. Horatius Flaccus, vol. II, *Satirae, Epistulae*, ed. quartam curavit W. Mewes, Berolini, 1892.

ORTEGA, A. 'El ingenio y la técnica al servicio de la poesía, seg. la mente de Horacio', *Helmantica*, II (1951), pp. 84–94.

OTIS, B. 'Ovid and the Augustans', *TAPA*, LXIX (1938), 188–229.

—— 'Horace and the Elegists', *TAPA*, LXXVI (1945), 177–90.

PALMER, A. [ed., with notes]. *The Satires of Horace*. London, 1883.

Bibliography

PARRELLA, P. *Introduzione allo studio dell'Arte Poetica di Orazio.* Napoli, 1948, pp. 38.

PASCAL, C. *La critica dei poeti Romani in Orazio.* Catania, 1919, pp. 144.

PATIN, A. 'Der Aufbau der Horazischen Ars Poetica', *St. zur Gesch. u. Kult. d. Alt.* IV (1910), pp. 41.

PAVANO, G. *Introduzione all'Arte Poetica di Orazio.* Palermo, 1944, pp. 125.

PERRET, J. *Horace,* 'Connaissance des Lettres', no. LII, Paris, 1959, pp. 255.

PHILIPPSON, R. 'Horaz' Verhältnis zur Philos.', *Festsch. Kaiser Wilhelms Gym.* Magdeburg, 1911.

—— 'Zu Philodemus und Horaz', *PW,* XLVII (1924), pp. 894–6.

—— 'Das Sittlichschöne bei Panaitios, (2) Das πρέπον', *P,* N.F. XXXIX (1930), 386–413.

—— 'Philomelos, (7)', *R-E,* XIX, 2 (1938), cols. 2525–6.

—— 'Philodemos, (5)', *R-E,* XIX, 2 (1938), cols. 2444–82.

PIERLEONI, G. 'L'Arte Poetica di Orazio e il De Or. di Cic.', *Atene e Roma,* VIII (1905), 251–9.

PIPPIDI, D. M. 'Horace *Art poétique* 309', *Rev. Clasica,* Bucarest, VIII (1936), 48 ff.

—— 'Les deux Poétiques d'Horace', *ibid.* XI–XII (1939–40), 132–46.

PLESSIS, F. and LEJAY, P. (eds.). *Q. Horatius Flaccus.* 1903.

POHLENZ, M. 'Die Anfänge der griechischen Poetik', *NGG* (1920), pp. 142–78.

—— 'Τὸ πρέπον. Ein Beitrag zur Geschichte des griechischen Geistes', *NGG* (1933), pp. 53–92.

POSTGATE, J. P. 'Albius and Tibullus', *AJP,* XXXIII (1912), 450–5.

PRESTA, A. *L'Arte Poetica di Orazio.* (Vitai lampas I), Rome, 1941, pp. 128.

PRICKARD, A. O. *Una forcatella di spine.* Winchester, 1922, pp. 31.

PUELMA-PIWONKA, M. *Lucilius und Kallimachos,* etc. Frankfurt, 1947, pp. 411.

RABE, A. 'Das Verhältnis des Horaz zur Philosophie', *Archiv für Gesch. der Philos.* N.F. XXXII (1930), 77–91.

RACKHAM, H. 'Horace, *Sat.* i. 4. 7', *CR,* XXX (1916), 224.

RADKE, G. 'Horaz. Auswahlbericht', *Gymnasium,* LXI (1954), 231–48.

RAMAIN, G. 'Horace, *Art Poétique*', *RP,* 3me sér. I (1927), 234–49.

RAND, E. K. 'Catullus and the Augustans', *HS,* XVII (1906), 15–30.

REENEN, J. H. VAN. *Disputatio philologico-critica de Q. Horatii Flacci Epistula ad Pisones.* [Thesis] Amstelodami, 1806, pp. 87.

REITZENSTEIN, R. 'Livius und Horaz üb die Entwick. d. röm. Schauspiels', *NGG*, 1918, 233–58.

—— 'Zur römischen Satire (2). Zu Horaz Sat. i. 10 und i. 4', *H*, LIX (1924), 11–22.

RIESE, A. 'Horatiana (3, "Die Abfassungszeit des Gedichtes *de arte poetica*")', *Ja. für cl. Phil.* XCIII (1866), 476–80.

ROSTAGNI, A. *Scritti Minori*: I, *Aesthetica*, Torino, 1955, pp. 520; II, I, *Hellenica-Hellenistica*, 1956, pp. 394; II, 2, *Romana*, 1956, pp. 410.

—— Aristotele, *Poetica*: Introd., testo e commento, Torino (1928), 2nd ed. 1945.

—— *Arte Poetica di Orazio*. Introd. e commento, Torino, 1930 (repr. 1946).

RUDD, N. 'Had Horace been criticised? A Study of *Serm*. 1. 4', *AJP*, LXXVI (1955), 165–75.

—— 'The poet's defence', *CQ*, XLIX (1955), 142–56.

—— 'Horace and Fannius. A discussion of two passages in Horace *Serm*. 1. 4', *Hermathena*, LXXXVII (1956), 49–60.

—— 'Horace, *Sermones* II, i', *Hermathena*, XC (1957), 47–53.

—— '*Libertas* and *Facetus*', *Mnem.*, ser. 4, X (1957), 319–36.

—— 'The names in Horace's Satires', *CQ*, n.s. X (1960), 161–78.

SBORDONE, F. *Tre poetiche: Aristotele, Orazio, Filodemo*. Napoli, 1952 [known to me only from Ardizzoni's summary, ΠΟΙΗΜΑ, pp. 119–20].

—— 'Il quarto libro di Filodemo', *Atti dell'Accad. Pontaniana, 1950–2*. Napoli, n.s. IV (1954), 129–42.

—— 'Il primo libro del Aristotele intorno ai poeti', *ibid.* pp. 217–25.

—— 'Filodemo e la teorica dell'eufonia', *Rendiconti della Accad. di Archeologia*, etc. Napoli, n.s. XXX (1955), 25–51.

—— 'Per un'edizione del Περὶ Ποιημάτων di Filodemo', *ibid.* XXXI (1956), 161–78.

—— 'Filodemo contro Eracleodoro', etc., *ibid.* XXXII (1957), 173–80.

—— 'Il papiro ercolanese 444', *ibid.* XXXV (1960), 99–110.

SCHÄCHTER, REGINA. 'De finibus poeseos et pedestris locutionis Philodemi quae videntur esse opiniones', *Eos*, XXVII (1924), 13–18.

—— Review of Jensen's *Philodemos über die Gedichte*, etc., *Eos*, XXVIII (1925), 165–70.

—— 'Philodemi περὶ ποιημάτων l. II fragmenta ex *VH X* collecta', *Eos*, XXIX (1926), 15–28.

—— 'Philodemus quid de psychagogia docuerit', *Eos*, XXX (1927), 170–3.

—— 'De Homero in Philodemi περὶ ποιημάτων l. II laudato', *Eos*, XXXI (1928), 439–46.

Bibliography

Schmid, W. 'Nugae Herculanenses' (iii), *RM*, xcii (1944), 50–4.

Schubring, K. and Petersen, L. *PIR²*, Pars iv (1958), 'Q. Horatius Flaccus', pp. 94–7.

Schweitzer, B. 'Mimesis und Phantasia', *P*, lxxxix (1939), 286–300.

Sellar, W. Y. *Horace and the Elegiac Poets*. Oxford, 1899; ch. iv, 'Horace as a literary critic'.

Shero, L. R. 'The satirist's apologia', *Univ. of Wisconsin St.* xv (1922), 148–67.

Sikes, E. E. *Roman Poetry*. London, 1923; chs. ii and iii, 'Roman criticism'.

Smith, W. K. 'The date of the Ars poetica', *CP*, xxxi (1936), 163–6.

Solmsen, F. Review of Rostagni's *Aristotele, Poetica, Gnomon*, v (1929), 400–14.

—— Review of Rostagni's *Arte Poetica di Orazio, Deut. Lit. Zeit.* liii, 1 (1932), 108–14.

—— 'Drei Rekonstruktionen zur antiken Rhetorik und Poetik, iii, Horaz ars poet. 391ff.', *H*, lxvii (1932), 151–4.

—— 'Die Dichteridee des Horaz und ihre Probleme', *Zeit. für Aesth. u. allg. Kunstwiss.* xxvi (1932), 149–63.

—— 'Aristotle and Cicero on the Orator's playing upon the feelings', *CP*, xxxiii (1938), 390–404.

—— 'The Aristotelian tradition in ancient rhetoric', *AJP*, lxii (1941), 35–50, 169–90.

—— 'Eratosthenes' *Erigone*: a reconstruction', *TAPA*, lxxviii (1947), 252–75.

—— 'Propertius and Horace', *CP*, xliii (1948), 105–9.

Spengel, L. 'Horat. ep. ad Pison. v. 24–30', *P*, ix (1854), 573–5.

—— 'Horatius de arte poetica', *P*, xviii (1862), 94–108.

Stégen, G. *Les épîtres littéraires d'Horace*. Namur, 1958, pp. 232.

Steidle, W. *Studien zur Ars Poetica des Horaz: Interpretation des auf Dichtkunst und Gedicht bezüglichen Hauptteils (1–294)*. (Thesis, Berlin), Würzburg, 1939, pp. 147.

Stemplinger, E. 'Horatius, (10)', *R-E*, viii, 2 (1913), cols. 2355–69.

Streuber, W. T. *De Q. Horatii Flacci ad Pisones epistola*. [Thesis, Basileae], 1839, pp. 104.

—— *Ueber die Chronologie der Horazischen Dichtungen*. Basel, 1843, pp. 42.

Syme, R. 'Piso Frugi and Cassius Frugi', *JRS*, l (1960), 12–20.

Szabó, A. *Neuere Lit. über Horazens Ars Poetica* [German summary], *Archivum Philologicum*, Budapest, lix (1935), 103–5.

—— *Horaz und die hellenist. Literaturwissenschaft* [German summary], *ibid.* pp. 254–6.

Tait, J. I. M. *Philodemus' influence on Latin poets*. (Thesis, Bryn Mawr), 1941, pp. 118.

Tate, J. 'Horace and the moral function of poetry', *CQ*, xxii (1928), 65–73.

—— Review of Steidle's *Studien zur Ars Poetica*, *CR*, liii (1939), 191–2.

Topitsch, E. 'Der Gehalt der Ars poetica des Horaz', *WS*, lxvi (1953), 117–30.

Tracy, H. L. 'Horace's Ars Poetica: a systematic argument' [Summary], *TAPA*, lxxvii (1946).

—— 'Horace's Ars Poetica: a systematic argument', *GR*, xvii (1948), 104–15.

Turolla, E. *Orazio*. Firenze, 1931, pp. 229.

—— 'Unità ideologica e tematica nel primo lib. delle ep. Oraz.', *Gior. ital. di fil.* iv (1951), 289–306.

Ullman, B. L. 'Horace and Tibullus', *AJP*, xxxiii (1912), 149–67, 456–60.

—— '*Satura* and Satire', *CP*, viii (1913), 172–94.

—— 'Dramatic *Satura*', *CP*, ix (1914), 1–23.

—— 'Horace, Catullus, and Tigellius', *CP*, x (1915), 270–96.

—— 'Horace on the nature of satire', *TAPA*, xlviii (1917), 111–32.

Vahlen, J. 'Zu Horatius de arte poetica', *Zeit. f. öster. Gym.* xviii (1867); repr. *Ges. Phil. Schr.* i (1911), 443–61.

—— 'Horatius' Brief an Augustus', *Zeit. f. öster. Gym.* xxii (1871); repr. *ibid.* pp. 461–91, with *Nachtrag* i, *ibid.* pp. 491–500, *Nachtrag* ii, *ibid.* pp. 500–11.

—— 'Zu Horatius' Brief an Florus (ii, 2)', *Zeit. f. öster. Gym.* xxv (1874); repr. *ibid.* pp. 511–15.

—— 'Über Zeit und Abfolge der Literaturbriefe des Horatius', *Monatsber. Berlin. Ak.* 1878; repr. *ibid.* ii (1923), 46–61.

—— 'Über Horatius' Brief an die Pisonen', *SBPA* (1906); repr. *ibid.* pp. 746–74.

Van Berchem, D. 'Poètes et grammairiens', *MH*, ix (1952), 79–87.

Villeneuve, F. *Épîtres*, Coll. G. Budé, Les Belles Lettres, 1941; *Satires, ibid.* 1946.

—— *État présent des études horatiennes*. Actes, Congrès de Nice, Paris, Les Belles Lettres, 1935, pp. 64–82.

Viola, A. *L'Arte Poetica di Orazio nella critica italiana e straniera*, 2 vols. Napoli, 1901–6.

Wagenvoort, H. 'Ad Hor. *Sat.* i, 4; i, 10; ii, i', *Donum Natalicium Schrijnen*. Nijmegen–Utrecht, 1929, pp. 747–54.

Bibliography

WAGENVOORT, H. 'Ludus Poeticus', *EC*, IV (1935), 108 ff.; repr. *St. in Roman Lit. Cult. and Rel.* Leiden, 1956, pp. 30–42.

WATKINS, R. E. 'A history of paragraph divisions in Horace's *Epistles*', *Iowa St. in Cl. Phil.* X (1940), pp. 134.

WEBB, R. H. 'Horace on the origin of Roman satire', *CP*, VII (1912), 177–89.

WECKLEIN, N. 'Die Kompositionsweise des Horaz und die Epistula ad Pisones', *SBBA* (1895), pp. 379–418.

—— 'Vindiciae zur Ars poetica des Horaz', *P*, LXVI (1907), 459–67.

—— 'Zur Ars poetica des Horaz', *Neue J-B f. d. Kl. Alt.*, etc., XXII (1919), 375–9.

—— 'Zur Epistula ad Pisones', *Bayer. Blätter...Gym.* LVIII (1922), 139–40.

WEHRLI, F. 'Horaz und Kallimachos', *MH*, I (1944), 69–76.

WEINBERG, B. *History of Literary Criticism in the Italian Renaissance.* Univ. of Chicago Press, 1961, 2 vols., pp. 1112.

WEINREICH, O. 'Zur röm Satire' (I), *H*, LI (1916), 386–411.

WEISSENFELS, O. 'Aesthetisch-kritische Analyse der Ep. ad Pis.', von Horaz. *Neues Lausitzisches Magazin*, LVI (1880), 118–200.

WELZHOFER, K. *Die Ars Poetica des Horaz.* Straubing, 1898, pp. 64.

WESSNER, P. 'Q. Terentius Scaurus', *R-E*, Zweite Reihe, V, I (1934), 'Terentius', cols. 674–5.

WHEELER, A. L. '*Satura* as a generic term', *CP*, VII (1912), 457–77.

WICKHAM, E. C. Q. Horatii Flacci Opera Omnia, vol. II, *The Satires, Epistles and De Arte Poetica.* Oxford, 1891.

WIELAND, H. *Beobachtungen zur Bewegungsführung in den Sat. und Ep. des Horaz.* [Thesis, typescript], Freiburg (Br.), 1950, pp. 73.

WILI, W. *Horaz und die augusteische Kultur.* Basel, 1948, pp. 414.

WILKINS, A. S. *The Epistles of Horace*, with notes. London, 1885.

WILKINSON, L. P. 'Philodemus and Poetry', *GR*, II (1932–3), 144–51.

—— 'Philodemus on ethos in music', *CQ*, XXXII (1938), 174–81.

—— *Horace and his Lyric Poetry*, 2nd ed., Cambridge, 1951, pp. 185.

WIMMEL, W. 'Kallimachos in Rom: Die Nachfolge seines apologetischen Dichtens in der Augusteerzeit', *H*, Einzelschr. XVI, 1960, pp. 344.

WITTE, K. *Horaz und Vergil: Kritik oder Abbau?* Erlangen, 1922, pp. 132.

—— 'Der Literaturbrief des Horaz an Augustus', *Raccolta...in onore di F. Ramorino*, Milano, 1927, pp. 404–20.

—— *Der Satirendichter Horaz: Die Weiterbildung einer röm. Literaturgattung.* Erlangen, 1923, pp. 39.

285

Bibliography

Witte, K. *Die Geschichte der römischen Dichtung im Zeitalter des Augustus*, II. *Horaz. I. Sermonendichtung*. Erlangen, 1931, pp. 288.

Zangemeister, K. 'Zum Horaz-Commentar des Scaurus', *RM*, xxxix (1884), 634–5; xl (1885), 480.

Ziegler, K. 'Tragoedia', *R-E*, Zweite Reihe, vi, 2 (1937), cols. 1967–79, 2052–63.

Zucker, F. 'Zur Textherstellung und Erklärung von Philodems V. Buch περὶ ποιημάτων', etc., *P*, lxxxii (1927), 243–67.

GENERAL INDEX

Academy, doctrines of, in Horace's *A.P.*, 136
ἄεισμα διηνεκές, 67 n. 1
Alexander Aetolus, tragedies of, 149
Alexander of Macedon, as a patron, 208
analytic procedure, applied to Horace's *Ars Poetica*, 1–40
Andromenides, on *poema–poesis–poeta*, 143 n. 1
Antiochus of Ascalon, 136 n. 3
Apollonius of Rhodes, 46 n. 5, 74 n. 1
Apollonius ὁ εἰδογράφος, 21
apologia, in Hellenistic and Augustan verse, 170 n. 1, 171–3, 185 n. 1
'appropriateness', see *decorum*
'appropriate style', in Aristotle's *Rhetoric* and *Poetics*, 96–9, 138, 229
Aristophanes and Horace, on archaic poets, 132–4; on Orpheus, 132–4, 225 n. 2
Aristophanes of Byzantium, mentions Neoptolemus of Parium, 45
Aristotle

(i) on Athenian temperament, 196–8; and his school on verse and poetry, 121–2, 162–3; on poetic attraction, 57; on poetic genres, 85, 87, 118–19, 144, 145, 203–4; on size of poems, 71; on style and content, 57–8

(ii) *De Poetis*, how related to his *Poetics*, 87–8, 120–50; and Philodemus, *De Poematis*, Book IV, 121 n. 1; speculative and historical features of, 121–2; discussion of *mimesis* in Book I and in *Poetics*, 121–2, 125; Books II and III, 122–3, 125; Book III, and Horace's *A.P.*, 126–8; was *catharsis* discussed? 123–5

(iii) *Poetics* and *Rhetoric*, concept of style, 86, 92–3; doctrine of appropriate style, 96, 97–9; and Neoptolemus of Parium, viii, 90–119, 135–50, 250

(iv) *Poetics*, how arranged, 84–9; and the structure of Horace's *A.P.*, 138; constituent parts of tragedy and the structure of Horace's *A.P.*, 19; ch. 6, and Horace's *A.P.*, 101–2; principle of poetic unity (chs. 7–8), and Horace's *A.P.*, 102, 108, 230–2, 245, 254–5; principle of poetic universality (ch. 9), and Horace's *A.P.*, 102–9, 130–2; 'modes of imitation' in *Poetics*, and Horace's *A.P.*, 39 n. 4; as rhetorical criticism of poetry, 80–1; not rhetorical criticism of poetry, 142 n. 1

(v) *Rhetoric*, how arranged, 81–4, 91; repetitions in, 250; arrangement and content of Book III, compared with Horace's *A.P.*, 93–4, 94–100; and the structure of Horace's *A.P.*, 20, 138; 'means of persuasion', 83; topic of τάξις in, 91; on style in tragedy and comedy, 97–9

(vi) and Horace, on metre, 96–7; and Horace, on poetic technique, 255; and Horace, on nature of subjects for poetic plots, 104–9; and Horace, on poetic ethos, 110–13, 139–40, 144, 250–2; and Horace, on poetry and philosophy, 130–2; and Horace, on subject-matter in poetry, 100–19; and Horace, on peace and the arts, 115–17, 196–9; did Horace know the *Poetics*? 100 n. 1, 140–1; his literary criticism fused with Horace's in the sixteenth century, 15, 79, 234; did Horace know the *Politics*? 197

Aristoxenus, on degeneration of music, 116–17; on Greek lyric poets, 172–3
ἁρμονία, 55–7
'arrangement', *ordo*, 11, 13, 24, 91, 99, 181 n. 2, 245, 254 n. 1; *see also* τάξις

287

General Index

ars–artifex, as a principle of arrangement in Greek and Roman treatises and in Horace's *A.P.*, 20, 21–4, 30, 31 n. 3, 36–40, 261–6, 269

ars–ingenium, 29 n. 2, 58, 70 n. 1, 73, 159, 160–2, 190, 218–20, 255–6, 268–9

Augustus, and Horace, 191–2, 207 n. 2, 208–9; requesting dedication of Horatian poems, 191 n. 3, 241–2

brevity of style, discussed in ancient literary criticism and Horace's *A.P.*, 261–4

Callimachus, and Neoptolemus of Parium, 45, 57, 73–4, 149–50; use of metaphors describing poetic style, 159 n. 3; on purity of poetic style, 159–61, 188 n. 4; language of the pioneer, 181–2, 231; attitude of, in Horace's *A.P.*, 109, 219; and long poems, 57, 71–2, 74, 159–61, 176, 203–4, 219, 232; on poetic skill, 255; on large subjects and poetic playfulness, 170; and Horace, 159–61, 176–7, 181–2, 188 n. 4, 195–6, 219–20, 231–2, 237, 255–6

Calvus, Horace on Catullus and Calvus, 160–1, 167, 237

carmen perpetuum, 67

Cascellius, Aulus, 240 n. 3

catharsis, 85, 123–5

Catullus, *nugae*, 170; Horace on Catullus and Calvus, 160–1, 167, 181 n. 3

censor honestus, the poet as a, 186, 218 n. 8

character, in Hellenistic tragedy, 111; discussion of, in Horace's *A.P.* and Aristotle, 110–13, 139–40, 144, 250–2; *see also* ἦθος

Charisius, cites Horace's *A.P.*, 233 n. 2, 243 n. 4

Choerilus, 208, 258

χρησιμολογεῖν, 129, 146

Chrysippus, isagogic writings, 22 n. 2

Cicero, on prose and poetry, 162–3; Cicero's and Horace's use of Greek doctrine, 3–4; and Horace, on choice of words, 188–9; Cicero's and Horace's literary criticism compared, 30 n. 4; and Horace, on ideal of style, 189–90

Cleophon, Aristotle on his tragedies, 98 n. 2

cogo, 191 n. 3

coherence, in prose and poetry, viii, 245 ff.

communia, meaning of, at Hor. *A.P.* (line 128), 103–4

'completeness' of tragedy, 85

concilio, 83

'content' in rhetoric and poetry, 7–10, 11–13, 24, 25 n. 4, 31–3; *see also* content and style

content–style, distinction, how applied by Horace, 7–13, 156–9, 162, 181, 223, 226, 245–8; by Neoptolemus of Parium, 59–62, 68, 69–73, 75–6, 92–3, 100–1, 137–8; impact of this division on arrangement of topics in Aristotle's *Poetics* and *Rhetoric*, 79–89; in (?) Neoptolemus' poetics, and Horace's *A.P.*, 249–50

conversational procedure, *see* Horace

critic, the poet as a critic of his own work, 186

criticism, literary, as material for Horatian poetry, ix, 3–4, 34–5, 40, 244 ff.; descriptive features of ancient criticism, 194; two types of ancient criticism, 88; by poets and professional critics, 153–4; and rhetoric, 19–20, 23–6, 30 n. 4, 35 n. 1, 39 n. 4, 79 ff., 90 ff., 137–8, 141–4, 186–7

dating, of works of literature, on internal criteria, 216–17, 242–3

decorum, Horace's theory of, and Panaetius, 35 n. 1, 96 n. 1, 136 n. 4, 228–30

288

General Index

διάθεσις, 92 n. 3
διάνοια and διανόημα, 92
Didymus, on metre, 97 n. 1
Diomedes, *Ars Gram.* III, traditional character of, 203 n. 3
drama, exemplary character of, in Aristotle's *Poetics*, 71, 87-9, 101, 203; history of, in Aristotle's *Poetics* and Horace's *A.P.*, 119; tragic and comic, 6-10, 19-20, 31, 71, 73, 87, 88-9, 98-9, 101 ff., 118-19, 138 ff., 141, 157 ff., 162 n. 1, 176-7, 192-3, 203, 204-7, 208-9, 214, 219-22, 238 n. 1

εἶδος, 58, 92-3
εἰσαγωγαί, 16 n. 1, 22-3, 35-6
elegy, 160-1, 205, 225 n. 1, 237
Ennius, *Annals* a *poesis*, 64, 67; as a poet, 163; *alter Homerus*, and the new poetry, 194, 209
epic verse, 7-9, 31, 71, 73-4, 87 n. 1, 88, 108-9, 118, 171-2, 176-7, 192, 203, 207-9, 214, 219-23, 224-5, 238 n. 1
Epicurean theory of language, 136 n. 2
Eratosthenes, and Neoptolemus of Parium, 45 n. 2
ethologia, 113
ἦθος, 92
exprimo, 191 n. 3

facundia, see style
Florus, addressed by Horace, 183

genitive absolute in polemic writing, *see* Philodemus

Heraclides of Pontus, 88 n. 2, 127, 142
Hermagoras, doctrine of rhetorical modes, 82 n. 3
Hermogenes, Horace on, 166-8
Homer, *Iliad* a *poesis*, 61, 64, 67, 67 n. 2, 68; biographical legend of, in Aristotle's *De Poetis*, Book III, 123, 125; Callimachus on, 71, 74; Horace on, as a teacher of morals, 222, 224; Aristotle and Horace on unity of plot in, 108 ff., 231-2; diversity of incident in plots, 231; omission of irrelevant detail in, 262
Horace
    (i) traditional and personal features of his literary criticism, 155, 179, 192, 213, 227-8 (*see also* (ii) *A.P.*, traditional and personal features); literary criticism, occasional in *Satires* and *Epistles*, systematic in *A.P.*, 153-5, 213, 215 ff., 225-6, 226-34, 244-8; tends to avoid technical terms of literary criticism, 247; on archaic and modernistic tendencies in contemporary literary criticism, 166-8, 193-5, 214; on poetry and morals in satire and other poetic genres, 160-77, 200-3, 214, 221-5, 235-6, 256-7; on the poet as a teacher, 200-3; on poetry and society, 199-209, 221-5, 235-6; on verse and poetry, 161-4, 176-7, 214, 220; on verse without substance, 257; on moralistic poetry, 257; on knowledge of character and moral values in poetry and philosophy, 185, 185 n. 2, 223-4, 235-6, 256-7, 258-9; contradictory attitudes as regards poetry, 169-71; disclaims poetic status when writing as a critic, 182-3, 192, 215-16, 242; and his readers, 168-71, 234-7, 245, 271; on Greek and Roman poetry, 196-9, 218, 256-7, 261; on national psychology, Greek and Roman, 196-9, 225, 225 n. 3, 256-7, 261, 265; on audiences in theatre, 260 n. 1; literary polemic by implication,

General Index

Sositheus, 149

Stoic, allegory, 133 n. 2, 136 n. 2; theory of language, 99 n. 1, 136 n. 2

style, concept of, in Aristotle's *Poetics* and *Rhetoric*, 86, 92; and content, impact of this division on arrangement of topics in Aristotle's *Rhetoric*, (?)Neoptolemus' poetics, and Horace's *A.P.*, 6–13, 19 ff., 32 ff., 57 ff., 90 ff., 138 ff., 226–7, 245–8, 250–2, 263–6; faults of, 264 n. 1; of verse, defined as 'combination of metres', 24 n. 3, 94; *see also* 'appropriateness', 'types of style'

Suetonius, on Augustus and Horace, 191 n. 3, 241–2

συνέχεια, 56–7

σύνθεσις, 57, 59, 92

συντέλεια, 56–7

σύστασις, 92 n. 1

Tarpa, Sp. Maecius, 240 n. 4

τάξις, 60, 81, 99 n. 2; *see also* 'arrangement'—*ordo*

technologia, τεχνολογία (Cicero, *Ad Att.* IV, 16, 3) 3, *see also* textbooks

textbooks, Greek, how used by Cicero, 3; by Horace, 3; on poetics, how arranged, 22–3, 36–40

Theodectes, 82 n. 1

Theodorus of Byzantium, 82 n. 1

Theophrastus, *Characters* and the moral qualities in Aristotle's *Ethics*, 112 n. 3; definition of comedy ascribed to Theophrastus, 98; his distinction between rhetoric, poetry, and philosophy, 83 n. 1; on σικελίζειν, 116 n. 2; his poetics, 142–3; on style, 93, 96, 262 n. 1

Thrasymachus, 82 n. 1

Tiberius, 183

tradition, and personal expression in Horace's *A.P.*, 155–6

transitions, *see* Horace

treatises, *see* textbooks

'types of style', doctrine of, 264 n. 1

unity of poems, 12–13, 86, 135, 137–9, 244 ff., 267–71

universality of poetry, 86, 105–9

ὑπόθεσις, 59, 92

usus, in vocabulary, 188 n. 3

Valerius Cato, 167 n. 1

Varro, are his literary doctrines attacked in Hor. *Ep.* II, 1? 193–4; on archaic drama, Greek and Roman, 205; and Horace on poetic metres, 97 n. 1; and Horace on vocabulary, 188 n. 5; on *poema* and *poesis*, 66–7; (?)on Roman satire and Attic comedy, 157 n. 2

Varus, Quintilius, 218, 240 n. 3

verum–verisimile–falsum, 263 n. 1

Virgil, *Aeneid*, a *poesis*, 67 n. 2; and Varius in Horace (*Ep.* II, 1 and *A.P.*) 208, 224, 238 n. 1, 240 n. 3; (*Sat.* I, 10), 167–8

vitiosus, in literary criticism, 159 n. 2

vocabulary, poetic, Horace on, 186–9

INDEX OF PASSAGES CITED

298

Index of Passages Cited